Educational Administration

EDUCATIONAL ADMINISTRATION

An Australian Perspective

edited by
Colin W. Evers
Monash University

and
Judith D. Chapman
University of Western Australia

LONDON AND NEW YORK

First published 1995 by Allen & Unwin

Published 2020 by Routledge
2 Park Square, Milton Park, Abingdon, Oxon OX14 4RN
605 Third Avenue, New York, NY 10017

Routledge is an imprint of the Taylor & Francis Group, an informa business

Copyright © Colin W. Evers and Judith D. Chapman, 1995

All rights reserved. No part of this book may be reprinted or reproduced or utilised in any form or by any electronic, mechanical, or other means, now known or hereafter invented, including photocopying and recording, or in any information storage or retrieval system, without permission in writing from the publishers.

Notice:
Product or corporate names may be trademarks or registered trademarks, and are used only for identification and explanation without intent to infringe.

National Library of Australia
Cataloguing-in-Publication entry:

Educational administration.

  Includes index.
  ISBN 1 86373 524 0.

  1. School management and organization — Australia. I. Evers, Colin W. (Colin William). II. Chapman, Judith D. (Judith Dorothy), 1948– .

371.200994

Set in 10/12 Bembo by DOCUPRO, Sydney

ISBN-13: 9781863735247 (pbk)

Contents

Figures and tables	vii
Preface	viii
Contributors	x
Introduction	xii
Colin W. Evers and Judith D. Chapman	

1	Theory in Educational Administration *Gabriele Lakomski and Colin W. Evers*	1
2	Educational Organisations as Systems *Gabriele Lakomski and Felicity Haynes*	18
3	Subjectivity and the Creation of Organisations *Peter C. Gronn*	34
4	Critical Theory of Educational Administration *Richard Bates*	49
5	Cultural Theory in Educational Administration *Lawrence Angus*	60
6	Ethics in Educational Administration *Fazal Rizvi*	81
7	Towards Coherence in Administrative Theory *Colin W. Evers and Gabriele Lakomski*	97
8	Cross-national Exchange and Australian Education Policy *Margaret Vickers*	110
9	New Patterns for Managing Schools and School Systems *Hedley Beare*	132
10	The Provision of Non-government Schooling in Australia: Retrospect and Prospect *Maurice Ryan and Helen Sungaila*	153

11 The Provision of Education and the Allocation of Resources 170
    Brian J. Caldwell

12 The Statutory Framework of Education and Legal Issues of
    Concern for Administrators 189
    Ann R. Shorten

13 Management of the Curriculum: Stability vs Change, Evolution
    vs Destabilisation 212
    Brian J. Spicer

14 Managing the Reform of Teachers and their Work:
    Perspectives, Prospects and Paradox 235
    Terri Seddon

15 Parents, the Community and School Governance 254
    Tony Knight

16 School Leadership: Securing Quality Teaching and Learning 274
    Clive Dimmock

17 Quality Assurance and Quality Management in Education
    Systems 296
    Peter Cuttance

Bibliography 317
Index 351

Figures and tables

Figures

7.1	A three-layer net with some connections shown	105
11.1	A model for the allocation of resources within schools	185
13.1	A strategic approach to curriculum management	216
13.2	Key competencies: an international comparison	224
13.3	An example of the program budgeting process for a department in an Australian primary school	228
13.4	Overview of models in context	232
16.1	Model of school leadership for quality teaching and learning: backward-mapping	280

Tables

11.1	Student-centred resource allocation to schools, Canada, 1993-94	181
11.2	Forecast total resource allocation, Canada, 1993-94	183

Preface

Despite a substantial growth in postgraduate courses in educational administration in Australia, in our view there has been no single text that addresses the needs of students considering educational administration in the Australian context. This book, with its focus on schools administration, aims to fill the gap. We have tried to consolidate, within one volume, contributions to both theoretical and applied contexts relevant to an understanding of the field.

In the theoretical chapters comprising the first half of the book, between an opening survey piece and a closing pointer to future directions, we cover the most influential perspectives. Some of these chapters make for demanding reading, but they reflect our decision to produce a compendium of current work rather than merely an introduction.

In selecting material for the second half of the book, on policy and practice, we faced the difficult task of balancing relevance in the current turmoil with importance over the longer term. Judgements like these are always controversial, the more so since they embody our guesses about the direction of the shifting scene in Australian education. We are hopeful that we have identified some enduring themes for understanding administrative practice in school contexts.

Because of the strength of Australian research in educational administration we expect the book will be of interest to a wider research community. For not only does the theory debate cross national boundaries, but many of the identified trends in practice have international counterparts—for example, decentralisation and participation, resource and curriculum management, and leadership. On these, and other matters, the authors in this book have not only surveyed viewpoints, they have also presented and argued their own positions.

In compiling this collection, we accrued a number of debts. We are grateful for the assistance provided by numerous colleagues who were willing to act as referees, and for the advice provided by the publisher's readers. A Monash University study leave from the Faculty of Education provided valuable time to research and design the project in its early stages. Helpful suggestions on work in progress came from our postgraduate administration students at both Monash and the University of Western Australia. We owe much to Gordon Young, whose wise counsel led to many improvements in the whole text. Finally, we are grateful to Heather Phillips for skilfully transforming a multitude of computer disks and endless editorial amendments into a seamless manuscript; and also to Erich von Dietze for assistance with proofreading and many of the final details of the project.

Colin W. Evers
Judith D. Chapman

Contributors

Dr Lawrence Angus Senior Lecturer, School of Graduate Studies, Faculty of Education, Monash University, Melbourne

Professor Richard Bates Dean of the Faculty of Education, Deakin University, Geelong

Professor Hedley Beare Professor of Education, Department of Policy, Context and Evaluation Studies, Institute of Education, University of Melbourne

Professor Brian Caldwell Professor of Education, Faculty of Policy, Context and Evaluation Studies, Institute of Education, University of Melbourne

Professor Judith Chapman Professor of Education, Faculty of Education, University of Western Australia

Dr Peter Cuttance Assistant Director-General (Quality Assurance), New South Wales Department of Education

Dr Clive Dimmock Senior Lecturer, Faculty of Education, University of Western Australia

Dr Colin Evers Associate Professor, School of Graduate Studies, Faculty of Education, Monash University

Dr Peter Gronn Senior Lecturer, School of Graduate Studies, Faculty of Education, Monash University

Dr Felicity Haynes Dean of the Faculty of Education, University of Western Australia

Dr Tony Knight Senior Lecturer, Centre for the Study of Curriculum and Teacher Education, School of Education, La Trobe University, Melbourne

Dr Gabriele Lakomski Associate Professor and Head of the Department of Policy, Context and Evaluation Studies, Institute of Education, University of Melbourne

Dr Fazal Rizvi Associate Professor, Department of Education, University of Queensland

Dr Maurice Ryan Lecturer, School of Religion and Philosophy, Faculty of Arts and Science, Australian Catholic University, Queensland

Dr Terri Seddon Senior Lecturer, School of Graduate Studies, Faculty of Education, Monash University

Dr Ann Shorten Senior Lecturer, School of Graduate Studies, Faculty of Education, Monash University

Dr Brian Spicer Senior Lecturer, School of Graduate Studies, Faculty of Education, Monash University

Professor Helen Sungaila Principal, McAuley Campus, Australian Catholic University, Queensland

Ms Margaret Vickers Lecturer, Graduate School of Education, Harvard University

Introduction

Colin W. Evers and Judith D. Chapman

The aim of this book is to provide a broad coverage of topics and issues in educational administration so that it addresses the needs of Australian postgraduate students. Because it is a work of many hands, we take the opportunity in this Introduction to provide some brief remarks that may help orient the reader to both the structure and content of this work.

We have found it convenient to group chapters into those primarily devoted to theoretical issues and those dealing with administrative contexts and practices. We do not regard this division as precise, because all discussion of practice is informed by some theory, and all theorising employs terms that figure in practice. Rather, it is a pragmatic division, though one that also enables us to display something of the structure within each grouping.

The first seven chapters, on theoretical themes, are organised to reflect the chronological development of theory in the field. Over the past four decades, educational administration has moved from being conceived almost exclusively as a species of behavioural science, to a domain that nowadays admits of considerable theoretical diversity. Much of this diversity has been developed in opposition to the dominant behavioural science tradition, usually exploiting some alleged weaknesses. Thus traditional science, with its methodological premium on objectivity, has difficulty accounting for human subjectivity and the importance of meaning, intention and interpretation. It also fails to offer a perspective on the ethical choices that administrators face, or to provide much guidance on the politics of organisational life.

In identifying and responding to these difficulties, theorists draw on a range of alternative sets of assumptions, although a common thread is a rejection of the model of science that underwrites the systems scientific approach. The opening chapter provides a review of the main elements of the theory debate, while Chapter 7 proposes an agenda for moving beyond the framework of argument between traditional science of administration and its critics.

INTRODUCTION

Doing justice to the diversity of applied and contextual issues presented us with a more serious challenge. Difficulties seemed to threaten all of the usual trade-offs between depth and breadth, current relevance and future importance, and whether to focus on the particular or the general aspects of issues. Our solution, in the end, was to adopt a mixed strategy. Chapter 8 places the Australian situation in an international context and subsequent chapters supply some analysis of patterns in both government and non-government sectors. We then consider basic issues of infrastructure—resource allocation, legal frameworks, curriculum, teaching, and community participation—and conclude with an emphasis on the emerging theme of quality as both a feature of leadership and an element of accountability through the mechanisms of quality assurance. These latter chapters reflect the more controversial editorial decisions we have made over priorities among issues and the path of future developments in Australian education.

A large book with modest structure should permit readers with particular interests to select material. We therefore provide, in the remainder of this Introduction, a brief guide to content by way of chapter summaries.

In Chapter 1 Gabriele Lakomski and Colin Evers trace the major theoretical developments in educational administration, from the initial influence of the US-based Theory Movement embodying a traditional conception of science applied to organisations as systems, through to the alternatives of subjectivism, cultural and interpretive perspectives, and critical theory, concluding with an account of an emerging new science of administration justified on coherence principles. The chapter reproduces key arguments from the literature to give a sense of the direction of theoretical development in the field.

Without doubt, the most influential framework for understanding administration has been the systems perspective. Lakomski and Haynes, in Chapter 2, sketch its origins, describe its central features and comment on changes that have taken place during its evolution, particularly the shift from closed systems to open systems. They conclude by urging caution in accepting the systems metaphor where it appears to offer generalisations beyond the reach of empirical evidence.

Although the subjectivist turn in educational administration was initiated by the Canadian writer T.B. Greenfield, it has had a profound influence on Australian theoretical work. Peter Gronn, in Chapter 3, analyses Greenfield's contribution, exploring the implications of his most distinctive thesis: that organisations are invented social reality. Gronn's chapter offers a particular focus on Greenfield's concern about values and his notion of organisation as an expression of moral order.

A founder of critical theory applications to educational administration, Richard Bates, highlights in Chapter 4 some weaknesses of a generic science of administration by drawing a contrast with *educational* administration. The former is said to embody a technological rationality, a concern for control, and the subordination of the individual to the social order. The latter, however, is centred on the achievement of education, which requires taking into account not just human technical interests but also interests in understanding and emancipation.

Lawrie Angus, in his very detailed discussion of cultural perspectives in educational administration (Chapter 5), canvasses themes raised by Greenfield, Bates and the functionalist scientific tradition of theorising corporate culture. Using insights from both Greenfield's critique of science and Bates's championing of the emancipatory interest, Angus urges the adoption of a relational view of culture. According to this, culture is something constructed as part of the social and political processes at specific sites.

All the major alternatives to systems science draw attention to its inability to account for the domain of ethics. Fazal Rizvi's work in Chapter 6 surveys and evaluates a number of the most important competing claims about the place of ethics in educational administration. He concludes that ethical concerns are at the heart of administration but that many familiar assumptions will need to be rejected before these concerns can adequately be dealt with. For example, the use of means–ends reasoning creates the expectation that values are separate from facts, thus mistakenly detaching relevant social, historical and economic factors from the ethical assessment of administrative policy and practice. For a more adequate framework, Rizvi draws on the work of Dewey and the pragmatist tradition in general.

An attempt to move beyond the current pattern of dispute between science and its critics is discussed by Colin Evers and Gabriele Lakomski in Chapter 7. They propose a theory of science that is much broader than traditional views and suggest that it should be the basis of a new approach to educational administration. Such an approach is able to permit ethics, human subjectivity and empirical elements to be included within the one comprehensive theory of educational administration, because Evers and Lakomski are also proposing a new way of justifying knowledge. Their chapter highlights features of an administrative theory that are the direct result of adopting a coherentist form of knowledge justification.

In Chapter 8 Margaret Vickers examines the impact of cross-national exchange on the development of Australian education policy. Her discussion concentrates on the interactions between the Australian government and the Organization of Economic Cooperation and Development (OECD), arguably the most influential of the international agencies whose work affects Australian education. To help structure and guide her discussion, Vickers examines recent work in the field of knowledge utilisation. Her analysis reveals the extent to which decision-makers drew on knowledge from overseas sources as they framed some of the key policy issues of the past decade—in particular, youth policy reforms and the reconstruction of the higher education system.

Hedley Beare in Chapter 9 develops the theme of cross-national exchange in his account of the restructuring of schools and school systems in Australia. Beare documents the movement away from school systems characterised by a 'large, predictable, plodding bureaucracy' towards the development of systems of 'network' organisations. He sees network organisations as characterised by a strategic core, which sets the boundary and makes system-wide policies, connected to operating units, to which the main work of the organisation is 'franchised out'. This kind of approach to public systems of education, Beare argues, requires new regulatory frameworks and new modes of operation hitherto unknown in the administration of public education.

Of course, alternatives to the highly bureaucratic approach to administering schools and school systems already exist in Australia. In the non-government sector there are at least eight school systems designed on premises radically different from those that underlie government school systems. These premises and other matters associated with the administration of non-government schooling are addressed by Maurice Ryan and Helen Sungaila in Chapter 10.

Non-government schools have been a significant presence in Australia since the earliest days of colonial settlement. Today, however, in the face of shrinking budgets, internal and external scrutiny and a growing convergence with the government school sector, there is a need to identify, develop and maintain their distinctive identity. Failure to promote a distinctive identity, according to Ryan and Sungaila, could lead to a questioning of the rationale for the separateness of non-government schools, a decline in their popularity and perhaps their demise. To resist such trends, Ryan and Sungaila suggest that administrators need to develop deeper understandings about the ways in which organisational identity is formed and nurtured. To facilitate this they delineate some practical strategies that administrators can use to promote a distinctive school identity, culture and ethos.

Such qualitative dimensions of organisational life, however, cannot be separated from matters associated with resources. In Chapter 11 Brian Caldwell gives a descriptive and critical commentary on the provision of education and the allocation of resources. Using the 'frames' of politics, economics and industrial relations, Caldwell examines the tensions among values that underlie much contention in the policy-making process. The balance of contention among values such as efficiency, equity and choice, he argues, is seen in the allocation of resources *to* schools and *within* schools. A new alignment of values underpins the major structural reform that is now evident in Australian education.

Yet as Beare points out (in Chapter 9), structural reform and new arrangements for the allocation and management of resources cannot take place without changes to regulatory frameworks. The importance of the statutory framework of education in Australia cannot be overemphasised, argues Ann Shorten in Chapter 12. The statutory framework determines not only how education is organised and financed but also the powers and responsibilities of participants in the educational process. In this chapter, Shorten describes the statutory framework of Australian education and outlines aspects of statute law and case law as they relate to education. Her survey highlights a number of legal issues of concern for educational administrators and teachers. Shorten emphasises that the law pertaining to education is always changing.

The challenges and dilemmas of change are developed further by Brian Spicer in Chapter 13. In 'Management of the Curriculum: Stability vs Change, Evolution vs Destabilisation', Spicer identifies the general structure, network and processes of curriculum development in Australia, directing attention towards various models of the curriculum development process and their interaction with societal directions. Spicer argues that curriculum, teaching and learning are the most important operational domains in education. This is clearly evident in the emphasis on quality teaching and learning in current Australian educational reform efforts.

Aligned with the concern for quality teaching and learning are policy interventions aimed at changing teachers and their work. In Chapter 14 Terri Seddon examines the conceptions of teachers and their work, which inform these policy interventions. She expresses concern that the educational managerial interventions that target individuals, and the award-restructuring interventions that target work but veer towards individualist managerial strategies for implementation, both end up separating subject and object, actor and system, individual and context, educational and industrial. This, she contends, is not where the work perspective starts conceptually nor where it ends politically. The work perspective offers a basis for new questions about teachers' work.

But this still leaves a central question unanswered: who should have authority over educational issues in a school? This question is addressed in Chapter 15 by Tony Knight. In attempting to unravel the gap between policy formation and policy implementation, Knight examines the micro-political processes of a school when it is implementing government policy designed to facilitate collaborative decision-making among teachers and parents. In his analysis Knight highlights the changing governance arrangements in Australian education. He argues for a closer relationship between parents and teachers as a way to enhance the educational experience of all students.

INTRODUCTION

Of course, essential to the achievement of this goal of enhanced student learning will be the nature of leadership at the school level. In Chapter 16 Clive Dimmock argues that top-quality schools place all students at the centre of what they do; they are driven by the philosophy and practice of helping all students learn as best they can. In such schools it is not only teaching and learning that assume new forms. Flexible organisational structures are designed to facilitate new learning and teaching practices. Leadership and management are reconceptualised in ways that respond to the delivery of quality teaching and learning. In this backward-mapping conception of leadership, school leaders must develop new roles, relationships and competencies in providing quality education.

An analysis of other approaches to quality—quality assurance and the management of quality—is presented in Chapter 17 by Peter Cuttance. He reveals the extent to which school systems since their inception in the late nineteenth century focused on the issue of quality through the establishment of inspectors. School inspectors, however, operated in a world of closed criteria and often in a punitive framework. This is in sharp contrast to the approach to assuring quality that is embodied in recent developments, such as the school review. The reviews operate in a way that provides maximum community ownership. They have an explicit objective to address the issues for the development of individual schools as well as contribute to the accountability of schools by making public their findings on the performance and development of schools. The reviews focus on the key management and educational issues for future developments to meet the educational needs of the community.

1 Theory in Educational Administration

Gabriele Lakomski and Colin W. Evers

If indicators of a profession's existence are the availability of university, in-service and Department of Education courses, national and international conferences and the emergence of a journal, then the birth of Australian educational administration as a profession occurred in about 1963. Of course, there were individuals or groups concerned with school administration before this, but as the focus of an identifiable theoretical activity and a set of articulated practices, Australian educational administration is barely thirty years old.

Australian educational administration borrowed its theoretical framework from North America, where professional status was much better established. The prevailing mood of the time was that of the Theory Movement, whose theoreticians are well represented in the texts of Australian educators such as William Walker (1970), who had gained his doctorate from the University of Illinois in the late 1950s.

The best indication of what constituted 'theory' in educational administration is found in the *Journal of Educational Administration*, the first truly international journal in the field, closely followed by the establishment of the North American *Educational Administration Quarterly* in 1964. The founder of the *Journal of Educational Administration*, William Walker, more than any other writer in the Australian context, must be credited with making available and personally contributing to the development of the theoretical–philosophical foundations of educational administration. While the practical concerns of educational administration have mostly been well represented in research studies, theoretical concerns have also been a focus of Australian research since the 1960s. Australian educational administration thus has a strong tradition of theory development, which continues to gain international acclaim.

The Theory Movement in Australia

Discussing the first Australian postgraduate course in educational administration, offered by the University of New England in 1959, Walker (1964) described the course as being comparative but also unambiguously theoretical in orientation. The 'how to do it' approach was not favoured, and Walker (1964: 21) was most concerned that the new profession was still 'rich in opinion and folk-lore, but sadly lacking in scientific foundation and fact'. Arguing against those who believed that personal experience in school administration was sufficient training, Walker conceded that 'the school of hard knocks' had produced some excellent administrators but insisted 'that they might well have distinguished themselves much earlier and much more often if they had been able to avoid a long period of trial and error learning. It is doubtful whether we can any longer afford to be as wasteful of our resources in material and personnel as we have been in the past' (Walker 1964: 12). This assessment shared by the prominent Australian educator William Bassett (1965) and others, clearly indicates the direction Walker believed the new profession of educational administration should take: it should be placed on a sound *theoretical* platform. It is largely because of Walker's work that the writers of what has come to be known as the Theory Movement (see Evers and Lakomski 1991: Ch. 3) were introduced to Australian educational administration and in turn shaped its early theoretical orientation. The clearest expression of the nature and function of 'theory' in administration is in Walker's (1965) landmark article, 'Theory and Practice in Educational Administration', published in the *Journal of Educational Administration*. Guided by the Deweyan motto that there is nothing more practical than a good theory, Walker is very clear on the kind of distinction to be drawn in educational administration: *the only relevant distinction is that between good theory and bad theory*. It is not the commonly advanced dichotomy of theory vs practice or even theory and practice. And even more strongly:

> Clearly, there is no question as to whether we should or should not employ theory in our administrative behaviour. Such a question is as meaningless as is the question as to whether we should or should not use motivation in our behaviour. The point is that all of us theorise, but that few of us develop *good* theory, that is, theory which reveals uniformities in the subject matter of the theory, which enables us to predict precisely in accordance with established criteria and provides guides to action which 'work', or more rigidly, as defined by Griffiths after Feigl, 'a set of assumptions from which can be derived by purely logico-mathematical procedures a larger set of empirical laws'. (Walker 1965: 20)

So the purpose and function of 'theory' is that it provides a coherent, systematic basis that can assist the administrator to predict a future state of affairs, and hence to guide action accordingly. In short, administrative theory guides people to better action or decision-making. Administrative action, including decision-making, in this context is considered to be rational or scientific.

This description already makes it clear what (administration) theory is not. Following Griffiths' (1959: 13–19) definition, adopted by Walker, 'theory' is not just a personal matter, nor a mere speculation or dream, nor is it to be equated with a philosophy. The important distinction for us is the third one. What Griffiths means to indicate by this distinction is that a philosophy has to do with (among other things) a well-developed set of values or 'oughts'. Roughly put, philosophy trades in values or 'oughts', whereas 'theory' trades in facts or 'is's'. The 'is–ought dichotomy' was actually the trademark of logical positivism and logical empiricism, the dominant philosophical orientation in the early decades of the twentieth century. Key members of the Theory Movement, such as Daniel Griffiths (1959), Andrew Halpin (1958 1966) and Jack Culbertson et al. (1973), accepted the logical empiricist doctrine of a strict separation of fact from value; and indeed this dichotomy has been best expressed by Herbert Simon (1976: 249–50) in his example from economics:333

> ... the proposition 'Alternative A is *good*' must be translated into two propositions, one of them ethical, the other factual:
> 'Alternative A will lead to maximum profit.'
> 'To maximize profit is good.'
> The first of these sentences has no ethical content and is a sentence of the practical science of business. The second sentence is an ethical imperative and has no place in any science.
> Science cannot tell whether we *ought* to maximize profit. It can merely tell us under what conditions this maximum profit will occur, and what the consequences of maximization will be.

According to this distinction, values ('oughts') have no place in science because they cannot be verified empirically, whereas facts can be by observation and deduction. The underlying belief—in Griffiths' theory and others—is that administration as a social activity can be studied *scientifically*; that is, the phenomena of social life are as amenable to scientific scrutiny as the phenomena of physics and biology; the only proviso is not to confuse matters of fact with matters of value. Administration, then, can be a science rather than remain an art based only on personal intuition and experience, or what Simon calls the 'proverbs' of administration. The science/art distinction in educational administration has its origins in the logical empiricists' separation of facts and values. Both dichotomies continue to pervade contemporary theorising in the field, the science/art distinction being the more overt.

For administrative theory to be scientific, according to Griffiths, it has to possess some specific characteristics. Like science generally, it has to be able to describe, explain and predict the phenomena with which it is concerned. Following the formulations of the logical empiricist Herbert Feigl, Griffiths believes that '[T]he study of administration can become scientific to the extent that it ascertains its *facts* by a meticulous scrutiny of administrative behaviour. This must then be followed by causal interpretation of the facts. On the basis of description and interpretation, accurate predictions can be made.' (Griffiths 1959: 22) Administrative scientific inquiry, like any other scientific enterprise, is guided by the criteria of objectivity, reliability, operational definitions, coherence and comprehensiveness. Of particular importance for the theorists of the Theory Movement was the concept of operational definitions, by which is meant observable measurable procedures that could be carried out in order to identify phenomena to which the relevant concepts refer. Griffiths (1959: 24) expresses the expectations of administrative scientific theory best when he writes that 'the practice of administration is the application of the theory of administrative researchers . . . and that the hypotheses to be tested must . . . be suggested by practitioners in the field'. Theory, among other things, is thus quite clearly conceived of as *a guide to action*. This is a point worth emphasising, because for an applied science such as administration it is precisely its capacity to guide action that proves its mettle. It is therefore not surprising that this issue has provided an important focal point for criticism by proponents of alternative, non-scientific conceptions of administration.

In addition to the scientific criteria listed above, a theory's role is to *explain* the phenomena under discussion. Having thus described the various criteria a scientific administrative theory must satisfy, Griffiths (1959: 28), following Feigl (1951), defines a theory as 'a set of assumptions from which can be derived by purely logico-mathematical procedures a larger set of empirical laws'. The definition of administrative theory provided by Griffiths shows three particular philosophical constraints that are characteristic of the Theory Movement:

1. 'Theory' is a hypothetico-deductive structure in which statements are partitioned into hypotheses and testable consequences, based on core assumptions, and eventually leading to 'a larger set of empirical laws'.
2. Operational definitions are created to provide empirical content for theoretical terms.
3. Administrative theory sharply distinguishes facts and values, where the latter are accounted for in terms of variables only.

These three constraints are indicative of the basic empiricist epistemological structure for the justification of theories. But in philosophy and epistemology, this kind of structure for justification is no longer considered sound, and empiricism as an account of science has been replaced by alternative post-positivist conceptions (Churchland 1986: especially Ch. 6; BonJour, 1985).

Systems theory

Seen through the eyes of Walker and Griffiths, the Theory Movement adhered to logical empiricism as its philosophical basis, while its conceptual framework was that of systems theory, which described (educational) organisations as *social* systems. (For a contemporary, prominent version, see Hoy and Miskel 1991.) Because the next chapter explicitly discusses educational organisations as systems, let us note here only some features. (For an excellent discussion, see Scott in Meyer 1978; Scott 1981; Chs 4 and 5; Harmon and Mayer 1986; Evers and Lakomski 1991: 59–73.) In general terms, systems are commonly described as consisting of interrelated objects, attributes and events (see Litterer 1969: 4) and are usually classified as either closed or open. A *closed* system is one that focuses primarily on its internal characteristics (for example, a lawnmower or a Weberian type of bureaucracy), while an *open* (or *natural*) *system* is defined in terms of its dependence on its *environment*—that is, the processes and events external to it (a school is an example). The 'environment' of an organisation comprises such elements as economics, politics, culture and technology, as well as other social and inter-organisational features (Scott 1978: 21) considered vital for the system's continued existence.

Prominent social system theorists such as Getzels, Lipham and Campbell (1968: 52) describe administration 'structurally . . . as the hierarchy of superordinate–subordinate relationships within a social system . . . Functionally, this hierarchy of relationships is the locus for allocating and integrating roles and facilities in order to achieve the goals of the system'. There are a number of important concepts to note here. Considering a school as a social system, two classes of phenomena can be observed (as in any social system):

1. There are *institutions* with certain roles and expectations that are supposed to fulfil the goals of the system.
2. There are also the *individuals* with different personalities and needs; it is their observed interactions that are called 'social behaviour'.

'Institution', 'role' and 'expectation' refer to the normative (or *nomothetic*) dimension of social system activity, while 'individual', 'personality' and 'need disposition' indicate the personal (or *idiographic*) dimension. The major task is to understand the relationship between these elements in order to explain observed behaviour and predict and control it. Understanding administrative behaviour therefore involves understanding the nature of the individuals who inhabit various roles and react to certain expectations. To re-emphasise this important point: *role* and *individual* are not synonymous. And as Harmon and Mayer (1986: 170) note, this separation 'is an important step of abstraction'. The significance of this is that because roles and role expectations cannot be directly seen, they 'must be inferred from phenomenological report or from the analysis of other kinds of data' (Getzels et al. 1968: 61).

Now within the justificatory framework of logical empiricism and Feigl's definition of theory, the 'science of managing behaviour' (as Walker put it) has to proceed by observing actual behaviour and then inferring roles and expectations from these observations. The point to be made here is that all observation is theory-laden, and it is human beings (and not abstract roles) who act. This means that an organisational role is in practice an *interpretation* of what should be done in a given circumstance (see Evers and Lakomski, 1993), and this interpretation, and thus the role, is shaped by a person's beliefs, wants and values. If this is so, then the distinction between the nomothetic and idiographic dimensions blurs, and the purported need to explain any relationship between them that was expected to deliver an account of 'organisational behaviour' becomes problematic. Organisational behaviour appears to be no more and no less than people's interpretations of what they should do under given circumstances, and the notion of role will often be too abstract to figure usefully in analyses of system behaviour. Insofar as we continue to talk of administrative roles, we do so by recognising that they are always value-laden. This was the very point made by Thomas B. Greenfield in his now-legendary address to the 1974 International Intervisitation Programme in Bristol, an address that changed the theoretical direction of educational administration. (The core essays of Greenfield's work are included in his 1993 collection entitled *Greenfield on Educational Administration,* edited by himself and Peter Ribbins.)

Greenfield's subjectivism

By renouncing the systems theorists' assumption 'that organisations are not only real but also distinct from the actions, feelings and purposes of people', Greenfield (Greenfield and Ribbins 1993: 1) challenges the core of the behavioural science of administration. Basing his argument largely on European (especially Weberian) interpretive social science, he stresses that it is human action and intention that first constitute what we call 'organisation'. Since 'organisation' is just another meaning we create for ourselves to explain what it is that we do in certain situations, according to Greenfield it is untenable to speak of organisations as if they had an *objective* reality outside of us, as if they were *real* in the sense that houses and cars are. It is in this sense that Greenfield speaks of organisations as 'social inventions'. They are 'invented' insofar as they are the products of our minds' activity, and it is in this sense that they are *subjective*. Hence, the systems theorists' talk of organisations as if they were houses whose basic structures remain intact while the human tenants come and go, is at best misleading and at worst amounts to reifying social reality. Expressed clearly in his 1974 Bristol presentation, this remains the core epistemological feature of Greenfield's research program and provides the basis for his alternative *subjectivist* perspective on educational administration. (For an elegant exposition of his ideas covering Greenfield's publications to 1982, see Gronn 1983. It can be said that Gronn has been largely responsible for making Greenfield's work largely accessible to Australian administrators. Gronn, 1994, updates and expands the earlier emphases.)

By rejecting a scientific view of administration, and by drawing expressly on the tradition of European and North American interpretivist social science, Greenfield also rejects the idea that educational administration can be an objective enterprise. In support of his view he draws on some crucial criticisms of empiricist science as developed in Thomas Kuhn's and Paul Feyerabend's work. The idea that all our experience needs to be interpreted has its correlate in philosophy of science in terms of the 'theory-ladenness of observation'. This is the basic idea that all observations are always couched in the language of some theory; there is no theory-free way of reading experience. This applies not only to ordinary common sense which, because of its unquestioned general acceptance is not perceived as theoretical, but also to the less accessible theories of science. Greenfield thus accepts that there is no sharp distinction to be drawn between theory and observation (see, for example, Greenfield 1979); and he also employs a second crucial argument against traditional science in order to support his subjectivist view. This argument, the *underdetermination* of theories by empirical data, follows directly from the theory-ladenness of observation. If there is no principled distinction to be made between theory and observation (or 'fact'), there are no 'hard data' that could be drawn on when arbitrating between competing claims to knowledge. Or to express this point differently, there are no secure foundations on the basis of which we can establish knowledge, and this strikes at the heart of all varieties of positivism. Because foundational support is not to be had, the whole business of justifying administrative theories becomes a lot more complex. Here Greenfield avails himself of Kuhn's insight that theoreticians live in different worlds which are, in the end, incommensurable—they are governed by their own internal standards of truth and objectivity. And because these standards are determined by each paradigm or large-scale alternative viewpoint, there is no way of comparing the standards of one with those of a competitor; standards in paradigm A do not *mean* the same thing in paradigm B, because the latter has paradigm B standards. It is this fundamental concept that underlies Greenfield's advocacy of an *anarchistic theory of administration*. Even if there was no problem with either empirical evidence or underdetermination, Greenfield (1979: 170) draws attention to a further difficulty: the problem of applying evidence to particular claims (because all claims are embedded in networks, and it is no easy matter to tell which part of the network empirical evidence bears upon). Test situations are always complex. Greenfield's case for subjectivism thus rests on some very powerful criticisms of traditional science: (a) the theory-ladenness of observations; (b) the underdetermination of theories by observation; and (c) the complexity of test situations. Bearing these in mind, the following argument summarises Greenfield's position:

1. If all the objective evidence there is for a scientific theory is empirical evidence, and
2. If empirical evidence is never sufficient for choosing among competing theories, then
3. Choosing among competing scientific theories of educational administration is ultimately a subjective matter, a matter of human will, intention and values. (See Greenfield 1991: 202–4; Evers and Lakomski 1993: 144.)

Much of Greenfield's criticism of traditional empiricist views of administration and science is valid, but in following Kuhn and Feyerabend he also perpetuates one significant problem: the identification of objective evidence with empirical evidence, as expressed in the premise above. This identification, we believe, is incorrect, as will be shown later.

Considering educational administration as a field of study, Greenfield moves theorising to a point where his criticism of *traditional* administrative theory and behavioural science is decisive. In doing so, he introduces some of the most important results of recent philosophy of science and epistemology. His subjectivist approach correctly stresses that humans are interpretive beings and that our knowledge of external reality is mediated through our beliefs and ideas about the world, and that in this sense, all our experience is *value*-laden. This insight remains a core belief of other, newer, modes of conceptualising educational administration, those that carry the label of 'alternative' because they see themselves as *alternatives to* the traditional *scientific* model of behavioural administrative theory: from Gronn's biographical approach to what has come to be known as the cultural perspective (for example, the work of Sergiovanni 1984a, 1984b; Sergiovanni and Corbally 1984; Beare et al. 1989; Westoby 1988); and critical theory as represented in the writings of Bates (1983, 1984, 1987, 1988, 1990), Angus (1988, 1994), Watkins (1986), and Foster (1980a, 1980b, 1984, and especially 1986), as well as Giroux (1983). This is not to imply that these alternatives share identical theoretical commitments, but just to indicate that there is some theoretical touchstone in terms of their acceptance of theory-ladenness and their rejection of positivist science's applicability in the social realm. In addition to these relatively modest shared assumptions there is, however, the common belief that educational administration cannot be a science. It would be fair to say that the first two premises that characterise Greenfield's position are shared by the alternative approaches, with important modifications being expressed in the conclusion, especially in terms of the nature of values held which provide the basis for choice. Here we refer especially to critical theory, which can be said to offer the only explicitly *political* framework for educational administration, based as it is on the neo-marxist critique of capitalism.

The cultural perspective

Greenfield's work represents a vital link in the chain of theory development in educational administration. His subjectivist criticism has prepared much of the theoretical ground for what has become known as the 'cultural perspective'. Although not yet a fully developed school of thought, it gives the most comprehensive alternative perspective to the traditional view. This is not to imply that the notion of 'culture' is new to either organisational thought or educational administration. It has already had a distinguished history in organisational theory, as discussed in Smircich's (1983) detailed overview (cf. Angus 1994 for a critical review of 'organisational culture'), while writers such as Jackson (1968) and Wolcott (1973) have long emphasised cultural phenomena in schools. Although there are many different features that one might emphasise as constituting 'culture', a comprehensive definition is provided by Beare et al. (1989: 173–4) in terms of the 'tangible, intangible and symbolic elements of organisational life'. These elements comprise a range of factors:

- The underlying philosophy and/or ideology espoused by the leaders and members.
- The ways in which that philosophy is translated into an operational mission or purpose.
- The respective value-sets of leaders and others (both within the organisation and those directly or indirectly affected by its operations) and the resonance between these.
- The quality (as well as the nature) of personal and interpersonal actions and interactions.

- The metaphors that consciously or unconsciously serve as frameworks for thinking and action.
- The sagas, myths, stories, folk heroes and celebrations that serve to generate or bolster incentive and motivation.

A cultural perspective thus focuses on issues and concerns very different from those emphasised in traditional scientific organisational theory. It is the cultural fabric of an organisation, in its many facets, that provides the only legitimate theoretical lens through which a social organisation such as a school can properly be described and its workings explained. According to cultural theorists, as language-using and meaning-constructing beings we need to avail ourselves of the tools of culture in order to make sense of our social environment. But sense-making and meaning-constructing are not the business of the natural sciences, which emphasise observation and hypothetico-deductive theories to explain behaviour. At the heart of the cultural view, in contrast, are all those aspects that do not, and indeed cannot, come into the scope of the scientific approach—aspects that are believed to accord us our quintessential human nature. While observable behaviour is not rejected as an important category, defenders of the cultural perspective argue that what is really important is the explanation of human *action*. In Sergiovanni's words (1984a: 3) 'humans do not behave; they *act*. Actions differ from behaviour in that they are born of preconceptions, assumptions, and motives. Actions have meaning in the sense that as preconditions change, meanings change regardless of the sameness of recorded behaviour.' Human action (as opposed to behaviour) is said to be fundamentally characterised by inner, mental phenomena, such as motives, intentions, beliefs and values. In this view, what really explains an action is the *meaning* we give to it, what we *intended* to do, or what *belief* or *value* guided us in pursuing one action rather than another. It is these internal non-observable characteristics that thus provide the only avenue to 'get at' what makes humans really 'tick'; and because these mental features are deemed to be so fundamentally human, the cultural view argues that it is *superior* to a scientific approach in terms of 'explaining' human action. This is the sense in which cultural theory understands itself as an *alternative*. A direct result of its presumed capacity to expose human motives and intentions is the belief in its increased ability to contribute to better decision-making in educational administration, a claim that goes to the heart of the criticism of orthodox administrative theory which, subject to its split of facts from values, could not provide any guidance on what administrators *ought* to do.

The justificatory framework that underpins the cultural perspective derives from European philosophical thought, such as *hermeneutics* (see Palmer 1969 for an excellent introduction), *cultural anthropology, phenom-*

enology and *interpretive social science* (see Rabinow and Sullivan 1977). An integral part of this tradition, and one that characterises it, is its emphasis on a different methodology, believed necessary to gauge hidden phenomena. This is the method of understanding *(verstehen)* as Weber (1949) conceptualised it. By means of this method it is believed possible to gauge human subjectivity and the creation of meaning, which are said to hold the key to understanding organisations such as schools. It is in this respect that the modern version of the cultural perspective differs from its forerunners.

We have to remember here that interpretive social science— to use this term as an umbrella for a number of approaches—shares with modern philosophy of science the vital insight that our observations are always theory-laden, or 'interpreted'. This is expressed in the idea of the 'hermeneutic circle', made famous by the philosopher Heidegger (1962). What is also shared is the conclusion that Greenfield reached: there are always many interpretations to be had of an event, a practice or an action, and the choice between them is a subjective matter. Nevertheless, interpretivists such as Gadamer (1976, 1979) and Taylor (1979) also worried about this, because the *correct* identification of the meaning of an event or action is important. So in order to be able to 'fix' the meaning of an event or a person's action, it is necessary to be able to take recourse to the meaning the agent gives to an action—in other words, his or her interpretation or motive for acting. The declared motive, or the interpretation, plays a foundational role in the sense of epistemic foundation, in that its identification is the *final arbiter* for the meaning of the action. Just as empiricist positivism's famous 'sense data' were supposed to provide the unshakeable foundation for sorting a valid theory from an invalid one, so an interpretation or motive within interpretive social science is expected to provide the epistemic justification for knowing *the* meaning of an action. And just as observations had to be secure (for any doubt would automatically eliminate them as a secure foundation), so a motive or intention had to be similarly beyond question. It therefore seems that the pattern of justification for a knowledge claim in the cultural perspective resembles that of empiricism, with mental, 'inner' phenomena replacing 'outer' observable items as the relevant foundational entities.

Here, practical and, ultimately, epistemological problems are encountered. If it is of the utmost importance that we unambiguously identify the relevant motive or intention in order to sort valid from invalid interpretations, then not only does the intention in question have to be accessible, but also we need a decisive procedure for identifying it. But following the principle of the 'hermeneutic circle', all we ever have are interpretations, and interpretations of interpretations. Hence foundational certainty is not available. Ironically, the (in principle) unlimited possibilities of successive interpretations is considered the strength of this approach rather than a weakness. It is this very possibility that cultural theorists believe establishes their approach as non-foundational, because it is interpretations 'all the way down'. Thus writers such as Sergiovanni (1984a, 1984b) speak of 'multiple perspectives' and more recently (1992) of different 'mindscapes' that are complementary because in his view there is no single way to truth or objectivity. What we have here is another version of the argument for different and incommensurable world views, which are all believed to be justified by their proponents, an argument we considered earlier.

Conceived as alternative to science, cultural theories of administration face an interesting methodological difficulty. Humans are enmeshed in a vast causal field, so that presumably what a person does is brought about by some prior set of relevant causes. Bidding at an auction, for example, requires the chemical transmission of electrical impulses from the brain to the muscles of one's arm in order that it be raised for a bid; and, we might suppose, the antecedent brain activity required for an arm rising in these circumstances has its own prior set of relevant causes; and so on. Let us call this sequence of events the physical detail.

Corresponding to the physical detail is some familiar mental detail: a person *wants*, say, a house, *knows* that a preferred one can be obtained by bidding at an auction, and *intentionally* makes a bid at the appropriate time. Cultural theory characteristically deals with the mental detail, while scientific theory deals with the physical detail, and the two modes of explanation are presumed to be quite distinct—indeed, the scientific mode is assumed to be inadequate as a methodology for accounting for social life.

The main trouble with maintaining a strong dichotomy between the scientific and the cultural is that there are no resources left over for explaining the obvious correspondence between physical detail and mental detail. Why should a person's arm go up at just the time he or she intends to make a bid? Why should the caused activities of a person's body bear any relationship to a person's mental activity of wanting, planning, believing and intending?

To avoid a mystery or the supposition that some kind of miracle takes place, we need a way of making the two accounts fit together. Our suggestion is that the brain has some method of acquiring and representing to itself the knowledge of its social circumstances, such as being at an auction, which is causally efficacious in producing the appropriate bodily movements at the right time. According to this view, mental talk and mental explanation are successful precisely because they capture the underlying causal regularities in the physical/social world. Indeed, most of the time such mental talk is all we have to go on, because scientific theories of the physical detail are still poorly developed in the crucial areas of human cognition and symbolic information-processing. As these theories are developed, we expect the methodological separation of the cultural from the scientific will appear less plausible (see Evers 1990a, 1993). Indeed, from our coherentist point of view there are no substantive distinctions to be drawn between the phenomena of the so-called natural sciences and those of the social sciences.

Critical theory

Advocates of critical theory in educational administration do not share *identical* theoretical commitments and assumptions with the cultural perspective, but they do agree with the first two premises that characterise Greenfield's subjectivism and which are also accepted in cultural theory. Critical theorists such as Bates, Foster, Watkins and Angus accept theory-ladenness and the kinds of subjectivist conclusions drawn (as expressed earlier).

The most important feature shared with their cultural theory cousins is their objection to empiricist science, which is routinely identified with science in general. Their major difference with cultural theory is that while they are able to employ the valuable insights of this perspective, they do so *on the background of the critical theory of society*, which is said both to facilitate a critical consciousness of social-administrative problems and to be able to suggest solutions for radical change by furthering human emancipation. So while cultural theorists believe that understanding a motive or intention provides the key for understanding human action, the critical theorist believes that such understanding alone is politically conservative and must be expanded to include the background of a society shaped by socio-economic inequality and resultant power struggles. Angus makes this point well in Chapter 5, when he notes that cultural theory (as discussed in the present context) concerns itself more with 'people problems' rather than power structures.

With regard to positivist administrative theory (that of Simon, Griffiths and Feigl, for example), critical theorists argue that the administrative orthodoxy has ignored issues of social structure, as well as economic and social inequality. Writers such as Simon are seen as lending support to the capitalist *status quo*, in that they describe organisations as if they were rational entities whereas their tight bureaucratic structures merely hide the real power struggles fought out 'behind the scenes'. This kind of instrumental rationality and bureaucratic control, so critical theorists maintain, merely serves to gloss over the interests of those in power in capitalist societies and denies legitimation to all the groups whose political values clash with those of the powerful. While critical theory in educational administration is primarily a critique of orthodox administrative theory, it also sees itself as an *ethic of change* and as superior to its forerunners in that the real (that is, political) world of organisations has been openly acknowledged.

It is obvious from this brief outline that the intellectual tradition of this alternative in educational administration differs from those discussed previously. Although heavily influenced by interpretive philosophy and social theory, its political commitments derive from neo-marxist thought as developed in the so-called Frankfurt School (for an overview, see Bernstein 1976). Within educational administration it is particularly the work of the second-generation critical theorist Jürgen Habermas (1972a, 1972b, 1976, 1979) that has become most influential (see Chapter 3).

As the most explicit political perspective in educational administration, the critical theory of society is broad in scope as well as the most ambitious of the alternatives. That it has become so prominent in administrative theorising is primarily due to Richard Bates's work in the Australian context, work that was subsequently taken up by Foster in North America. Bates's core thesis, in keeping with the original theory's primary objective as critique, is that the traditional science of administration is fundamentally manipulative—that is, it serves both to delude and to control people in organisations. The first sentence of his influential 1983 monograph states boldly, 'Educational administration is a technology of control' (1983: 8). And while the primary task of a critical theory of administration is to lay bare the delusion and thus empower agents to see through the administrative control mechanisms, it is also its task to change them. Theory (or critical reflection) and praxis are thus to become one 'in the interest of a better world' (Bates 1984: 272).

The wider political context in which critical theory is located is Habermas's account of the rise and success of modern bureaucracies which are a characteristic form of capitalist development. Capitalist development, in turn, is fundamentally shaped by the continuing growth of science and technology, an idea Habermas takes over from Max Weber's theory of rationalisation and develops in his famous essay on 'Technology and Science as "Ideology"' (Habermas 1972a: especially p. 82). This essay is an important source for Bates's claim of the manipulative character of science. However, what is clear in this context is that Habermas believes that science is *instrumentalist*, or in his terminology '*purposive-rational*'. Technology and science become ideological the moment they are extended into the realm of social phenomena. To put the point another way, an instrumentalist (or positivist) definition of science is accepted as a valid account of natural science but loses its legitimacy when applied to social phenomena. When (the methods of) positivist science *are* extended into the social domain, as happens routinely in capitalism, social ends, values and beliefs can no longer be discussed freely in the public domain; rather, they are replaced by a technocratic consciousness, which concerns itself only with the most efficient means of reaching predetermined ends. The ends themselves are no longer part of the legitimate public discourse. This is the danger Bates as well as Foster see in orthodox administrative theory. As Foster (1986: 79) points out:

> An administration based on a purposive-rational conception of action becomes an administration of means and forecloses discussion of ultimate goals and values. The science of administration, to the extent that it is based on a positivistic methodology that does not incorporate qualitative understandings, furthers the goals of a technocratic administration. Positivism is a subject of concern for both administration and critical theory and relates closely to the distinction between purposive-rational action and communicative interaction.

While in critical theory purposive-rational action is the legitimate means for the control of nature, *communicative action* is its appropriate equivalent in social life, because there the goal is to reach mutual understanding. The need to appropriate and transform nature, expressed by Habermas's 'technical interest', and the need to understand one another, encapsulated in the 'practical interest', are, according to Habermas, integral to the history of the species. In addition, humans have always sought to rid themselves of any form of domination and oppressive social structures. This third, most fundamental but also derivative interest, is called the 'emancipatory'. Since it is through language that we understand one another, and since according to Habermas it is in the structure of language itself that we find the *moral norms of action*, he postulates an *ideal speech situation* by means of which ideological distortion can be overcome. Habermas (1972a: 118) is aware that this speech situation is an ideal, insofar as capitalist structures will never allow speech to be free of ideological distortion. Nevertheless, we still can strive for unhampered communication in the structuring of communicative encounters.

The three interests, also called 'knowledge-constitutive', are ascribed the status of '*quasi-transcendental*' and are Habermas's epistemological taxonomy which justifies three sciences: the empirical-analytic, interpretive-hermeneutic, and emancipatory social sciences. What becomes obvious from this characterisation is that science has no purchase on social reality—meaning that objectivity and truth are similarly excluded when it comes to justifying statements about social phenomena including claims of injustice and inequality. This difficulty, of course, has been recognised in interpretive social science. The social science correlate of objectivity is expressed in the conception of *intersubjectivity*—that is, the discursive agreement about the validity or otherwise of statements about states of affairs. In Bates's (1990: 31) view, intersubjectivity provides a good warrant for objectivity in the social domain, because we can appeal to 'a public tradition of ethical discourse . . . [which] provides a basis other than mere personal preference . . . ' There are a number of worries here: one in relation to Habermasian science, accepted by Bates and Foster and other critical theorists in educational administration; and another in relation to the move to intersubjectivity. Both raise serious problems for critical theory's claim to be the change theory *par excellence*, whether in its original form or adapted for educational administration (see Lakomski 1988).

Concerning the status of science, critical theorists influenced by the early work of Habermas tend to conflate science with positivism. More specifically, logical empiricism is assumed adequately to describe science and its processes. However, since logical empiricism is known to be flawed, it is assumed that these failings also accrue to science. But this is the wrong conclusion to draw. For the demise of logical empiricism in the early 1960s led to the development of new theories of knowledge and its justification, including the development of post-positivist accounts of the nature of science. The first casualty of these new views is the rather narrow notion that science is mainly a manipulative technology of control.

The shift to intersubjectivity as a move designed to secure objectivity in ethical judgement is the second casualty. On Habermas's analysis, human communication presupposes the conditions of the ideal speech situation—conditions that involve the assumption of truth-telling, equity of access to participation in the speech community, and democratic procedures for reaching a consensus. However, the science of information theory suggests that these conditions are too strong. For example, truth-telling was not required for the development of the communication systems of a range of animal species. Nor is it a requirement in mathematical formalism, which underwrites the current information technology revolution. Instead, information theory gets by with the much weaker requirements of *statistical regularity*. (This is why weather forecasts that are consistently wrong can convey more information than those that are wrong only half the time!)

We are happy to defend objectivity in ethics, but not this way. For we think that critical theory's account of science, and its arguments for limiting the applicability of science to human affairs, are both less plausible than the scientific knowledge that is being discounted.

Coherentism in educational administration

The preceding discussion of theory development in educational administration made it clear that, departing from the Theory Movement, all major alternatives are in opposition to a science of administration. Indeed, in spite of their disagreements, they are united in arguing that administration cannot in principle be a science. We noted that the conception of science employed by subjectivism, by cultural and critical theory, shows all the hallmarks of empiricist science. The common strategy employed is to quarantine science, in the sense of keeping it out of the social realm where its methods are believed to be inappropriate, misleading or distorting of the phenomena under study, while accepting that empiricist science is perhaps valid for the investigation of sticks and stones and bricks and bones. Although the alternative approaches discussed here quite rightly criticise central features of orthodox science, their conclusion that therefore there cannot be a science of administration is premature. Empiricism is a discredited account of science, and the criticisms raised against it do not apply to all conceptions of science. Rather than seeking yet another alternative approach to educational administration, Evers and Lakomski (1991) argue that it is far more profitable, theoretically and practically, to develop a better, post-positivist account of administrative science, which does not need to jettison objectivity nor exclude values. Such a post-positivist proposal includes an account of justification where evidence, unlike its empiricist versions, does not equate with just empirical adequacy. In order to justify a theory, there also need to be consistency, simplicity, fecundity, comprehensiveness and coherence, to name the most important features of what is known as a *coherence theory of justification* (Quine 1960; BonJour 1985). This kind of justification stipulates that an administrative theory (or any other, for that matter) be a continuous part of our most global theory of the world, that it be part of our seamless web of belief. (For an introduction to holism and coherentism, see Quine and Ullian 1978.) Because the web of belief will include our accounts of nature, administrative theory can be both scientific and naturalistic. And because ethical claims admit of coherentist justification in the same manner as non-ethical claims, they are also part of the web of belief and thus also a continuous part of administrative theory. The new science of educational administration, based on coherentist principles, is thus a science much broader in scope than orthodox approaches, and one that is able to accommodate the insights and objections of the main alternatives.

2 Educational Organisations as Systems

Gabriele Lakomski and Felicity Haynes

The scientific study of schools as formal organisations has traditionally relied on theoretical tools and frameworks derived from the study of organisations in general. Organisation theory evolved from the *classical* doctrine, associated with the work of Frederick Taylor (1947), which was largely concerned with the internal structure, or *anatomy*, of formal organisation (see Scott 1983). The anatomy of an organisation was seen to consist primarily of four features: (1) the division of labour; (2) the scalar and functional processes; (3) structure; and (4) span of control. These concepts have become the stock-in-trade of organisation studies but, although still useful, have come to be seen as presenting too narrow a focus for understanding the nature and functioning of an organisation. What was missing was any acknowledgement of the fact that it is humans who people organisations and that the most important aspect aiding our understanding of organisations is understanding the complex interplay of individuals who work in and shape the organisation (for example, in the famous Hawthorne studies; see Roethlisberger and Dickson 1939). However, it needs to be stressed that it was the *neo-classical* school of organisation theory, commonly identified with the *human relations movement* and the name of Chester Barnard (1938), that first focused on the human element. It is an important feature of the human relations school that it drew on the behavioural social sciences, which presented theories explaining various aspects of human behaviour. This, of course, was invaluable for a discipline centrally interested in understanding how it is that humans act in and interact with formal organisational structures. As a consequence of this influence, neo-classical organisation theory, whether in industrial or educational contexts, could attend to such issues as communication, motivation, climate, change, leadership and conflict—concerns that had not come into the purview of its classical ancestor. It was the human relations movement, in particular, that provided the framework for the behavioural science of administration, discussed in Chapter 1.

Both the classical and neo-classical views are so complex that they cannot be covered in the present chapter. (For good discussions and overviews of the history of organisation theory, see, for example, Hoy and Miskel 1991; Ogawa 1985; Ecker 1985; Campbell 1987; Harmon and Mayer 1986; Perrow 1983, and Burrell and Morgan 1982; Gronn 1982.) Nevertheless, it would be fair to say that the overriding difference between the two schools is their respective emphasis on *formal* vs *informal* organisational features. The study of the informal leader, for example, is a most important research issue generated by the neo-classical tradition. And this topic could only become an issue because the interactions and interrelationships between the formal and informal organisations were considered of prime importance by the neo-classical school. The major emphasis signalled by the shift from classical to neo-classical thinking is therefore the move away from the study of the components of the organisation to the study of the relationships among its parts. This reorientation had become possible, in part, because of an accompanying shift of viewing organisations conceptually as *social systems*, which, as will be explained in the following, are by their nature 'open'.

Although already embedded in the neo-classical view, the idea that organisations are best viewed as *social* systems is the main characteristic of modern mainstream organisation theory. This also holds for educational administration. Hoy and Miskel's text, *Educational Administration: Theory, Research and Practice* (fourth edition 1991), is arguably the most prominent representative of the social systems approach. While advocating an open rather than closed systems perspective (the latter being associated with the Theory Movement), Hoy and Miskel nevertheless align themselves theoretically with the behavioural science approach. Arguing for the scientific nature of educational administration, and maintaining an empiricist definition of science (albeit in modified form), they are the modern descendents of the Theory Movement. There is little indication in the fourth edition of their widely used text that they have rethought their epistemological views. Thus they continue to be important representatives of what Evers and Lakomski (1991: 60) have termed the 'new orthodoxy' in educational administration. It is therefore worthwhile giving their social systems theory of educational administration a closer inspection.

While the idea of treating educational organisations as social systems appears plausible and may be helpful as a heuristic device, we still need to ask whether the systems metaphor enables us to understand organisations better. In other words, does the systems' view have *explanatory* value? There is reason to believe that it has important limitations. For example, the generality of the systems metaphor, advocated as its great strength, is also its Achilles heel because great generality can also signify that a claim is compatible with almost any state of affairs and hence is empirically vacuous. This consequence has to do with problems of functionalism and functionalist explanation, which are inherent in the open systems perspective. But before we can address the issue of its explanatory nature, it is necessary to consider some of the major features, claims and assumptions of the systems perspective itself, because it is these that also shape educational organisation theory. The best way to do this is by beginning with a brief outline of general systems theory as the parent discipline, and considering its relationship to modern organisation theory. In the following, then, let us explore what it means to speak of a social organisation as an *open system* and what the differences are between a closed system and an open system. (For a fuller treatment, including explicitly rational and natural systems, see Scott 1981. On loosely-coupled systems, see Cohen and March 1974; Weick 1969, 1976, 1982.)

General systems theory and modern organisation

In his characterisation of the relationship between modern organisation theory and general systems theory, Scott (1983: 60–1) points out that modern organisation theory is primarily defined in terms of its 'conceptual-analytical base, its reliance on empirical research data and, above all, its integrating nature. These qualities are framed in a philosophy that accepts the premise that the only meaningful way to study organisation is to study it as a system.' This view rose to prominence and became the conceptual foundation of contemporary organisation theory primarily because of the pioneering work of Ludwig von Bertalanffy (1973), the founder of general systems theory. His work is of such importance that some of the major features of his general systems thinking are sketched below. This also allows us to trace the origins of theoretical problems that continue to plague contemporary advocates of the systems perspective in the field of educational administration (Hoy and Miskel, for example).

General open systems theory was designed to explain no less than 'the world as organisation'. Von Bertalanffy conceived it in the hope of 'attempting scientific interpretation and theory where previously there was none, and [providing] higher generality than that in the special sciences.' (von Bertalanffy 1973: 14). Motivated by his observation of the inadequacies of the 'mechanistic approach' then employed in classical physics, especially when applied to solving theoretical problems in the biosocial sciences, and struck by structural similarities (and their isomorphism) in different fields, von Bertalanffy believed that a 'general systems theory', as a general theory of organisation, would be able to provide an overarching framework for all the sciences. A general systems theory was to provide precisely what its name denotes: 'the formulation and derivation of those principles which are valid for "systems" in general' (von Bertalanffy 1973: 32). More specifically, general systems theory, as outlined in the program of its society founded in 1954, was expected to perform the following functions:

> (1) investigate the isomorphy of concepts, laws, and models in various fields, and to help in useful transfers from one field to another; (2) encourage the development of adequate theoretical models in the fields which lack them; (3) minimize the duplication of theoretical effort in different fields; (4) promote the unity of science through improving communication among specialists. (von Bertalanffy 1973: 15)

These functions are underwritten by a 'systems philosophy', which von Bertalanffy outlines in the preface to the revised edition (1973). Its most important features for us in the present context are its ontological and epistemological elements. While we may agree that systems of various kinds can be identified by direct observation, such as 'a galaxy, a dog, a cell and an atom', there are also other systems such as conceptual and abstracted ones not directly observable but equally real—that is, 'corresponding with reality'. But, von Bertalanffy warns, 'the distinction between "real" objects and systems as given in observation and "conceptual" constructs and systems cannot be drawn in any commonsense way.' (von Bertalanffy 1973: xxi) This difficulty poses 'deep problems', which are not addressed by him in the present context. A definition of systems is given as 'sets of elements standing in interrelation' (von Bertalanffy 1973: 38), a definition which, he states, acquires more precise meaning when we consider that 'systems can be defined by certain families of differential equations'—that is, mathematically.

But how do we get to know systems of either kind? Von Bertalanffy stresses that his systems epistemology differs quite markedly from both logical positivism and empiricism, while retaining their scientific attitudes. Rejecting the physicalism and reductionism of both forms of positivism, and believing knowledge to be 'an interaction between knower and known', he opts for what he terms a perspective philosophy in which science is 'one of the "perspectives" man with his biological, cultural and linguistic endowment and bondage, has created to deal with the universe he is "thrown in", or rather to which he is adapted owing to evolution and history.' (von Bertalanffy 1973: xxii) Finally, now that the closed system of classical physics has been replaced with its equally confined image of humans existing in a world of 'physical particles governed by chance events as ultimate and only "true" reality', von Bertalanffy (1973: xxii) believes that 'the world of symbols, values, social entities and cultures' can also be considered as real, seeing that all reality is 'a hierarchy of organised wholes'. Thus, general systems theory, according to von Bertalanffy, has a humanistic orientation that is directly opposed to the narrow vision engendered by classical systems theorists, which, he warns, runs the danger of mechanising society.

Even in its early days general systems theory was criticised for its lack of explanatory value, among other things. Von Bertalanffy acknowledges the difficulty but also points out that at this stage of theory development, 'explanation in principle', an expression borrowed from the economist Hayek, has to suffice (von Bertalanffy 1973: 36). Just as economists are not able to predict fluctuations in the stock market accurately while explaining general economic phenomena well enough, so system-theoretical explanation has to await further developments. 'Explanation in principle . . . ,' he notes, 'is better than none at all.' We shall return to this point later.

Heavily influenced by biology, his home discipline, von Bertalanffy was quite careful, however, to note the limitations of the (biological-organismic) systems metaphor in any attempt to explain *social* activity. When looking for similarities between very different kinds of systems, von Bertalanffy (1973: 35–6) warns that one always also finds important dissimilarities:

> Analogies as such are of little value since besides similarities between phenomena, dissimilarities can always be found as well. The isomorphism under discussion is more than a mere analogy. It is a consequence of the fact that, in certain respects, corresponding abstractions and conceptual models can be applied to different phenomena. Only in view of these aspects will system laws apply. This is not different from the general procedures in science. It is the same situation as when the law of gravitation applies to Newton's apple, the planetary system, and tidal phenomenon. This means that in view of certain limited aspects a theoretical system, that of mechanics, holds true; it does not mean that there is a particular resemblance between apples, planets, and oceans in a great number of other aspects.

Despite such delimiting comments, von Bertalanffy believed that his general systems theory, because it was truly interdisciplinary, had the potential to contribute to the unification of all science. Eschewing reductionism, he describes his philosophy of perspectivism in the following way:

> The world is, as Aldous Huxley once put it, like Neapolitan ice cream cake where the levels—the physical, the biological, the social and the moral universe—represent the chocolate, strawberry, and vanilla layers. We cannot reduce strawberry to chocolate—the most we can say is that possibly in the last resort, all is vanilla, all mind or spirit. *The unifying principle is that we find organisation at all levels* [emphases added]. (von Bertalanffy 1973: 49)

Finally, there are also some educational implications deriving from the

general systems theory. On the one hand, von Bertalanffy argues that general systems theory helps to train scientific generalists who are able to work in an interdisciplinary way, and on the other, he believes that his theory also helps in regard to developing ethical values. His solution is not to advocate straight-out scientific control of society, which, in his words, is 'no highway to Utopia' (von Bertalanffy 1973: 52), but to pay attention to the individual, a humanistic concern that, interestingly, he shares with Greenfield, although of course he would disagree with Greenfield on other matters.

Having thus traced some of the more important features of general systems theory, and identified some difficulties, let us note for the moment that both general systems theory and contemporary organisation theory consider organisations as 'wholes'. The major difference between them is that general systems theory, as the more comprehensive framework, is concerned with examining every level of system, whereas organisation theory restricts itself to human organisations in particular. (Scott 1983: 65, provides a useful classification of systems, following the economist K. Boulding.) Perhaps another way of expressing the relationship between the two is to say that modern organisation theory, in terms of its theoretical structure, is a specific social science application of general systems theory. This also means that problems inherent in one are likely to show up in the other, as we shall see.

Characteristics of general and open systems

The discussion of general systems theory and system features does suggest that the theorists employing this concept know and can define what makes up a 'system'. Recall that in Chapter 1 a definition was offered in terms of systems consisting of interrelated objects, attributes and events. This is a very general definition, but, as Burrell and Morgan note, it appears to be all that is available. They observe that 'Despite its popularity . . . the notion of "system" is an elusive one. Many books on systems theory do not offer a formal definition . . . and where a definition is attempted, it is usually one of considerable generality.' (Burrell and Morgan 1982: 57) Given the brief exposition of general systems theory and von Bertalanffy's own definition, Burrell and Morgan's concerns are not surprising. Bearing in mind the generality of definition, it appears that *interrelatedness* is a system's most important characteristic. This is followed by *holism* as the second most fundamental characteristic. We can already note some interesting methodological problems here. For example, changes in any one of the interrelated objects, attributes or events will result in changes or adjustments across the whole system. This means that it is very difficult, or near impossible, to assess what affected what, and to determine exactly what accounts for the changes in the system. Also, the second important characteristic, *holism*, brings its own difficulties when examining a system. Often expressed in the phrase 'the whole is bigger than the sum of its parts', the problem, as Litterer (1969: 4) acknowledges, is the following:

> Is a set of bricks just a wall, or is it a part of a building, is the building part of a city, is the city part of a nation? Any element contributes to a system, but all too typically that system is part of another system, and the question then is, 'What is the system under study?'

Litterer answers his own question: 'This depends to a considerable degree upon the interests of the observer or person who is concerned with defining a system.' (1969: 4). Here, let us note simply that because different observers bring different interests to the study of social phenomena, the question of determining 'the system under study' becomes very elusive indeed and, on this reading, is one that cannot be answered decisively by system theorists, as Litterer (1969: 4) appears to concede when he notes that 'The definition of system . . . is somewhat arbitrary.' Despite the uncertainties of definition, it is nevertheless true that complex systems such as banks, automobile companies and governments have stability and continue over time. This third characteristic is described in terms of open systems being *goal oriented*. What is meant by this is that all systems, open or closed, tend to return to a position of equilibrium after they have been disturbed. The return to equilibrium is interpreted as the system's seeking to achieve this goal. There may be more than one point of equilibrium in complex systems, meaning that the system may have multiple goals, which, however, cannot all be attained simultaneously, and this indicates that the system may be in conflict.

A fourth characteristic of general systems is that they are self-regulating, and *regulation* includes three different kinds: adjustment, control (which includes feedback) and learning. Fifth, open systems, as Litterer (1969: 5) points out, are almost by definition characterised by their acceptance of *inputs* from the environment, usually described in terms of energy and information, as well as by the *outputs* they give back to their environment. A sixth characteristic, *transformation*, indicates that what systems deliver back to their environment is not what they received, because transformation has taken place. Seventh, what is termed *hierarchy* is a system characteristic that suggests that complex systems may contain simpler and smaller ones. The study of the latter is one of the main tasks of general systems theory. The eighth characteristic is called *entropy*. Following Katz and Kahn's (1983) characterisation, it is the concepts of *entropy* and the *second law of thermodynamics* in particular that demarcate open (social) systems from closed ones. Expressed simply, the second law of thermodynamics means that systems tend to run down (see Harmon and Mayer 1986: 162–3). Katz and Kahn (1983: 100) provide the example of an iron bar heated at one end by a blowtorch. The iron bar is now in an unstable state, with fast molecules in the end being heated and slow molecules in the other, the cool end. After the blowtorch is switched off, a steady state is eventually reached (in that the distribution of fast/slow molecules in the iron bar becomes random) and the bar reaches the same temperature overall. The iron bar cools, until its temperature approaches that of the room in which it is located; when this has happened the system has returned to equilibrium. However, unlike closed physical systems, social systems tend to become more complex over time rather than simpler. This characteristic is called *differentiation*. An open system does not run down, because it imports energy from its environment. This constitutes the major difference between the two types of system. Because of this specific characteristic, open systems experience what is called *negative entropy*. As Scott (1981: 109–10) explains it, 'By acquiring inputs of greater complexity than their outputs, open systems restore their own energy and repair breakdowns in their own organisation.' Finally, given that open systems are goal-seeking entities, they are also characterised by the principle of *equifinality*. As Harmon and Mayer (1986: 164) put it:

> The idea is that an end state can be reached by a variety of paths and from widely different initial conditions. Essentially this [equifinality] is a notion of causality, but one that differs radically from that embodied in, for instance, the work of Frederick Taylor . . . From the systems perspective, 'the one best way' does not exist.

Now that we have briefly looked at some of the major features of general and open systems, and also considered some differences between closed and open systems, let us see how the open systems perspective works in educational administration. This is best done by considering first why theorists objected to the closed systems view when applied to organisations such as schools.

The systems perspective in educational administration

Not surprisingly, the closed systems perspective was never popular in organisation studies because of its many perceived limitations. It has mainly been applied to theorists such as Max Weber, Frederick Taylor and Herbert Simon because their work emphasised the internal structure and functioning of bureaucracies and/or (industrial) organisations and did not pay sufficient attention to the influence of the external environment. In fact, the criticism levelled against these theorists, commonly described as advocates of the *rational model of organisations*, was not expressed directly in terms of closed vs open systems models, but in terms of their narrow *scientific* approach to the study of organisations. As a result of these criticisms, some writers, such as Griffiths, argued for a more flexible scientific approach in educational administration that would expand the traditional empiricism of the Theory Movement, while others such as Greenfield, Hodgkinson, Foster and Bates reasoned that administration is not to be understood as a science at all but ought to be seen as a humanism or an art. So when Griffiths (1979) took stock of what the traditional science of administration had accomplished, he noted that one of its major shortcomings was that it had not included discussion of women, unions and racial minorities in administration. This is another way of saying that orthodox administration science's primary focus on rational-bureaucratic features excluded the external environment from consideration (see Lawrence and Lorsch 1967, for a first major study on the importance of the environment). The closed systems model therefore sanctioned only very limited *empirical* research. The dynamic interplay between environment and organisation could not be studied as the major factor of organisational change. This was acknowledged by Bidwell (1979: 111), who in a recanting of his earlier, closed systems, views (for example, Bidwell 1965), describes organisations as follows:

> Closed-systems theories have approached organizations as if they were machines. The organization-as-machine is a system that remains undisturbed by events outside its boundary, unless a prime mover of some kind—most often in these theories either an entrepreneur or top-level administrator—intervenes to change parts of the system or change the ways existing parts act on one another. Moreover, the action of such a prime mover is used to account for the machine's existence in the first place.

The features Bidwell alludes to here—the system's static and apparently self-contained nature, the assumption of a 'creator' or 'designer' whose rational purposes determine the system's goals, and the exclusive focus on its internal workings—are the very features that are too narrow to encapsulate real-life social organisations. As Bidwell (1979: 111) notes in relation to schools, the closed system idea could not account for change, for school productivity, and for 'the connectedness of schools and their environments'. From a closed systems perspective, the influence of the economy on organisations, for example, would not be an issue that could be raised. If we assumed a closed system model, Victoria's 'Schools of the Future' project would be inexplicable because Australian economic rationalism, the relevant 'environment', could not be drawn on as an important source of 'input'. The kind of study possible from a closed perspective would emphasise how well or how badly schools manage to restructure themselves internally—that is, how efficiently or inefficiently they manage their human and other resources. While this is, of course, one way of saying that the environment is disregarded, there is another added cost. Internal restructuring takes place without regard for the effects it might have on the environment. Katz and Kahn (1983: 101) spell out in more detail what the consequences are:

> The effects of such [internal] moves on the maintenance inputs of motivation and morale tend not to be adequately considered. Stability may be sought through tighter integration and coordination, when flexibility may be the more important requirement. Coordination and control become ends in themselves, desirable states within a closed system rather than means of attaining an adjustment between the system and its environment. Attempts to introduce coordination in kind and degree not functionally required tend to produce new internal problems.

In addition to the preoccupation with internal functioning and its resultant consequences, there are two more features of closed systems thinking that are particularly detrimental: 'the neglect of equifinality and the treatment of disruptive external events as error variance' (Katz and Kahn 1983: 101). Equifinality means that there are many ways of reaching an objective; there is no single best way. Insofar as there might be social conditions that are fixed and known, there may well be one best way, and Katz and Kahn (1983: 101) mention the coaching of baseball players as an example. However, this is the exception rather than the rule in social organisations, as was indeed recognised by Simon (1976) and expressed in his well-known phrase of 'satisficing' (this concept makes him rather less of a closed systems thinker than commonly assumed).

The second detrimental feature mentioned by Katz and Kahn, that of treating disruptive external events as error variances, means that they are controlled out of studies of organisations because they are considered to be irrelevant from the organisation's point of view. This means that troublesome external factors are simply bracketed out, defended against or ignored. In the open systems perspective, because environmental inputs of any kind are integral to system functioning and maintenance, disruptive factors are also included as an important source of input.

A final, and most important worry for closed systems thinking is that it has a very limited view of organisational learning. What is meant by this is captured in the feature of regulation, particularly the feedback function which in closed systems is a single feedback loop. An organisation's feedback function is important because it delivers information about external changes back to the organisation so that it can react or change as required. This learning function has not been developed in closed systems thinking but is of central importance in the open systems view.

Despite the conceptual advantages seen in the open systems metaphor, even Katz and Kahn, whose book *The Social Psychology of Organizations*, initially published in 1966, can be described as the classic open systems primer for organisation theory, note that organisational openness must still be developed:

> Open is not a magic word, and pronouncing it is not enough to reveal what has been hidden in the organizational cave. We have begun the process of specification by discussing properties shared by all open systems . . . (Katz and Kahn 1978: 33).

This warning notwithstanding, the general consensus in organisation theory is that the debate between the two versions of systems theory is, as Meyer (1978: 18) expresses it, closed 'on the side of openness'. This shift is considered quite significant because, as Katz and Kahn (1983: 100) observe, it allowed a refocusing of the *scientific* study of organisations. That is, leaving behind the laws of traditional physics which sanctioned the closed systems view, they believe, did not mean giving up the scientific study of organisations. Rather, the turn to the biological sciences with their emphasis on living open systems enabled a new and more promising scientific way of studying social organisations, which, after all, are also living entities. Hence, the open systems metaphor appeared to be more appropriate for all manner of organisations, including schools. As Hoy and Miskel (1991: 21) put it:

> . . . schools are social systems that take resources such as labor, students, and money from the environment and subject these inputs to an educational transformation process to produce literate, educated students and graduates.

As in the (1987) third edition of their text *Educational Administration*, Hoy and Miskel, in their fourth edition (1991), again make clear that they consider their theory of educational administration as a continuation of the behavioural science approach, with the open systems perspective providing the relevant conceptual framework (Hoy and Miskel 1991: 23, 25). As well as reconfirming their commitment to this perspective, they also remain loyal to the view of theory they advocated previously. While noting that there was initial agreement in the field that Feigl's definition of theory 'was an adequate starting point', they also cite Willower's criticism that Feigl's view 'is too rigorous as to exclude most of theory in educational administration' (Hoy and Miskel 1991: 2). They settle, as they did before, for Kerlinger's definition of theory as the most useful:

> Theory is a set of interrelated concepts, assumptions, and generalizations that systematically describes and explains regularities in behavior in educational organisations. Moreover, hypotheses may be derived from the theory to predict additional relationships among concepts in the system. (Hoy and Miskel 1991: 2)

Hoy and Miskel believe, as did Griffiths, Walker and others before them, that administrative theory guides action, that it is in the business of explaining the nature of educational administration, and that it contributes to the solving of administrative problems. Their major departure from the Theory Movement does not therefore involve abandoning its philosophical assumptions but rather adopting an open systems view, of which they have high hopes. This is indicated in the introduction to their second chapter, 'The School as a Social System', where they cite Getzels, Lipham, and Campbell approvingly: 'There is little point in general models if they do not give rise to specific conceptual derivations and empirical applications which illuminate, in however modest a degree, significant day-to-day practices . . . ' (Hoy and Miskel 1991: 28) Adopting the social system perspective is considered to be the appropriate way to achieve these aims. Also, the system perspective's utility is supported by their belief that the challenges faced by the behavioural science approach in the 1990s require that 'theory and research will have to become more refined, useful and situationally oriented', to which they add in the latest edition, 'and will need to address emerging gender issues' (Hoy and Miskel, 1991: 25). This is a welcome addition, yet one may wonder why, at a time of extraordinary theoretical and philosophical debate, there is scant attention to values and cultural concerns in the latest edition, and still no discussion of Greenfield's or Hodgkinson's contribution to administration theory. It also seems odd that their section entitled 'Philosophical and Sociological Foundations of Organizational Theory' has been dropped, at a time of philosophical and epistemological criticism.

In keeping with general systems thinking, Hoy and Miskel (1991: 28) define a social system as follows:

> It is a model of organization that possesses a distinctive total unity (creativity) beyond its component parts; it is distinguished from its environment by a clearly defined boundary; it is composed of subunits, elements, and subsystems that are interrelated within relatively stable patterns (equilibria) of social order.
> (See also Thelen and Getzels 1957: 351.)

In addition to drawing on the work of Litterer (1969), Getzels and Guba (1957) and Bidwell (1965), the authors draw on the classic systems theory work of Getzels, Lipham and Campbell (1968) in the fourth edition. This means, then, that for Hoy and Miskel the basic two elements of a social system are also (a) the institutional, and (b) the individual (this is represented graphically on p. 29 of their text). Getzels et al., as discussed in the first chapter of this volume, describe administration 'structurally . . . as the hierarchy of superordinate—subordinate relationships within a social system . . . Functionally, this hierarchy of relationships is the locus for allocating and integrating roles and facilities in order to achieve the goals of the system'. Hoy and Miskel are also concerned to explain organisational behaviour in terms of relating institutional elements—that is, roles and expectations (the nomothetic)—with individual elements, such as different personalities and need dispositions (the idiographic) found in any organisation. These two elements together provide 'the basis of a social-psychological theory of group behavior in which a dynamic transaction between roles and personality interacts' (Hoy and Miskel 1991: 35). Thus, the summary of their basic model is as follows:

> Behavior (B) in the system is explained in terms of the interaction between role (R), defined by expectations, and personality (P), the internal needs structure of an individual; that is, $B = f(R\ P)$. (Hoy and Miskel 1991: 35)

Although there may be a balance between role and personality factors in some systems, it is to be expected that the proportion of one to the other differs depending on the type of organisation. The authors suggest that highly bureaucratic organisations are characterised more by role factors, and that less highly structured ones display more personality attributes. Behaviour in all social systems, nevertheless, is determined by both institutional and personal needs. Hoy and Miskel refine their basic model, adding the concept of the work group. In fact, in formal organisations 'the work group is the mechanism by which bureaucratic expectations and individual needs interact and modify each other' (Hoy and Miskel 1991: 38). In the school context, for example, teachers might have developed informal procedures for disciplining students; these informal norms might then, in turn, become the hallmarks for judging good teaching, which is equated with keeping good control. Now since a social system is an open system, determining boundaries is difficult because the environment encroaches on what happens inside the organisation. This raises an important question: 'Which features of the environment are most salient for constraining behavior in schools?' Hoy and Miskel (1991: 40) answer their own question by admitting that 'There is no quick or simple answer' because all kinds of external factors impinge on the operations of schools. The most useful way to predict the behaviour in schools is to study the interactions of the three elements (institutional, work and individual) in terms of their consistency:

> We posit a congruence postulate: *Other things being equal, the greater the total degree of congruence among the elements of the system, the more effective the system.* (Hoy and Miskel 1991: 41)

An effective school, in their view, is one in which expected performance and actual performance are consistent (Hoy and Miskel 1991: 51). Although, in their second chapter, the authors no longer speak in terms of goals, a section deleted for reasons of 'parsimony' (Hoy and Miskel 1991: 53, footnote 2), the goal model of organisational effectiveness is still maintained. Thus, in their Chapter 12, Hoy and Miskel (1991: 375) continue to accept Etzioni's definition: 'An organisation is effective if the outcomes of its activities meet or exceed organisational goals'.

With regard to the congruence model, Hoy and Miskel also suggest that it provides a good basis for organisational analysis and problem-solving. In order to improve school outcomes, school decision-makers

> gather information on the performance levels of their schools, compare the information with the desired performance levels, identify discrepancies and difficulties, search for causes of the problem, develop and select a plan to alleviate the problems, and implement and evaluate the plan . . . The model is particularly useful in diagnosing conflict or lack of congruence among the key elements of the system. (Hoy and Miskel 1991: 51)

Determining or improving congruence is not just a matter of intuition, according to Hoy and Miskel, who suggest that 'the theory and research in the remainder of this book should be extremely useful in this regard' (1991: 51).

Although this is only a brief outline of a more complex approach, the essential elements of the model are clear enough for us to make some critical observations. In the final section, then, let us address the issue of the systems theory's explanatory utility and identify other difficulties for this perspective in educational administration.

The utility of the (open) systems metaphor

Because the conceptual framework for Hoy and Miskel's theory of educational administration is that of general systems theory, it is to be expected that problems inherent in the general theory will also show up in its organisational application. Furthermore, the fact that the writers still subscribe to a version (albeit modified) of a logical empiricist account of science has its own unhappy consequences. But let us begin by noting one problem that has already been addressed in Chapter 1. In following on from Getzels et al., Hoy and Miskel adopt a structuralist—functionalist framework for understanding schools, although they add a third element, that of the work group. Hence, the difficulty of explaining observed behaviour found in the former reappears in Hoy and Miskel's account. To begin with, one cannot observe a role or role expectation; it has to be inferred. Furthermore, how a person perceives his or her role depends on how he or she *interprets* what needs to be done in a given situation. The point is an unexceptional one; it is not a role but a human being who acts on the basis of certain beliefs or values. Because 'filling' a role is essentially the interpretive act of an individual, the distinctiveness of roles and role expectations as categorically separate from the personal or idiographic dimension, disappears. This means for Hoy and Miskel's model that explaining behaviour as a function of the interaction between the institutional and the personal dimensions is problematic because the institutional is laden with the personal. The result is that the generality of systems theory is compromised by the particularity of its major categories.

This tension between the generality demanded by traditional science, and the particularity demanded by the conditions of applicability, appears in several other guises. Take, for example, the definition of 'system'. Given von Bertalanffy's definition of systems as 'sets of elements standing in interrelation', everything and anything would appear to qualify as a system *in the absence of specifying the nature of the relations in question*. But once we begin to specify the relation by stipulating, for example, that collections of objects have to stand in a *causal* relation to each other, many sets of elements would not qualify as systems.

This difficulty with definition spills over into von Bertalanffy's point about isomorphism across different fields. Because relations between sets of elements are initially not specified, the fundamental question is: on the basis of which assumptions can they be seen *as* isomorphic? How does von Bertalanffy (and other systems theorists) *know* which phenomena to count as 'similar' and which as 'dissimilar'? This is the crucial epistemological point he attempts to answer by talking about a 'perspective' philosophy, which according to Litterer amounts to saying that it is the interest of the observer that ultimately defines what the system under discussion is. Such interests are, of course, theoretically motivated (see Lakomski 1986). For a trained biological scientist, what systems count as isomorphic would be determined by the relevant concepts, theories and models of that discipline. For a scientist from the behavioural sciences, psychological theories and constructs would be the relevant markers as they are for Hoy and Miskel. Or, to use von Bertalanffy's example, what is considered as the 'relevant' aspect that ties together Newton's apple, the planetary system and tidal phenomenon is 'relevant' in terms of the relations stipulated to hold by the law of gravitation. However, notice now that the plausibility of systems theory as a heuristic device depends on the integrity of the background substantive theory used to sort and classify phenomena (for more detailed criticism, see Evers and Lakomski 1991: 68–73; 1993: 143).

This is also the fundamental problem of functionalist explanation. Insofar as scientific knowledge and theory is implicitly drawn on to specify what are seen as relevant relations among phenomena or objects, systems theory (including its educational administration relative) piggybacks onto generalisations first developed elsewhere. Therefore, talk of the respiratory system, or of the heart as an organ that pumps blood through the body, is of explanatory value precisely because the detailed scientific work has already been done. Useful talk of 'system' comes *after* rather than before empirical study. But now talking of schools as social systems, for example, presumes that the detailed work needed to explain the extraordinary complexity of human interaction and interrelations has already been done. In the end, our caution about the utility of the systems metaphor in administrative studies stems from our belief that this presumption is false. The upshot, ironically, is that the powerful generalities that systems theory was supposed to deliver will arrive only when the particularities have been attended to.

3 Subjectivity and the Creation of Organisations

Peter C. Gronn

It is now nearly two decades since a Canadian professor of educational administration, Thomas Barr Greenfield, first launched a blistering attack on the United States' version of this field of study, known as the Theory Movement or the New Movement, at a conference in Bristol, England. In twelve articles between 1973 and 1982 he assailed the field for what he claimed was its almost total reliance on systems theory's conceptions of organisations and the predominance of quantitative research methodologies among educational administration researchers. As part of an alternative approach, Greenfield endorsed subjectivist ways of understanding organisations, and non-rational images and ways of knowing and experiencing organisational life, especially ones that highlighted such themes as alienation and anarchy (Gronn 1983: 10).

These criticisms continued in Greenfield's subsequent writings, but his major emphasis shifted increasingly to attacking the prevailing conceptions of social science and to thinking of organisations as comprising moral orders rather than natural systems. One of Greenfield's abiding concerns, which figures more prominently as part of his emphasis on organisational morality, was the split that he saw the field of educational administration making between facts and values, and the denigration of the latter in a quest for universalistic theory and knowledge. Greenfield was concerned that nobody really asked the following sorts of questions:

> What does constitute progress? What is the good and how may it be attained? How does education contribute to the social good and to personal well being and happiness? How should schools be organised to achieve such goals? What are the moral choices that face educational administrators? (Greenfield 1991b: 209)

Instead, he believed, educational administration was reduced more and more to technologies of effectiveness and training in mechanical procedures.

Greenfield pleaded incessantly with theorists to understand schooling and education from the points of view of those who experience them and to see that the everyday world is suffused with intertwined facts and values and, more particularly, to see that 'the business of committing people to values is the basic stuff of both education and administration' (Greenfield 1991c: 217). One corollary of the neglect and denial of values is to reshape the curriculum of administrative studies so that it returns to the humanities and includes liberal studies in disciplines such as law, history and philosophy (p.219).

After a brief outline of his connection with educational administration in Australia, the chapter discusses Greenfield's arguments about subjectivity and organisations found in his eight most recent publications (1983, 1984, 1985a, 1985b, 1986, 1991a, 1991b and 1991c). Firstly, we shall look at what is meant by the claim that organisations are the outcome of human actions, intentions, meaning, will and experience. Secondly, we shall examine the tension in Greenfield's subjectivism between the idea that values are always in contention with one another and yet at the same time there somehow exists a moral order. Thirdly, we will consider the extent to which Greenfield's view of anti-leadership is compatible with his claim that leaders and administrators are also meant to be entrepreneurs for values.

Greenfield and Australian educational administration

What is the link between Greenfield's views and the provision of educational administration in Australia? Unlike their North American counterparts, postgraduate preparation programs for educational administrators in Australia are of fairly recent origin. In fact it was only at the very point when Greenfield first launched his assault on traditional educational administration in the United States that the field was really undergoing expansion in Australia. His criticisms occurred simultaneously with the dramatic subjectivist shift, an anti-behavioural reaction, by then well and truly under way throughout the social sciences and stimulated by publications such as Berger and Luckman's *The Social Construction of Reality* (1972). Because no single approach to educational administration had had sufficiently long to take root in Australia and attain the status of an intellectual orthodoxy, Greenfield's iconoclasm earned him a receptive following, particularly among a younger generation of scholars, just as it had already done for him in the United Kingdom.

The first attempt in the United States to use the social sciences for the formal preparation of administrators had begun back in 1950–51 when the Co-operative Program in Educational Administration was inaugurated with the financial support of the W.K. Kellogg Foundation. But it was the University Council for Educational Administration seminar at the University of Chicago in 1957 that had launched the so-called 'Theory

Movement' (Culbertson 1981: 37, 26). Australian awareness on any large scale of American management practice first occurred during the Second World War, but only in the 1950s did university programs begin in business administration (Byrt 1989: 80–92) and only in 1959 was the first Diploma of Educational Administration offered at the University of New England (Cunningham and Radford 1963: 20). William Bassett (1965: 33, 35), who had been responsible for the development of the New England diploma, could still write in the mid-1960s that 'the need for administration training in education has hardly been recognized' in Australia and that 'we are at the beginning of this movement'. Some twenty years later, after numerous senior officials in departments of education had gone to North America (particularly to the University of Alberta, Canada, where Greenfield himself trained) to undertake doctoral studies in educational administration, and by which time Greenfield had visited Australia twice, the number of colleges and universities offering educational administration in Australia had increased to twelve (Duignan and Teather 1985). Greenfield's name is still well known and his ideas receive wide currency in this country.

Because values figure so prominently in Greenfield's epistemology, it goes without saying that the one component of Australian education for which his views about schools as moral orders might have particular appeal is the non-government sector. Values for Greenfield certainly meant more than just those that find expression in religious doctrine, but in Australia it so happens that the Roman Catholic and non-Catholic independent-sector schools have long devoted considerable energy, both for marketing purposes and in an effort to safeguard the traditions for which they stand, to defining the core values on which their independence rests. It is not surprising, therefore, that the sponsors of at least one of Greenfield's visits to Australia were the principals of Roman Catholic schools. And now, with the rising cacophony of multicultural voices for which Australian government schools have no choice but to cater, Greenfield's message about the significance of values and value conflicts in a era of social pluralism and moral relativism is of direct concern to those responsible for departmental schools.

Creating organisations

What is an organisation? According to Greenfield, this question is legitimately worded, and the answer to it has always been straightforward. An organisation is a cultural artefact rather than some kind of naturally occurring physical entity or phenomenon. It is the product of human intelligence, design and will. Unlike rocks, plants, animals and wind, therefore, organisations are socially constructed, built up and maintained.

Anyone encountering Greenfield's arguments for the first time will be struck by what seem to be statements of the obvious and by the impression that he always appears to be writing in strident reaction to something else. The explanation for these rather odd characteristics is that Greenfield usually saw himself as having to begin by dispelling unwarranted but commonly held misconceptions in educational administration. The particular understanding of organisations that was part of the administrative science into which he was originally inducted during postgraduate study at Alberta, and to which he adhered for some time, was known as the natural systems view. This traditional theory, which lay at the heart of the Theory Movement, privileged images of controlled environmental equilibrium, rationality, goodness, order and depersonalisation, so that:

> organizations may be studied scientifically and objectively without engaging the images, passions, and biases of the observer. Organizations are one thing and those who observe and study them are something else. With these notions about organizations, it would be possible for observers to establish universally validated truths about organization free from the personalities of the scientists. (Greenfield 1984: 147–8)

Organizations were therefore able to be known and understood as part of a value-free objective social science.

Two important assumptions underpin Greenfield's social construction of reality view. The first is that there is the world of nature, which is distinct from the world of culture and society. The natural world is substantially given, whereas the social world is wholly made. The second assumption is that while knowledge may be derived from both worlds, it is obtained in quite radically different ways. Nature is typically the realm of brute data, or 'facts that press themselves upon our understanding so forcibly that no one can question their existence' (Greenfield 1984: 151), whereas society can only be understood through the interpretation of the meanings that individuals choose to give to their experiences. The facts of organisational life are, therefore, non-brute data, which 'rest upon the interpretation and upon the interpretation of interpretations in a process that continues without end and without ever reaching the definitive statement, the final judgement or the ultimate social truth' (Greenfield 1984: 151).

The characteristic way in which the members of an organisation go about constructing that entity is through the process of negotiation over the meaning of their shared experiences. This is done as part of the ordinary everyday interpersonal relations, which people transact in living out their formal roles, through such mechanisms as speech, gesture and written discourse, so that

> The organization arises from a web of cross-connected wills as active

agents live their lives and strive to make the world as they know it or as they want it to be. (Greenfield 1984: 152)

Always, therefore, people are in conflict to some degree with one another as they pursue their particular interests and desires.

Instead of a systems organisational model, in which organisational members were meant to blindly adapt to prescribed roles in the interests of effectiveness—a process that administrators were supposed to facilitate (Greenfield 1985b: 5246) and which implied that in doing so an administrator's role was isomorphic with that of the scientist in engineering knowledge and control of the natural world—Greenfield (1986: 71–3) proposes a distinct alternative. In a series of points he argues that 'people do not exist in organizations', rather 'organizations exist in and through individuals'; that organisations are best thought of as moral orders which are 'arbitrary, nonnatural, and often backed by enormous power, even by violence'; that any science of administration must recognise the personal and subjective complexities that comprise organisational life; that conflict between individuals adhering to contending values is endemic in organisations; that the administrators of organisations need to be thought of in moral terms as builders of commitment, rather than as rational technicians; and reflecting upon moral issues must become the 'essential and pervasive purpose' of administrative studies.

Other organisations

Coterminous with the view of organisations as socially constructed is Greenfield's claim that the environments within which they are usually thought of as being embedded are subjectively defined realities. On the other hand, to speak as adherents of the natural systems model do, of organisations as being *in* environments is to persist in seeing organisations as things other than people, to reify them and to depersonalise the administrator's role within them (Greenfield 1983: 6).

> It is a belief that sees organizations as something separate from human endeavour and that seeks a solution to human problems in the adjustment of an illusion (the organization) to an undefined residual concept (the environment). Those who believe that something called an organization can adapt to something else called an environment do so under the illusion that there are laws governing organization in environments that elevate the process of adjustment to a science and those who practise it to the status of benefactors of mankind.

The fallacy enshrined in the perception of organisations being *in* environments is the assumption that there is something to adjust to, when all there is, in fact, is other organisations.

Organisations react or adapt, then, not to environments but to other similarly structured entities, which owe their origins to the ideas of people and are likewise socially constructed. But the implication of this is that if there is no cohesive objective force known as an environment that can be pointed to, then the idea of other organisations simply standing in its stead necessarily reduces itself down to lots and lots of other people, acting in concert, resorting to committed human effort and driven by moral imperatives, to create their own separate, unique and sustainable moral orders (Greenfield 1983: 34–5). Accordingly, whenever organisations react to one another, 'such interaction is the reaction of certain individuals grouped around one set of ideas to other individuals grouped around other sets of ideas' (Greenfield 1983: 7). It is precisely when such organisations (by virtue of being people) strive to realise or bring such ideas to fruition that it is possible to speak of a moral order.

One of the problems with Greenfield's line of argument is that it risks organisations being viewed as purely mentalistic phenomena, when in fact, of course, they have a material reality. It is on this point that Greenfield's anti-realist epistemology gets him into strife. Take schools. If a group of individuals conceive the idea of founding a new school to embody a particular pedagogical world-view, for as long as they carry the idea around in their heads it is precisely that: something in the mind. But when at last a building is erected, a uniform and insignia adopted, teachers employed, money raised, publicity produced and records kept, their idea is made real. The school suddenly exists as an actual physical object, which is given shape and form and is no longer simply a mere mental category. For sure, it is minds, or at least ideas and values in those very same minds, that began the shaping and continue to do so. But Greenfield had little to say about the physicalness of any organisation—be it Oxford University, Telecom, Qantas, Coca-Cola or Eton College—and what this means for the ideas about it that people continue to carry around with them. The difficulty is not so much that the physical embodiments of the organisation somehow have a life of their own independent of the people who enliven them, but instead that the material form any organisation takes, its 'thingness' so to speak, and the relationship between that physical property and the idea it is supposed to embody, seems to be of no account at all for Greenfield, or at least the importance of the relationship between the two is not made clear. So, 'as soon as one person assists another to fulfill an idea in the head of the first, an organisation appears', he writes (1983: 6), but 'it has no reality in itself except as human effort gives it life', whereupon he leaves the matter at that.

Schools as moral orders

So what does it mean to depict an organisation as a moral order or universe? For Greenfield this entailed understanding organisations as ethical systems rather than as physical ones, in which peoples' actions and decisions are ultimately explained and justified by reference to the underlying values that these socially constructed entities are intended to realise. For each and every one of us, values 'are the ultimate subjective reality' (Greenfield 1985a: 25).

Greenfield's condemnation of the Theory Movement rested largely on its adoption of a model of scientific inquiry that took for granted a distinction between facts and values, and which then decreed that values had no place whatsoever in social and organisational research. This version of science is often mistakenly known as 'logical positivism', when in fact it is really a species of 'logical empiricism' (Evers and Lakomski 1991: 46–60; Phillips 1983: 6). Part of Greenfield's objection rested on the claim that any alleged scientific theory which logical empiricism yielded was not some kind of neutral instrument for ordering an otherwise disparate body of facts but was *itself* 'a moral vision of the world' (1991c: 216), so that each and every statement about facts and values made by apologists for logical empiricism were *themselves* valuational (1991c: 209). For Greenfield, therefore, there can, in the end, only ever be values, which means that a value acts like the hook on which everything else hangs, with the consequence that a scientific standpoint and a philosophical standpoint are simply incommensurable or irreconcilable.

Whereas scientific inquiry (as traditionally conceived in educational administration) excised values from theory, or at its best recognised that organisational purposes and ends were someone else's job to define (Greenfield 1985a: 10, 16), Greenfield proposed jettisoning any claim that administration was a science and substituting for it a view that it was substantially an art and a value-based activity (1985a: 21). The influence of Hodgkinson (1978 and 1983) on Greenfield's thinking became more and more marked as this view solidified, and it found its most succinct expression, perhaps, in Greenfield's (1991a: 7) brief foreword to Hodgkinson's (1991) book, in which Greenfield asserted unequivocally that 'the central problems of administrative theory are not scientific at all, but philosophical'. Indeed, the central questions of administration 'deal not so much with what is, but with what ought to be; they deal with values and morality'.

Making values count

Where, then, do administrators fit in the scheme of things, and what, in fact, do they do? Greenfield's answer to this question, which he himself posed (1985a: 6), is that they do precisely what Chester Barnard, the eminent American scholar-practitioner whom he was so fond of quoting, claimed (1982) they always have done: 'administrators make choices about the purposes of the organization and then build the commitment of people to the organization so that its purposes may be achieved'.

To conjure up a vision of a hypothetical administrative world ordered purely and simply by 'the facts' was, to Greenfield's way of thinking, to eliminate responsibility, both for what administrators themselves do and for what those for whom they have responsibility do as well. In this kind of scientific utopia, which Greenfield found so obnoxious, the administrator is transformed into an odourless, colourless and tasteless functionary, reduced to the status of a mere factotum or, better still, a moral eunuch or cipher (Greenfield 1985a: 14). According to Barnard, however, for an administrator to be conceived of as someone not exercising any sense of responsibility was to be defined as someone without convictions, a person lacking a belief in, or commitment to, anything. The essence of the executive functions, as Barnard called them, was that 'they impose the necessity of *creating* moral codes' (1982: 274, original emphasis) for oneself and other people, so that moral creativity was what ultimately distinguished supreme executive responsibility (Barnard 1982: 279). Indeed, so strong was Barnard's view of the essence and significance of the executive's role as an ethical leader that he went as far as to claim that organisations endure only 'in proportion to the breadth of the morality by which they are governed' (1982: 282).

Those kinds of dilemmas which defy purely scientific resolution for Greenfield and which necessitate difficult choices among conflicting values are 'the great issues of the day in education' (1991a: 6). Examples are: how big should a school be (e.g., while small might be beautiful, just how viable is it?); who should be enrolled (e.g., should it be single-sex or co-educational? a multiracial institution? and one designed to reproduce a social caste or achieve a mix of social classes?); the behaviour and convictions it condones; the decision as to what is included in its curriculum and what is withheld; what facilities are needed; and the purposes for which such a school exists. Other issues, which defy proper resolution by resort to any imagined uncomplicated administrative fiat or edict, he lists as: busing, multiculturalism, bilingualism, streaming, equal opportunity, drugs, sexuality, allegiance, community and personal morality, the achievement of excellence in all spheres, the place of prayer and religion, the role of the state, the attainment of economic well-being and the survival of the culture (Greenfield 1991a: 6).

Greenfield saw that people in mainstream organisation theory for whom the world is ordered by facts, and by facts alone, made few concessions towards the importance of values, expunging all but three: organisational survival and efficiency (1983: 28) and effectiveness (1991b: 209). While the point that values simply have to creep in (no matter how sophisticated the attempt to excise them) was by no means a trivial criticism of those of a counter-persuasion from his own, Greenfield was content, nonetheless, to let these few instances of lapses from a value-free science he had unearthed pass by, in order to prise open the moral order.

Securing commitment to values

Is there any tangible proof that administrators stand for values and that those values make a difference? And how exactly do they manage to engender commitment to such values? Taken purely at face value, the notion of 'order' implies agreement, regularity, shared understanding, or perhaps some kind of contractual rubric (a set of rules of conduct or procedure). Yet this turns out not to be the case for Greenfield, and it is on this crucial point that he parts company with Barnard.

In Barnard's case, organisation is virtually impossible to sustain without cooperation, so that a formal organisation is 'a system of consciously coordinated activities or forces of two or more persons' (1982: 73) for which cooperation is a *sine qua non* (1982: 83). Although the failure to cooperate has perhaps been the outstanding fact of human history, so that humankind has for the most part been disorganised (1982: 5), a cooperative state of affairs was nonetheless, Barnard believed, an eminently reasonable and rational one to be in because it facilitated the attainment of agreed-upon ends or purposes. Any such willingness to cooperate is in turn dependent upon a system of inducements and an economy of incentives or, failing either of these, upon various methods of persuasion (1982: 149). Incentives for Barnard include a number of material attractions and enticements, whereas methods of persuasion include coercion and the inculcation of motives. Barnard could point to very few enduring examples of cooperation ever having been sustained by coercion, but inculcating belief in a common purpose he deemed to be an absolutely vital executive function (1982: 87).

For Greenfield, on the other hand, the quality of organisational life always bordered dangerously close to being a continual Hobbesian state of nature: solitary, poor, nasty, brutish and short. One of his favourite images is what he calls the organisational war (1984: 165):

> Everything within the [organisational] order—no matter how stable and unchanging it appears—rests upon struggle and personal contention among individuals. The war is never over. No victory is ever decisive; no defeat, however devastating, is ever final. No matter what happens in today's battle, no matter how satisfying the victory or how humiliating the defeat, there will be another round tomorrow.

There are two sorts of wars for the members of organisations—wars within and wars without—and any moral order is but the uneasy and precarious outcome of somebody's success in ensuring commitment to the realisation of his or her particular ideas or values. At best, a moral order seems to represent a temporary, unstable consensus, and at worst a begrudging, niggardly acquiescence.

Now it is the particular job of the administrator or leader—Greenfield seemed to use these two terms interchangeably—to create or bring about that moral order. To this extent he agreed with Barnard, but he diverged from Barnard in two significant respects: firstly, in the significance he attached to power and, secondly, in his espousal of what he called 'the anti-leadership position' (Greenfield 1984: 165). On the first point, the crucial thing to bear in mind is that, whereas for Barnard an organisation was an instrument for the exchange of utilities with other organisations in a kind of ongoing market relationship, for Greenfield an organisation was simply an instrument for the expression and exercise of naked power (1983: 40). Barnard had remarkably little to say about power as such and, as has been pointed out, he considered coercion and force to be of little value and he also believed that executives could only very rarely get away with the exercise of arbitrary authority (1982: 163), for reasons that will become clear in a moment.

The contrast between these two theorists could not be more dramatic than as regards their second point of difference over leadership. Barnard's model of organisation implies a community of interest between leader and led—an implicit social contract between the two, based on trust in the leader's ability to inspire faith. Because Barnard was so adamant that authority is sanctioned not from above but from below, in what is really the organisational equivalent of the doctrine known as the consent of the governed, executives have no choice but to be men and women of genius because so much of their success depends upon their personal attributes. For Greenfield there was no social harmony at all; organisational authority simply cannot be trusted and so there is only bitter, never-ending conflict. Thus (Greenfield 1983: 41–2):

> Organizations are realized through massed hierarchical power. They are tools for achieving the ends of those who enjoy a perceived right to command others, whether that right rests on force, tradition, election, appointment, or personal choice.

In this view the noisy combatants simply retire to lick their wounds at sunset and gird themselves during the brief lull afforded them for more of the same the following day.

At the same time, however, Greenfield was acutely aware of what the withdrawal of consent can do—it can render organisations as limp as 'beached whales' (Greenfield 1983: 42)—for his next sentence after the observation about hierarchical power reads 'Organizations are conversely enfeebled to the extent that individuals decide to withdraw their powering from them' (1983: 40–1). Here Greenfield clearly had his eye on the loss of regime legitimacy, so common throughout the world in the 1970s and 1980s, whereas Barnard had in mind the strength of sentiment among work groups and informal organisation which his contemporary, the Australian, Elton Mayo, had hit upon in research at the Western Electric Company. But because Greenfield drew a different conclusion from this recognition of the power of veto of lower-level participants than did Barnard, and because he was deeply suspicious that leadership is always 'on the side of society and legitimation' so that those who challenge leadership's verities 'do so at their own risk' (Greenfield 1984: 165), he was led logically to take a position of anti-leadership. In essence, therefore, 'administration is about power and powerful people', he concluded (1986: 74), and any new science of administration 'must be free to talk about the values that power serves, but free it cannot be if it is closely dependent upon the Sovereign'.

Anything goes?

Power, then, 'is what holds any normative order together; it is the glue of organization' (Greenfield 1983 : 46), and it follows from what has been said about power that the price any individual pays for organisation membership and allegiance may be the sacrifice of at least some of the values to which he or she stands committed. So when Barnard (1982: 233) wrote about 'the necessity for indoctrinating those at the lower levels with general purposes, the major decisions, so that [cooperative systems] remain cohesive and able to make the ultimate detailed decisions coherent', it is easy to understand why Greenfield might have squirmed uneasily. Instead of surrender and submission, what Greenfield proposed (1984: 165) is the recognition that, in the end, there is only 'a plurality of values in human society [which] denies ultimate legitimacy to any action'. This is a glimpse of a world in which there are values in contention with one another and in which 'we are all leaders to some degree'. On this point Greenfield staked out for himself a position of pure and unequivocal relativism, which might also be described as anarchy and possibly even dismissed by his less charitably-minded critics as moral chaos.

Two immediate consequences for research flow from this relativist standpoint. The first is that social scientists must come to know first-hand what it is that administrators know: administration.

> But that will require the study of decisions, will, intentions in all their depth, perplexity, and subjective uncertainty. The new science will surely also require giving up the notion that decisions and organizations

themselves can be controlled by science. Greater insight such science may offer but greater control, no. (Greenfield 1986: 75)

This in turn means, as Greenfield acknowledged (1984: 166), that in regard to the moral order itself, scholars are limited to describing the context within which personal action takes place, or arguing about 'the rightness of the moral order we depict'. Greenfield's research agenda therefore included things like the discovery of the way the social reality of organisational life is built up and maintained, and the contribution administrators make to that; the role of language in sustaining social reality; consideration of what is 'good' and 'right' in administration and how this is learnt; and uncovering the 'existential realities of leading and following', the wielding of power and the making of decisions 'when much is on the line' (1986: 76).

The second consequence is that researchers must come to know administrators themselves. These have now become people who, from the point of view of a particular organisational order, Greenfield cast in the role of representatives of, or as entrepreneurs for, its values (1984: 166; 1991c: 222). While this colourful metaphor is left undeveloped, Greenfield pleaded (1986: 76) for researchers to take seriously such things as the character of administrators (something readily accessible through history and biography) and the careers of administrators: exactly who does administer schools, for example, and what motivates them to climb the administrative ladder? What happens to them as they climb? And where do their various upward pathways lead? Finally, does any semblance of truth still remain in the old adage that in education it is women who mostly teach and men who mostly administer?

Leaving aside these implications for the moment, if, as Greenfield later argued (1991c: 217), committing people to values is 'the basic stuff' of both education and administration, then his unreconstructed relativism presents him with very real difficulties. Of course he is not the only scholar to advocate an anti-leadership view. Yet no matter whether this more recent disdain for leadership (under any guise) is packaged, either as some kind of existential horror at the prospect of the 'learned helplessness' it is said to induce (Gemmill and Oakley 1992: 115), or because there can never really be virtuous leaders, only effective ones, and 'effective leadership requires villainy' (Bailey 1988: 10), anti-leadership in whatever form is, quite frankly, untenable. Greenfield's two problems therefore, were firstly, that he considered values to be all of a piece, when this seems to be patently false; and, secondly, he provided no way of discriminating between the values with which an administrator has to deal and values that he or she might want to endorse. Yet implicit in Greenfield's own commitment to allowing all contending values a place in the sun was a kind of meta-level value that to do so was a good thing and therefore (presumably) superior to any other meta-level value that represented its direct denial. And implicit also in an indirect reference to the treatment afforded his own views (see below) is his claim that heterodox opinion is by and large ignored in educational administration. If such opinions are ever published, they are 'well countered with extended bulls of orthodox refutation' (Greenfield 1991b: 210), whereas he believed that all opinions have a right to be heard and that everyone benefits by tolerating a process known as trial by what is contrary.

So the question is, then, which values? And how are we to know? Hodgkinson (1983: 36–41) is the only theorist in educational administration who has tried to tackle these questions by rank-ordering values (concepts of the desirable, he calls them) in a hierarchically arranged paradigm. Influenced by Hodgkinson's endeavours and his own editorial experience at *Curriculum Inquiry* over a number of years, Greenfield began to refer to values making possible the attainment of 'what is good', to claim that 'everyone wants the good', and to assert that 'a hierarchy of the good is therefore inevitable, as is the demand to ground it in authority and to further it through leadership' (1991b: 215). These few fleeting references and just one other—the idea that if 'we are to find and act upon *better* values' and aim at '*something higher*', then the notions of authority and hierarchy require redemption (1991c: 222, 223 original emphasis)—are the sum total of the final hints Greenfield gave his readers of which values, in the end, he believed really count.

In fact, it now seems that, when taken together, these passages actually signal or portend a dramatic shift in emphasis, particularly a recognition by him that ethical relativism entails unendurable social costs and, therefore, severe limitations. Significantly, and for the very first time, towards the end of an extended review of his own experiences in training at Alberta, Greenfield offered this even more telling observation (1991c: 222, emphasis added):

> The spirit of the times: encouraged by charters and codes of human rights the individual seeks maximum advantage for self, ignoring the consideration that one person's rights are enforced at the cost of another's loss of them. *The furtherance of individual rights often comes at the cost of civility and social order.* Can anyone look at contemporary life and not think that we live in a dog-eat-dog world? As the symbols of authority in schools have been attacked and removed, the power of *the institution* to teach and educate has been denigrated and diminished. The spirit of the times encourages individuals to be irresponsible, calling it freedom.

Here, suddenly, a premium has been put on the pursuit of individuality: the costs are borne by traditional and time-honoured institutions, such as schools, and these are costs which any society cannot and should not have to bear. For Greenfield, then, the wheel had begun to turn full circle, because the needs of organisations appeared to have been put before those of the individuals who comprise them. Organisations, he conceded, can indeed represent or stand for better values and not merely deny, repress or obliterate them as was once thought. No longer need any individual stand fast against the world, for he or she at last can find a home. The rebel had come in from the cold.

Conclusion

In their recent discussion of his work, Evers and Lakomski (1991: 81) note that in the controversy within educational administration sparked off by Greenfield, 'while almost all [of his] critics acknowledge the centrality of epistemology to its resolution, there is a conspicuous reluctance to engage in explicit epistemological theorizing'. And what is more, 'there is further noncommunication over the reality of organizations'. Apart from a handful of respondents in the United States, Greenfield's work has generally been ignored in that country. The bulk of his readership is instead found in the United Kingdom, Australia and Canada. Greenfield himself wrote (1985a : 24):

> I have asked myself why my critique has been greeted in this way and slowly the answer is drifting back to me from friends who think that they know me well enough to let me glimpse the truth. I am regarded as someone who has been disloyal to the organisation [the field of educational administration]: I have questioned its basic tenets and the appropriateness of the means it has chosen to achieve its ends.

The significance of this introspective remark lies less in its literal truthfulness (or otherwise) and more in what it reveals about the kinds of circumstances confronting all apostates and how experiences of rejection almost inevitably find their way into what they write about the world.

In one way or another, then, in virtually all that he wrote during the last two decades, Greenfield strove to shrug off every vestige of the scientific world-view into which he was schooled. When, many years later, he was invited back to the Department of Educational Administration that had nurtured him as part of an elite corps at Alberta, he was careful, as he put it (1991c: 216), not to try and bury that Department but rather only 'the pseudo-science of administration' for which, in good faith, it was a pioneer in the 1950s. In what was for so long a one-man campaign to move educational administration out of the narrow lockstep, logical empiricist view of science it was content to bask in, Greenfield had recourse to all manner of unorthodox images and all sorts of unconventional material to give added bite to his scholarly writing, including extracts from newspapers, diaries, poems, novels, plays, the cinema, the Bible and even ancient mythology. All of this was used to try to communicate graphically a sense of the fragility of human existence and, by contrast, the awesome power frequently at the disposal of administrators.

Educational administration, as he came to know it, was always built on the foundation of theories of organisation, and so that is why he spent so much time writing about those places in which administrators work. And then, because he came to believe that science was the wrong way to come to terms with the world, he devoted himself to pointing out that values were the only things in life that really counted. For these reasons, so much space has been devoted to organisations and values in this chapter. Given the centrality of subjective experience for Greenfield, then there is no way that students who embark on understanding his contribution to their chosen field of endeavour can avoid asking themselves what they value in education and how they can then best appreciate, and accord due recognition to, the values of those whom they administer.

4 Critical Theory of Educational Administration

Richard Bates

Is it possible for a system of administration to be truly educational? If so, what might an *educational* system of administration look like? If systems of administration are typically concerned with the productive capacity of economic organisation or the steering capacity of political organisation, can they have anything other than an adversarial relationship with systems of education concerned with learning and motivation and the cultivation of norms and values related to social development? These are the questions with which a critical theory of educational administration is concerned and to which this paper provides an introduction.

Weber's paradox and educational purposes

It was Max Weber who pointed out that the increasing rationalisation of society through technologies of administrative control might eventually construct an Iron Cage which imprisoned us all. Weber was, of course, writing well before the development of the computer-based data banks and computer-mediated communications systems, which have extended the reach and power of both commercial and state administrative capacity in such extraordinary ways. Nonetheless he saw the general shape of what was to come. Weber's attitude towards the historical development of such enormous administrative capacity was ambivalent. On the one hand, the processes of rationalisation involved had already produced a 'disenchantment' with magic, sorcery, witchcraft and superstition, replacing them with science, learning, technology and art. This he describes as rational progress, and it is difficult, from our standpoint, to disagree with his positive valuation of such changes. On the other hand, the administrative rationalisation of production and of social control lead also to the incorporation of individuals within the unyielding structures of the Iron Cage of rationalised economic and political organisation, with a consequent loss of meaning and loss of freedom in everyday life.

Weber despairs at this seemingly inevitable consequence of what at first had seemed such a liberating historical process. That society should end in a state of 'mechanical petrification' populated by 'sensualists without heart', who excluded all feeling and emotion from their actions, seemed a poor reward for the enormous energy expended by the Protestant revolution. The paradox of a cultural revolution that transformed the psychology of individuals and allowed them new freedom to develop alternative ways of life but leading to forms of economic and social organisation that denied the very premises of that revolution, was one that Weber could not solve.

Marx 'solved' the problem by insisting that, instead of changes in consciousness determining changes in the basis of production, it was changes in the means of production that produced changes in consciousness. Thus the 'freedom' engendered by the Protestant revolution was simply an illusion produced by alterations in the means of production resulting from the continuous battle between capital and labour.

Towards the end of his life Weber seemed to be influenced by such a view. Rather than assuming that the rationalisation of cultural and psychological phenomena was the driving force of economic and social change (an assumption that underlay his work on the emergence of Protestantism and capitalism), he assumed the converse. As Michael Pusey suggests, following Habermas,

> the shift in Weber's perspective is clear. The rationalisation process is no longer primarily a cultural and 'psychological' process: we are no longer tracing a process that unfolds, as it did before, in the dimensions of *culture* and *personality*. The perspective has changed, and it is now the functional imperatives of the state and the economy that together drive the rationalisation process in a gloomy path that leads ultimately to spiritual, intellectual and moral extinction. In Weber's view it is a process in which the original ethical and religious-cultural motivations are dissolved into a 'pure utilitarianism'. (Pusey 1987: 53)

The arguments surrounding these difficulties were central to the agenda of the Frankfurt school of critical theorists. Marx's analysis of commodification and Weber's analyses of rationalisation and disenchantment were linked and extended by them. As Pusey suggests,

> the Frankfurt School brings Marx and Weber together in a many sided study of *reification*, of 'false consciousness' and of ideology in late capitalism—in its art (Benjamin), in its popular culture (Adorno), in economics (Pollock), in psychology and the family (Adorno, Fromm) and in science (Marcuse). (Pusey 1987: 33)

The essence of the problem remains: what is the relationship between culture and personality, on the one hand, and the structures of economic and political organisation, on the other? Does the increasing rationalisation of economy and society inevitably produce a loss of freedom and loss of meaning in everyday life?

The problem is a central and crucial one for education, because education is fundamentally concerned with the construction of meaning and identity—that is, with psychological and cultural processes. At the same time, education systems are major 'steering mechanisms' through which the structures of economic and political organisation are managed—that is, they are heavily subject to processes of rationalisation taking place in the economic and political spheres.

Evidence of mounting pressure for the subordination of education systems to increasingly rationalised systems of production and control is all but universally apparent, but perhaps particularly obvious in Western countries. Here the general economic malaise is frequently asserted to be the result of failures in education. Education must therefore be transformed. The model for transformation is that of the increasingly rationalised structures of economy and polity (despite the fact that the majority of the population regard these structures as failing). Education must produce a more skilled workforce and impose tighter social discipline so that the economy can be more competitive. The role of the state is reduced to that of a steering mechanism whose task is to ensure compliance on the part of educators and educated alike. (For a discussion of this issue, see Bates 1993.)

Recently the state (at least in Western countries) has developed numerous mechanisms in order to demonstrate its steering capacity. In terms of the economic imperatives of increasing productivity and competitiveness, these invariably involve a reshaping of the curriculum to make it more work-related; a reshaping of pedagogy so that greater creativity and innovation are developed; a reshaping of examinations and assessment to ensure that 'standards' and competitive hierarchies are maintained; a reorganisation of schools to ensure their greater efficiency in the development of a 'culture of production'; and a reshaping of teacher education to eliminate all but the most practical of activities directed towards production.

At the same time the political imperatives of increased steering capacity insist that increased social discipline must be achieved through a reshaping of the curriculum to conserve 'traditional' values; a reshaping of pedagogy so that compliance and submission are achieved through discipline; a reshaping of examinations and assessment to ensure the maintenance of competitive individualism; a reorganisation of schools to bolster their moral authority; and a reshaping of teacher education to eliminate 'radical' theories and ensure complicity in the assertion of tradition.

The result of these not wholly consistent demands is a great deal of confusion, both in schools and in the wider society (Bates, 1992a). Such contradictory processes of rationalisation have as one of their main effects the reduction of motivation and commitment among both teachers and pupils as the resultant educational activities are further separated from the realities of their everyday lives. But the production of motivation and commitment among the young is one of the fundamental requirements of the education system. Weber's paradox is alive and well and living in the schoolroom.

Theories of educational administration

Traditional theories of educational administration are unable to address this paradox because they are fundamentally technologies of control articulated in terms of a functionalist account of social order (Bates 1983); they are accounts that assume that the needs of the system are paramount and that the 'system' will do whatever needs to be done to ensure that it moves towards 'equilibrium' with regard to both internal and external forces. The system is therefore reified and the individual subordinated to its requirements. The economic and political needs of the system take precedence over the psychological and cultural needs of its inhabitants. The purposes of educational administration are taken for granted as being those of adjusting the individual to the society or economy, or both.

The result, in education, as elsewhere, has been the development of methods of administration which are quite at variance with the psychological and cultural needs of citizens. Economic, social and political systems have been reified and their inhabitants subordinated to their supposed needs, aims or objectives. Administrative theory has addressed the 'needs' of organisations in terms of their efficient functioning. But, as Greenfield suggested, organisations (that is, systems of administration)

> have no ontological reality, and it is no use studying them as though they did. They are an invented social reality of human creation. (Greenfield 1980: 31)

Greenfield put a great deal of effort into understanding organisations as inventions, as changeable social realities which people attempt to shape and reshape in their own image. Moreover, when studying such organisations, Greenfield insisted that they be interpreted rather than reified.

> The basic problem in the study of organisations is that of understanding human intention and meaning . . . Action flowing from meaning and intention weaves the fabric of social reality. (Greenfield 1980: 26–7)

And so it does. And particularly important in this process is the role of values. Values, however, are often in conflict. Thus organisations become battlegrounds where people fight over which values are to determine what actions.

> Conflict is endemic in organisations. It arises when different individuals or groups hold opposing values or when they must choose between accepted but incompatible values. (Greenfield 1986: 72)

If organisations, far from being reified, are treated as battlegrounds over values, then the role of leaders is the articulation of such values into the heat of the battle.

> To help us begin to think of leaders in moral terms we should recognise that they are the representatives of values: indeed, they are both creators of values and entrepreneurs for them. (Greenfield 1986: 73)

Indeed, if we abandon the positivist view of organisations and adopt Greenfield's subjectivist view:

> What we are left with . . . is contention among values, or more accurately, among those who espouse different values. In this view we are all leaders to some degree. We all have legitimacy in the degree to which we act out our own values and can involve others in them. (Greenfield 1984: 165)

However, if the problem with the functionalist view is that there shall be no values other than those of 'society' or 'economy' then the difficulty with Greenfield's subjectivist view is that it provides no grounds for adjudicating between the differing values of various competing groups. Understanding organisations through the analysis of motivations, intentions and values and the struggle between them does not therefore lead to any resolution of action, for

> understanding leads not to technique and technique to control; understanding leads only to greater understanding and (if we follow the insights of Eastern religions) to escape, through insight, art, suspension of the will and ultimately to oblivion. (Greenfield 1984: 151)

The interpretivist answer to Weber's paradox seems therefore as unsatisfactory as that of the positivist. The yearning for oblivion seems a rather inadequate response to the disciplinary powers of reified organisations!

But is there an alternative? The answer from a reconstituted critical theory is yes, maybe.

Critical theory and the institutionalisation of reason

One of the starting points of Habermas's reconstitution of the work of the early Frankfurt theorists is his recognition of the impasse produced by the conflict between a reificatory positivism and a subjectivist interpretivism. His book *Knowledge and Human Interests* is a critique of positivism and its limiting of our conception of reason through the construction of a particularly narrow conception of science and an insistence that the resulting 'scientism' is the only form of knowledge possible. *Knowledge and Human Interests*,

> seeks to show how positivism has mutilated our reason and swallowed it whole into a limited theory and practice of science ... It is ... not an attack on science but an attack rather upon an arrogant and mistaken self-understanding of science that reduces all knowledge to a belief in itself. (Pusey 1987: 20)

Habermas criticises this intensely self-regarding view of science as taking too little account of three major criticisms. Firstly, that observation itself (on which positivistic science is said to be based) is far from pure and unmediated but is shaped by *a priori* categories and concepts that the observer brings to bear during the very act of perception. Secondly, that rather than knowledge being constructed solely from data, knowledge is socially constructed and mediated by culture. Thirdly, because of the positivists' insistence on eliminating the social and cultural from their theorising, they cannot give a convincing account of the process of reflection (and therefore explain the 'self-correcting' procedures of scientific progress) without admitting the incompleteness of their theory.

From these criticisms Habermas develops a tripartite theory of cognitive interests to which every speaking and acting subject is presumed to appeal. These cognitive or 'knowledge-constitutive' interests relate, firstly, to our interest in controlling nature (our *technical* interest); secondly, to our interest in understanding each other (our *practical* interest); and thirdly, to our interest in distinguishing between power and truth (our *emancipatory* interest). It is this third interest that is constituted by our search for reason and fully rational knowledge in the face of ideologically frozen representations of social, political, economic and scientific 'reality'. The emancipatory interest is the one that drives us towards the detection and elimination of false beliefs in areas concerned with technical and practical interests—the detection of false science and of false tradition.

It is this emancipatory interest that is so evident in Weber's account of the processes of 'disenchantment' associated with the Protestant revolution. The transformation of sorcery and witchcraft into science and religion was clearly an emancipatory achievement. Moreover, and very importantly, it was a dramatic instance of *learning*. Indeed, Habermas's examination of the processes of social evolution places the emancipatory interest, the capacity to detect and correct false science and false tradition, the capacity to *learn*, at the heart of human progress. As Pusey suggests:

> Accordingly, we must reconstruct social evolution as a progress that

depends on expanded possibilities for *learning* and so for the creation of culture with an emancipatory potential: as the progressive institutionalization of the claims of reason against arbitrary power. (Pusey 1987: 29)

Here Habermas makes two claims that are fundamental to a critical theory of educational administration. Firstly, that learning is to be defined in ways that incorporate an emancipatory interest and, secondly, that social evolution is dependent upon such forms of learning.

Learning, language and power

Now, of course learning is also dependent on technical and practical interests as well as the emancipatory interest. So, Habermas argues, is the very act of discourse—of communicating with each other. Habermas's theory of communicative action argues that three validity claims are made whenever speakers engage in discourse. That is, communicative action

> relies on a cooperative process of interpretation in which participants relate *simultaneously* to something in the objective, the social and the subjective worlds even when they thematically stress only one of the three components in their utterances. (Habermas 1987: 120)

Rational communication is therefore not simply a matter of individuals relating to each other on the basis of egocentric calculations. Nor can theories of communicative action based solely on notions of stimulus and response, of sticks and carrots, explain the processes they seek to illuminate, for such theories omit one or more of the dimensions that are implicit in communicative action (Habermas 1986). Communicative action is inescapably socially coordinated through the medium of language and always contains implicit reference to objective, social and subjective assessments of the shared world of the people concerned.

This does not, however, mean that all speech is therefore rational communication. For instance, there is a whole background of understandings, attitudes, language and convictions that are assumed by individuals from their local tradition. Natural languages carry such knowledge in symbolic forms, which are often unexamined.

> This stock of knowledge supplies members with unproblematic, common, background convictions that are assumed to be guaranteed; it is from these that contexts for processes of reaching understanding get shaped, processes in which those involved use tried and true situation definitions or negotiate new ones. Participants find the relation between the objective, social and subjective worlds already preinterpreted.
> (Habermas 1987: 125)

Habermas calls this 'preinterpreted' world the life-world. It forms the same sort of substratum or foundation for action and consciousness in the social world that Freud's notion of the Unconscious provides for the Conscious in individual psychology. As with the Unconscious, the life-world is 'so unproblematic that we are simply incapable of making ourselves conscious of this or that part of it at will' (Habermas 1987). However, just as an individual in a therapeutic situation can begin to relate certain aspects of the Unconscious to puzzling aspects of Conscious behaviour, so through processes of *mutual learning* we can relate to the life-world in a more rational and ordered way. Indeed, Habermas suggests that social evolution is characterised by the progressive rationalisation of the life-world. Weber's analysis of the shift from sorcery and witchcraft to science and religion is a classic example of such rationalisation during the process of social evolution.

Within the modern world of capitalism, however, rationalisation has taken on an unbalanced form; that is, science and technology are fused together and subordinated to economic development in ways that seek to reduce or eliminate more widely held social purposes. In terms of our earlier discussion, the technical interest subordinates the practical interest and defines the emancipatory interest as solely economic. Habermas labels this phenomenon the dominance of *technocratic consciousness*. This is an ideology that seeks to promote a particular relationship between power and truth.

> technocratic consciousness reflects not the sundering of [particular] ethical situations but the repression of ethics as such as a category of life. The common positivist way of thinking renders inert the frame of reference of interaction in ordinary language . . . as the reified models of the sciences migrate into the sociocultural life-world and gain objective power over the latter's self-understanding. The ideological nucleus of this consciousness is the elimination of the distinction between the technical and the practical . . . Technocratic consciousness makes this practical interest disappear behind the interest in the expansion of our technical control. (Habermas 1972: 112–13)

The result is a society irrationally geared to capital accumulation and therefore to the private interests of the few rather than to the public interests of the many—to collective interests and needs. Technocratic consciousness cannot address such public collective interests because of its exclusion of the practical interest in how we are to live together.

Moreover, the progressive rationalisation of technological consciousness and its repression of ethics destroys the very elements of the life-world on which it depends for underpinnings of social solidarity. Traditional values and institutions such as the family, church and school, which articulated the ethical components of the life-world, begin to fail. As they do so, attempts are made to modify or sustain them in forms consistent with the dominant technocratic consciousness. The difficulty is that such technocratic consciousness can only address technical interests.

Thus the practical and emancipatory interests that are necessary for rational social evolution are further eroded. Habermas, at this point, makes a further strong claim that:

> the sanity, well being, and the very identity of each individual ultimately depends upon shared, or at least, reciprocally communicable, self-understandings, upon which 'ego-defining structures', that join up your inner world with mine in such a way as to make mutual understanding, negotiation and relationship possible. (Pusey 1987: 100)

Moreover,

> Habermas insists that the desiccation of traditions, the manipulation of world views, forced social change and the forced acceptance of carrot-'n-stick inducements all combine to distort 'the communicative structures' and 'ego-securing' structures upon which mass loyalty and generalised motivations of the population depend. (Pusey 1987: 100)

Such mass loyalty depends not on technocratic consciousness but on a conviction that in principle what is being done to us is ultimately justifiable—that technocratic consciousness is indeed compatible with the practical and emancipatory convictions implicit within the life-world.

As Pusey puts it,

> The point is that motivation, participation, and conforming loyalty *all* depend ultimately on our shared and taken-for-granted assumption that validity claims implicit in every administrative and social action *could*, in principle, be made good, or 'discursively redeemed' in a rational discourse that is ultimately beyond manipulation. (Pusey 1987: 102)

The great contemporary struggle is, then, that between the 'system' constructed through technocratic consciousness in the interests of the few (a system coordinated through the mechanisms of power and money) and the 'life-world' which incorporates all three interests, technical, practical and emancipatory.

An educational administration?

We are now in a position to ask again, in a somewhat more informed way, what an *educational* administration would look like. If social evolution is secured through the progressive rationalisation of the life-world through means of mutual learning, which simultaneously incorporate the technical, practical and emancipatory interests that are implicit in any notion of rational communication, then it is possible to conceive of an *educational* administration. It would, however, be one somewhat different from the current forms of administration, which are captured by the 'system' and dominated by a technocratic consciousness solely concerned to promote technical interests and subordinate them to the economic motives of capitalism.

Firstly, as learning takes place through language, an educational administration would pay great attention to the forms through which language is articulated in educational institutions. It would be concerned, for instance, to ensure that a conscious commitment to the uncovering of technical, practical and emancipatory interests was part of the language of discourse of the school, class, university, etc. It would endeavour to correct any lopsided analyses that were *solely* technical, practical or emancipatory and to encourage a balanced consideration of all the elements required for rational discourse.

Secondly, an educational administration would be committed to learning as the development of a *public* form of discourse, one that allowed issues emerging from the life-world to be dealt with as a public responsibility rather than as an opportunity for private gain.

Thirdly, an educational administration would defend the autonomy of the school from the encroachments of technocratic consciousness and seek to organise itself in the defence of democratic aspirations.

These are, in fact, easily recognised principles, which can be identified in much of the work of great educators such as Dewey. As such, then, they have historical roots, which are recovered by a critical educational theory of administration. They can also be recognised as hostile to the self-regarding importance of educational and administrative theories associated with technocratic consciousness; as hostile to a solely hermeneutic concern with practical interests, which leads to a regressive pursuit of understanding to the exclusion of engagement in social action; and as hostile to the excesses of forms of education based solely on notions of emancipation. (For an excellent discussion of some of these issues, see Young 1990.) The question is therefore one of balance and comprehensiveness. How can such matters be attained through processes of administration?

Schools are administered through the construction and maintenance of four message systems: curriculum, pedagogy, assessment and discipline (see Bates 1992b). A critical educational theory of administration would be committed to ensuring that technical, practical and emancipatory interests were considered with regard to each of these message systems. Moreover, the resulting structures of organisation and control would have the maintenance of such considerations as their major purpose. In addition, the very processes of administration themselves would need to be justifiable (though not continuously justified!) in terms of the public, democratic commitments to mutual learning, which are fundamental to rational social evolution. Message systems of the educational organisation would also need to be grounded in the technical, practical and emancipatory concerns of the communities within which it was embedded, thus ensuring a connection between its activities and the progressive rationalisation of the life-world of which it was a part.

All this suggests a dramatically different form of administration of educational institutions from those we are used to seeing. However, in educational practice, challenges to conventional notions of educational administration are more prevalent than we might expect. Teachers are resistant to the privatisation and marketing of education, for quite good reasons (for a discussion of such resistance, see Blackmore 1992). Basically these reasons concern their recognition of the potency of the considerations outlined above, even though they might articulate them in rather different ways. Their concern is well articulated by Bob Young:

> The penetration of classroom life by system imperatives steered by bureaucratic power and market incentives can only destroy the pedagogical relationship by industrialising it. Just as the individual teacher needs to exercise pedagogical tact and restraint, so the administrator needs to exercise administrative tact and restraint. There is an irreducible field of pedagogical freedom without which the pedagogical relationship is not possible. Indeed, without such freedoms there can be no act of teaching as such . . . (Young 1990: 131)

The point is that a truly educational administration has a responsibility to protect those areas within which a pedagogical relationship is possible, a relationship concerned not simply with the production and encouragement of technical reason, but also with practical and emancipatory reason. The role of educational administrators in protecting such space against the encroachment of technocratic consciousness is vital to the process of social evolution through mutual learning. The difficulties of doing so are well documented in the longstanding conflicts between teachers and administrators and in the stresses experienced by principals, for there is a fundamental tension between the pedagogical impulse of teachers and the forms of administrative control of education.

> The point is to protect areas of life that are functionally dependent on social integration through values, norms, and consensus formation, to preserve them from falling prey to the systemic imperatives of economic and administrative subsystems growing with dynamics of their own, and to defend them from becoming converted over . . . to a principle of sociation that is, for them, dysfunctional. (Habermas 1987: 372–3)

A critical theory of *educational* administration would have precisely such a goal.

5 Cultural Theory in Educational Administration

Lawrence Angus

It is interesting that there has been such a dramatic rush to incorporate cultural concepts within educational administration during the past decade. In seeking to embrace notions of organisational culture, corporate culture or 'cultures of effectiveness', writers on educational administration are joining with, and indeed imitating, their colleagues in the world of business administration. Such imitation is not new. Reasons why the wider business and academic communities are fascinated with corporate culture are complex. One possible explanation is that the interest has been sparked by the apparent success of Japanese business and industry, and the belief in the West, particularly in the United States, that cultural aspects of Japanese management can be incorporated into Western practices to improve corporate performance (Goll and Zeitz 1991; Ouchi 1981; Smircich 1983a). Western nations have generally been looking for ways out of a severe economic downturn, and this is reason enough for them to look to imitating Japanese successes.

As Meek (1988), in a seminal article on organisational culture, points out, however, the economic slump has had the effect of making more apparent than previously the structural inequalities inherent in capitalist society. Not that this situation has resulted in any direct challenge to the legitimacy of structures of Western capitalism; political and economic alternatives have generally been discredited, given the democratic revolutions in the former Soviet Union and eastern Europe and the retreat from Euro-Communism. Meek does seem to insist, however, that apparent inequality of organisational power and remuneration can led to dissatisfaction among calculative, knowing workers, and that this can emerge as a management problem. Meek therefore suggests that the emergence of 'the present preoccupation with organizational culture is probably related to socio-economic factors in Western society' (1988: 453). This is because the cultural approach allows an emphasis on 'people problems' rather than power structures and so may induce greater employee satisfaction. It allows the adoption of strategies that cohere with particular cultural environments, and of a rhetoric that suggests an apparent concern with the wishes and values of organisation members who are to be incorporated into the corporate 'vision'. Administrators are expected to become symbolic managers, manipulators of culture and belief, who attempt to impose corporate control over institutions in the increasingly decentralised organisational form which is considered necessary for organisational efficiency and, most importantly, legitimacy, in the increasingly complex post-industrial society (Parker 1992).

In this chapter I shall examine the current enthusiasm for notions of 'corporate culture' in educational administration, as well as other traditions of cultural work that have been important in educational analysis. Because of limitations of space, however, I shall not discuss in detail the implications for our understanding of culture of recent work in gender theory or postmodernism; that analysis will require a separate paper. In my discussion here, I shall limit my endeavour to an analysis of the strengths and weaknesses of various culture concepts and the ways in which they have been employed in educational administration. Building on this analysis I shall construct an argument in favour of the adoption of a relational perspective on school culture—one that relates schooling and other spheres of society, and which regards schools as sites wherein the construction of culture is a social and political process.

Cultural concepts in educational administration

Despite the impression created in much of the current literature in educational administration that organisational theorists have only recently discovered it, cultural analysis has a long tradition in organisational research, management theory and the literature on education and society. Unfortunately, these traditions, and their conceptual advances and limitations, seem to have been largely overlooked in much of the current literature on educational administration. Before proceeding with an analysis of current conceptions of school culture, therefore, it may be worth examining briefly some of these traditions of cultural scholarship.

In educational circles, the notion of culture sits easily with the long-held popular wisdom of teachers and administrators that when you walk into a school you almost immediately pick up a 'feel' for whether it is a 'good' school with a distinctive character or 'climate'. The notion of 'school climate' links with a particular tradition of administrative theory—that of the human relations school of scientific management. This group of theorists took the concept of culture seriously as they presented a revision of the classical model of organisation (e.g. Mayo 1933; see Perrow 1979, for an overview). They emphasised the need for the motivation of subordinates, rather than their coercion and argued that organisational success depends on the 'social integration' of an organisation. From this point of view, it is essential for managers to understand the human condition in order to influence organisations. For, although the needs of employees were to be taken into account, 'to the extent that personal sentiments, values, and goals are in conflict with formal regulations and organizational objectives, the job of managers is to reconcile individual and organizational needs' (Werlin 1988: 52). This strongly pro-management position of the human relations school 'resulted in biased research that studied the "irrational" behaviour of lower ranking personnel and supported unquestioningly the "rational manager" model' (Gregory 1983: 361). The objective was to diagnose and control the organisation and its culture, and therefore subordinates. Current literature on school culture and corporate culture generally takes a similar stance and, although it rarely acknowledges it, fits squarely into the human relations tradition.

It was not until the work of Greenfield that a significant scholar in the field of educational administration took seriously the notion that organisation participants construct their own organisational culture and indeed their own organisation (Greenfield 1980: 27). Greenfield opposed the 'scientific' school of educational administration which, he argued, had adopted a narrowly positivistic approach in which organisation had come to be regarded as a 'thing', capable of being measured and controlled. Instead, he regarded organisation merely as a process of people organising themselves. From this perspective, organisations such as schools 'have no ontological reality beyond the specifications of individuals whose attitudes, values and motivations define organization' (Greenfield 1983: 50). Organisations such as schools are therefore sites of cultural negotiation among those people who have a stake in them:

> ... what many people seem to want from schools is that schools reflect the values that are central and meaningful in their lives. If this view is correct, schools are cultural artefacts that people struggle to shape in their own image. Only in such form do they have faith in them; only in such form can they participate fully in them. (Greenfield 1973: 570)

This insight is extremely important because it suggests that the focus of attention in attempting to understand schools as organisations, and their administration, should be on ordinary participants and their day-to-day social interaction rather than on management, techniques of management control, and a search for universal laws of administration. Greenfield seems to have been most interested in the interpretation of organisational participants' values and experiences. However, the notion that organisations are sites of cultural interaction also raised broader questions about the nature of social processes in schools, the politics of administration, educational change, and the relationship between schools and society. In particular, it raised questions about the management of culture in schools. These are precisely the questions that, standing on the shoulders of Greenfield as it were (cf. Apple 1988), Bates and several colleagues began to pursue in the early 1980s.

Although acknowledging an enormous debt to Greenfield, Bates was critical of Greenfield's apparent reduction of organisations to collections of voluntarist individuals who create organisations such as schools out of their own free will and collective sense-making. Such a view, he argues, largely ignores, or at least oversimplifies and underestimates, the influence on organisations of power, history and the social, economic and cultural structures within which schools (and all organisations) are embedded. In other words, school culture is not simply the creation, or the property, of individual school members. It is influenced by, and simultaneously influences, authority structures, the dominant culture(s) and, in general, the 'needs' of society and economy. Educational administration, then, is intimately connected with power and politics and is itself a political process. Because educational control is therefore linked to broader social control, for Bates the most significant aspect of educational administration in this process is its capacity for enhancing or challenging institutionalised power and control. The essential issue is summed up in Bates's claim that educational administration typically amounts to the management of culture and knowledge (see, for example, Bates 1980, 1982, 1983).

Culture concepts in sociology of education

In emphasising the significance of culture and cultural control in educational administration, Bates, unlike most within the field, was drawing not only on the pioneering work of Greenfield but also on strong traditions of cultural analysis within the sociology of education. Most obviously, Bates reflected the concerns of the British 'new' sociology of education which was, in the 1970s, grappling with questions about the significance of power, ideology and the construction of knowledge in the relationship between education and society (see, especially, Young 1971; and also important critical (Wexler 1987) and even self-critical (Whitty 1985) analyses of this field). Bates pursued these concerns by investigating the role of administration in legitimating structures of knowledge and providing differential access to 'what counts as culture and knowledge' to children of different social backgrounds. As such, educational administration, Bates argued, provides ideological and cultural legitimation to prevailing power relations in society. In short, it generally confirms the status quo but could, if a critical perspective were adopted, contribute instead to greater social justice, liberty and equity. In order that scholars and practitioners might be assisted in developing a critical cultural perspective, Bates posed a number of specific research questions which reflected the perspective of the 'new' sociology:

1. What counts as knowledge?
2. How is what counts as knowledge organised?
3. How is what counts as knowledge transmitted?
4. How is access to what counts as knowledge determined?
5. What are the processes of control?
6. What ideological appeals justify the system? (Bates 1980: 9)

By framing these questions in educational administration in terms of 'what counts', Bates stresses the contested nature of meaning in educational organisations. In this way Bates goes well beyond Greenfield as he makes it clear that 'meaning is the result of intersubjective negotiation within organizations (as Greenfield had suggested), but what "counts" as meaning is determined within contexts—both organizational and social—of unequal power relations' (Anderson 1990: 43). The 'new' sociology of education (a title that sounds somewhat pretentious now), so influential on Bates' conception of culture, also drew from and built upon at least two other related traditions of cultural analysis in the sociology of education. One of these was work in the areas of teacher culture and pupil culture. The other was work in social and cultural reproduction.

Still a seminal text in the first of these fields is Waller's (1932) classic study of *The Sociology of Teaching* in which he concludes that 'education is the art of imposing on the young preformed definitions of the situation current and accepted by the dominant group'. He regards the school as a gigantic agency of social control in which pupils, acting upon 'youth culture', resist the 'teacher culture' of adults, and the dominant culture, but gradually become absorbed into it. Renewed interest in ethnographic studies in the 1970s led to continued investigation of teacher and pupil cultures and the apparent conflict between them (Jackson 1968; Hargreaves 1980; Woods 1980a, 1980b, 1984). Although many of these studies dealt also with cultural negotiation between teachers and pupils (e.g. Woods 1980b), some more recent ethnographic work, especially that of Walker (1988, 1993), has shifted the focus specifically to the articulation of these cultures rather than seeing teachers and pupils merely as 'fighting groups' (Waller 1932: 109–10).

One point on which there is general agreement is that teacher and pupil cultures intersect at least in their common perception that the essential role of the teacher is to control pupils (e.g. Everhardt, 1983). While culture may be constructed and experienced differently from different positions within the school, as Brizman (1986: 444) explains, 'What dominates the perceptions of both teachers and students is the individual teacher's ability to control the class'. In other words, generalised teacher and pupil cultures influence each other in complex ways such that each shapes, enculturates and socialises the other:

> Years of classroom experience allow students to have very specific expectations of how teachers should act in the classroom. Students, for example, expect the teacher to maintain classroom control, enforce rules and present the curriculum. Students expect teachers to be certain in both their behaviour and their knowledge, and students articulate these expectations if the teacher in any way deviates from this traditional image. In this sense students do coach their teachers in ways which reinforce school structure and, as such, constitute an immediate source of teacher socialisation. (Brizman 1986: 445–6)

Brizman raises two especially important points here. The first is that students are not simply passively socialised by schools, nor are they inert victims of cultural reproduction in schools. They are active agents in the process (see also Angus 1982, 1984, 1986a). Indeed, despite their structural position, in at least one important respect teachers may well be disadvantaged in the battle of cultures. This is because although teacher and pupil cultures act on each other, in teacher culture teachers are typically highly individualised while being subject to the demands of bureaucratic control and school structures (Bullough et al. 1984; Connell 1985; Hargreaves 1982; Lortie 1975). The research generally concludes that teacher culture is 'practical in its orientation, largely uncritical and unreflective, and is concerned more with means rather than ends' (Sachs and Smith 1988: 425).

The second point raised above by Brizman is one that few researchers into teacher culture seem to have appreciated, but it is vital for understanding school culture. Brizman implies that research findings that teacher culture is characterised by such things as individualism and practicality have merely identified cultural myths. The point is to look behind the myths at how teachers' work is influenced by institutional practicalities and school structures. When this is done, Brizman (1986: 448) argues, we can begin to see how the myths of teacher culture 'valorise the individual and make inconsequential the institutional constraints which frame the teacher's work. [In the research] the teacher is depicted as a self-contained world. [But] such myths transform the teacher's actual isolation into a valued autonomy which, in turn, promotes the larger social value of rugged individualism'. According to this argument:

> Teaching style, then, turns out to be not so much an individually determined product as it is a complex movement between the teacher, the students, the curriculum and the school culture. The myth that teachers are self-made serves to cloak the social relationships and the context of school structure by exaggerating personal autonomy. (Brizman 1986: 452)

Brizman's analysis is useful, particularly in the way she connects student and teacher cultures with school structures, power relationships and the social context of schooling—elements that are often overlooked in interpretive and interactionist, as well as managerial, descriptions of culture. All of these are interrelated in complex ways (Angus 1988) and are relevant to the important and varied body of work on cultural reproduction in education. Scholars in this tradition, influenced by a number of Weberian, neo-marxist and critical perspectives, reject the implicit assumption of mainstream approaches that schools are socially and politically neutral institutions simply to be managed in the most efficient manner. Instead, schools are regarded as social and cultural institutions, sites of power relationships, in which schooling serves the interests of dominant groups largely through the reproduction of relations of class, race and gender. While the variety of specific positions within this tradition makes generalisation difficult, reproduction theorists generally focus upon 'macro-structural relationships and how these relations in the form of structural determinations shape, as well as limit, the actions of human beings . . . [R]eproductive positions reject consensus as the normative glue of the social system; instead, they focus on the way in which dominant classes are able to reproduce existing power relations in an unjust and unequal society' (Giroux 1981: 13).

Two significant contributions in the reproduction theory tradition, which illustrate the diversity of this field, deserve special mention. The first of these is that of Bowles and Gintis (1976) who, from a classical Marxist position, addressed a twofold problematic: 'to understand the role of the school in reproducing the social division of labor and to explain how it is that people accept such sorting and selecting' (Apple 1992: 132). Bowles and Gintis (1976: 131) concluded that:

> The education system helps integrate youth into the economic system . . . through a structural correspondence between its social relations and those of production. The structure of social relations in education not only inures the student to the discipline of the workplace, but develops the type of personal demeanor, modes of self-presentation, self-image, and social class identification which are crucial ingredients of job adequacy. Specifically, the social relationships in education . . . replicate the hierarchical division of labor.

Bourdieu, from a rather different theoretical position, has for many years worked specifically on issues of cultural reproduction in the precise sense through a focus on the formation of social consciousness and individual identity. Schools play a major part in this cultural activity but in a way in which, according to Bourdieu (1977), provides differential access to socially-valued cultural resources for students of different backgrounds. This is part of a broader social process in which, as Miller (1991: 14) explains, 'The contours of social inequality are structured through patterns of unequal access to symbolic capital, [and] through unequal cultural competence as defined . . . by those in economic, political and cultural control'. Schools contribute to this wider process, without necessarily meaning to, because

> the education system demands of everyone alike that they have what it does not give. This consists mainly of linguistic and cultural competence and that relationship of familiarity with culture which can only be produced by family upbringing when it transmits the dominant culture. (Bourdieu 1977: 494)

The work of Bourdieu and that of Bowles and Gintis was taken up in various ways by researchers who pursued the notion of the 'hidden curriculum'—the idea that students learn in schools subtle cultural messages which devalue the cultural experiences of some students and privilege those of others. The work of Jackson (1968) was also important in this regard and prompted other curriculum theorists to seek to uncover the 'hidden curriculum' of life in classrooms. The criticism levelled at much of the work of these scholars and their followers, although it does not apply so strongly to Bourdieu (see Miller 1991), is that they assumed an almost direct correspondence between the informal messages of the school and the social and economic needs of a stratified capitalist society. As Apple summarises this criticism, a focus on the hidden curriculum led to inquiry

> based on a theory of homologous structures, in which norms and values of one set of institutions (schools) mirrored in a relatively straightforward and uncontradictory way—those 'required' in another (the paid labor market [in the case of Bowles and Gintis, and the broader social structure in the case of followers of Bourdieu]). Only the hidden curriculum was important in one's explanation. The formal corpus of school knowledge [for instance] was inconsequential. (Apple 1992: 132)

Despite such criticism, it must be said that work on the hidden curriculum and cultural reproduction in schools opened the way for sophisticated analysis and theorising about the nature of schools as organisations, the complexity of their cultures, and the problematic relationship between schools and society. These insights, although they may have been expressed in a somewhat crude and reductionist manner in some cases, helped us to understand schooling as a social, political and cultural process that is far from neutral. It is precisely this fundamental lesson that is ignored in the currently dominant perspective on organisational culture.

Defining organisational culture

Culture is an extraordinarily complex concept and extremely difficult to define. Indeed, because there are so many traditions of cultural analysis, one problem emerging from the current interest in organisational culture is that incompatible notions of culture are employed by different theorists (Erickson 1987). The predominant perspective sees organisational culture as an aspect of institutions that may be manipulated by management in order to enhance organisational commitment and efficiency. That is, the organisation and its leadership are seen as generators of particular cultural attributes that are associated with corporate solidarity and a sense of mission or corporate vision (Deal and Kennedy 1982; Ouchi 1981). Such a perspective on organisational culture allows virtually no concern for culture as a shifting and contested notion that is continually being constructed and reconstructed, and which must be subjectively understood. Instead, emphasis is upon managerial concerns with the manipulation of and intervention in organisational culture to shape it in ways that are conducive to the realisation of organisational goals. Not only is there a lack of appreciation of the importance and complexity of cultural politics, but also there is a taken-for-granted assumption that organisational culture will reflect unproblematically norms and goals which are internalised to form stable, integrated organisational structures.

It is perhaps no surprise that theorists have trouble defining organisational culture. Even if they stay within the tradition of cultural anthropology (e.g. Geertz 1973), they will find that Kroeber and Kluckhohn (1952) have identified some 164 ways in which culture has been defined. Despite the variability and complexity, however, organisation theorists seem to have become relatively comfortable with culture concepts to the point where a general view of organisational culture has emerged as largely non-controversial. As Dent explains:

> we are now used to conceptualizing organizations as bodies of thought, variously described as myths, causal schema, theories-of-action, interpretive schemes, ideologies, paradigms and so forth. The concept of culture, drawn from anthropology and ethnography, has entered the organization literature as a framework for extending this ideational understanding of organizations. (Dent 1991: 708)

There is now general agreement, according to Mitchell and Willower (1992: 6), that organisational culture is typically taken to be 'the way of life of a given collectivity (or organization) particularly as reflected in shared values, norms, symbols and traditions'.

Meek (1988: 463), following Smircich (1983a), helpfully divides theorists of organisational culture into two camps. The first treats culture as a variable—as something the organisation has, which is able to be manipulated and controlled. The second regards culture as something the organisation is—as 'the product of negotiated and shared symbols and meanings; it is produced from human action'. The first definition offers a broadly functionalist account of culture, while the second is interpretive. Literature employing the second definition is likely to be somewhat more analytical and to employ the notion of culture as a 'root metaphor' (Smircich 1983a) for understanding organisational life. In this literature culture is regarded as 'the pattern of basic assumptions that the group has invented, discovered or developed in learning to cope with external adaptation and internal integration' (Schein 1986: 9).

Much of the literature directed at administrators adopts this second broad definition in its account of culture as a concept, yet takes on the first definition, that culture is an artefact that can be manipulated and controlled, when advocating or prescribing managerial action. For instance, in the educational administration literature, school culture—which includes values, symbols, beliefs, shared meanings, customs and traditions, legends and sagas, stated and unstated understandings, habits, norms and expectations, common meanings and shared assumptions—is thought to enable the unified school to become 'effective' and achieve its objectives (Sergiovanni and Corbally 1984: viii). In successful and effective schools, it is argued, culture should be aligned with a vision of excellence. By providing a source of common meaning and significance for school participants, such a culture, which is to be created by management, creates common values and a common direction (Sergiovanni 1984: 10). It is the job of administrators, according to this literature, to provide the 'vision' and control the culture.

Limitations of functionalist definitions

What is lacking in both of the above ways of understanding organisational culture (regardless of whether it is something an organisation has or is) is any sense of the relationship between the organisation and other organisations, social spheres and social experiences. The focus in both cases is internal to the specific organisation, where it is assumed that there is a natural tendency towards consensus and harmony. Social conflict and the external cultural, social and economic context in which organisations are embedded, are generally ignored. However, these provide the essential problematic in critical approaches (Angus 1993a, 1993b; Bates 1987; Anderson 1990) which generally see organisations as manifestations of cultural forms (Smircich 1983b) or rules (Clegg 1981) and also as sites of cultural contestation (Benson 1977; Clegg and Dunkerley 1980). In other words, these critics argue, in institutions such as schools, rather than a uniform concept of organisational culture simply being imposed from above, or bequeathed from the past, contest occurs over the construction and assertion of cultural forms. Organisation members, as active and knowing agents, have the capacity to influence organisational culture and structure, while also simultaneously adapting to, and influencing to some extent, strongly institutionalised cultural expectations, both within the organisation itself and more broadly in society.

It is probably correct to say that 'there is no single comprehensive theory that fully explains the complexity of the school as an organization' (Shaw 1992: 295). There are problems with various traditions, yet all of them provide important insights. The predominant functionalist concept of culture, however, which has been enthusiastically and uncritically appropriated into educational administration, reduces the complexity of culture to an almost absurd level of simplicity by emphasising only that culture creates consensus, harmony, shared beliefs, shared values and shared culture. Writers seem to assume without question that sharing in fact exists, and to ignore the capacity of people to challenge and depart from, as well adapt to, organisational rules. The functionalist perspective even dismisses the capacity of organisation members to comment critically on their situation (Golden 1992: 1–2). As Golden (1992: 2) points out, 'the majority of writers . . . systematically overlook this aspect of culture, focussing instead on the ways in which individuals adapt to, and reinforce, the organization's rules for action'. There is presumed to be a unitary ('the') organisational culture rather than a complex of subcultures, in which organisation members may well switch back and forth (Schultz 1991).

The notion of organisational culture which is narrowly stereotyped in management literature is borrowed from the structural-functionalist theoretical tradition without the accompanying debates and criticisms (Meek 1988). The interests that are served by this are, most apparently, those of management, but also the dominant social and economic interests in our society. These interests are served partly by the privileging of leadership within organisation literature and partly by the current fascination with business management. Indeed, business has become a dominant metaphor in educational administration (Kempner 1992; Mitchell and Willower 1992). This is illustrated by, for example, the fascination with, and space devoted to, Peters and Waterman's 1982 book *In Search of Excellence: Lessons from America's Best-run Companies* in a number of texts (e.g. Caldwell and Spinks 1988). The 'adoration of business' in educational administration has led to the situation in which 'business operations, management, and leadership are often used by administrators and scholars in education as models of success' (Kempner 1992: 110). More specifically, the literature on school effectiveness typically emphasises 'the rational, structural, machine-like aspects of school organizations' (Shaw 1992: 295). This partly explains why, in current approaches to educational governance, management and leadership have become so significant.

Leadership, organisational culture and the management of meaning

The combination of a narrowly functionalist cultural perspective and an obsession with leaders has had the effect that, in most management literature, organisational culture is regarded virtually as a 'controllable variable' (Killman et al. 1985: 423). For example, in what the editors claim represents the 'state of the art' in literature on corporate culture, Killman and colleagues in *Gaining Control of the Corporate Culture* (1985) urge leaders to 'take charge' and manage the culture. Various chapters emphasise that strong cultures can be created by management (Schein 1985); that these emanate from the beliefs, values and philosophies of senior management and serve to unite lower level workers (Lorsch 1985; Martin 1985); and that these workers, through rewards and sanctions, can be brought to internalise management wishes and directions (Allen 1985). A similar argument is advanced in educational administration by Smith and Peterson (1988) in their influential text on *Leadership, Organizations and Culture*. These authors treat culture as a dependent variable of leadership. It is consistent with this position to conceptualise corporate culture as 'the major beliefs and values as expressed by top management that provide organisational members with a frame of reference for action' (Goll and Zeitz 1991: 191). Leaders therefore create their own organisational environments (Kirby et al. 1992: 303). The leader's values, in this view, virtually *are* the organisation, or, as Bottery (1988: 342) puts it:

> whoever is in charge of the organization has the right to dictate its aims; these aims can be relatively easily decided upon and implemented; as the organization's aims are more important than those of individuals within the organization, it is perfectly acceptable to treat people as means to the organization's ends.

The work of Sleezer and Swanson, who recommend 'culture surveys' as a tool for managers to use when they 'are faced with the challenge of changing the organizational culture to support new ways of accomplishing work' (1992: 22), is an example of this orientation. Sleezer and Swanson further advise that 'because time is money, the longer it takes a manager to solve a problem, the greater the cost to the organisation'. Therefore, in order to get the culture right as efficiently and cost-effectively as possible, 'management can use culture surveys to communicate its vision of the organization's culture and the performance expectations that operationalize the vision' (Sleezer and Swanson 1992: 23–4). Presumably, subordinates are expected to simply accept this communication, adopt the new vision, and blithely alter their organisational values and practices to suit the new culture. This vision of compliance and tranquillity seems to fly in the face of virtually everyone's experience of organisational life, in which 'organizations are often arenas for dispute and conflict . . . Organizations are not one homogeneous culture, but are "multicultural", and culture can be a source of conflict' (Meek 1988: 461).

In educational administration, what is considered appropriate leadership has been heavily influenced by culture concepts in United States management literature, such as *In Search of Excellence* (Peters and Waterman 1982), and the school effectiveness literature (e.g. Purkey and Smith 1985). In particular, scholars such as Caldwell and Spinks give special attention to the so-called 'higher-order attributes of leadership, namely the capacity to articulate and win commitment to a vision for the school and ensure that vision is institutionalised in the structures, processes and procedures which shape everyday activities' (1988: 21). Appropriate cultural expectations of those associated with a school are assumed to be embodied in the particular values and vision of the leader. The elitist implication of this is that leaders are more visionary and trustworthy than anyone else. The general approach seems totally consistent with the tradition of managerial reforms which have attempted to secure the consent of subordinates and build it into otherwise unchanged forms of management control (Braverman 1974; Clegg and Higgins 1987; Wood 1985).

Shrewd leaders are expected to manipulate culture, people and situations so that the leader's 'vision' is willingly shared by followers. Active leadership is therefore required in order to incorporate the desires and needs of followers into a corporate agenda that is set by the leader. The approach draws heavily on the work of such scholars as Weick (1976), Burns (1978), Vaill (1984), Bennis and Nanus (1985) and Deal and Kennedy (1982). It is believed that leaders of vision are able to bring about a negotiated order, or organisational culture, which accords with their own definitions and purposes and ensures that any change is directed into reasonable, predictable channels by their own overriding moral force. Other organisational participants, such as teachers, parents and students, if mentioned at all, are generally viewed as essentially passive recipients of the leader's vision. By asserting and defending particular values, leaders so strongly articulate and endorse their own vision that it becomes also the vision of followers and thus bonds the leader and followers together in a shared covenant, which then informs the non-negotiable core beliefs and values of the organisation. This core, according to the argument, amounts to an organisational culture which effective leaders can manufacture and manipulate.

Most traditions of cultural analysis would probably agree that organisational 'leaders', such as principals, rightly seek to influence organisational arrangements and that they are generally in a better position than most other organisational participants to do so. As such, they are to some extent 'managers of organizational meaning, the custodians of organizational legitimacy, and the definers of organizational and social reality' (Anderson 1990: 43), as the corporate culture theorists advocate. But the functionalist view wrongly assumes that 'leaders' have virtually unlimited management power. One point that should be startlingly obvious, however, is that although administrative leaders are able to influence organisations in various ways, particularly because of their access to resources and information, leaders have no monopoly on the development of organisational meaning (Smircich 1983b: 161). Everyone, whether they like it or not, is a part of this process (Angus and Rizvi 1989). Moreover, there is a range of cultural influences on an organisation such as a school over which a 'leader' can have little if any control. The list would include history, national culture, international cultures, professional cultures, gender cultures, class cultures, the economy and many more.

It is perhaps surprising that so much management literature starts out embracing the notion of culture as shared values, interpretations and meanings, yet ends up advocating that such sharing is the result of organisational participants unproblematically accepting values, interpretations, meanings and culture defined for them by a leader. The fact that the literature can reach such a startling conclusion is perhaps partly due to the long-standing concern in educational administration for order, control and predictability (Bates 1980, 1987). It would seem ludicrous to an anthropologist, for instance, to suggest that a leader could define the culture of a group in what is a complex interactive process. It seems clear that management can be only a part of the total organisational culture.

If for the moment we accept the view that organisational meaning and culture are created not by a manager but are constantly emerging, being made, in the context of the total organisation and all that influences it, then we must accept that the making of meaning is a highly problematic and uncertain process. In any case, meanings have to be learned. Such learning often results in meanings that are largely taken for granted and can become institutionalised as 'rules' (Clegg 1981) which 'guide people in appropriate or relevant behaviour, help them to know how things are done, what is expected of them, how to achieve certain things, etc.' (Mills 1988: 360). But even learning of this type is not simply soaked up by people without question. Meaning is mediated in institutional frameworks, both organisational and social, and is the result of contested social practices in arenas of unequal power relations.

Where organisational legitimacy seems to prevail, therefore, it is less likely to be the result of open consensus than the product of 'the control of those resources which render meanings and identities seemingly unproblematical for the practical, historically conditioned, purposes of particular individuals and groups' (Coombs et al. 1992: 69). Such production of meaning always remains part of 'the competitive struggles over material and symbolic resources whose asymmetrical distribution routinely privilege the claims of some agents (and especially managers) in their exercise of control' (Coombs et al. 1992: 69).

Drawing on the work of Willis (1977), Apple (1992: 138) explains this point nicely:

> making meaning is not merely an individual act but also a profoundly social act, one structured by location and situation. However, locations and situations are not merely to be understood as determinations. They are also, and profoundly, 'relations and resources to be discovered, explored and experienced'. As Willis (1977) goes on to say, race, class, gender, age and membership are not simply learned; they are lived and experimented with, even if only by pushing up against the oppressive limits of established order and power.

The making of meaning, therefore, requires agency, energy and struggle, and is likely to mean making it against other meanings, including dominant meanings. For Giroux, this is a critical point. Given that schools have generally promoted the interests of capital and of dominant social groups, he argues, educational administrators should turn their attention to the way in which 'the issue of how teachers, students and representatives from the wider society generate meaning tends to be obscured in favour of how people can master someone else's meaning, thus depoliticising both the notion of school culture and the notion of classroom pedagogy' (Giroux 1984: 37). What Giroux is alluding to here is the subtle way in which power works in schools and society, which is ignored in the mainstream literature on organisational culture.

Culture and power

Giroux and others have long argued from a critical perspective that bland discourse of management, with its emphasis on control, regularity and predictability, and relatively routine and apparently neutral activity, in various ways reinforces the socio-cultural system through the 'hidden curriculum' (Jackson 1968) and the 'message systems' (Bernstein 1977) of curriculum, pedagogy and evaluation, as well as management. Certainly, both administrators and other organisational participants are caught up in the 'culture of administration' in which, 'though they downplay it and whether they want it or not, principals, for example, typically have more power than teachers, students, parents, and others' (Sergiovanni 1991: 43). Therefore, 'despite commitments to empowering and shared decision making, relationships between school administrators and others are often inherently unequal' (Sergiovanni 1991: 43). However, the domination of managers, or any other form of domination for that matter, is not automatic.

A focus on power relationships may help organisation researchers to illuminate the dynamics of organisational culture in action and the ways in which domination occurs in practice. And because power relationships extend beyond any single organisation, such a focus also encourages us to connect the organisation in dynamic ways with other, larger social contexts and explore relations between them. This point is particularly important for the critical social science perspective on organisational culture.

> The critical school views organizations as constructed realities but stresses the fact that this construction is not a free, voluntary process. The critical school views the system of meanings that exist at the surface or participant level as resulting from deep social and material forces. Creation of meaning is not an arbitrary process that occurs through friendly negotiation and talk. The social reality legitimizes particular social relations, structures and conditions, and it is explained by the deep social and material forces. To understand organizational reality, then, is to ascertain why a particular meaning system exists by examining the conditions that necessitate its social construction and the advantages afforded to certain interests. (Deetz and Kerston, in Anderson 1990: 44)

In organisations, as in other spheres of social life, we can probably say that cultural forms may become hegemonic when understandings are so strongly entrenched that they become internalised as guides for appropriate action. But an organisational culture does not simply bear down upon individuals in an institution so that a monolithic sense of organisation is unproblematically sustained. Organisational culture, as part of the social world, must be continuously constituted. It is therefore always imperfectly reconstructed among contested discourses and subjectivities. Institutions like schools should therefore be seen as cultural sites (Willis 1977; Giroux 1984) in which entrenched expectations and hegemonic understandings act as background rules influencing the actions of organisational participants (Clegg 1981; Giddens 1976, 1984). And while a particular organisational culture may be associated with specific institutions, these institutions are also influenced by, and partly mediate, broader social structures and societal cultures.

Organisational 'rules' (Clegg 1981) have a strong existence in the form of institutionalised expectations and organisational features such as bureaucratic rationality (Rizvi 1986). When taken for granted they amount to pervasive, but unrecognised, structures of power (Angus and Rizvi 1989). They need not be hard and fast rules, and they may be mediated or broken, without much thought or quite deliberately, in organisations in different ways in different situations involving different people. Such 'rules', like social organisation, may be messy and confusing, indeterminate, partially understood or understood in different ways. According to Giddens (1976: 121), rules of this kind may still amount to structures that are 'both constituted *by* human agency and yet at the same time are the very *medium* of this constitution'. Giddens emphasises both the dynamic relationship between structure and agency and the important point that structures do not merely constrain but also *enable* meaningful choices that may lead to action. Rules, then, largely in the form of institutionalised expectations and values, influence the nature and quality of individual and group participation in organisational life in complex and variable ways. A gender regime in a particular organisation, for example, could be seen as an illustration of such influence (Angus 1993a). In examining any set of rules, structures or authority relations, however, it is important that, as Clegg (1988: 11) reminds us, we keep in mind that 'organizations are arenas of struggle and loci of calculations in which social relations of and in production are worked out with a degree of indeterminacy'.

Mills makes the relevant and obvious point here that 'people do not leave their cultural perspectives at the gates of organizations' (1988: 355). They bring their beliefs, values, social conditioning and location within wider social dynamics and power relationships with them. This means that:

> schools must be seen as institutions marked by the same complex of contradictory cultures that characterize the dominant society. Schools are social sites constituted by a complex of dominant and subordinate cultures, each characterized by the power they have to define and legitimate a specific view of reality. Teachers and others interested in education must come to understand how the dominant culture functions at all levels of schooling to disconfirm the cultural experiences of the 'excluded majorities'. (Giroux 1984: 37)

Schools therefore influence and are influenced by the cultural milieu of the society in which they are embedded. From this perspective, they are simultaneously sites in which cultural negotiation and contestation occurs, sites of cultural dominance, and sites which, actually as well as potentially, wield power in society. This assumes that a focus on internal micro-cultures of schools and organisations is needed (S. Ball 1987). But such a focus should also examine the way in which organisations contribute to macro-cultures, and how inter-organisational dynamics influence wider power relations and widely shared beliefs across sectors of society and national macro-cultures (Abrahamson and Fombrun 1992).

In this process some institutional theorists (e.g. Meyer and Rowan 1977) argue that organisations such as schools may tend to reflect the dominant society because they need to be seen to conform with, and to adopt strategies that are consistent with, their cultural environments in order to maintain legitimacy and survive within them (Abrahamson and Fombrun 1992). However, this does not rule out the potential of schools to challenge and comment critically on social norms and practices. As Galbraith argues, it is through 'persuasion, education or the social commitment to what seems natural, proper or right' that institutions such as the corporation, school, church and state 'cause the individual to submit to the will of another or of others' (Meek 1988: 461). Such conditioning is fundamental to the functioning of modern, complex society and so we may conclude, with Meek, that while we should understand the modern organisation as a form of social control, we also need to recognise that 'it is not a form of social control created by management, but a process in which management, workers and the community at large are participants alike' (Meek 1988: 462).

Schools, because they are expressly intended for the education of citizens, are, along with the media perhaps, particularly well placed to contribute to the production of macro-culture. Although they certainly possess a degree of autonomy, schools and the education system 'must still articulate with other sectors of the social formation' (Johnston 1991: 32). This articulation is, of course, accepted without question in the dominant tradition because, in it, 'culture' is integrated into a systems perspective in which schools are seen as being necessarily functional in socialising the young to take their place in society and the economy. Functionalist scholars are therefore less likely to be troubled than critical social theorists such as Apple (1991) about the way in which many current educational reforms—largely informed by new right thinking (Angus 1992; Pusey 1991), which has become pervasive in social, political and educational debates—are directed at 'providing educational conditions believed necessary for increasing profit and capital accumulation' (Apple 1991: 22). A similar logic, present in the Victorian rhetoric of 'Schools of the Future', for instance, promotes 'programs of choice to make schools like the idealized free-market economy' (Apple 1991: 23).

The current use of market analogies in educational administration has profound cultural significance, for, as Bowles (1991: 11) argues, 'markets are as much political and cultural institutions as they are economic'. This is because markets 'not only allocate resources and distribute income, they also shape our culture, foster or thwart desirable forms of human development, and support a well-defined structure of power' (Bowles 1991: 11). This is what all cultural institutions do, although not necessarily in such a deterministic manner as Bowles seems to imply. Although he points out that the notion of markets has become particularly widespread in all forms of public and private provision in recent years, Bowles is not claiming a particularly new insight. As he reminds us, 'anthropologists have long stressed [that] how we regulate our exchanges and coordinate our disparate economic activities influences what kind of people we become' (Bowles 1991: 12). Because of current obsession with 'the market' and the insidiousness of market arrangements throughout society, 'we learn to function in these environments, and in so doing become someone we might not have become in a different setting' (Bowles 1991: 13).

The influence in schools of the notion of 'the market', which in recent education policy has been strongly asserted as the appropriate metaphor for both the competitive relationship between schools and the relationship of schools to their communities, is becoming increasingly apparent. It is significant, for instance, that a number of well-regarded scholars in educational administration have recently closely linked organisational culture, leadership, market and school effectiveness (e.g. Caldwell and Spinks 1988; Beare et al. 1989). For some, school culture seems to amount to little more than market image. In this case, managing the culture is managing the appropriate image so that a commodified package that is acceptable to consumers is presented to the market (Beare 1982; Millikan 1984). This represents a good example of the importation into education of business management methods, which directly influence educational practices and school culture. Moreover, the institutionalisation of market thinking as right and proper for school management and organisation is an example of the relationship between culture and power. Market rationality, like other elements of culture, serves particular interests over others and connects with broader forms of social power and control.

Organisational cultures, in particular sites, at least partly reflect structural features of society at large, and also contribute to those structural features. Institutions are created within, and exist in relationship with, the social formation of society. This implies that society, despite its diversity, is characterised by micro- and macro-cultures that are socially and historically constituted. Their ongoing constitution is always problematic and provisional, however, and occurs largely as a result of differential power relationships, cultural expectations and access to resources. Institutions such as schools contribute to macro-cultures in problematic ways because social relations in particular sites, as in society, cannot be simply assumed but must be continuously reconstituted as part of everyday life. Oganisational culture is extraordinarily complex and dynamic—too much so to be rendered manipulable by organisational managers. This is not to say, however, that organisational culture cannot be influenced by organisational members or leaders who join with colleagues in asserting or challenging particular values in specific locales.

Conclusion

In this chapter, with a particular focus on the notion of organisational culture, I have reviewed ways in which cultural concepts have been employed in the literature of education and management, and I have endeavoured to analyse the implications of these for understanding educational organisation. Like Anderson (1990: 53), I am forced to agree with Smircich that it is not clear to what extent the term organisational culture (as generally used in management) 'refers to anything more than an ideology cultivated by management for the purpose of control and legitimation of activity' (Smircich 1983a: 346). Quantz and his colleagues reach a somewhat similar conclusion. They believe that the emphasis on organisations as cultures has potential but that this potential has been limited because 'in its most common form organizational culture theory has become just another means for the managerial manipulation of organizational "output"' (Quantz et al. 1991: 6). Important learnings can be gained from this work, but these authors feel that 'we can learn even more when we approach schools not as the embodiment of a unitary organizational culture, but as an arena for the politics of culture' (Quantz et al. 1991: 6). The implication of such conclusions is that the field of educational administration needs more studies of the dynamics of organisational life and micro-political activity, as well as studies of the connections between schooling and society. It would be especially important for such studies to investigate the ways in which administrators contribute to 'meaning-making' in schools, and how administration mediates wider social influences (Anderson 1989; Angus 1986b, 1988).

Such a perspective would imply also that ongoing critique of conventional notions of culture and leadership in schools is needed (Angus and Rizvi 1989; Foster 1986; Smyth 1993). The focus could be on the responsibility of schools to enhance the interests of all their members. This would be perfectly consistent with notions of 'sharing' in organisational culture; but instead of sharing coming about because of the imposition of uniform culture from above, it might be a process of shared responsibility among participants for the production of organisational culture. It would not deny cultural contestation and negotiation in school sites but would see all members as important participants in cultural politics. Indeed, administrators might recognise that participation is a cultural phenomenon, and that active participation is most likely to exist in a cultural milieu that accepts and encourages it—and sustains it in everyday practices—as an organising principle of institutional life. This view connects with notions of democratic education and the stated goal of schools to prepare citizens for participation in democracy. If this responsibility also was taken seriously, we might well see greater concern in educational administration for 'just' as well as 'effective' schools (Quantz et al. 1991; Starratt 1991).

One can only imagine the difference there would be in the field of educational administration if justice and democracy became the organising concepts instead of efficiency and effectiveness. This does not mean that the alternative perspective need be inefficient or ineffective (Rizvi 1986). If scholars in the field did embrace such a perspective, however, there are several traditions of cultural work that might inform their analyses. I have already referred to the socially critical tradition in educational administration, work on teacher and pupil culture, the 'hidden curriculum', and social and cultural reproduction. The feminist tradition has also resulted in work that challenges hierarchical administration and advocates relational forms of school organisation (Angus 1993a; Blackmore 1987). A further tradition is that which has explored the nature of teachers' work in the context of school organisation and investigated the emergence and assertion, and institutionalisation in some cases, of democratic school practices (e.g. Apple 1991). Emerging postmodern approaches, although these are too complex for me to go into here, also raise interesting possibilities for the analysis of organisation and culture (e.g. Parker 1992). In all of these approaches, although the position of the specialist administrator may be somewhat decentred, the basic questions about organisational culture can still be asked. Such as: What holds a group of people together as an organization? Through what processes do they change? (Smircich 1983b: 162).

The current state of restructuring of education in virtually all industrial countries adds urgency to the task of reconceptualising the culture of schools. The pattern of restructuring is depressingly familiar with a number of common features such as:

> centralized control (although under the rhetoric of devolution); decrease in educational expenditure; accentuation of horizontal and hierarchical divisions in education, reversing some of the apparently progressive settlements of the 1960s and 1970s; greater emphasis on vocationalism and instrumentalism; commodification of education; increase in privatization and links with the private sector; increased deskilling of the teaching force; a reorganization of the patterns of teacher education; and a reconstruction of the 'crisis' of schooling. (Davies 1992: 135)

With such characteristics it is unlikely that equitable and humane school cultures will be officially promoted. The nature and dynamics of school culture in this environment need to be investigated, along with alternative and oppositional cultures. Most importantly, the relationship between school culture and power needs to be interrogated so that the contribution of schooling to social understanding, social control and social justice can be better understood as we begin to better understand how culture works in and through institutions such as schools.

6 Ethics in Educational Administration

Fazal Rizvi

In recent years, there has been a great deal of interest in the role that values, and particularly ethical values, play in administrative theory and practice in education. This interest signifies the extent to which the traditional view of educational administration no longer enjoys the support it once did. The dominance of the Theory Movement has waned, as the positivist view of science has given way to the idea that issues of power and interests, and ethics and values, cannot be divorced entirely from issues of knowledge, and from the uses of knowledge in educational administration.

While it is now widely recognised that ethical values are integral to administrative theory and practice, it is less clear what these values are and how they might be rationally debated and justified. In this chapter, I want to do two things. First, I want to show how ethical concerns are central to the work of administrators, and that the positivist aspiration of value-neutrality in educational administration is hence both mistaken and misguided. Second, I want to discuss three recent attempts to develop a post-positivist theory of values relevant to the concerns educational administrators have. These attempts, by Hodgkinson (1991), Foster (1986) and Noddings (1984), seek to show how educational administrators might address value issues and resolve ethical problems.

I argue that while each of these accounts are successful in demonstrating the value-neutrality thesis to be fundamentally mistaken, they nevertheless remain trapped within positivism's dualist framework. Ultimately, each remains committed to a basic distinction between fact and value. This dualism, I suggest, leads each to seek universal ethical principles in an *a priori* manner, essentially disconnected from the observable empirical considerations that are relevant to educational decision-making. I argue that this limits the usefulness of their theories to administrators confronted with ethical problems in education.

Positivism and values

The traditional view of educational administration is located within an orthodoxy that separates facts from values—one that views administrative work as neutral with respect to particular ethical positions and particular policy regimes. Not unlike that fictitious television character Sir Humphrey Appleby, it expects administrators to be able to serve any political master. For it takes administration to be a technical matter, concerned with finding the most appropriate means for achieving a given end. Thus, it eschews ethical concerns, regarding them as matters that lie outside the domain of administrative theory and practice.

In educational administration this view was most clearly articulated by the Theory Movement in the 1960s. One of the chief architects of the Theory Movement, Griffiths, in 1985, argued that the movement saw ethical evaluation and empirical explanation as involving two different kinds of propositions, which, for the sake of clarity, should be kept analytically distinct. This did not, of course, mean that administrators could not make evaluative judgements. It was just that they should recognise that ultimately their judgements could not be empirically grounded.

This view of administration was developed largely within the framework of a positivist theory of knowledge. It accepted positivism's imperialistic restrictions on what counted as legitimate knowledge. According to positivism, statements of facts and statements of values are categorically distinct, and only facts can be rationally assessed. Values, in contrast, are seen as non-scientific, subjective and, in a sense, arbitrary. They express the choices that individuals make, and are thus incapable of being either true or false. Lacking scientific status, they cannot be rationally debated.

However, because values express judgements of taste, likes and dislikes and preferences, they have a practical character. They prescribe certain courses of action. But if administration is ultimately a practical activity, how can it possibly eschew values? The positivist answer to this question involves the use of a distinction between substantive and procedural values. Administration, it is suggested, is concerned with *procedural* values, concerned with the questions of *means*, and not with the *substantive* questions of *ends*. An example might help to clarify the point. Administrators wedded to positivist assumptions would argue that, as administrators, it is not their role to ethically appraise an educational policy, such as student participation in educational decision-making. Instead, their role is confined to procedural issues. Their responsibility is to determine the most efficient and effective manner in which the policy of student participation might be implemented.

The Theory Movement thus highlights the principle of value neutrality. It seeks knowledge that is testable and has a high degree of predictive reliability. Its focus is on knowledge of the underlying regularity in the functioning of educational organisations. It suggests that, armed with this knowledge, it is possible for administrators to control people's behaviour in order to obtain maximum organisational efficiency and effectiveness. Educational administration is thus viewed as a technology—a study of techniques of control over environmental variables that affect organisational performance.

For example, in Hoy and Miskel (1987), perhaps the most widely used text in educational administration, the primary focus is on causal connections between input variables such as motivation, personality and expectations, and output functions such as behaviour, performance and effectiveness. Causal connections are believed to furnish generalisations, which can (because of their predictive capacity) be used to control environmental variables in any organisation. Issues of control are thus central to the entire range of theories, such as the systems theory, the theory of bureaucracy, the role theory and the decision-making and leadership theories, which Hoy and Miskel employ in order to describe the terrain of administrative work in education.

However, Hoy and Miskel insist that empirically grounded findings provided by administrative theory are applicable only to the determination of means. They are incapable of establishing the ends that an educational organisation might pursue. Accordingly, they suggest that the main task of school administrators is 'organisational problem analysis in schools' (1987: 81). This may involve diagnosing difficulties, gathering information on performance level of students and schools, comparing the information with the desired performance levels, addressing motivational issues, searching for sources of problems, and devising, implementing and evaluating plans of action for the solution of those problems—but significantly, *not* determining or assessing, in ethical terms, the ends a school might want to pursue.

Neutrality and the nature of administrative work

In recent years this view of administrative work has been subjected to a great deal of criticism. It has been argued, for example, that the aspiration of keeping the issues of means and ends conceptually apart cannot survive the recent criticisms of the positivist view of science. The writings of such philosophers of science as Thomas Kuhn, Hilary Putnam, Paul Feyeraband and Willard Quine have been used to show how pragmatic value criteria are involved in determining the adequacy of all scientific claims, including those in the social realm, and that therefore the idea of a neutral social science is impossible.

But beyond these general arguments, it has been argued that administrative work in education cannot eschew ethical concerns because the concept of education is itself inextricably bound up with the specifically cultural and political notions of human improvement and emancipation. As Bates (1986) has noted, educational organisations cannot avoid issues of the preservation, communication and transformation of culture. Culture is a basic resource of administrative practice in education. For Bates, schools are 'negotiated realities' in which facts and meanings are controlled and resisted through the main message systems of curriculum, pedagogy and evaluation. Viewed in these terms, educational administration is fundamentally concerned with ethical values; how these become institutionalised in educational structures and procedures; and how it might be possible to challenge or transform them.

In a theoretical perspective somewhat different from that of Bates, Skilbeck (1988) has also shown how the management of institutional life is linked to wider developments in culture. He has argued that rapid changes currently taking place in society have made it impossible for administrators to disengage from ethical issues involved in complex decisions affecting the values that are transmitted to the young. Culture is pervaded by values and is articulated within and through institutions such as the school. And because schools are formative, reinforcing and corrective, ethical values form an inextricable part of their organisational discourse and practice.

If one of the central purposes of education is the cultivation of values, moral character and the capacity in students to engage in moral deliberation, then administrators cannot avoid the consideration of aesthetic, economic and ideological purposes that are served by education. It is only within the framework of these purposes that educational administrators can prioritise and manage scarce institutional resources, which have alternative uses and claimants. As educational purposes are always politically open, issues of power and control can never be too far away from the work of administrators.

Because educational purposes and the means to achieve them are subject to endless debate throughout the educational community, the way that administrators encourage and engage in or suppress this debate marks their administrative style and defines what Hodgkinson (1991: 37) refers to as 'the entire chemistry of an organisation'. Importantly, for Hodgkinson, this chemistry is a value chemistry made up of such stuff as feelings, actions, beliefs, purposes and commitment. Hodgkinson is surely correct, then, in concluding that administration involves 'ethical action in a political context, or purposeful human conduct, or behaviour informed and guided by purposes, intentions, motives, morals, emotions and values as well as the fact or the "science of the case" ' (1991: 43).

However, if ethical values are central to administrative work, then how might they be characterised and justified? In what follows, I want to discuss three different approaches to ethical deliberation, not only because they represent perhaps the most influential post-positivist interventions in the field in recent years but also because I want to argue that none of them has been able to escape some of the dualist assumptions of which they are critical.

Hodgkinson on ethics

Along with Greenfield (1986), Hodgkinson has been one of the most perceptive and incisive critics of the traditional view of educational administration. He has insisted that it is fundamentally mistaken for administrative theory to aspire to a scientific status. Administration, he has argued, is not a science but an art; concerned not with certainty, predicability and technical correctness but with human choice, practical wisdom and responsibility. In short, with values. According to Hodgkinson, administration is best viewed as a philosophy-in-action, which seeks to address the problem of reconciling two divergent interests—those of the individual and those of the collectivity or organisation. This, he insists, requires a theory of values because educational administration is essentially motivational and valuational.

Hodgkinson's theory of values is an integrative one, seeking to bring together the various ways people think about ethical matters. His is an account of values that posits an elaborate justifactory schema organised in an hierarchical form. In a way very similar to Maslow's hierarchy of needs and Kohlberg's stages of moral development, Hodgkinson provides an analytical model for classifying three types of values. At the bottom are Type III values, grounded in individual affect and constitutive of the individual's preference structure. Moving up the hierarchy, Type II values are variously defined as expressions of the will of the majority in a given collectivity or as judgments of the consequences of particular practices. These values emerge essentially from utilitarian and social contract considerations that presuppose a social context and a given scheme of social norms, expectations and standards. Finally, there are the Type I values, grounded in formal principles such as the Kantian categorical imperative (Kant 1781). These are universal values possessing certain non-natural properties. Hodgkinson maintains that these values are absolute, dependent neither on particular facts nor on particular traditions. As such, they cannot be justified on any empirical grounds but only in a metaphysical or transrational manner.

Hodgkinson's theory of values is central to his view of educational administration. It provides administrators with a mechanism by which to judge between competing interests and claims. The theory, or 'value paradigm', as he calls it, is thus a conceptual tool that can be used to resolve organisational conflict or make judgements about the ethics of organisational purposes. This conflict resolution logic dictates that lower-type values are subordinate to higher values, and that the highest form of administrative leadership is that which is able to exercise authority in terms of a commitment to Type I values. Hodgkinson's own ethical project is to encourage administrators to move towards Type I values.

Hodgkinson provides numerous examples to illustrate the applicability and usefulness of his value paradigm. He is not reluctant, however, to acknowledge that the realities of organisational life, the trials and tribulations of school administrators and the social, economic and political forces, constitute a 'complex equilibrium of power in schools'. In the expedient world of educational administration, he recognises, ethical deliberation may sometimes be considered irrelevant or at least a luxury. But, he insists, it is precisely because our contemporary cultural condition is so confused that ethical deliberation has become a necessity. If we are to overcome the deep contradictions that currently exist in education, we need a theory of values that enables us to judge educational processes in valuational terms.

Now, while Hodgkinson's case concerning the indispensability of ethical issues in educational administration is certainly a strong one, the same cannot be said of his theory of values. Here, a number of problems can be identified. For example, as Evers and Lakomski (1991) have argued, Hodgkinson's account of the nature of his Type I values is highly problematic. Where do these values come from, and how does one identify or choose among different Type I values? As Evers and Lakomski (1991: 107) argue, because Type I values do not specify a unique set of values, the question of their content is left open. But such an approach leaves the problem of values choice unresolved. The practising administrator is no wiser about how to differentiate between two competing interests, each claiming to have been derived from Type I values. And how indeed are we to separate the charlatans who simply claim that they administer with the authentic Type I values from the sincere who have a genuine commitment to transrational values?

Also, Hodgkinson's theory of values does not provide an account of personal psychology that might explain how an individual might move from a lower-type value to higher ones. Hodgkinson recognises that for a theory of values to be useful, it must be both valuational and motivational. But his account of motivation is far too cryptic to be adequate. In a more comprehensive account the issue of organisational power is crucial, not simply in terms of its distribution but also in terms of the way it defines the possibilities of organisational development and reform. If we are to make educational institutions more ethically responsive, we need to consider how issues of leadership are related to the exercise of power and authority.

Hodgkinson's theory of values suffers from many of the same problems as other rationalist accounts of morality, such as the one provided by Kant (1781) and, more recently, by analytical philosophers of education such as Richard Peters (1966). The most serious of these problems is that without any specific criteria about how to give content to the form of the allegedly transrational Type I principles, we have no way of telling when and how our application of those principles is correct and appropriate. In Hodgkinson's theory, the transrational principles appear at a level of generality that makes their application in specific contexts difficult to formulate and achieve. This is both a practical and philosophical problem.

Also, at the practical level it is difficult to categorise values in hierarchies in the manner Hodgkinson seeks to do, for the transrational values (Type I), on the one hand, and the consensual and consequential values (Type II), on the other, cannot be separated in any clear-cut way. In assessing the relative merits of competing consequences, we cannot be theory-neutral and value-free. Theories and principles are inevitably involved in judging one consequence as more acceptable, or as more appropriate or as morally superior, than another. And indeed sometimes we prefer to subscribe to one principle rather than another because of the consequences we assess to follow from its adoption.

We are constantly working out, revising and reconstructing the principles by which we might administer. Furthermore, we deliberate over these principles not in the isolation of our contemplative privacy but, as Wittgenstein (1953) has shown, in public. Values are social in this way, located in specific historical contexts. They are embedded in specific material relationships; they can change as organisations come to recognise their impact and consequences. Principles do not therefore have abstract existences, as Hodgkinson's view would seem to suggest. Rather, they are embodied in our practices and in our institutions and traditions.

Hodgkinson's theory thus pays insufficient attention to the social and historical character of values. His is a view of administration that seems to be premised on the assumption that certain individuals obtain the will and capacity for moral enlightenment unattainable by the majority. But administration lies not only in the acts of individuals but also in social relations. It is not only a property of an individual but is linked to the way an organisation is socially and historically defined.

Foster and the ethics of emancipation

This insight is central to the way Foster (1986) has explored the issues of values in educational administration. His work is located within the philosophical tradition of critical theory, most notably the writings of the German social theorist Habermas. Following Habermas (1979), Foster argues that the traditional view of administration is based on a very narrow view of the interests that human beings have. Humans, he maintains, are not only concerned to control their environment; they are also interested in understanding each other, and in collective improvement and emancipation. And it is the idea of emancipation, Foster believes, that should be central to the work of all administrators, especially educational administrators.

Foster rejects the view that values are simply the expressions of the attitudes, commitments, preferences or choices that individuals make and that therefore cannot be rationally assessed. Instead, he insists that certain ethical values, such as truth, freedom and justice, are universal and are capable of objective justification. He justifies this claim in terms of Habermas's account of universal pragmatics.

Habermas's theory of universal pragmatics is designed to delineate a set of universal capacities and standards that all human beings possess. Habermas argues that these standards can be identified by examining the presuppositions of our communication, by asking the question 'what makes human communication possible?'. His answer to this question enables him to identify a set of formal criteria that form the basis of all human communication. Communication between people, he insists, cannot get off the ground unless we are already committed to certain universal ethical principles. As Habermas (1979: 177) argues:

> In adopting a theoretical attitude, in engaging—or for that matter in any communicative action whatsoever—we have always (already) made at least implicitly, certain presuppositions, under which alone consensus is possible: the presupposition for instance that true propositions are preferable to false ones, and that right (i.e. justifiable) norms are preferable to wrong ones. For a living being that maintains itself in the structure of ordinary language communication, the validity basis of speech has the binding force of universal and unavoidable—in this sense—transcendental-presuppositions.

This argument leads Habermas to reject the claim that values cannot be rationally determined. For at least truth, justice and freedom, he suggests, are values to which all human beings would aspire in a state of perfect rationality—or, as he puts it, in an 'ideal speech situation'. He argues that any proper understanding of the conditions of undistorted communication can give us an appreciation of how it is that certain ethical claims can be true or false.

It is important to point out, however, that Habermas does not regard an ideal speech situation as an empirical state; it is rather an analytical construct which enables him to identify the standards by which human speech and conduct can be judged. To envisage an ideal speech situation is to reflect carefully on the presuppositions of human communication. Against those who regard all values as relative, Habermas argues that we are at least committed to the norms of truth, justice and freedom. These norms are not choices—not even universalisable choices—but standards which we can use to guide and justify conduct in a manner that is not arbitrary. Habermas insists that these norms would inevitably and universally be adopted in an ideal speech situation, in a constraint-free consensus. In contrast, he asserts, ideology is a form of systematically distorted communication, in which people are kept away from understanding each other and thus from leading an ethically informed life.

Habermas rejects ethical relativism as just another instance of systematically distorted communication, for it carries an implication that there are no constraints on reason and evidence and that there is no limit to the number of ways in which an ethical problem could be approached. Habermas regards this way of thinking as fundamentally misguided. As Connolly (1988: 62) suggests, for Habermas the doctrine of ethical relativism (and also of pluralism) 'weakens the self-confidence of social critics and increases the already impressive leverage available to those who obscure and defend established practices of oppression'.

Foster believes that Habermas's theory of communication has profound implications for the critical theory and practice of educational administration. More importantly, he suggests, Habermas provides a framework within which educational administrators can once again put ethical and cultural issues at the centre of their work. The Theory Movement was concerned exclusively with techniques; the critical view, in constrast, regards techniques as secondary to the ethical concerns that should lie at the heart of any educational enterprise. What ends educational organisations pursue, who are they designed to benefit, whose interests do they undermine, and how they contribute to a socially just society are questions that should be asked of all administrative practices in education. For Foster, critical theory also implies that schools should develop democratic structures in which rational and free discourse could take place, without the hindrance of authoritarian bureaucratic procedures.

Administrators, in Foster's view, have a major responsibility to develop structures that both enable and prepare teachers, students and parents for democratic participation. Ultimately, Foster argues, critical theory provides 'an attitude, a way of conceptualising reality, and a way of addressing social change through individually formulated actions' (1986: 90). This attitude is essentially concerned with encouraging the widest participation in educational decision-making—raising legitimate questions regarding how and why our schools and society fall short of the norms defined by an ideal speech situation.

In any assessment of Foster's views on ethics and educational administration, one question suggests itself above all: can the idea of ideal speech situation do the theoretical work required of it? My answer is that 'it cannot', for many of the criticisms directed against Habermas apply equally to Foster. While the idea of ideal speech situation has *prima facie* appeal, the rationalist universal ethics it implies is highly problematic. Held, for example, has argued that:

> the ideal speech situation itself is not a sufficient condition for a fully open discourse, nor, by extension, for the critical assessment of barriers to this type of discourse in society. The conditions of the ideal speech situation fail to cover a range of phenomena, from the nature (content) of cultural traditions to the distribution of material resources, which are obviously important determinants of the possibility of discourse and, more generally of a rational, free and just society. (Held 1980: 396)

Other critics have also doubted the possibility of undistorted communication characterised by openness, unbiased attitudes and rational dialogue, directed towards reaching consensus. Gouldner (1976: 140) has gone even further, suggesting that the model of ideal speech situation is too strict and that by placing unrealistic demands on the conditions of rational discourse, it may actually provide barriers to democratic politics. In any case, as Bubner (1982: 108) has argued, critical theorists have not succeeded in explaining why individuals should be motivated to enter into a situation of undistorted communication, even if such a state were possible.

In his later work, Habermas (1986) has attempted to revise some of his earlier views by developing a theory of communicative action which states that because human beings learn in a collective fashion, the learning processes that advance communicative rationality should provide a framework within which ethical progress might be pursued. Implicit in this account is the assumption that an engagement in appropriate discourses will lead inevitably to the participants becoming committed to the values of truth, rationality and justice. In so far as Foster's views also remain tied to this assumption, he is working within an Enlightenment tradition that regards intellectual progress as a basic condition for moral progress. In this sense, the theory of communicative action does not seem to have overcome some of the rationalist assumptions implicit in the ideal speech situation model.

Foster has clearly not explained why principals in schools, who are already advantaged by the existing power structure, would, for example, feel inclined to engage in communicative dialogue. And even if they might decide to engage in dialogue, there is no guarantee that their deliberation would result in appropriate action. Dialogue itself does not ensure that the potential for an ethical practice is realised. The question that remains unasked by Foster is which social, political and material conditions are conducive to dialogue, and which are not. What is clear is that critical theory is based on a number of *a priori* assumptions, which bear little resemblance to the *realpolitik* of organisations.

Noddings and the ethics of caring

Both Hodgkinson and Foster have emphasised the role that rationality plays in ethical deliberation. Reason has been presented as a universal value. Both Hodgkinson's Type I values and Foster's emancipatory values derive their claim to validity on the basis of an exercise of reason. It is this exclusive emphasis on rationality that Noddings (1984) finds objectionable in her account of ethical deliberation. Critical of the Enlightenment project, Noddings rejects the Kantian assumption (implicit in the theories of both Hodgkinson and Foster) that reason's function and power are *sui generis* and that reason does not make appeal to the criterion 'external to itself'. She is highly critical of the rationalist's view which suggests that particular ethical problems are best comprehended and assessed against a commitment to a set of 'detached' universal ethical principles. What this perspective on ethical values overlooks, she maintains, is the realm of the affective. For Noddings, the affective does not only serve to explain the nature of the motivation that leads individuals to behave in certain ways but, more significantly, it is a factor that is constitutive of morality itself. In rejecting the abstract, formal and universal view of morality, Noddings thus seeks to reinstate the importance of the context, the particular and the affective. In her theory of ethical deliberation, a notion of 'caring' is central.

Noddings's theory of values is based on the research of a number of recent feminist scholars, most notably Carol Gilligan (1982). Both Gilligan and Noddings argue that the dominant male tradition in philosophy adopts an 'aloof, distant and impartial' perspective on ethical knowledge, which serves to portray women as morally deficient. They claim instead that, typically, women approach ethical problems differently—not so much with a determination to apply a set of universal ethical rules to particular cases, but with a caring disposition allegedly distinctive of their mode of experience and sense of identity. Women's ethical deliberation is thus more contextual—more immersed in the affective dimensions of the case, and more sensitive to the concrete histories of people's lives and cultural formation.

Noddings argues that ethical problems are often contemplated in a context of uncertainty and risk. Women resolve their ethical dilemmas by 'looking and seeing' the possibilities, attempting to reconcile differing needs and interests in terms of the intuitive knowledge they often have about how others would feel about the action they might pursue. Noddings insists that pure reason never yields moral principles that are self-justifying and authoritative; rather, our choices seem to appeal to specific content and feelings to resolve problems. Ethical conduct is relational in this way, for it recognises and confirms certain norms of friendship, care or treatment of equal worth. As Ben Habib (1987: 87) argues, 'In treating you in accordance with the norms of friendship, love and care, I confirm not only your humanity but your human individuality', something that reason functioning as a self-sufficient instrument of ethical deliberation cannot grasp or capture in itself.

In the context of education, Noddings would like to see her 'caring' perspective extended to all instances of deliberation involved in school administration. She argues that it is important to recognise that individuals cannot abstract themselves from their histories, attitudes and desires. Viewed in this way, ethical deliberation becomes an everyday occurrence, a mode of living and working in schools. It involves a preparedness to accept that in an area as sensitive as education, such supposedly 'private' human dispositions as sentiment and love play a significant role, and that in educational administration it may therefore not be possible to draw a distinction between public and private aspects of morality.

What follows from this is that all administrators—both male and female—should be encouraged to approach ethical issues in the same way as women do instinctively. An ethic of caring, according to Noddings, has major implications for the way schools are organised. It requires, she suggests,

> an attempt to eliminate the special language that separates us from other educators in the community (especially parents), a reduction in the narrow specialisation that carries with it reduced contact with individual children, an increase in the spirit of caring—that spirit that many refer to as 'maternal' attitude. (Noddings 1984: 198)

This suggests a certain 'deprofessionalisation' of school administration, necessary for reducing the alienation that current management practices have helped to create, not only among students but also among parents and teachers.

While Noddings' argument is clearly an advance on the rationalist positions, it too has been subjected to many criticisms, from both feminists and other writers. Blackmore (1991: 114) has argued, for example, that the caring perspective is open to the charge that it 'is merely practising exclusivity by privileging a universal female *relational* morality over a universal male morality of *self-interest*'. Noddings' view does not therefore escape the ethical universalism she wants to criticise; nor has it escaped the dualism between facts and values, as it is simply reintroduced as a dichotomy between reason and passion.

That men and women differ in the way they deliberate over ethical concerns is a claim that is difficult to sustain empirically, because their ethical experiences and dispositions vary widely. More seriously, as Grimshaw (1991: 495) argues, the idea that women 'reason differently ... runs the risk of recapitulating old and oppressive dichotomies'. For we know that historically the dualism between reason and passion has worked against the interests of women by consigning them to a private realm far removed from the public exercise of real power.

Despite her assertions to the contrary, there is something primordial about Noddings' account, which seems to assume that the female moral voice is grounded ultimately in biology, and only secondarily reproduced through sex-differentiated social experiences. Her account implies that gendered experiences are not socially constructed but represent certain biologically fixed categories that are transhistorical. Moreover, it also does not make it clear how, and the extent to which, men can in fact be socialised into an ethic of caring. Ultimately, then, Noddings' account of ethical deliberation remains trapped within a framework that is both essentialist and dualist. For as Parsons (1990: 81) argues, while it is important to give due recognition to the gendered construction of ethical language, Noddings' allocation of a sex-differentiated metaphysics of ethical experience rests upon a dualism that impedes 'the possibility of one seeing the other point of view by leaving their nature behind'. And as Murphy (1993: 89) suggests, 'by keeping alive the idea of certain human qualities and capacities that are allegedly paradigmatically female, Noddings advocates a female essentialism that rapidly begins to rekindle the traditional stereotypical views of men and women'.

Beyond dualisms

What is clear is that both the rationalist and caring perspectives on ethical deliberation are dualist, unable to escape such traditionally accepted opposites as reason and passion, facts and values, and means and ends. In my view, we need to look beyond these dualisms because ethical deliberations cannot be divorced from consideration of the concrete circumstances in which decisions are made—in other words, the facts of the matter. Deliberation is never a matter of disembodied reflection, but takes place within a framework of specific historically constituted relations. And while these relations are subject to historical change, ethical deliberation comes up against social and natural realities that are not entirely of our making.

This is a point that was made forcibly by John Dewey, a philosopher whose critique of dualist thinking is still relevant in the development of a workable alternative to the rationalist and caring perspectives I have examined in this chapter. In his writings, Dewey questions the very conception of the rationality that gives rise to dualisms. He argues that such a rationality involves a gross oversimplification, of, for example, how means and ends can be separated. The rationality of clear ends and distinct means is really an *ex post facto* rationality; it is the result of a construct we have placed on completed actions as a simplification of what we would have liked those actions to be. There is in such a construct all the presumption of a simple and idealised structure, which is a long way removed from the reality of social situations. In those situations, means and ends are never as easily separated as the model suggests. The ends achieved are not always preconceived by the actors in the field, but often reflected upon in retrospect rather than in prospect. Indeed, frequently the nature of ends is understood only in the context of a practice. When administrators consider their activities, for example, they do so in the hurly burly of the day-to-day activity rather than in terms of a rationality that dictates that they separate the specification of ends from the specification of means. There is no dichotomy possible between means and ends, for in the conduct of an activity we are continually grouping and regrouping these elements, viewing them afresh as new circumstances present themselves.

An assumption implicit in the dualist thinking is that if the organisation of the goals is done by one individual for others, then somehow the psychological organisation of the activity is more efficient. But this assumption overlooks the fact that the very nature of an activity requires that individuals do their own organising, their own interpreting of the goals to fit them into the context in which they find themselves, the same context in which they have to devise the means.

In *Human Nature and Conduct*, Dewey (1957) expresses the complex nature of the relationship between ends and means in the following way:

> Our problem now concerns the nature of ends, that is ends-in-view or aims. The essential elements in the problem have already been stated. It has been pointed out that the ends, objectives, of conduct are those foreseen consequences which influence present deliberation and which finally bring it to rest by furnishing an adequate stimulus to overt action. Consequently ends arise and function within action. They are not, as current theories too often imply, things lying beyond activity at which the latter is directed. They are not strictly speaking ends or termini of action at all. They are acts of deliberation, and so turning points in activity. (Dewey 1957: 207)

Dewey thus denies that ends exist outside activity. His idea of ends as turning points in activity places them integrally within the continuum of human experience. In contrast, the rationalist view would seem to be committed fundamentally to a theory–practice dualism.

Dewey's philosophy implies further that the rationalist view leads also to narrowness because 'fixed and separate ends reflect a projection of our own fixed and non-interacting compartmental habits' (Dewey 1957: 215). For Dewey, the doctrine of fixed or predetermined ends diverts attention from the examination of consequences. It does this by emphasising not the ends themselves but the degree of efficiency with which the ends are achieved. The correlation is between the ends and the means, not between the ends and their consequences. Also, Dewey argues that the creation of purpose can only occur when the individual has the opportunity to formulate his or her own purposes, act upon that formulation, and receive the consequences thereof. But a fixed-ends approach emphasises not the process or the activity of creation but rather the product.

An end, in this Deweyan sense, is therefore best seen as arising out of natural effects or consequences; they are the result of acts that at first are just hit or stumbled upon but which on reflection are desired for themselves. Even when a clear definition of ends is provided, it also has to be actualised in practice. It has to be understood within a broader system of beliefs and practices. For as Wittgenstein (1973 edn, para 85) points out, no rule, no matter how specific, ever dictates its own application, and we understand a particular prescription only when a place for it is already prepared for in our system of beliefs and practices. Thus ends become contextualised and projected—not removed from the activity in question, but turning points in that activity. They are continuously negotiated, modified, challenged and acted upon in specific ways in specific circumstances. Whereas the traditional rationalist model sees ends existing outside activity, the idea of ends is thus better seen as turning points integrally linked within the continuum of human experience.

Conclusion

In this chapter I have argued that ethical concerns lie at the heart of administrative theory and practice, and that the positivist aspiration of value-neutrality is misguided. I have then examined three post-positivist accounts of ethical deliberation in education and have suggested that, despite the many insights they offer, each remains committed to a dualist framework. Each of the accounts presented by Hodgkinson, Foster and Noddings seeks to identify a set of universal ethical principles in order to provide administrators with a framework within which to make ethically sound decisions and judge particular practices.

In contrast, with the use of Dewey's writings, I have suggested that the philosophical character of such universal principles is unclear; and that they are neither necessary nor sufficient for administrators to be able to address value issues and resolve ethical problems in education. They are not necessary because ethical rules are already embedded in particular practices, and, in any case, the principles can be grasped only by those who are already inclined towards the norms they prescribe. And they are not sufficient because the enunciation of the principles does not in itself ensure that an ethical practice will follow. Ultimately, both the rationalist and caring perspectives are trapped within a dichotomy between theory and the enunciation of principles, on the one hand, and the practical contexts of application, on the other.

Following Dewey, I argue that it is perfectly possible to develop a view of ethical deliberation in educational administration that is not dualist. Because ethical principles are already embedded in our practices, what we need are conceptual resources with which to examine these principles, in terms of their historical formation, their coherence with other beliefs we hold and the consequences they have for our social relations. Such an examination is necessary in order to determine which principles are worth preserving and which need to be replaced by others.

7 Towards Coherence in Administrative Theory

Colin W. Evers and Gabriele Lakomski

Much of the recent theoretical debate about educational administration has concerned the adequacy of traditional conceptions of science to provide a plausible science of administration. Thus, while traditional science focuses on the objectivity of observable phenomena, such as behaviours, subjectivist critics draw attention to the importance of human intentions, purposes, motives and beliefs—to the dynamics of a hidden, inner, mental life. The study of organisational culture, in particular, seems to draw heavily on a repertoire of such hidden phenomena, with its typical appeals to interpretations, meanings, and understandings.

As we have seen in earlier chapters, other critics lament the failure of science to provide ethical guidance, to offer suggestions on what ought to be done beyond, say, the choice of efficient means to achieve morally unanalysed goals (although the appeal to efficiency itself has moral consequences). Some writers, such as Hodgkinson (1991), think that science is in principle unable to offer administrators ethical guidance because it can deal only with facts, and there is thought to be a fundamental distinction between facts and values; ethical knowledge is simply different from factual knowledge. This alleged distinction is reinforced by a tradition in critical theory that posits a distinction among three types of knowledge-constitutive interests (see Chapter 4). In this taxonomy, the scientific is primarily concerned with meeting a human interest in manipulating and controlling the physical world. According to critical theorists, it is because science-influenced conceptions of reason and knowledge are dominant that one type of knowledge, the scientific, has come to serve as a model for all knowledge.

Further criticisms of science allege its inability to theorise on gender issues, to support political analyses, or to adjudicate conflicts of interest (Griffiths 1979). And if success in all of these tasks were to be achieved, it might still be argued that the dominance of science as a 'master narrative' has now been eclipsed in this post-modern age.

In our view, most of these criticisms of traditional science of educational administration are sound. However, the response we recommend is not to look for alternatives to administrative science, or even to augment it with non-scientific knowledge. Rather, our response is to urge the development of a better, broader and more inclusive account of science, one that is able to accommodate, for example, human subjectivity and ethics.

In what follows, we sketch some of the philosophical background to a number of theoretical disputes in educational administration and provide a brief account of the framework for our own coherentist position. We then offer three examples where our coherentism provides fresh insights into issues in educational administration. These discussions are rather speculative, very much a reflection of work in progress, and of course controversial. We hope, nevertheless, that they show something of the scope and explanatory promise of this research program. (For more on the program, see Walker and Evers 1984; Evers 1987; Evers and Lakomski 1991, 1993. For criticisms, see Bates 1993; Gronn and Ribbins 1993; Hodgkinson 1986; 1993; Willower 1993 and Maddock 1994.)

Philosophical background

Philosophical assumptions have always had a significant coordinating function in the development of distinctive positions in educational administration. For example, assumptions about the nature of theory have determined what is included and what is omitted from the scope of administrative theory. Similarly, assumptions about the nature of ethics help to determine whether the moral evaluation of organisational goals can be considered part of administrative theory or not. However, for us, the most important general assumptions are about the nature and justification of knowledge, dealt with most systematically in that branch of philosophy known as epistemology. Where some kind of justification is demanded for administrative choices, decisions, practices and theoretical commitments, the relevant background epistemology, or theory of knowledge and its justification, will be significant in determining the structure and content of administrative theories.

Content is shaped by the common practice of omitting from theory any claims that are in principle unknowable. And structure is shaped by characteristic patterns of justification. To see how these points operate, consider the traditional science of administration, with its background epistemology of logical empiricism. According to logical empiricist canons, claims are justified by appealing to some empirical foundation for knowledge, usually observation reports that can in principle be intersubjectively made by several observers, in order to secure objectivity (Feigl 1974). Because a person's inner mental life cannot be directly observed by others, subjective experience drops out as objectively unknowable. Similarly, if it is agreed that all observations are of facts, and facts are separate and distinct from values, then value claims will not admit of justification either and so can be omitted from theory without loss.

The matter of structure is a bit more complex and involves spelling out the nature of empiricist appeals to foundations. Roughly speaking, empirical foundations provide knowledge whereby theories are *tested against experience*. If observations match what the theory predicts, the theory is said to be confirmed. If contrary experience is reported, the theory is disconfirmed and in need of revision. According to this epistemology, theories that are extensively confirmed and have no disconfirmations are more justified than those that have only a few confirming instances. To meet the demands of testability, theories are structured in a certain way. Because the aim is to test deduced observable consequences against experience, justification imposes a hierarchy on the sentences used to express a theory. At the top of the hierarchy are the theory's most general empirical claims, because these are needed to deduce more particular claims. As we move down the hierarchy we go from the most general universal law-like claims to the most particular singular observational claims. The theorists of the Theory Movement clearly regarded administrative theory as possessing this kind of pyramidal hypothetico-deductive structure (as we saw in Chapters 1 and 2).

Weaknesses in empiricist epistemology have been known and discussed for a long time in educational studies. Perhaps the best known critic is John Dewey, who argued against the whole idea of justifying knowledge by appeal to foundations, whether empirical or otherwise (Dewey 1929). However, we think that the current flourishing of alternatives in educational administration is primarily because of the influence of Thomas Kuhn's (1970) attack on empiricism and the widespread acceptance of his paradigms perspective on theoretical diversity. In the late 1950s and early 1960s Kuhn (among others) was able to show that the results of testability were never sufficient for rationally choosing among competing large-scale theories (or paradigms). Rather, such theories have their own internal criteria for interpreting, evaluating and responding to experience. The business of justification was therefore claimed to be *paradigm relative*.

Thomas Greenfield harnessed these arguments to great effect in his critique of administrative science, and so did many other critics. Moreover, by the early 1970s, the paradigms perspective was becoming orthodoxy in educational research methodology (Walker and Evers 1988). This coincidence was mutually reinforcing. Subjectivism in administration meshed with a range of qualitative methodologies, critical theory with, for example, action research, and cultural theory with interpretative research, each having its own epistemology. To the extent that it was seen to be valid, science was displaced to become just one more paradigm, though perhaps suitable for theorising about only a fairly narrow range of phenomena where quantitative methods were useful, but certainly not about something as broad and complex as administration.

Although the above sketch glosses over much relevant (and controversial) detail, two features are worthy of comment. First, traditional science approaches to administration are methodologically unable to exploit many valuable sources of knowledge, particularly those accessible to qualitative modes of inquiry. In education especially, this represents a major loss for policy analysts, decision-makers and practitioners who, as a matter of course, have to extract knowledge from, and act upon, scant or partial information from complex changing scenes. Second, however, because alternatives fostered by the paradigms framework were developed in opposition to traditional science, there is the risk of scientifically accessible knowledge being discounted. An attack on the pretensions of science quickly becomes an argument for a dichotomy, or partition, between natural science and social science. Our general concern here is that partitionist epistemologies actually lose already-scarce information.

In response to this pattern of theoretical dispute we have sought to challenge its basic assumptions by attacking narrow foundational epistemologies, including logical empiricism, and defending a holistic rather than partitionist approach to knowledge (Evers and Lakomski 1991). A central point is that the logical empiricist account of science is mistaken, but that there are more adequate post-positivist accounts that allow for a more flexible and inclusive view of science, able to be developed to accommodate the demands of administration.

The detail and defence of our version of a post-positivist science is complex and has been given elsewhere (see Evers and Lakomski 1991). However, the key moves can be sketched briefly and informally. Essentially, we see the successful attacks on logical empiricist epistemology as a case for asserting the narrowness of that epistemology's standards of evidence. In short, there is more to justification than appeal to some foundation of public, sensory evidence. Administrative theories need also to be consistent. Simplicity is a further theoretical virtue because, without it, any event can end up being explained by just treating a description of the event as primitive and adding it to a theory. We want to explain a large class of things by invoking a small class of principles. Comprehensiveness is another virtue. A slight addition to a theory may be warranted if it makes for a big increase in explanatory power. And there is a premium on coherence, in the special sense that all parts of a theory should fit together, or consistently share the same explanatory resources, or enjoy explanatory unity. Except for contradiction, these canons of *coherentist* justification come in degrees. A further constraint on theories is that they should be learnable; that is, they should cohere with accounts of how knowledge of them may be acquired. We conjecture that the best accounts of learning are provided by natural science, which means that, to that extent, administrative theories should cohere with natural science. In this sense our post-positivist theory is a species of scientific naturalism justified on coherentist principles. Putting it all together, our research agenda is to develop a science of educational administration that is more coherent, and hence better justified, than its rivals.

This rather abstract account of theory and knowledge, given above, needs to be interpreted within the context of application. The following three examples illustrate how the impact of this epistemology on the content of administrative theory can be progressively sharpened and refined. Our first example draws attention to some modest advantages of coherentism's methodological requirement to mesh administrative and educational theory in educational administration. Our second example uses some assumptions of our preferred learning theory to reshape how the relationship between theory and practice might be more fruitfully construed. Finally, we suggest a relationship between organisational learning and ethics that is rich enough to provide a moral framework for educational organisations.

Administrative and educational theory

For the writers of the Theory Movement, educational administration owes much more to administrative studies than to educational theory. Educational content is generated primarily by the nature of the organisations under study—namely, organisations such as schools, universities and government and non-government educational bureaucracies (or networks) and systems. There are at least two reasons for this. Firstly, educational organisations are regarded as *particular* kinds of organisations. If theory has the pyramidal structure suggested by logical empiricism, then what occurs in educational organisations will admit of deeper explanation by appeal to the features of organisations in general. That is, a comprehensive traditional administrative science will subsume the particular under the law-like, or general.

Secondly, because of the dominance of decision-making models in administration, logical empiricism's means/ends account of rationality tends to detach consideration of organisational goals and purposes from accounts of organisational life and structure. That is, goals and purposes appear as external givens, with the main emphasis of theory being to determine optimal or satisfactory means (see Chapter 6). One consequence of combining this view of rationality with the quest for empirical generality is that the resulting administrative theory will come up with similar prescriptions for organisations that have widely differing aims. Hence the current use of private-sector corporate management models as guides for the restructuring of schools and school systems (see Chapter 9). However, a failure of explicit congruence between educational theory and administrative theory can lead to a failure of educational organisations to achieve certain educational outcomes.

Consider a school that is concerned to prepare students in three ways—to provide vocationally relevant skills, to socialise students into the surrounding culture(s), and to develop each student as an autonomous agent—though with a special emphasis on the third (Hodgkinson 1991). The school's educational theory specifies certain conditions under which student autonomy flourishes. Let us suppose, in keeping with a broadly progressive tradition, that these conditions for developing autonomy are the same as the conditions for exercising autonomy (Walker 1981). So this development/exercise equivalence means that the social relations for becoming autonomous are the same as those required for a person to act autonomously. Now let us suppose further that, however else these social relations are characterised, they at least involve respecting a person's freedom to choose within limits that are equally applicable to all. A systematic expression of this account of personal autonomy usually implies that the social relations of schooling are best instantiated in an egalitarian, participatory and democratic organisation. Indeed, it is arguable that the school's educational aims could not be achieved in any other way. Requiring educational ends to cohere with organisational means for their realisation thus blurs the means/ends distinction (as Rizvi has argued in relation to ethics).

Where the administration of learning is not readily separable from the educational processes of learning, as is clearly the case on some accounts of learning to be autonomous, it is especially important that administrative and educational theories be known to cohere. Of course, ignoring a demand for coherence does not prove that the two can be detached in fact. Rather, it means that some different view of education is likely to be implemented, or instantiated organisationally, *although without educational scrutiny or evaluation*. Much of the literature on the 'hidden curriculum' posits a causal role for the organisational framing of learning on what is actually learnt. Similarly, the use of benchmarking as a decision tool for the allocation of educational resources will *de facto* favour the implementation of one set of educational aims and objectives over another where there are differing associated costs. Indeed, the adoption of traditional administrative science approaches to educational administration will generally favour some educational programs over others. For example, applying economic interpretations of efficiency and effectiveness to schools (perhaps with the intention of achieving theoretical generality across organisations) will place a premium on vocational interpretations of educational purposes, because the corresponding criteria for justification will be economic.

We see two main advantages in explicitly meshing administrative and educational theory into a coherent theoretical package. First, because the administration of education brings about specific educational practices, the effectiveness of educational administration can be evaluated by appeal to an entirely relevant body of knowledge: educational theory. A partitionist approach thwarts this possibility. Second, it provides a framework for adjudicating educational priorities against administrative priorities. This raises the option of permitting the main educational purposes of an organisation largely to determine how it is to operate, rather than using administrative principles to determine what is educationally possible. These advantages may seem modest, but they do have some purchase by raising the matter of proof against the prevailing fashion for generic administration.

Theory and practice

Discussions of administrative theory usually begin with a recounting of the advantages of theory for practice (Halpin 1957). Thus, good theory is said to provide useful knowledge, which may lie beyond what an administrator has learned from experience. Or it may permit the rigorous development of further knowledge to guide practice, or the anticipation of unseen problems. And all these claims can be reasonable. However, behind the benign formulations lurks a deep and difficult issue generated by the common acceptance of a fundamental dichotomy concerning how knowledge is to be represented. A long tradition of conceiving knowledge as propositions represented by symbols, usually in the form of sentences of a natural language, implies an obvious solution to the representation problem for theories; theories can be represented explicitly by some symbolic formulation. However, there is no clear account of how knowledge of practice can be represented. Instead, we have some familiar dualisms, which correspond roughly to the theory/practice split: for example, mind/brain, mental/manual, reason/cause, mainstream education/special education, knowing that/knowing how, propositions/skills, and so on.

Difficulties arise because the representation of theoretical knowledge highlights logical and quasi-logical relations among semantically significant symbols, whereas the activities of practice flow from being enmeshed in a causal field. The problem is most acute in two areas of human activity. The first is learning, where we may plausibly say that the best accounts portray learning as a complex set of processes, which produce certain changes to the central nervous system. That is, human reasoning is a causal process. And the second is motivation, where we need a causal story that connects up the semantical decoding of symbolic tokens with desired responses. Until we can find some way of making a reasons-based account of theory cohere with a causal account of practice, the theory/practice nexus will continue to generate serious problems. This will be especially the case in administration; it has traditionally acknowledged the importance of theorising decision-making, which, if seen as the business of making reasoned choices among desired alternatives, is the point where both reason and motivation converge.

Because we learn from both theory and practice, our proposal is to approach the symbolic representation issue from the causal learning side rather than approaching the learning issue armed with the usual notions of representation. We therefore have to tackle the question of knowledge representation from the causal side as well—from the way the brain represents knowledge. Fortunately, advances in this area have been very impressive over the past ten years, to the point where researchers in cognitive science can now build plausible models of neural information processing—called 'neural nets'—which are capable of quite powerful feats of learning (see Bechtel and Abrahamsen 1991, for an introduction; Rumelhart and McClelland 1986, for the most influential text; and Evers 1990a, 1994, for applications to educational studies).

Consider the sort of neural net displayed in Figure 7.1. Although biological realism has been sacrificed for simplicity, this net still has considerable learning powers. Perhaps the most startling example of network learning discussed in the early literature is NETtalk, a network that learns to pronounce English text (Sejnowski and Rosenberg 1987). Its architecture consists of 309 'neurons' arranged in three layers: a 203-node input layer (29 groups of 7), 80 hidden nodes, and 26 output units, with each neuron in one layer connected to every neuron in the next layer. Each letter of text is presented to the appropriate part of the input layer as a seven-place vector consisting of that letter plus three letters on either side (or more precisely, letters, punctuation and word-boundary markers). Each letter thus has a small window of context. Inputs are then multiplied by numerical weights between layers, summed and checked against a set threshold value, and then passed from the output layer to a speech synthesiser for pronunciation. Differences between output and correct pronunciation are fed back into the network by a formula, which adjusts weights to minimise error. At first the network produces just a babbling noise. After a short while it recognises discrete words. Gradually, under the steady pressure of weight adjustment it produces clearly recognisable speech, being correct about 95 per cent of the time on the 1024-word training text.

Note that no *rules* for text to speech mappings have been coded into the network. Rather, it is the case of an efficient learning device

extracting the relevant regularities from experience. The network's knowledge, or *theory*, of these regularities is located in, and distributed across, the 18 000-plus weights in this configuration. Not having a symbolic theory formulation of text to speech mappings is no barrier to acquiring a powerful 'neural' theory of these mappings.

Much human knowledge from experience must be along these lines. Under the steady pressure of feedback from practice we build up non-symbolic internal representations of the main regularities we find useful in our interactions with the world. Now in educational administration, where current symbolic theory formulations are of only modest power, we would seem to have little alternative but to regard a considerable amount of day-to-day knowledge as acquired and represented in this fashion. Teaching may be another example, and Paul Churchland (1989b: 133) applies the same reasoning to culture:

Figure 7.1: A three-layer net with some connections shown

Each connection has an associated weight for changing the signal transmitted from one layer to the next.

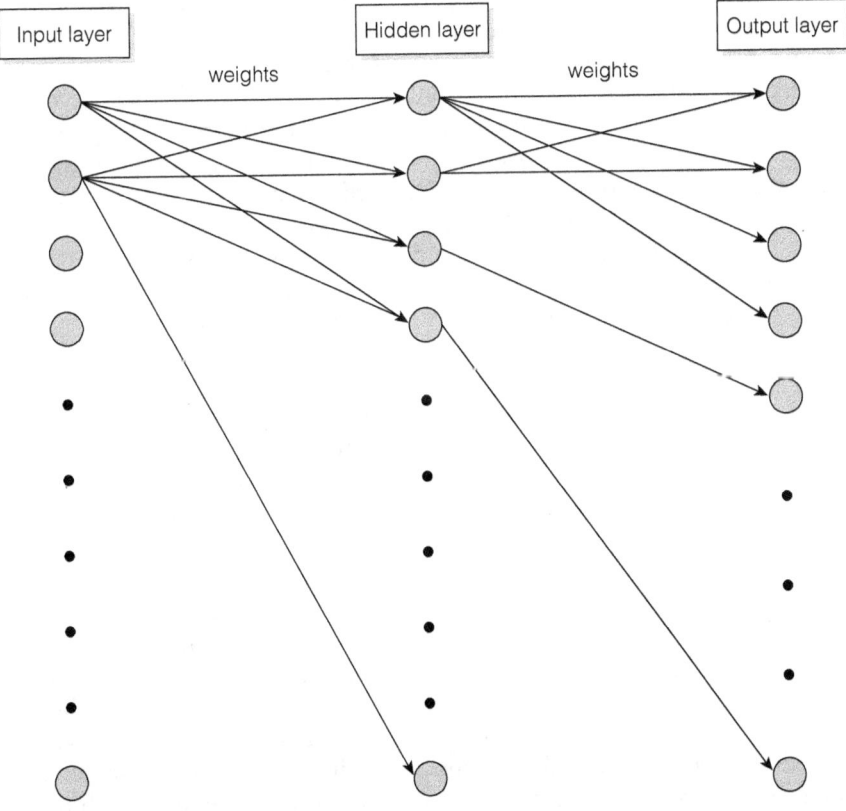

The set of weights that constitutes a child's developing consciousness is continually being shaped by the linguistic, conceptual, and social surround. The developing brain comes to reflect the elements and structure of that surround in great detail. For that is what networks do. What shapes them is the stimuli they typically receive, and the subsequent corrections in their responses to which they are typically subject. Small wonder we become attuned to the categories of the culture that raises us.

Just as the notion of theory can be extended to admit theory formulations in neural stuff, so the notion of practice can be extended to include the processing of symbols. These extensions have the effect of making any so-called division between theory and practice a matter of pragmatic emphasis over promoting learning, rather than principled bifurcations. For example, symbols have the advantage of being public, though causally more remote as a source of behaviour. Networks effortlessly represent exceptions as well as regularities, whereas symbolic formulations fare best on exceptionless rules.

It is tempting to conclude that the training of administrators can occur entirely by engaging in a class of practices that excludes dealing with symbolic theory formulations altogether; one becomes an administrator by doing the things an administrator does, or a teacher by getting out there in the classroom. (This is a version of the development/exercise equivalence we canvassed earlier in relation to autonomy.) Tempting but wrong. For whereas networks represent and store learning from past experience, and permit extrapolations, the manipulation of sentences permits inferences to be made about matters that are counterfactual, or beyond the range of experience. Knowledge can be extended in some cases simply by the sound (neural) processing of a good representational structure. Clearly, it is important to maintain all sorts of possibilities for learning where information is scarce and situations are complex and changing.

The connection between symbols, cognition and organisational design has been the major preoccupation of Herbert Simon (1976, 1983), without doubt the most influential theorist of administrative studies during the past fifty years. In Simon's work, understanding administratively relevant human subjectivity is a matter of developing a psychologically realistic account of human rationality. However, Simon's models have all been within the symbolic paradigm and hence within a correspondingly narrow view of rationality. We think that the recent arrival of neural network models of thought will provide vastly greater scope for meshing natural science with a view of human subjectivity. The use of terms such as 'intention', 'meaning', 'understanding', 'interpretation', 'belief', 'desire' and 'deciding' capture familiar categories for describing inner mental processes. But these are all terms embedded within our commonsense theory of folk psychology. Just as science has revolutionised our understanding of the external world over the past four centuries, so we expect the new cognitive science to provide the beginnings of a revolution on our inner world. Our sketch of how the terms 'theory' and 'practice' might be embedded within the less familiar categories of this new approach gives some indication of how that revolution might proceed.

Ethics in educational administration

Different epistemologies can generate quite different accounts of ethical knowledge. For Plato, moral knowledge depended on one's intellectual apprehension of abstract objects called 'forms'. Being aware of the form of the Good thus provides knowledge for distinguishing good from evil. Philosophers possess this kind of awareness beyond the common measure, and so according to Plato, in the *Republic*, a just society will be one ruled by philosophers or philosopher-kings. Here, in a systematic educational treatise, we find defended a meritocratic distribution of administrative and political power; an epistemically based hierarchy of access to knowledge, especially moral knowledge, is isomorphic to an organisational hierarchy of authority. Christopher Hodgkinson (1991) defends a similar link between knowledge and power, though one based on the requirement that leadership and moral insight intersect.

The place of ethics in traditional science of administration has been shaped by its long association with empiricism, which tends to identify knowledge with what corresponds to observable facts, and ethics as claims concerning one's subjective reactions to those facts. Subjectivist critics such as Greenfield have challenged the exclusion of ethics from administrative science by attacking science's profession to objectivity (see Chapter 3). Our response has been to defend the unity of knowledge and the objectivity of ethics (Evers and Lakomski 1991: 166–91).

We begin with the familiar Deweyan point that all experience is interpreted, or filtered, by the brain's past learning (or initial configuration of material dispositions that we now call weights). In the terminology of philosophy of science, all observation is laden with theory. Some interpretations or theories are better than others, however; they lead to more successful predictions, or explain more phenomena, or manage to do both while being simpler than alternatives, or cohere better with what is known about human learning and other bodies of (provisionally) accepted knowledge. This approach to knowledge helps to explain why, in science, we might reasonably suppose that electrons exist, or atoms, or molecules, even though they are not directly observed by the senses. It is partly because their supposition leads to simpler, more comprehensive, accounts of otherwise disparate, disconnected phenomena. Chairs and tables are also known inferentially, as posits, to integrate and simplify accounts of experience—for example, we suppose they continue to exist when observed by no one. The difference between these two sorts of posits is one of degree, not kind. Imagine, to use Quine's metaphor, knowledge as a web of belief (Quine and Ullian, 1978); at the centre of the web can be found the most theoretical parts of our knowledge (atoms and molecules), and towards the periphery, closer to observation, are the less theoretical parts (chairs and tables).

Now if we suppose, with Churchland, that there is no special or additional faculty for acquiring moral knowledge, that it is learned by the same cognitive machinery responsible for everything else that we know, then it is simpler to conclude that the apparent distance of values from observations merely reflects their theoreticity. That is, value claims are part of the one continuous fabric of knowledge, to be justified by their contribution to the fabric's overall coherence in relation to systematic alternatives.

Controversy over values often reflects the sheer complexity of many moral issues, especially in applied fields such as medicine, law, education, or administration. With the abandonment of any sure or certain foundation for knowledge, the resulting fallibility of all knowledge also contributes to controversy. As fallibilists in epistemology we therefore see the business of justification as merging with the task of improving and revising existing, provisionally accepted claims, including moral claims; of promoting, as Dewey saw, the growth of knowledge. Whatever disagreement there might be about value positions, our theory of knowledge requires the maintenance of a social and ethical infrastructure that supports the further growth of knowledge and which can lead to the revision of all value positions (including those assumed necessary for sustaining inquiry).

For us, this social and ethical infrastructure coheres best with the organisational learning tradition of administration (Argyris and Schön 1978). Politically and ethically it has much in common with Dewey's liberal democratic values, or Karl Popper's 'Open Society', championing respect for persons and differing points of view, tolerance, the value of criticism and critical feedback, education and learning, and equitable participation in the epistemic community.

Although compatible with a wide range of organisational designs, there is a premium on developing feedback loops for correcting and improving decisions. The emphasis is not so much on the soundness of visionary and authoritative leadership, which always contains the possibility of error, but on the mechanisms of quality assurance—the steady pressure of regular checks of expectations against outcomes, goals against performance, and the coherent adjustment of both against the total fabric

of organisational purposes and possibilities (see Chapter 17). We therefore favour an *educative* model of leadership; that is, one in which leadership is concerned with promoting individual and organisational learning (Duignan and Macpherson 1992). In educational organisations where the process of feedback requires acquaintance with a broad and diffuse set of community expectations, more democratic forms of community participation can be defended, perhaps by invoking the notion of quality improvement through stakeholder participation (Evers 1990b).

After investigation, it is a fairly commonplace result to find that proposed structures of human knowledge acquisition and cognition are isomorphic to proposed organisational structures. Our epistemology is certainly no exception in sustaining this consequence. However, because our coherentism justifies the claims of administrative theory by assessing their contribution to the overall coherence of a more global account of experience, the outcome is a much closer integration of administrative concerns with the ethical, educational, scientific and social theories relevant to administration (Evers 1987). And because the resulting administrative theory both coheres with natural science and employs the same pattern of coherentist justification, the aim of our research program may be regarded as the development of a new post-positivist science of administration. The background and examples given above should indicate how we see that development progressing.

8 Cross-national Exchange and Australian Education Policy

Margaret Vickers

In an information-rich world of instantaneous communications where like-minded governments are facing similar problems, it is not surprising that policy-makers are looking beyond their own shores for guidance on how to deal with the pressing problems they face. In Australia, as in the rest of the English-speaking world, interest in the impact of policy borrowing and cross-national exchange is growing. For example, Finegold, Richardson and McFarland (1993) describe how Britain's appropriation of American education and training policies intensified in the last years of the Thatcher government, reflecting a growing internationalisation of the policy-making process. Boyd (1992) notes with concern that economic discourse has replaced the earlier focus on equity in educational provision and is now the dominant paradigm for policy discussion in education and training in the English-speaking world. This trend is evident on both sides of the Atlantic as well as in Australia and New Zealand (Boyd 1992).

To date, very little systematic research has been published on how ideas from abroad influence Australian education policy, although the recent work of Beare (1991) and Beare and Boyd (1993) has begun to fill the gap. Despite the dearth of analytic studies, even the casual Canberra-watcher should be able to identify cases where overseas developments have been cited to justify recent policy changes in Australia. Broadly speaking, this chapter aims to examine how cross-national exchange influenced the development of Australia's education policies during the 1980s. To help structure and guide this discussion, the chapter also examines recent work in the field of knowledge utilisation and explores the extension of particular concepts from that field to the issue of how information from abroad may be used in the policy process.

In the absence of a substantial body of research on this topic, the goal of the chapter is a modest one. It will examine how educational decision-makers at the federal (Australian Commonwealth) level drew on knowledge from overseas sources as they framed some of the key policy ideas of the last decade. Rather than looking at every possible form of cross-national exchange that might have influenced Commonwealth education and training policy over this period, the specific cases discussed here focus on the role of the Paris-based Organization for Economic Cooperation and Development (OECD), arguably the most influential of the international think-tanks.

It is not difficult to demonstrate that the OECD played an important role in the sphere of Commonwealth education policy during the decade. From the 1983 *National Economic Summit Conference* to the 1988 *Higher Education White Paper* and beyond, extensive use was made of OECD statistics that pointed to a gap between the education participation rates of Australia in comparison with other OECD member countries (AGPS 1983; Dawkins 1987, 1988). In 1987, while he was actively pursuing his higher education reform plan, the Hon. J.S. Dawkins chaired a high-level OECD conference on *Education and the Economy in a Changing Society* (OECD 1989a). In Paris he announced that Australia's universities would be expected to play a leading role in improving the nation's economic competitiveness. On returning home, Dawkins implemented the most extensive program of reconstruction that has ever been imposed on Australia's higher education sector.

To take another example, from the very inception of the OECD's *International Educational Indicators Project*, Australia has played an active role, assuming the position of lead country for key components of that project (OECD 1988). Over the past few years the Commonwealth has invested considerable resources in this project. The project is still running, and its aim is to develop international indicators so that administrators can measure the 'educational progress' of their systems and compare the performance of their systems with those of other member countries (OECD 1992b: 8). At the same time, the Commonwealth is using its participation in this project to mobilise support for the national performance-monitoring system it would like to establish in Australia (AEC 1990, 1991).

In the area of youth policy, the OECD link has also been important. Some years back, in 1983, the Commonwealth invited an OECD team to Australia to review the nation's youth policies. In its final report the team recommended reforming the curriculum and assessment practices of secondary schools, increasing high school completion rates, restricting access to junior unemployment benefits, and introducing a system of allowances that would provide economic incentives for young people to remain in school (OECD 1986). The OECD also recommended that an 'entitlement year' be created for all young people not continuing past the final year of compulsory schooling. Although the entitlement year recommendation was not acted upon, all the other recommendations of the report were fully implemented and the goals suggested by the OECD were accomplished by 1988 (Department of Employment, Education and Training 1989).

Two of the three instances sketched above—the youth policy reforms and the reconstruction of the higher education system—are developed as case studies and discussed in greater detail later in the chapter, but even in these very brief sketches the importance of the OECD's influence on Australian education policy during the past decade may be seen.

In one sense, this influence seems paradoxical. Why should the OECD have such powerful effects on educational decisions in Australia? The Paris-based Organization does not have a mandate to decide on the directions that Australia's policies will take. By way of contrast, when developing countries seek World Bank loans, they are required to follow World Bank advice, even if that advice is not sensitive to historical traditions and local needs (Payer 1982, 1991). But the OECD is not the World Bank, and when the OECD offers advice to its member countries they are free to take it or leave it.

In particular policy areas—notably, defence—Australia's leaders have often been pressured to adopt policies that conform to American or British strategic interests (D. Ball 1980, 1987; Sexton 1981). No such imperative need force the hands of Australian educators. On the contrary, teachers and academics at all levels have shown a considerable capacity for innovation and an admirable independence of spirit. For example, although the Australian Council for Educational Research was responsible for importing a certain amount of American-style standardised testing to this country (Connell 1980), Australian teachers have successfully resisted other pedagogical invasions.

To take another example, after some years of exposure to imported 'basal readers', which had their origins in the American behaviouristic tradition, Australian primary teachers rejected this approach and (together with their New Zealand counterparts) developed and adopted the 'whole language' approach to initial reading instruction. Australian innovations such as these are now being treated as welcome imports in the United States. The 'whole language' approach is being enthusiastically promoted as a way of improving reading comprehension in American elementary schools (Cazden 1992).

Still further examples illustrate Australia's capacity to develop and export exemplary educational practices. Australia was one of the first countries to use distance education at both the school and higher education levels, and it remains at the cutting edge of this technology (Dahloff 1986; Brumby 1989). American reformers concerned with the deleterious effects of standardised testing in their high schools are increasingly drawn to the 'authentic' methods of assessment that have been developed in Victoria, South Australia and Queensland for high school graduation and university admission (Resnick and Wirt, in press). In both cases, the antipodean origins of these approaches are fully acknowledged, and in the United States, Australia is rapidly gaining a reputation as a country whose educational system is worth emulating.

These examples suggest a contrast between the professional activities of teachers and the preoccupations of Commonwealth educational administrators. This contrast reflects what Pusey (1981: 224) called the 'permanent tension between teaching and administration'. As Pusey explained, the more teachers pay attention to the needs of individual children in the always unique context of particular classrooms, the more these needs take precedence over the aspects of learning and curriculum that can be standardised and therefore subjected to administrative control. Thus, while teachers argue that they need greater professional autonomy in order to do their jobs well, system managers assert that unless the criteria for the assessment and evaluation of performance are standardised it will be difficult to improve the efficiency of the education system.

The conflict between these two positions was perhaps most graphically illustrated by the abolition of the Australian Schools Commission and the amalgamation of the education and labour portfolios in 1987. In its charter, the Schools Commission framed education as an explicitly social project, and its operations drew heavily on the contributions of practically engaged educators. This 'bottom-up' process, in which workable ideas from the field were garnered and gathered into the national debate, has now been replaced by a 'top-down' managerialism, whose long-term objective includes the development of a national system for monitoring student achievement (N. Johnston 1991).

With the creation of the mega-department of Employment, Education and Training (DEET), the function of the education system was recast in a framework that principally related it to the needs of the labour market. This shift is reflected in similar developments throughout the OECD world. Thus, the framework for educational discussion in both Canberra and Paris is now dominated by a transnational paradigm in which education is reconstructed as 'human capital' formation and is largely viewed as a strategy for improving national economic competitiveness.

Because the OECD's overall strengths relate to its economic expertise and its capacity to bring together ministers and experts covering multiple portfolios—education, labour market, economic affairs and finance—it makes sense for the Organization to focus on education–economy relationships. However, the OECD does not advocate viewing education as solely an economic good and is quick to express concern that education policy should not become an instrument of economic policy and short-term objectives. Rather, the Organization explicitly acknowledges a broader conceptualisation of education and its purposes. Its program of work includes several activities related to curriculum innovation and school improvement, while even the programs that focus specifically on links between education and work do not neglect pedagogical aspects of the topic. For example, the project on *New Directions in Vocational and Technical Education and Training* is based on a sophisticated and carefully planned sequence of investigations, which pay attention to the cognitive psychology of integrated learning as well as analysing the economic aspects of work-based learning (Durand-Drouhin 1991; Raizen 1991; Sako 1991).

Unfortunately, within Australia, it would appear that Canberra's education bureaucrats have focused selectively on aspects of the OECD's agenda that emphasise the economic functions of education and have used this agenda to increase the centralised managerial control the Commonwealth exerts at all levels of the system. By filtering out much of the information flowing from the more pedagogically oriented projects, the inclusiveness of the Organization's agenda has been somewhat obscured and Australia's teachers have been deprived of a potentially valuable source of support and inspiration.

Exactly what role does an international organisation such as the OECD play in educational policy formulation in Canberra? Is it really as powerful as it appears? One possibility is that the Commonwealth relies on the OECD for guidance; that is, OECD-based analyses are used to determine which alternative, among the various options available, is most likely to work. It is also possible that, most of the time, Canberra's bureaucrats already know what they want to do, and the function of the exchange with the OECD is primarily to gain legitimation for some predetermined course of action. If this is true, then Australia's policies are decided at home and not in Paris, and the OECD is much less powerful than Canberra's politicians would have us believe.

Studies have shown that when politicians want to mobilise support for change it is essential that they attribute their ideas to some authoritative source. Citing the work of Orfield and Baker, Eliason wrote:

> Organised knowledge production in the form of research tends to be endowed with a high degree of prestige, respectability and credibility . . . To associate the state's operations and decisions with a process of such prestige is expected to enhance . . . overall state legitimacy. (Eliason et al. 1987: 258)

As noted at the beginning of this chapter, very few systematic investigations have been undertaken on the effect of cross-national exchange on the development of Australian education policy. However, the use of knowledge from local research in the policy-making process constitutes a relatively well-researched field. In order to set up a theoretical scaffolding for the remainder of the chapter, the next section provides a brief review of this literature.

The politics of knowledge utilisation

Over the past fifteen years, Weiss (1977, 1979, 1989), Rule (1979), Lindblom (1980), Huberman (1983, 1989) and others have conducted a wide range of investigations examining how knowledge from research enters into the policy-making process. A key argument advanced by these authors is that the process of knowledge utilisation is almost never simple and direct. Their argument contrasts with the simple, technocratic view of knowledge utilisation, which conceptualises policy-making as a rational process—a process in which information and research results are sought out by decision-makers in order to help them decide which option, among a number of alternatives, is most likely to solve a particular problem. According to this simple view, the role of information is pivotal and decisive. It is as though decisions are made by benevolent despots who have their hands firmly on the controls and only need advice on what to do.

Policy decisions, however, are rarely this simple. Numerous interest groups and institutions may have a stake in a decision, and there is rarely a sole individual who has the power single-handedly to carry out a complex policy. As Rule (1979), Buchanan (1987), Cronbach (1980), Lindblom (1980) and others have pointed out, stakeholders usually disagree about fundamental beliefs and values concerning the issue at hand. Furthermore, the nature of the issue may be poorly defined, making several different explanations possible. Sensible alternatives may be proposed, but be rejected because they are costly or are unacceptable to certain factions within the governing party. In reality, policy decisions result from a complicated conjunction of forces; and alongside these forces, technocratic analysis and research-based knowledge are often pushed into minor roles.

While technocratic approaches to decision-making give primary emphasis to the use of research to identify the most workable option among a set of alternatives, political models emphasise that knowledge from research carries many other functions in the decision-making process. On the basis of an empirical study of how research influences congressional decision-making in the United States, Weiss (1989) describes four ways that research knowledge is utilised. It can be used to provide warnings that problems are arising, which cannot be ignored. Information from a variety of sources can provide guidance if it indicates that particular options really work in practical settings. Perspectives from research studies can also lead to enlightenment; that is, they can create new ways of conceptualising a problem and can profoundly influence the set of solutions considered appropriate. Finally, research can be used to mobilise support for particular policy proposals. Information in this context becomes a means of persuasion, aimed at strengthening support for an already-chosen policy and countering the arguments of dissenters.

Occasions certainly arise when the key question is not 'what shall we do,' but 'how shall we get it accepted'. Politicians may then use knowledge from research to legitimate a position they already hold, mobilise the support of fellow party members, weaken the case of their opponents, or reassure those who are expected to implement a proposal that the change will actually work (Weiss and Vickers 1992). Academics and decision leaders are comfortable with the idea that research helps solve particular policy problems, yet the use of knowledge from research to support a predetermined position is neither unimportant nor illegitimate. For example, if a politician, who is already committed to increasing the availability of publicly subsidised childcare, makes effective use of a research report that demonstrates the benefits of such a policy, then the research will have served a useful purpose. As Weiss (1979) noted, it is only when the findings from research are distorted and misinterpreted that the political use of research becomes questionable.

The model outlined above proposes that knowledge has several legitimate functions in the decision-making process. It suggests that at different stages of this process, knowledge is used for very different purposes by people who are trying to put new policies in place. The next few paragraphs expand on the multiple meanings of knowledge utilisation identified by Weiss (1989) and briefly discuss how these might apply in the context of cross-national exchange. Later in this chapter we shall explore the use of cross-national exchange for policy-making through the analysis of two Australian case studies.

In the chronology of decision-making, many groups vie to determine whether an issue will get onto the political agenda in the first place. Diverse forms of information, such as letters to the minister or local representatives, protest meetings and newspaper exposés, can be used to provide the signal that trouble is brewing. But research and statistical data provide especially compelling warnings; they have a relatively objective quality and a measure of precision, which most competing forms of information lack. Monthly employment statistics, for example, provide data on trends—whether conditions are getting better or worse, and which demographic groups are bearing the brunt of unemployment. As Weiss wrote, 'sudden shifts can signal serious trouble and may be particularly potent in triggering a policy response' (1990: 106).

A warning that something is amiss overseas is not necessarily so compelling. In general, political agendas are determined by local rather than off-shore crises. During the past decade, however, the very existence of a disparity between Australian educational and economic indicators and those of other advanced industrial nations has often been used to suggest that something is amiss (Dawkins and Costello 1983). John

Dawkins' prologue to the Green Paper provided a clear example of this. In launching the debate on the future of Australia's higher education system, he drew considerable attention to the gap between Australian higher education participation rates and those of Japan and the United States (Dawkins 1987: 1–12).

Such 'warnings' do, of course, carry an element of 'interpretation'. It is not at all obvious that the superior economic strength of Japan and the United States in comparison with Australia can be simply attributed to the differences in higher education participation rates in these countries. Nevertheless, participation rates in the United States were set up as a target against which the performance of the Australian system should be measured. Rather than simply warning Australians about the existence of a gap in educational participation rates, these data were actually being used to justify placing the Dawkins plan high on the government's political agenda.

Once an issue is on the agenda, attention turns to how it should be conceptualised. High levels of youth unemployment, for example, may be interpreted as indicating short-term cyclical problems in the labour market. An alternative interpretation is that the unemployment is due to structural shifts in the economy. In the latter case, short-term measures would be ineffective, and major investments in youth education and training need to be considered. In the mid-1970s these alternative interpretations were not nearly as self-evident as they appear today. Conceptual shifts like this often take place as a result of the gradual diffusion of ideas from the research literature into the policy-making community.

The diffusion of research-based ideas into the policy context can provide a new way of looking at things and is part of what Weiss (1986) called enlightenment or knowledge creep. Over time, one socially constructed set of meanings replaces another, and the nature of the discourse around a set of issues shifts. For example, as a particular set of concepts moves into popular parlance and becomes accepted by policy-makers, public servants and interested citizens, it tends to change the premises that are taken for granted. This process may influence the issues seen as problematical, as well as having a profound influence on the set of solutions considered appropriate.

Information from overseas likewise broadens the conceptual frameworks in which policy decisions are taken, and in this sense it provides a special form of 'enlightenment'. Differences between the social and political traditions of countries usually prohibit the wholesale importation of approaches that are effective elsewhere. However, comparison can help a decision-maker to think about policy processes and outcomes in a broader and more refined perspective. As Antal et al. wrote:

> An awareness of alternatives challenges the political and cultural assumptions on which a nation's policies are based. This brings to light underlying, often unquestioned premises. Researchers conducting comparative research often find that they learn as much, if not more, about their own political system by studying others. Not only do they find new policy options in other countries, but they also discover latent policy constraints and opportunities within their own system. (1987: 15)

But comparative policy research is complex and expensive to conduct. In addition, much of the cross-national research conducted by academics is not sufficiently problem-oriented to meet the policy-makers' needs. International organisations (such as the OECD) that are both government-based and research-oriented provide a unique function in this context.

Another role of information is to provide guidance. Within a particular country, evaluation studies may be used to indicate which variations of a policy are more successful. Policy-makers may be guided, for example, by studies that compare the effectiveness of different labour market programs in terms of the longer-term employment records of young people. To be useful to a policy-maker, such evaluation studies need to take into account the relative costs of different programs and their respective durations. These studies also need to be sensitive to hidden costs, such as the difficulty of administration. If the studies are comprehensive and well designed, the comparative information they yield can be especially useful as policy guidance.

Sometimes, however, experimental evaluations are difficult to contrive. If broad systemic changes are being considered, it may not be possible to examine their effects by dividing some section of the population into separate treatment groups and determining the different outcomes that follow from the treatments. In circumstances like these, close study of fully operational programs in another country may indicate the likely outcomes of borrowing certain programs and may even provide better information than contrived evaluation studies. This is because evaluation experiments are usually established on a very small scale, and it is frequently impossible for the researcher to measure all the factors that should be taken into account when implementing a policy. The study of fully operational programs in another country suffers from none of these limitations.

Finegold, Richardson and McFarland (1993) argue that, 'In spite of the problems of transplanting one nation's policies into another country's historical and institutional settings, the process of transnational borrowing is likely to become more common in the years ahead.' Suggesting that cross-national exchange is possibly becoming more cost-effective than local evaluation studies, they note a 'general internationalization which has taken place in the world's academic and policy communities. As the cost and time associated with sending people between countries has fallen it has become more practical to include other nation's experiences in the policy equation' (1993: Ch.1). Nevertheless, if another country's experience is to provide effective guidance, it is essential to understand how the social and political ecology of the borrower's country differs from that of the country from which the policy is being borrowed.

At every stage of the policy-making process, those advocating particular policy changes need to find ways of establishing the legitimacy of their proposals and mobilising support. Knowledge from research can play a key role in this process. As Weiss wrote:

> Whether or not advocates (of a policy) were influenced by research in adopting the proposal initially, they can use research to build a winning coalition. Research becomes a means of persuasion. It can (a) reinforce the conviction of policy originators that their plan is a good one, (b) stiffen the support of current allies, (c) help to persuade the undecided, and (d) perhaps even sway the beliefs of opponents, weakening their adherence to their old position. Of course, good arguments are counters in the policy game. (1990: 107)

There are very few significant changes a government can introduce that do not threaten the vested interests of some particular faction or group. If the threatened group is a powerful one, it will take considerable courage and determination for the politician who decides to take it on. When pursuing an unpopular course of action, it strengthens a politician's case considerably if he or she can demonstrate that governments in several other countries have found it necessary to follow the same difficult path. As the cases presented below illustrate, among all the ways that cross-national research may be used in the policy-making process, deploying it to legitimise policy change is perhaps the most powerful.

The Commonwealth and the OECD: a special relationship

The previous section of this chapter provided a framework for discussing the politics of knowledge utilisation and mentioned the four meanings of research use identified by Weiss (1989) in her study of committee members in the United States Congress. The remainder of the chapter uses this framework to analyse the role of the OECD in Australian policy-making. While it should be acknowledged that the literature on knowledge utilisation is based almost entirely on studies of the American policy-making process, extrapolation from this literature to the Australian setting does not appear to be a major problem (Biddle and Anderson 1991).

Before proceeding, however, there are two important questions that must be addressed. First, can a framework originally developed to describe how research-based knowledge enters into the policy-making process legitimately be extended to cover knowledge that is cross-national in substance and not entirely research-based in its origins? Some extrapolations from local research to cross-national research have already been suggested in the preceding section. It is reasonable to include the OECD in this field, because much of the Organization's work can legitimately be described as 'research'—it involves disciplined investigation based on the collection and analysis of evidence. Therefore, the proposed extension of the knowledge utilisation literature to cover cross-national exchange with the OECD is not altogether far-fetched.

Research at the OECD takes a variety of forms. For example, the secretariat gathers statistical data and generates econometric models, conducts surveys, analyses policy trends, and commissions papers by respected researchers. Officially, documents generated through these activities are available only to expert advisers or government officials in member countries. Unofficially, individual OECD secretariat members also maintain contact with a small circle of policy boffins—academics and other people in the know—who provide them with informal advice. Expert advisors appointed by the OECD, government officials, and government nominees also attend OECD conferences in Paris and the more issue-oriented OECD seminars, many of which are hosted by member countries.

Work at the OECD tends to be organised in terms of projects, which run for a duration of three years at a time, subject to renewal. Each project is headed by an *administrateur*, a professional employee whose qualifications for the job include recognised credentials and considerable expertise on relevant topics. Over time, these secretariat members become even more expert. Through their extensive range of contacts they come to know what is consensually accepted as true by the majority of experts in their field, across the majority of member countries. Because of this, official OECD reports not only reflect experts' views on an issue but also help to shape a transnational consensus, which often carries considerable authority among the closed circle of government officials and boffins connected to the OECD.

Unfortunately, most of this knowledge-building activity occurs within a closed circle. Many of the documents generated by particular projects remain officially 'restricted' for years. For those who are neither government officials nor expert advisers, restricted OECD documents are difficult to obtain without personal access to someone inside the Organization. By the time restricted documents emerge in book form, the issues they address may no longer be on a government agenda. If the subjects addressed by a publication have already been dealt with, then the opportunity for public discussion is past. A further problem is that books from the Paris-based OECD press are often expensive and poorly distributed; they are not likely to be discovered on a Sunday afternoon's browse in the bookshops of Carlton or Glebe.

The second question concerns the pathways through which ideas travel. Comparing the Australia–OECD link with American domestic policy-making, it is evident that the way information moves from the source to the policy-maker is quite different in these two contexts. That is to say, there is a sharp contrast between the freedom of access the American policy-making community has to research reports and academic expertise, and the very restricted access Australian decision-makers (particularly those outside the upper echelons of the Australian Commonwealth) have to information from the OECD. To understand how the stylised facts, statistical information and consensual positions developed by the OECD enter into the Australian policy-making processes the special relationship the Commonwealth enjoys with the OECD must be examined.

The OECD is an inter-governmental membership organisation, and it is the Australian Commonwealth (but not the states) that has the formal responsibilities and privileges of membership. Australia has an ambassador to the OECD, who is appointed by the federal government, located in Paris, and assisted by federal public servants whose tasks include reporting back to Canberra on OECD activities and acting as a liaison with the OECD secretariat.

Member countries make agreed-upon financial contributions to the OECD, and this provides fiscal stability for the major divisions and directorates of the Organization (Education, Manpower, Social Affairs, Trade, and so on, each roughly corresponding to a major government portfolio). In this sense, the process is rather like dining at a *prix fixe* restaurant. Member countries pay the full price even if they are not interested in active participation in all the projects the OECD is pursuing. In relation to their financial contributions, countries are not at liberty to pick and choose among the different projects represented in each directorate's program of work. However, the extent to which a country invests the time and energies of its senior personnel in particular projects can and does vary considerably.

Under the foreign affairs power, the Commonwealth is responsible for deciding on Australia's level of participation in each project. This provides it with a definite strategic advantage. If a particular project of the OECD's Education Division or the Centre for Educational Research and Innovation (CERI) is not high on the Commonwealth's agenda, Australia will remain unrepresented, or be represented on the project by state-level bureaucrats or academics with expertise in the field. For example, in 1991–92 the state of Victoria was delegated to be Australia's official representative to the CERI project on *The Environment, Schools and Active Learning* because the Commonwealth was 'not strategically involved' in that issue (Alan Ruby, personal communication, 6 October 1992).

In general, the Australian Commonwealth has participated most actively in projects that connect education to the economy and has shown relatively less interest in projects concerned with teaching, curriculum and learning. For example, CERI sustains projects on *School Development and New Approaches to Learning* and on *Teacher Education, School Organization and Educational Leadership,* but these projects have not gained star billing with the Commonwealth in recent years (OECD 1987a). Even in relation to the Education Committee's project entitled *The Search for Quality: Policies for Educational Reform,* the Commonwealth's commitment has been lukewarm. Noted Australian academics have played important roles as expert authors and advisers for these projects, but official participation from Canberra has never been at an especially high level.

There is a clear distinction between the OECD activities that the Commonwealth has chosen to support and those it has chosen not to support. However, a low level of support for an OECD project on an issue such as 'the quality of schooling' does not imply that the Commonwealth intends to ignore the issue altogether. On the contrary, when Monash University's School Decision Making and Management Centre proposed a national seminar on the quality of Australian schools, the Commonwealth agreed to assist, and the seminar (which was informed by the OECD report *Schools and Quality)* was conducted in conjunction with DEET (Chapman et al. 1991). The point is, however, that the Commonwealth sets its own priorities regarding the extent to which it will commit itself to particular OECD projects. Where it does make a substantial investment in a project, it is usually looking for some political return on that investment.

Thus, for example, if the Commonwealth wants to raise the profile of a particular agenda item, a commitment of time and energy at the highest levels may be in order. When the OECD's Education Division ran its *International Conference on Education and the Economy in a Changing Society* in March 1988, John Dawkins, Minister for Employment, Education and Training, accepted the Organization's invitation to act as Chair. His foray on the Paris headquarters of the Organization proved to be expedient for him, as the higher education case study, outlined below, demonstrates.

Since 1987 the OECD projects favoured in Canberra have all focused on the *national* elements of DEET's agenda: the creation of a unified national system of higher education, the definition of nationally agreed goals for schooling and common curriculum structures, and the creation of the Australian Standards Framework. As already noted, it is these issues, rather than the steady work of teachers on improving the effectiveness of school and classroom practices that have become the key concerns of the Commonwealth (N. Johnson 1991, in Chapman et al.). The year 1987 proved to be a watershed for the Commonwealth, because this was the year when the Schools Commission was abolished and DEET was created. With the demise of the Commission and the former Department of Education, most of the top structure of the former Department of Education found itself in what was euphemistically known as the 'departure lounge' while their jobs were taken over by hard-nosed managerialists from the central departments of Treasury, Finance and Prime Minister and Cabinet.

Pusey (1991) captured the essence of what was happening at this time when he characterised the powerful cadre of newly appointed managers as the 'economic rationalists'. According to Pusey, when these men moved out from the central departments to take over the service departments they were intent on rolling back social democratic or welfarist currents in public administration in favour of corporatism, minimal government, and market forces. The form of discourse they developed redefined the core functions of the education system in purely economic terms. This discourse relied heavily on cross-national comparisons and asserted that 'human capital' formation plays a critical role in the relative success of our trading competitors.

The cases presented in the next section suggest that on occasions, Canberra's relationships with OECD do reflect the ideological thrust of Pusey's analysis. However, the cases also show that the relationship of the Australian policy development process to the OECD is complex and multifaceted. As Weiss (1989) argued, knowledge carries many functions in the service of policy.

Case studies in cross-national exchange

Case I: The OECD and Australian youth policy

During the first four years of the Hawke Labor government (1983–86) the major objectives of Australian youth policy were substantially reconceptualised. Superficially, it appeared that a variety of different policies had been implemented during the 1972–82 period in an attempt to bring youth unemployment under control, but all of these had one thing in common—the assumption that youth unemployment was essentially a short-term problem. Whitlam's Labor government (1972–75) promoted job creation and generous benefits, whereas the government of Fraser (1975–83) cut back on the benefits and offered subsidies to encourage private-sector employment. The differences among these measures largely reflected the political ideology of the party in charge, but both parties assumed that the next rotation of the business cycle would probably set things right.

At the end of the 1972 to 1982 period it was evident that the traditional policies of both the left and the right were inadequate for solving the youth unemployment problem. A new theoretical basis was needed, and the OECD played a crucial role in helping Australia's policy-makers define what this would be. In the early 1980s the OECD warned that the relationship between education and employment was changing in fundamental ways because of changes in both the internal and international economic order in most member countries.

For example, in its 1985 report *New Policies for the Young*, the OECD expressed its concern that mainstream education and training institutions may be failing to prepare young people adequately for life and work in the late twentieth century. This concern is prompted by the effect of technological change; structural change, especially the rapid growth of the service sector; and the internationalisation of manufacturing, which has led to the displacement of low-skill labour to the newly industrialising countries. The report states, 'These changes are probably permanent, and will affect the occupational structure of the labour market and the nature of new jobs and, in turn, affect the kind of educational and technical preparation required for these jobs' (OECD 1985: 10).

The pathway through which the OECD's analysis of this problem first entered the Australian policy arena was a little unusual. In 1982, Peter Wilenski, who had been a Commonwealth department head during the Whitlam years, held a professorial position at the Social Justice Project at the Australian National University. At the invitation of the OECD he went to Paris in 1982 to write a paper on the problems of youth policy. Working at the OECD he developed a plan for a universal youth allowance, which would have 'a clear bias towards keeping young people out of the full-time work force and retaining or returning them into some form of training or education.' Although such a scheme would have merit, Wilenski noted, it would 'require a considerable effort to improve the post-compulsory education system' (Wilenski 1982: 31).

He suggested that the scheme could be financed largely by abolition of the existing range of piecemeal financial arrangements directed at subsidies to employers, student scholarships, transitional and labour market schemes, unemployment and welfare benefits, allowances to parents of dependent children over the age of sixteen, and so on. There is a need to be far more realistic, his paper suggested, about what labour market schemes can achieve. It may be appropriate, he suggested, to 'pursue clear and limited objectives through the [combined] training and employment approach that has been set out in so many OECD documents' (Wilenski 1982: 23).

In March 1983 the Hawke government was elected, and Wilenski was appointed head of the Department of Education and Youth Affairs. The transformations in Australian youth policy implemented over the subsequent three years bore a remarkable resemblance to the plan he had drafted at the OECD. Shortly after his appointment he invited a team of OECD experts to conduct a comprehensive review of policies affecting young people in Australia. At the same time he authorised the Office of Youth Affairs (OYA) to take responsibility for coordinating all Commonwealth activities for youth, and asked OYA and the Social Welfare Policy Secretariat (SWPS) to jointly review income-support arrangements for young people.

The purpose of the income support review was to rationalise the plethora of piecemeal allowances made to or on behalf of young people and to produce a comprehensive youth allowance, which would provide stronger incentives for education participation (OYA/SWPS: 1984). By the end of 1985 the work of the income-support committee had in fact largely eliminated the piecemeal financial arrangements associated with different labour market programs, student scholarships, allowances to parents of dependent children over sixteen years of age, and so on, and had created the AUSTUDY system of benefits, which gave much stronger support to the objective of increasing education participation.

Working closely with Ralph Willis, the Minister for Employment and Industrial Relations, Wilenski also recommended that a committee to review youth labour market programs should be set up with Peter Kirby as its director. Under Fraser, labour market programs and employee subsidy schemes had been the central instruments of youth policy, but following Kirby's (1985) review of youth labour market programs, many of these programs were eventually abolished and the emphasis was shifted decisively toward mainstream education and training activities.

Early in 1985 when the OECD produced its final report, the consistency of its findings with those of the Kirby review and the income-support committee was evident. While there is a short-term problem of high unemployment among Australian young people, the OECD said, there is a long-term problem as well. Low levels of educational attainment and occupational skills and unequal access to education and training opportunities will, in the long run, mean that Australia will lack the skill and educational requirements the economy needs to compete in world markets. The OECD review team stated that:

> The highest priority for the Australian youth agenda should be to raise educational attainment, increase broad-based occupational skills, and assure that education and training opportunities are accessible without regard to sex or socioeconomic status. (OECD 1986: 80)

The team argued for broad-based reforms to secondary schooling and argued that upper secondary education should do more than simply prepare young people for higher education. It should also be geared to young people going on to technical training, apprenticeships and immediate employment as well. This would require a broader curriculum and a more flexible approach to assessment, an approach not dictated by admissions requirements of the universities.

As the OECD review process drew to a close, the Hawke government committed itself to shifting the focus of youth policy away from job creation towards education and training. But the claims of young people seeking work could not be dismissed easily, especially given the level of concern expressed by youth advocacy groups and Labor Party supporters (ANOP 1984). The changes achieved by 1989—substantial increases in education participation, the implementation of AUSTUDY, and the abolition of unemployment benefits—would have been unimaginable in 1983. But the combined weight of the OECD review, the confluence of views expressed in the Kirby report and the income-support review created a climate in which the government's plans could be enacted.

This case illustrates how the OECD contributed to the development of new perspectives on youth policy in Australia. It represents an instance of 'enlightenment,' in that it introduced a new way of understanding the youth unemployment problem—one that contrasted sharply with the interpretations that had previously dominated local discussion.

In the early 1980s the OECD secretariat had already begun to recognise that major changes were occurring in the labour markets of industrialised economies (OECD 1989a). In most member countries, confidence in the value of labour market schemes as an alternative to mainstream education and training was waning. The OECD analyses indicated that the most rapidly growing occupational areas would be those that demanded higher educational skills, and that governments were doing a disservice to young people if their programs merely helped them get jobs (often dead-end jobs) when what they really needed was a solid base of skills to equip them for the future workforce.

Regardless of whether a political party is in government or in opposition, some of its more eminent thinkers may be actively engaged as consultants and expert advisers to the OECD. In this case, Wilenski's experiences at the OECD allowed him to argue convincingly that there was a need for change in the direction of Australia's youth policies. When Hawke took office in March 1983, his government was ready to work towards a new understanding of these issues—an understanding reflecting perspectives it had evidently gleaned, at least in part, from the OECD.

Case II: Dawkins' reconstruction of the Australian higher education system

Between 1987 and 1989 John Dawkins executed a virtual revolution in the organisation, funding and control of Australia's higher education system (Stokes and Edmonds 1990). So radical were the changes introduced by the plan that they precipitated a questioning of the concept of the Australian university itself (Harman and Meek 1988). Ideologically, Dawkins' agenda was based on the construction of a nexus between the need for improved national economic productivity and changes in the role of the higher education system. Dawkins' view of higher education was in conflict with the position traditionally held by most Australian academics. Indeed, many saw the Dawkins plan as an unprecedented attack on academic freedom (Stretton 1988).

In the context of this chapter, two specific questions about these developments are of particular interest. First, given the strong opposition by the academic community, how did Dawkins get his proposals for restructuring the higher education system onto the government's legislative agenda and engineer the broad acceptance needed for their implementation? Second, did the OECD have an important influence on the development of the Dawkins plan, or did he simply make use of the Organization to mobilise support for a program of change to which he was already committed?

The question of how the Dawkins plan got onto the government's agenda in the first place is an interesting one. At the time, the Australian higher education system was not in any particular state of crisis. There was no evident public pressure for changes of the kind Dawkins proposed. On the contrary, most aspects of the Dawkins plan were immediately unpopular with both students and faculty and provoked sharp criticism as soon as they were announced (Smart 1989; Sloan 1989). With hostile stakeholders and an indifferent public, it would not be easy for Dawkins to mobilise support for his proposed reforms.

Dawkins met this strategic challenge by establishing a new form of discourse about the rightful function of Australia's higher education system. As one of the government's key economic ministers and former Minister for Trade, Dawkins was naturally predisposed to view the higher education system as one that should be reshaped to serve the nation's economic interests. The discourse he established did not address the interests of students and faculty—the groups that make up the system. Instead, it shifted the focus of concern away from the interests of academics towards what Dawkins called 'the national interest'. As Schattschneider (1960) explained, if an issue is defined as being of national importance, then sectional or private interests can be overridden. Thus, faculty members at Australia's universities were seen as self-serving when they complained that the Dawkins plan would erode their working conditions. Their complaints about restrictions to academic freedom were seen, not as a reflection of public-spirited concern, but as a desire to protect ivory-tower privileges to which ordinary citizens were not entitled.

Dawkins repeatedly cited OECD sources to legitimate this new form of discourse about the rightful functions of the Australian university. It should be stressed, however, that the OECD never actually advocated that Australia *should* implement such an extensive restructuring of its higher education system. A key function of the OECD is to observe and report on emerging trends around the world, but the Organization has neither the power nor the resources to impose policy changes on the member countries. The OECD report, *Universities Under Scrutiny*, published in 1987, states that despite their differences, 'universities in OECD countries today confront common problems which derive from a single fact: they are being called on to play an ever more important part in the restructuring and growth of increasingly knowledge-based economies' (OECD 1987a: 8).

According to this report, new economic functions feature significantly among the many new roles universities will be expected to carry in most OECD countries. The public purse can no longer be expected to finance these new functions by creating fresh institutions to meet new demands. To support national economic development, the report argued, universities will be expected to reallocate existing resources, and this may mean cutting back on some of their traditional activities. Dawkins interpreted these statements, not as a simple description of trends, but as a rallying call to action. It could be argued that in his particular use of the arguments reported in *Universities Under Scrutiny* Dawkins was making the report say more than its authors had intended. The OECD secretariat had reported a *trend* towards closer relationships between governments, institutions and firms—it had not advocated that governments should take it upon themselves to curtail the autonomy of the universities and impose new functions upon them.

The arguments presented in *Universities Under Scrutiny* appealed to Dawkins. In establishing the conceptual framework for his plan, he made extensive use of the report and quoted it twice in his two-page foreword to the Green Paper, arguing that the connection between the role of the higher education system and economic development and productivity is now well recognised internationally. The implication was that economic development is an issue of national and international importance, while the working conditions of Australia's universities are merely a private and parochial concern. In March 1988, while discussion of the proposals in the Green Paper was still in full swing, Dawkins took the opportunity to further remove the higher education debate from the sphere of parochial interests. He seized upon an invitation to go to Paris and chair an OECD conference on *Education and the Economy in a Changing Society*.

In his opening statement Dawkins placed the Australian government's position in a global perspective by focusing on the growing importance of micro-economic policies in dealing with the post-oil shock problems that affected most Western economies. The industrialised countries, he argued, now need to rely on human skills rather than natural resources as the basis of their national wealth. He went on to argue that the productivity of Australian industry is low by international standards, in part because of inappropriate management and work practices, but more particularly because of the low skill base of the Australian economy. The government, he said, now realises that Australian industry needs 'a highly skilled workforce, not only possessing the skills currently required by employers, but also capable of responding quickly to the demands created by technological and structural change' (cited by Gittins 1988). He explained that in the Australian case, higher education institutions would be expected to play a central role in responding to this challenge.

Dawkins delivered these pronouncements in Paris just as the higher education debate back home was entering its most intense period. His timing was critical. It was March 1988, and the universities were starting back after their three-month long summer recess. The Green Paper had been released in December 1987, after the final examination term and the end of the academic year. Nevertheless, the universities had been asked to respond to the plan's complex and wide-ranging proposals by 30 April 1988. Just as the faculty were reassembling to address this difficult task, Dawkins seized the high ground by pronouncing that throughout the OECD world there was a general consensus that higher education would need to play a more active role in supporting national economic recovery.

By the end of the 1988 academic year Dawkins had achieved most of his goals. The introduction of the Higher Education Contributions Scheme (HECS) had been approved, numerous colleges and universities had been amalgamated, a system of accountability requirements and educational profiles had been set up, and the whole framework of higher education research had been reorganised. In order to legitimise his agenda of reform, Dawkins had decided to redefine the Australian university as an institution whose key function would be to serve the national interest.

It appears that, in this case, information from the OECD was used by Dawkins to legitimate reforms he had already decided to impose. Instead of debating his plan at home with an appropriate cast of characters, Dawkins used the international context of the OECD as an arena in which to play out his drama of ideological redefinition. The complaints that Australian academics made about anticipated increases in class sizes and reduced entitlements were easily represented as selfish grumbles, once the functions of universities had been redefined in terms of the national economic interest.

By citing elements of the OECD report *Universities Under Scrutiny* out of context, Dawkins represented the traditional freedom of the academic community as a luxury that Australia could no longer afford. Given Australia's geographical isolation and the fact that access to OECD debates is restricted to those inside a closed circle, it was difficult for Australia's citizens and academics to challenge Dawkins' interpretations of the OECD's work.

Conclusion

Recent work on the utilisation of social science knowledge has shown that its influence on policy decisions is anything but direct. Mechanistic views that see policy as developing logically from research findings simply do not correspond to what happens in the real world of politics. Policy decisions are the result of a complicated conjunction of forces, and alongside these, information is often forced into a minor role.

A key feature of the framework advanced by Weiss (1989) is its emphasis on the many meanings of knowledge use: not only do politicians use information to help them decide what to do, but information also carries multiple functions in the political process. This chapter has attempted to examine the applicability of the Weiss framework beyond the field of domestic politics, by asking what political purposes are served by the cross-national exchange of information. Do we find that overseas research is also used by local politicians for the same purposes—warning, guidance, legitimation and enlightenment? Do some of these functions become more important, while others become less important, when decision-makers attempt to borrow policies and ideas from other countries?

Quite probably the answer to these questions depends on which country is doing the borrowing, and from which other country or international agency they are borrowing. A more modest approach has been adopted in this chapter, and that is simply to ask how Australian policy-makers use information from the OECD. The case studies analysed above suggest that while Australia makes use of OECD data in all four ways, the 'enlightenment' and 'legitimation' functions are rather more salient than the warning and guidance functions. This conclusion is in some ways obvious. Legitimation is a logical use of the authority of an organisation such as the OECD. It is especially useful to Commonwealth politicians and bureaucrats who already know what they want to do but need to consolidate their support. Because most OECD discourse takes place at a fairly high level of abstraction, its main value is the identification of 'paradigm shifts' rather than the identification of particular programs or strategies that work. Either way, the role that knowledge from the OECD plays in the Australian policy-making process is clearly a political one.

The use of knowledge to mobilise support for policy decisions is not a matter of concern in itself. It is only when the findings from research are only partially represented that the political use of knowledge from research (or from cross-national exchange) becomes questionable. Given both the geographical isolation of Australia and the privileged access to information from international organisations such as the OECD, the Commonwealth carries a special responsibility to ensure that the information it contributes to the national debate is a comprehensive and even-handed representation of what the Organization has reported.

9 New Patterns for Managing Schools and School Systems

Hedley Beare

The 1980s and 1990s saw a wholesale restructuring of both public and non-government school systems around the world. The patterns of management in operation up to the 1970s were all but wiped out by the 1990s and were virtually gone for ever. The extent of the change is best illustrated by the new language and imagery used to describe educational management, as though one world-view had been replaced by another. By the early 1990s the almost universally accepted mode was for self-managing schools, called 'school-based management' (SBM) in the United States and 'local management of schools' (LMS) in Great Britain. Clearly, the idea that had been extant for decades—of tight prescriptive control of schools, teachers and teaching by and within a centrally devised education system—was in the process of being superseded by new designs found in post-industrial organisations, mostly in the private sector. The new models were being put in place not in education alone but throughout the public services.

The death of those outmoded ideas for running schools and school systems was hastened by the most persuasive of factors: there was simply not enough money to support the survival of schools in the ways the community had grown used to. Further, the new world economy, which effectively interconnects national economies and makes them dependent on each other, forced schools everywhere to become self-consciously international, basing their operations on outward-looking curricula and on 'international best practice'. Indeed, quasi-economic measures of student performances, especially test scores, became a prevalent political device for demonstrating the need for school reforms. Thus educators, in whatever contexts they practise their profession, must now learn to use the new kinds of structures emerging in education, or they will not be able to prevail.

The economic imperative for educational change

Viewed in retrospect, the policy perspectives for education—indeed, for the whole community—changed in several profound ways in the 1980s, the simplest manifestation being that an economic rationale was used to justify almost every major policy initiative, national and local. The need to compete in the international marketplace, especially alongside aggressive new performers such as Japan, South Korea, Taiwan, Singapore, Indonesia, and India (to name several in the Asia sector) became so overwhelming that it made the subordination of other considerations to that single cause almost a matter of national loyalty.

The reasons for the obsession with economic considerations are not hard to find. By the 1990s national economies across the world had become interlocked and dependent on each other. Fluctuations on the New York, London and Tokyo stock exchanges, for example, continued to cause daily fluctuations in the value of other currencies. The level of foreign exchange affected the level of a country's foreign indebtedness, especially in developing countries, and influenced the revenue from exports and the costs of imports. Australian mineral production rose and fell with the needs of Japanese and South Korean industries. Government subsidies paid to European farmers affected the price of grain in the markets supplied by the United States, and the threatened trade war directly undermined the markets served by other participants in primary industries. The stalling of a general agreement on trades and tariffs (GATT) caused international anxiety. Whether there would be tariff walls raised over trade in rice caused anxiety among Asian nations. In a real sense, then, and especially since the 1980s, national governments, including the largest and the least, partially had ceded control of their own financial affairs to the international marketplace. There had developed what Ohmae (1991) labelled a 'borderless world'.

The Western economies, which for centuries had dominated the global economy through industrialisation and large-scale factory production, felt acutely the impact of the new international economic conditions when they found themselves competing against newly industrialised countries (NICs), which had access to cheaper labour and the most recently developed technologies. 'Smokestack industries' were being replaced; manufacturing industry was shedding labour, using comparatively fewer people because of increased automation. For instance, the American states of Illinois, Indiana, Michigan, Ohio, and Pennsylvania, which had produced fortunes through steel, coal, building motor cars and railroads, became known as the 'rust belt'.

In consequence, there were important sectoral shifts in the proportion of the workforce in the various occupations. Whereas in the 1950s over two workers in every five had made their living in the manufacturing sector, by the 1980s it had fallen to below one in five. Four jobs in every five, it had been predicted, would be located in the information and services sector of the economy, but widespread unemployment resulted, often among well-educated workers, when those openings did not transpire. Thus many economies, including that of Australia, were in deep recession by the early 1990s.

The occupational sectors that *were* growing by 1990 were those in which both the older and the newer professions were found, which are characterised by the kind of specialisations acquired through a post-school or tertiary education, which assume twelve years of education as the basis for the vocational skills practised in those sectors, and which demand not merely substantial and formal training but also a paper qualification, a credential, as the passport to occupational practice. A typical example is tourism, which requires quite different work practices from those exercised in manufacturing industry, and which by the end of the twentieth century is predicted to become the world's largest export dollar earner. Education is itself a major part of the information and services sector, a factor that had led its commodification by the early 1990s.

In country after country, just at the point when the fundamental transition was being made out of an economy heavily dependent on manufacturing industry into a post-industrial, internationally oriented economy, schools came under intense pressure and were subjected to adverse criticism. In part this can be understood because education is the key factor that makes such a shift in the economy possible, for the general capacity of a country's entire workforce has to be raised to a point where the members can enter occupations that govern success in the new international economic conditions.

While it might have been true of the innovations of the 1970s, the school reforms of the late 1980s and early 1990s were therefore not driven by educators but rather by political and economic factors. In many respects, educators had lost control of the agenda (Harman, Beare and Berkeley 1991: 20–4). Furthermore, national governments were more powerfully interventionist in education than they had ever been, often overriding the powers and sensitivities of local and provincial governments, even to the extent (as in Great Britain, for example) of threatening the survival of local authorities. The same fear of declining competitiveness in international markets impelled private enterprise, especially the large businesses engaged in the global economy, to become vocal about educational standards and the competencies of those seeking employment. Education, in short, had become an important political and economic factor.

Not surprisingly, the eleventh and twelfth years of schooling and the immediate post-school vocational training programs became a particular focus for attack. The policy manifestations were:

- Increased retention rates into year 12; in Australia these rose from about 25 per cent in the early 1980s to nearly 90 per cent in the early 1990s.
- The reconstruction of the curriculum in the senior secondary years, with the simultaneous pressures to make the curriculum offerings broader so that they would suit the wider spectrum of students taking them, and to make the courses more intellectually rigorous.
- An attempt to control, systematise and consolidate and even to make conformist the assessment and certification procedures at year 12, in spite of the more diverse student groups and ranges of ability.
- Consolidating several school campuses and aggregating costly personnel into one large senior school complex; this was a device to ensure that a sufficient range of options was available to students.
- A replacing of the earlier infatuation with the school-to-work transition with another more important one, namely the transition from school to universal post-school education and training; put bluntly, the jobs for unskilled school-leavers had been wiped out or were going offshore.

Evidences of the transformations are easy to find. By 1992 two-thirds of the membership of the Australian Council of Trade Unions (ACTU) were from 'white collar' or public service unions. The second largest affiliate of the ACTU was the Federated Teachers Union, whose national President was also the ACTU vice-president. The Carmichael Report, from a committee chaired by a former Deputy Secretary of the ACTU, had advocated a wholesale reconstruction of the apprentice training scheme; and a series of national reports, chaired by leading businessmen Finn, Mayer and Deveson, sponsored a 'core competencies' and skills approach, not only for occupational training, but also, by implication, for secondary and tertiary education also. There were similar developments in Britain and Europe.

One major effect of these policy directions was to make educators, schools and school systems acutely aware that from now onwards they operated in an international setting, for their students found themselves increasingly in an international workplace where they functioned alongside or in competition with people from other countries. What was learnt at school by young people of their own age in Japan, Canada, South America, India or Thailand was relevant to them, and it was no longer good enough to compare their school records only with the peer group in their own school, or their own state, or their own country.

Probably the most important outcome was the emergence of the notion of education markets, crystallised by the influential and widely cited book by Chubb and Moe (1990). The market analogy produced a new set of metaphors to describe the process of schooling, educational management, educational outcomes and the nature of educational productivity. Because education was positioned in one of the critical sectors of the economy (namely the information and services sector), and because economic justifications were used so widely by policy-makers, business leaders and politicians, it was hardly surprising that education was so widely spoken of in business terms, or that it was referred to as an export earner, or that it was described as an industry which buys and sells knowledge and competencies. Such a description may have omitted some deeply treasured parts of a liberal education and defined learning in bald, instrumental language, but it nevertheless became the favoured metaphor that emerged from the 1980s.

The next step was logical, namely to advocate a privatised mode for delivering the education service. Schools and school systems, especially those supported by public funds or which were government-provided, were constantly told to emulate the style of operation that characterised private, stand-alone enterprises. Immediately some of the characteristics of schooling that had for decades been taken for granted came into question, because so much about schools and schooling derive from the ideas and metaphors that grew out of the industrial society. Those models were unlikely to be sustainable in a post-industrial state.

Two Australian cases

To demonstrate what have been the operational consequences of this paradigm shift in education management and policy-making, consider the two cases of Australia's newest public school system (in the Australian Capital Territory) and of its largest (the New South Wales system).

In 1974 Australia's eighth public school system came into existence, the newly created Schools Authority in the Australian Capital Territory. (The seventh, the Northern Territory school system, had been built only three years earlier.) Australia had previously existed with six, centralised, state-school systems from the 1880s, before the states federated and brought the national parliament and constitution into being. It was to be a hundred years later before any further such systems were created, even though the nation was five and a half times more populous by then, and both its economy and its station in world politics were vastly different.

The Canberra schools formed a self-consciously innovative system, built on a blueprint that broke the pattern prevailing elsewhere in Australia. Designed by a select committee, it was modelled on a combination of local school boards in the United States and the local educational authorities (LEAs) of Great Britain. The chair of the committee, Professor Phillip Hughes, later became the first chairperson of the ACT

Schools Authority; he was subsequently appointed a professor at the University of Tasmania, where he taught educational administration, and he later led teams to redraw the structure of the Tasmanian education department and the administration of curriculum in Queensland. His personal history demonstrates how the Australian innovations became disseminated.

Canberra's system gave parents and the public a significant voice in its affairs. Every school had a managing council from the outset, for example, and most of its policy-making apparatus included teacher, parent, and public members. It aimed to be a highly participative system in the 1970s; by the end of the 1980s, however, new waves of reform had wiped out many of those features.

One of the major achievements of the new ACT system was the reconstruction of senior secondary education through the creation of secondary colleges, catering for the last two years of general education. These provide new Year 12 (matriculation) certificates that incorporate continuous school-based assessments, modularisation of the curriculum offerings to allow alternative learning paths for students, a productively fresh approach to curriculum development, and an 'open campus', non-custodial, self-determining culture for senior secondary students. This radical break with tradition was planned through the Campbell Report, a remarkable document drawn up by a panel representative of the stakeholders in Canberra schools and chaired by Dr Richard Campbell of the Australian National University, who several years later also became chairman of the council that governed the ACT school system. Although secondary colleges are now common, Tasmania was the only other system in Australia at the time that had them.

But even Australia's most recently designed school system did not escape the managerial reconstructions of the 1980s. The ACT Schools Authority, the system's governing board on which sat parents, teachers, and government appointees, was dismantled and replaced after territorial self-government by a fairly typical Department of Education. Subsequently, Health, Education and the Arts were combined into a single ministry. These changes were symptomatic of the turbulence which surged through Australian education in the ensuing decade and a half.

The reconstruction of the giant New South Wales Education Department best summarises the new policies for education, principally because it was the last of the decade. New South Wales had held off the radical reforms through the 1980s, only to be hit with a complex of reports and restructuring almost as the climax to the decade. When the long-standing Labor government in New South Wales was replaced by a coalition led by Harvard Business School graduate Nick Greiner, his new Education Minister (Dr Terry Metherell) ordered the first management review of the Education portfolio in its entire history of 110 years. Concurrently,

New South Wales education was also comprehensively reviewed by a Select Committee set up by Metherell and headed by former national Education Minister Sir John Carrick; and a curriculum shake-up was foreshadowed in a ministerial document entitled *Excellence and Equity*, which led to a shake-up in the Higher School Certificate provisions.

The management review of the Education portfolio, a formidable task, was conducted during 1989–90 by Dr Brian Scott, one of the nation's top business consultants. The final report, a solid volume of 348 pages, was appropriately called *School-Centred Education* (and subtitled, significantly, 'Building a More Responsive State School System'); it was presented to the Minister at the end of March 1990. It is worth noting how frequently the educational reviews of the 1980s and 1990s were carried out by persons drawn from the business sector.

In any case, the same kinds of reforms that were visited on education through the 1980s and 1990s were being imposed on other government instrumentalities as well. As Pusey (1991) has pointed out, it could well have been the consistency of the advice that politicians were receiving; 'economic rationalism', the free market analogy, and the philosophies of the New Right were the orthodoxies among senior bureaucrats. As well, 'managerialism' was driving much of the public administration ideas, summed up in the term pervasively used in this period: 'corporate management'. The public service reforms had this common agenda:

- Cut out every non-essential activity or office.
- Ensure (indeed, police the fact) that national and state priorities were strictly observed.
- Downsize wherever possible intermediaries and middle management.
- Concentrate responsibility in the unit that delivers the service (in education's case, the schools).
- Require accountability, usually through negotiated performance indicators and regular 'audits' (professional as well as financial).
- Require 'value-added' quality (the essential question, then, was 'Does this office or operation add value to the final product or service?').
- Inculcate a 'productive culture' (you are paid for the quality of the job, not just for being on the job).
- Make the services compete for their customers, and survive because they deliver the quality the customer wants (or will pay for).

The principles were never enunciated as clearly as this, although they were clearly implicit in governmental restructuring. Further, they presented problems for a human service such as education, but each enterprise was expected to translate them and make them work in an appropriate way.

That a management review of New South Wales public education and the ministerial portfolio was needed should have been self-evident, for the NSW Department of School Education is a huge enterprise by any standard, with an operating budget in the 1991–92 fiscal year of $3.2 billion. It catered for a student population in excess of three-quarters of a million which made it larger than any school system in the United States or Great Britain; it exceeded in size, for example, the New York, Los Angeles, and Chicago school districts, the former Inner London Education Authority and the Scottish Clydeside district. Indeed the New South Wales and Victorian state school systems were among the three or four largest corporations in Australia, and by 1990 they were using corporatist language to describe themselves.

The New South Wales and Victorian school systems between them account for two-thirds of the nation's schoolchildren. There are *six* state and territory systems to serve the remaining one-third. It should be noted here, however, that Queensland is well on the way to displacing Victoria as the second most populous state of Australia, but the growth is masked by the fact that Queensland is the only state in Australia in which the capital city does not contain the majority of the state's population. In addition, it seems only a matter of time before the population of the Australian Capital Territory exceeds that of Tasmania. In short, there is already in Australia striking diversity in the configurations in its schooling provisions.

The public schools: the passing of bureaucracy

The term 'corporate management' emerged almost as a signal that bureaucracy was to be superseded. There were several meanings read into the term, some explicit and some implicit. First, the word 'corporate' was literally meant; corpus, a body, has many parts, with a central nervous system and a central brain; but because the bodily members are different and function in different ways, it is important not to impose conformities and administrative regularities that constrict action appropriate to only one member. Second, the word did mean that the public sector should model itself on the corporate sector, on private enterprise, and learn to be resilient, flexible and innovative. Third, the terms became formal with the passage of time. Thus the Victorian Premier defined 'privatisation' as selling a government enterprise to private interests, thereafter to operate as a private firm. 'Corporatisation' meant reconfiguring the government enterprise so that it operated like a business corporation while remaining a government instrumentality; it was not expected to follow slavish public service regulations or to operate like a typical bureaucracy. 'Commercialisation' implied that the government enterprise remained within the fabric of government but was expected to operate like a business, to meet its own costs and to make a profit. Some government enterprises, such as schools, could be corporatised without being commercialised. Union pressure prevented much privatisation, and it was never really contemplated for schools, as it was in both Britain and the United States.

The result of the revised mode of operation for schools and the new approaches to systemic administration and policy-making threw up new configurations within which Australian schools were set. The same modes are evident in other countries—New Zealand and Canada, for example—but the Australian cases demonstrate that the 'one-best-way' approaches of the past had been laid to rest by the end of the 1980s, and a new orthodoxy had arrived.

There is no compelling argument that giantism on the scale of New South Wales or Victoria is good for schoolchildren and suitable for the delivery of a sensitive education service. Scott's hope was that the New South Wales system be made 'more responsive' and that its structure should affirm 'the basics of a truly school-based and school-supporting approach to management'. His report produced not only regions but clusters of schools (150 of them) each with its own Cluster Director, and each with the potential to become a local school system in its own right, or at the least a de facto, loosely coupled, locally influenced subsystem. Physical size does not necessarily indicate significance or importance.

Nor indeed does geography. It is questionable whether the states as we have known them since federation ought to continue in their present form and with their present powers, although it would be difficult to unsettle the vested interests that hold them in place. But it is now problematical whether public school systems confined by state boundaries artificially created a century and a half ago ought to continue into the twenty-first century. The fact that every reconstruction in the 1980s favoured some form of local school governance, a degree of regionalisation, and (more interesting still) some kind of school clustering is evidence of a growing conviction that schooling should be a public service locally administered but conforming with national priorities.

Must schools continue to be factories of knowledge?

One of the problems is that the patterns of schooling familiar to the 1980s had developed from ideas associated with the industrial societies of the nineteenth and twentieth centuries. The huge cities that have grown up around the globe during the past century are a direct result of the industrial revolution. It is significant that most of the world's problematical 'supercities'—Mexico City (now the world's largest), Shanghai (estimated to be nearly 26 million by the year 2000, more than the entire population of the South Pacific including Australia, New Zealand and Papua New Guinea), Tokyo (24.2 million by the year 2000), Peking (22.8 million), Bombay (17.1 million), Calcutta (16.7 million), Jakarta (16.6 million), Seoul, Madras, Manila, Bangkok, Karachi, New Delhi, Teheran, Osaka and Dacca (all estimated to exceed the 10 million barrier by the turn of the century) to name some in the Asia/Pacific region—are located in newly industrialising countries. Put simply, to drive the mass production of factory-based industries, the workforce must congregate in suburbs around the industrial cities.

The large and usually urbanised secondary school was not only created by such industrialisation but has also played a decisive role in making the industrialised society possible. The big school was designed and organised like a factory; its buildings have the factory configuration, and its analogy for learning is the conveyor belt, a progression through defined stages to a finished and labelled product. We therefore should not expect schooling in that form to survive into the post-industrial society. The problem is what form it should now take.

The post-industrial economy ought to allow us to be more intelligent about the way we plan and run the cities of the future and the schools located in them. Nor should we go on building the kinds of cities that reproduce the multiple social diseases of the industrial economy. Can schools be made to bring forth the new design for society?

If the industrial economy and the supercity have done anything effectively, it is to create social class and divisions, and schools have been been powerful agents in that process. Liverpool, Manchester, Birmingham; the port of London or New York or Singapore or Shanghai or Hong Kong; Rotterdam, Pittsburgh, Detroit, Chicago, Woollongong, Newcastle—all these grew up as cities that were vast enclaves of working-class people clustered around the engines of industrial growth, like factory production, steel, shipping, motor vehicle construction. All across the Western world, the boom and bust of those industrial enclave cities have characteristics in common:

- a large, industrial area—ugly, run-down, with hectares of land occupied by factories, industrial barns and warehouses; or partially derelict docklands now laid waste by computerised bulk-handling and containerised cargo facilities;
- a 'central business district' (CBD), as though it is necessary (it no longer is, of course) for commercial and business houses and the headquarters of major firms to be physically and geographically close to each other;
- a run-down inner rim of suburbs, once the homes of the well-to-do but now vacated by the rich, who have moved to the outer rim of garden suburbs; the inner suburbs became slums, often owned by

absentee landlords and over-occupied by poorer families, who live in constricted space in order to meet the rent;
- inner suburbs now being taken over by the yuppies, the younger, two-income, no-children, professional couples, who need a commuting pad close to the central business district and the downtown's facilities such as theatre and restaurants; and
- large sets of suburbs usually divided along social class or socio-economic status lines.

Schools have faithfully assisted in creating these patterns. One lesson from the Industrial Revolution is that cities and schools could be planned more cleverly than that. Indeed, the large industrial cities constitute the planet's major polluter and the environment's grossest enemy.

Schools, especially larger secondary schools and colleges, have sometimes been the catalyst for developing a new kind of city or urban community. Their 'concept plans' indicate that they were designed to be at the heart of community, to be agents for the creation of a new kind of town centre. Wherever a secondary school or college is brought into existence, the opportunity for a new kind of community opens. To capitalise on that opportunity, educational planners need to be twinned with those involved in urban planning and community developers. The scale of the task also demands a new kind of educational manager.

The post-industrial society has also made obsolescent the dependence on the controls or facilities available in the state, locality, or system to which the school has been attached. Many schools around the world have opted for the International Baccalaureate; and there is really no insurmountable reason why a school in one state could not choose to present its students for some or all of the Year 12 offerings and credentialling available in another, or to use the educational services located in another part of the country. Thus as the state systems pared down their professional and consultant services, schools were led to explore the available market to purchase services from whatever source they found to be satisfactory. Those services were increasingly being provided out of Education Support Centres, rather than a city-based head office, and they were forced to operate like free-standing firms, not as units controlled within an hierarchical framework, surviving on the quality of the service they gave.

In keeping with the privatisation analogy, the constant policy of the 1980s and 1990s was to turn each school into a free-standing entity, to require it to have some form of local policy-making council, to give it a lump-sum or 'global budget' and a great amount of discretion on how the money was allocated, to de-zone in a way that made schools compete for students and to survive by satisfying their client community, and to make each school perform like a private enterprise. In short, schools became unhooked from systemic structures and were made self-managing.

The trend around the Western world seemed to be consistent, towards deregulation of schools, freeing them to act as self-contained entities loosely linked in a network of schools. In Great Britain the conservative governments under Prime Ministers Thatcher and Major pushed through the Education Bills of 1988 and 1993, which reworked the governance of schools and introduced the 'opting out' provision, which allowed individual schools to disengage from their local authority and become grant-maintained with funds provided direct from the national government. The powers of the local education authorities were weakened as the individual role of the schools was strengthened. The largest and most visible system in the country, the Inner London Education Authority, was abolished and broken up into metropolitan boroughs. Her Majesty's Inspectorate was remodelled, school inspections were privatised, and a scheme for universal inspection introduced. In the New Zealand reconstruction following the publication of the Picot Report and the ministerial White Paper *Tomorrow's Schools*, each school was asked to draw up a charter that became the basis for its funding, each school was to have a board of trustees, and each school was to conduct its own affairs under negotiated conditions and was held to account through regular reviews and educational audits. 'Restructuring' was a word constantly used in the United States from the late 1980s onwards to characterise the second wave of reforms after those prompted by the 1983 report *A Nation at Risk*, which resulted from a national taskforce commissioned by the US President. Restructuring came to mean a variety of measures, but they were consistent with those in other countries and were best symbolised by the wholesale reconstruction of the huge Chicago system to incorporate autonomy for each school.

What became evident at the end of the 1980s was therefore the recognition that every school is a significantly large and complex enterprise. When the payroll in any normally sized school, the value of its buildings and equipment, the budget for its maintenance and supplies, and its other recurrent expenditures are aggregated, the school comes to be seen as literally a multi-million-dollar enterprise. Compared with any other business in the area, the school usually emerges as the largest enterprise in town; it usually occupies the largest piece of real estate in the locality; it is much more complicated to run than any other local business because its purposes are more complex, more public and more politically sensitive; it directly affects a far larger proportion of the community than does any other enterprise; and because by its very nature it requires the delicate exercise of human relations, not merely among the enterprise's own staff but also with a large, very particular, and highly volatile set of customers or clients, its managers (especially the principal) are not 'middle management', nor a subordinate part in a big bureaucracy, but among the most highly skilled and qualified executives in the community.

Structure and style of education systems

During the 1980s every state and territory system of education in Australia went through management reviews and reconstruction. Throughout the 1980s more than fifty documents or government reports were issued dealing with the restructuring of Education ministries. From these major policy documents, which every state and territory produced during the 1980s, some fundamental rethinking about the nature of educational administration emerged, concentrating heavily on structural reform with the following common features:

1. *Efficiency and good management as priorities*: A universal priority was efficient management, with an emphasis on cost-management, cost-effectiveness, efficient allocation and use of resources, and a deliberate reaffirmation of governmental priorities. Economic considerations were overpowering.
2. *Simple, political control*: The structures tried to re-establish clear and simple lines of control. Some powers were re-centralised, and ministerial responsibility was underlined. Part of the tidying up, even by Labor governments, involved wiping out any semi-autonomus statutory authorities and replacing them with bodies directly responsible to the Minister, through a departmental Chief Executive.
3. *Portfolio and policy coordination*: The Minister's office and the headquarters staff became responsible for portfolio coordination, the consolidation of the processes for policy-making and policy advice. Clearly, Ministers prefer uncomplicated decision-making. The details of implementation and day-to-day administration were devolved.
4. *Lean head-office management*: There was a dramatic cutting back of the numbers of people in head office. The systemic structures were broken up, the large central bureaucracies were dispersed and replaced by lean, head-office management.
5. *Devolution of responsibility*: Every state and territory system experimented with some form of regionalisation. 'Devolution of responsibility' was a frequently used term in the reconstructions. A strong common theme in all the restructuring was that schools must be given greater responsibility to order their own affairs. Terms such as 'the self-managing school' and 'the self-determining school' were used, and the role of the principal as an effective manager was emphasised.

6. *Excellence before equity*: The documents talked about 'better schools' or 'excellent schools' or just 'excellence', suggesting that the school's management must be responsive to the clients' wishes in a kind of free market for educational services, and that the school should observe best international practices. A 'resource agreement' of some kind was now implied, in which the school had to demonstrate that it had exercised good stewardship of its resources. Excellence was to be judged on outcomes, not on inputs or internal processes.
7. *National priorities*: The national government emerged as one of the key players in deciding educational policies and practices, imposing its own priorities on education, sometimes for defence purposes, but more often because the justification was economic. Those educational provisions that affected the country's economy became a legitimate concern of national government.

To understand the movement to remake public school systems, we need to understand the private business model that was being copied (Deal and Kennedy 1982; Toffler 1985; Handy 1985; Caldwell and Spinks 1988, 1992; Beare 1990; Peters 1992; Murphy 1991). It assumes at least four characteristics. The first is that the organisational pyramid, the typical bureaucratic hierarchy, is replaced with a 'network organisation', a system of interconnecting, semi-autonomous operating units. Each is relatively small consisting of fewer than a hundred members, and the internal arrangements and modes of operating are left to be determined by the unit.

The second characteristic is that the units are under a contract to provide a designated service of a required quality for the parent company. In short, the units provide a service for an agreed price. It is not necessary for the parent company to own all the subsidiary units; they can be 'spin-off companies', or units to whom a function is 'franchised out', or 'firms within a firm'. They are simply paid for doing a job. The parent company ensures that it gets value for money through an accountability mechanism, which uses mutually negotiated 'performance indicators' and a regular audit or quality checks. Thus there are formal reporting-back procedures, an agreed format for giving that feedback, and a unit at head office that handles these regular audits. Operationally, the audits free the networking units from unnecessary interference in the way they work. The units are judged on outputs, on services delivered.

Thirdly, the head office of the parent company is thereby transformed into a 'strategic core'. It is physically incapable of controlling the units in the traditional sense; it simply coordinates them. The core staff of the company become responsible for making the strategic decisions for the whole; for undertaking long-range planning; for coordination and articulation of the system; for raising, determining and parcelling out the company's global budget; for instituting quality controls; for ensuring staff development; and for managing the company's culture.

And fourthly, the company is collegially, not hierarchically, ordered. It is effectively a 'federation of subsystems'. Indeed, the head office staff do not necessarily outrank the staff in the units, for they perform different roles. It is possible to interchange the parts without interfering with individual career lines or with the company's well-being. The chief executive, then, could be a role that is shared around among the managers of the operating units, who might take it in turns to occupy that central position.

System after system in Australia began to move in this direction, paring down the big central bureaucracies, divesting them of educator staff, and reassigning them to regions, clusters and schools. Because this kind of divestiture of the centre does not affect education in the direct way that limiting the number of teachers in schools would do, it is a politically easier way to conserve finances. What schools lose, of course, are allies at head office, support in terms of curriculum and professional services, a range of free professional advice, and protection from the political winds. If the present trend continues, there will be very few staff left at the centre.

In this model, schools gain increased legal and professional responsibilities in the form of a global budget, wide discretion over funding, the responsibilty to select their own staff as well as to fill their promotion positions (from the Principal down), the management and upkeep of their physical plant, and so on. Put simply, Australian public schools are more and more resembling the private schools in their governance and operation. Most of the money allocated for education now resides in the hands of individual schools. In Great Britain more than 90 per cent of the money voted from Whitehall to the local education authorities must be passed on direct to the schools; and the same trend is clearly evident in Australia and New Zealand. Individual schools will therefore have to go into the marketplace and buy any specialist services that are required to supplement the work of their own teachers and general staff. It will also become common for schools to form coalitions, like the New South Wales 'clusters' or the South Australian and Tasmanian 'districts', whereby they will share their expertise, pool resources, or 'contract in' services by each contributing to the cost of a specialist consultancy. Already the School Support Centres (in Victoria) and the Education Resource Centres (in New South Wales) are taking on the role of broker for a set of schools; indeed, the intention in the Scott reforms in New South Wales was that the ERCs should be owned and managed by school clusters.

By the early 1990s, then, there appears to have developed a consensus about the general model for the public school systems in Australia. The model was based upon ideology rather than research, but it had grown out of free market economics, many public reports in several countries, and an awareness that bureaucratic systems were artefacts of industrialisation, of a past era, and were ill-suited to the political realities of the internationally conscious, post-industrial states.

The Catholic schools: a different organisational format

Are there other options? Well, yes; by the 1990s at least eight school systems in Australia were operating on premises radically different from those that underlie the government school systems. I refer, of course, to the Catholic systems. The Catholic school system in New South Wales is the fourth largest in Australia, exceeded in size only by the government systems in New South Wales, Victoria and Queensland. Put another way, the New South Wales and the Victorian Catholic systems rival in size the Western Australian and South Australian government school systems. By 1990 Victorian Catholic schools contained more students than the combined total of all schools in Tasmania, the Australian Capital Territory and Northern Territory (Casey 1990: 49, 52).

Catholic schools have a different mode of developing both school-based approaches and regionalisation. Their regions are dioceses, and the twenty-eight in the eight states and territories all have a strong degree of autonomy. The State Catholic Commissions are essentially coalitions of convenience, the means to enable the dioceses to act collectively. Even within a diocese, a parish or a group of parishes may run schools with relative independence. Those parochial schools resemble a local system, a cluster, or a network of schools (Casey 1990: 6).

Three of the guiding principles built into the operation of Catholic schools are subsidiarity, pluriformity, and complementarity. The principle of subsidiarity was first introduced in a papal encyclical of 1931; it declared that 'it is a grave evil and a disturbance of right order to transfer to the larger and higher collectivity functions which can be performed and provided by lesser and subordinate bodies' (McBrien 1980: 1044). The economist Schumacher made the same point in his celebrated book *Small is Beautiful: Economics as though People Matter* (1973). Subsidiarity requires that, in designing a system, you start at the parochial level, not from the 'centre' or the 'top' (wherever that is). Any collectivity, before it usurps the power vested in the local body, must show cause why it can discharge that function better, more efficiently, more humanely, more skilfully.

The second principle, pluriformity, is a logical consequence. The Catholic systems allow diversity, a plurality of forms. If a parish or cluster or community believes that a certain configuration best suits its needs, conformity will not be imposed from without. Variety is not only tolerated, but also encouraged and celebrated. The centre (in this context, the metaphor does not fit well) must respect, indeed honour, the special character of each person, each school, each community, and instead of controlling its actions, will actively foster the special expression each will take.

The third principle, that of complementarity, means that each part of the enterprise will dovetail, will complement, help, and encourage the other parts, will not impede them, will not get in the way of their functioning. Complementarity defies centralism, then. It encourages a sense of community, the collegiality that produces cooperation among equals, and it spurns pyramids of interlocking power such as we associate with the typical bureaucracy. Complementarity means that centralised action is consensual, based on the cooperation of all the parts, an alliance forged for the greater common good.

When these kinds of principles become the guidelines for the operation of the system, there develops a structure of organisation that is refreshingly different from the centralised formats so long taken for granted in the government systems. The organisation charts of the Catholic systems—if they are drawn at all—do not resemble the boxes and lines of control that prevail in the public service. And why should they? Indeed, why should all the government schools need to function in such a deadly consistent stereotype?

Even more interesting are the schools run by religious orders. These are systems independent of the dioceses, and they transcend the boundaries of the states and territories. There could be schools and systems of the same kind, but run by government, or foundations, or private companies, or community groups; the Steiner schools are a case in point. Particularly during the 1980s, many of the non-government, non-Catholic schools developed several campuses or began to operate three or four subsidiary schools, thereby becoming sets of schools, school-systems-in-little. This is the way that many of the small, district school systems developed across the United States; the high school became the centrepiece for the system, with the high school principal also carrying the role of superintendent of schools. Consolidation has changed that pattern in recent decades, but it is possible that the principals of larger secondary or elementary schools throughout Australia could lead a movement towards genuinely district-based educational provisions, to the development of a plurality of school systems, no less.

Viewed positively, therefore, the decades of the 1980s and 1990s stimulated more imagination on the part of those who run schools, especially forcing educational managers to picture alternative ways of organising and providing an education service.

Serving the national interest

It is not possible to review the recent reforms of education in any Western country without acknowledging the dominant role played by national governments and federal agencies (the two are not synonymous, and are often rivals). When Prime Minister Whitlam set up the Australian Schools Commission in the early 1970s, his action signalled that it was a time to develop some nationally coordinated, new approaches for Australian schools; it also introduced a powerful new player into a domain that had been the states' preserve from the earliest colonial days. Although it was a creature of the national government, the Schools Commission nevertheless had the independence of a statutory authority and its members were drawn widely from across the communities with both a stake and an interest in education. It was bound to be an uncomfortable body.

Paradoxically, it made strong the Australian Education Council (AEC), the council of the Ministers of Education from around Australia. This was a state ministers' creation, which had existed since the 1930s, and it was a useful political foil to the Commonwealth bodies. When, therefore, Minister Dawkins abolished the Schools Commission in the late 1980s, the AEC moved quickly into the vacuum and took over the role of national coordination. The federal minister was by this time a full member of the AEC and therefore in a position to participate in the new venue for national approaches to schooling. The AEC came into its ascendancy just at the time when the school systems had emerged from a decade of reconstruction in which they were subjected to instrumentalist approach to education. By the beginning of the 1990s, many of the Education ministries were led by people recruited from areas outside Education. They were by and large very able, but many did not have the special understanding of the educative process which is supposedly the preserve of the educational professional. As a consequence, educational policies began to take on quite new complexions. There was pressure, for example, to draw up a national set of goals for schooling; it was an economists' kind of initiative—define the goals, set tests to see whether the goals are being achieved, reward those who meet the targets and punish those who do not. There followed in logical order national guidelines for the curricula based upon the goals, a standardising of the approaches, and the creation of a national Curriculum Corporation to put flesh on the bones of the guidelines. The logical conclusion would be a single, unified, national school system. In fact, the national daily *The Australian* suggested as much when it reported the AEC's decision about the national curriculum guidelines. The Australian Education Council's compliance with national educational goals was described as 'a national approach to school curricula in the first step to a centralised system' (*The Australian*, 22 June 1990, p.1).

To be fair, there are aspects to schooling that need to be dovetailed in the national interest. National goals, national guidelines, national curriculum regularities, some national cooperation and coordination are not in themselves bad, but the model can be pushed too far and become educationally counterproductive. In any case, the tendencies to centralise policy-making in the national interest and at the same time to decentralise in a way that makes schools self-determining pose an unresolved dilemma.

Teachers and the educator profession

All of these developments caused a rethinking of the very notion of an educator profession. So much happened to change the traditional role of the teacher and educational manager that taskforces (for example, the National Project on the Quality of Teaching and Learning (NPQTL) in the early 1990s) began to ask again what are the areas in which it is essential that the educator profession maintain its dominance; whether it is possible to unlock the traditional roles and positions that have always belonged to teachers; to analyse what are appropriate professional functions (and what are not), to reconstitute the roles, and then to negotiate the kind of configurations and career openings for educators that will guarantee the best educational delivery. In the process, notions such as class size, pupil–teacher ratios, and even the notion of classes have to be reconsidered.

It emerges that teachers can function as providers of professional services rather than as employees, to supply schools with expertise of various kinds without having to be subject to the complicated fabric of governmental or systemic career structures. School management could become the activity of a core staff, which recruits instructional services from professional companies of teachers. Teachers, especially those in hard-to-provide categories, could have their firm negotiate a contract for them, including a fee for service at rates the market will pay, and they could opt for however many hours they wished to work. It seems likely, for example, that an adequate number of science, mathematics and commerce teachers could be secured only by paying them a rate that will attract them out of other industries.

The most profound change may come from the way professional people plan their own careers, for there are high rates of stress being felt in occupational areas such as teaching and social welfare. In a provocative discussion of the working patterns likely to emerge in the 1990s, Charles Handy (1989: Ch.2) argued that the terms 'retirement' and 'full-time work' are rapidly losing their meaning; that by the year 2000, 70 per cent of all the jobs in Europe would require cerebral rather than manual skills; that firms will tend to favour buying-in on contract the services they require; that the core staff are the only ones likely to be salaried and permanent employees, and that they will be professional, highly cerebral and highly trained. Theirs will be an intensive and shortened life at the top. 'Most of them', Handy (1989: 37) pointed out, 'will be in their thirties and forties, putting in their . . . hours in huge annual chunks'. It will be 'a shorter life but a more furious one'.

> The next generation of full-time core workers . . . , be they professionals, managers, technicians or skilled workers, can expect to start their full-time careers later—and to leave them earlier. This is the crucial point. The core worker will have a harder but shorter job, with more people leaving full-time employment in their late forties or early fifties, partly because they no longer want the pressure that such jobs will increasingly entail, but mainly because there will be younger more qualified and more energetic people available for these core jobs. (Handy 1989: 37)

Work will not stop for these people, but it will be a different kind of job, when they take on work to satisfy themselves, but it 'will not be a job as they have known it'. When these people step out of their intensive period of employment, they will be ready for a series of intellectually demanding assignments, but they will take them on in their own time and on their own terms. It is likely that, if the education profession were suitably configured to use them, it could gain the services of a large number of experienced, highly educated, and wise operators. Teaching could become their last job, rather than their first. Handy warns:

> Organizations may have to learn to be more flexible in the way they run things, more willing to recognize that they are buying the talents of someone but not necessarily all their time. And that will apply to schools no less than to any other organization. (1989: 39)

Conclusion

In summary, then, the break-up of the pyramidal, hierarchically ordered bureaucracies, documented by Mintzberg, Toffler and Handy in particular, are being replaced by 'network organisation', with a strategic core (which sets the boundaries and makes the system-wide policies for the system) connected to operating units to which the main work of the organisation is 'franchised out'. An accountability mechanism for regular audits accompanies the change. This kind of 'corporatising' has been copied by public school systems throughout the Western world, including Australia and New Zealand. In setting up public school systems along these lines, there have been some necessary revisions to entrenched modes of operation. In a sense, the Australian school systems have been disaggregated.

In contrast, the non-government school sector began to act in the reverse, aggregating into larger operating units and expanding onto other campuses, creating what amount to new school 'systems'. Thus the New South Wales Education Reform Bill of the late 1980s made provision for the registration of new independent school systems, as well as new independent schools. Catholic school systems adopted a different model again, based upon subsidiarity, pluriformity, and complementarity, and recognising the primacy of the parish school. In essence, the Catholic systems exist to support the parish school.

Overarching all these developments is the growing importance of national policies, increasingly being determined in a setting described as 'new federalism', a venue in which equal partners each with sovereign powers mutually arrive at policies that are thereafter jointly implemented.

In short, there has now developed a diversity in the nature and shape of schools and school systems. These flexible and light-limbed models have superseded the large, predictable, plodding bureaucracy, which once supported the now superseded industrial economy.

10 The Provision of Non-government Schooling in Australia: Retrospect and Prospect

Maurice Ryan and Helen Sungaila

Educational administration is about providing a better future. The future, however, demands survival. For the non-government schools, survival requires a distinctive identity in the face of shrinking budgets, internal and external scrutiny, and a growing convergence with the government school sector. This contemporary convergence, especially since the 1970s, has historical precedence: private schools at one time *were* the government schools. In the last decades of the twentieth century, there is once again an emerging consensus about the answers to many of the foundational questions concerning Australian schools: what are the schools for? how can they best be organised and governed? what should be taught in them? how? and by whom? The answers to these questions have important implications for the work of educational administrators in all sectors. As the forms of governance grow to mirror each other, a challenge emerges: how is any school to develop and maintain a distinctive identity?

This chapter provides an account of the relation between non-government schools and public administrations in Australia in the past 200 years. In reviewing the past, we can gain clues to the future provision of non-government schools. A prospective view of non-government schools offers all educational administrators ways to respond to contemporary shifts, especially the need to survive and the quest for distinctiveness.

1788–1870: church and state in partnership

In the early days of colonial New South Wales, schools were deemed to be the responsibility of the churches or, more specifically, the Church of England. The British government had made no provision for schooling in its settlement plans; priority was given to the demands of establishing a gaol. Two schools established in 1792 for the children of officers and convicts were supervised by the Reverend Richard Johnson, on the assumption that it was traditionally part of an Anglican clergyman's role to run a school in his parish. Schools were seen primarily as moral guardians and custodians of the young who would otherwise have little else to occupy their time other than petty crime.

For the most part, the colonial governments remained uninvolved with early colonial schooling. Successive governors varied in their enthusiasm for schools. Lachlan Macquarie vigorously fostered their development, not the least because he saw the opportunities for social control. His general order concerning the establishment of charity schools in 1810 expressed the earnest wish that such schools would make the young 'dutiful and obedient to their Parents and Superiors, honest, faithful and useful Members of society and good Christians' (Barcan 1965: 32). A presumption was common among administrators that schools would continue along the lines established in Britain: schools would be Anglican. In 1820 Earl Henry Bathurst, in charge of the Colonial Office in London, suggested that a national system of schools be adopted that would facilitate bringing up the young 'in habits of industry, regularity, and for the implanting in their minds the principles of the Established Church' (Austin 1961: 8).

Roman Catholics objected to the Anglican domination of schooling and, with the arrival of Father John Therry, set about establishing Catholic schools, each under the guidance of a local Catholic priest. As such, they were 'parish schools', even though formal parish structures were rudimentary. After 1830 successive colonial administrations made small grants available to the churches for purchase of land, buildings and salaries, with the structure and organisation of the schools being left to the churches. In effect, the government schools in the colony were the church schools.

From this brief review of early efforts to establish schools, several themes emerge. First, a strong association of schools with the churches was forged. The role of the colonial government was supplementary and supportive rather than directive. Second, church schools were closely identified with the clergy. Church schools were seen to have a variety of purposes beyond basic instruction. They offered a primary opportunity for inculcating moral virtue, ensuring faithful church membership and providing shelter from the iniquities of the penal colony. Third, the separate denominations were unable to cooperate in the provision of schools.

Governor George Gipps signalled in 1844 a theme that would recur in the story of schooling in Australia. Gipps' efforts throughout the 1830s and 1840s to introduce a general system of schools to cater for all colonial children were impeded by the refusal of leaders of the separate denominations to agree on a suitable system. He lamented in 1844 that 'without the co-operation of the Ministers of Religion it seems to me scarcely possible to establish any system of Education with a prospect of its being extensively useful' (Austin 1961: 43). Gipps's remarks testify to two important issues. One was the lack of government jurisdiction over a matter presumed to belong to the churches; colonial governments refused both authority and responsibility for the direct management of schools. The other issue was the inability of the churches to cooperate on schooling matters. The remarks might have sounded a warning to the church authorities for the days when men of more liberal stamp would have control of colonial administrations. Such tolerance displayed by Gipps was not to last for long.

With the separation of colonies (South Australia in 1836 and Victoria in 1851), the policies for government-funding of schools became more complex and inconsistent. The criteria for funding schools varied markedly from one colony to the next. To provide organisation for the development of schools, colonial governments established in each colony two Boards of Education—one for denominational schools, the other for the growing number of government schools—whose function consisted of administration and school inspection. The denominational boards, however, reported to the local clergy, who maintained ultimate control of these schools. The establishment of these boards resulted in a shift of government attitude towards the provision of schools. The existence and work of the denominational boards represented a hiatus for the non-government schools, for not only did the schools enjoy an increase in funding to build, staff and run their schools, but also they were able to do so without government interference in their internal organisation. It was a generous proposition, which was to be short-lived.

The type and amount of assistance varied among the colonies: grants for school buildings, teachers' residences, rents for premises, equipment, and guarantees for teachers' salaries. While the boards provided greater systematisation to the non-government provision of schools, flaws were still apparent. Many school buildings were poorly equipped, and many teachers were poorly trained, largely because of the rapid expansion in the colonies after gold was discovered. Some schools were built close to each other, while other districts had no schools at all. Colonial governments, only slowly coming to a realisation of their role in providing schools, looked unsympathetically on the duplication of schools and their uneven distribution throughout the colonies. As a consequence, the separate boards (National and Denominational) were merged under one authority and provided one integrated and unified system of schools under government patronage.

Until 1870 the churches and colonial governments had therefore achieved almost a century of cooperation in the provision of schools. This partnership, while often stormy, had succeeded within narrow limits to provide elementary schools for a significant proportion of colonial children. A break in the relation between the churches and colonial governments on the matter of schooling was imminent. The break came first in Victoria in 1872 with the passing of the first free, compulsory and secular Education Act in the Australian colonies. Other colonial governments followed suit in the following decades.

1870–1960: Catholic schools as the non-government schools system

The reasons why the schooling of children became the battleground for ideological conflict in the last quarter of the nineteenth century are complex and beyond the scope of this chapter, although a few issues are worth highlighting. For one, the same shifts occurred contemporaneously in other colonial outposts of the European empires. At one level the struggle was between traditional images of authority and vigorous new concepts drawn from nineteenth-century reflection on liberal democracy, which was played out at the edges of the empire. A majority of the men who moved into the colonial parliaments shared a nineteenth-century conviction that denominational religion, while intellectually bankrupt, remained socially useful and necessary. For the most part, the liberal reformers were not anti-religious; many professed a form of personal religion or an interest in spirituality. The separation of church and state on the matter of schools cannot be seen as a rejection of religion, *per se*. Rather, the liberals were motivated by a desire to create in the new colonies a common citizenry without the old European divisions. Schools, therefore, should be kept free from the influence of denominational religion, which could be provided by the separate churches for their own people, at their own expense. The bickering between the denominations served only to confirm the views of the majority of colonial legislators.

As well, the rationalising of schools must be seen as an economic necessity. While schools were viewed as useful for the development of an articulate and vibrant democracy, they had to be economic. The most efficient means to ensure adequate provision of schools, according to the reformers, was the vesting of authority in a responsible government minister. Henry Parkes, speaking in the debate on the New South Wales Public Schools Bill in 1866, summarised the views of economic rationalists who saw that 'whilst ministers of religion are cavilling over a division of the spoils, [many children] are destitute of all instruction'. His estimate of the number of such children was 100 000 and he argued that 'it is the duty of the Government, on the clearest grounds of statesmanship and political economy, to make every effort possible to reach a larger number of these destitute and neglected children' (Griffiths

1957: 119). The nature of colonial society was changing from a rigid and authoritarian one to an increasingly liberal and democratic one. Schools were among the first institutions to grapple with the implications of this shift. Utilitarian economics and liberal secularist views were the major forces that shaped the provision of schools for the next century.

The decision to exclude private and church schools from the public purse was deeply felt. Manning Clark described the action of separating church and state schools as amounting to 'one of the most momentous decisions, and probably the most disastrous' in Australian history.

> It meant the neutrality of the teachers in the State schools on all questions touching personal faith: it meant the permanent division of Australian education into three types of schools—the Catholic, the Protestant, and the State: it meant the pauperization of the Catholic schools, and left them an aggrieved minority. What was just as grievous was the decision of each colony to adopt a highly centralised system of administration for the conduct of education. Thus one part of the administrative machinery was created for a centralised democracy: to permit, in turn, the development of the tyranny of the majority. (Clark 1962: 662)

The Education Acts of the late nineteenth century caused the kind of deep division and persistent acrimony their sponsors wished to avoid in the new colonies.

The Roman Catholic community protested the exclusion of their schools from the public purse and decided to fund their schools from their own resources. Catholic opposition to the Education Acts of the 1870s and 1880s established a pattern for the provision of a non-government schooling sector in Australia for the next century. The Catholics were the only significant church group to oppose the abolition of state aid to religion; the school systems of other Christian denominations, though diverse and lively prior to 1870, dissolved in the wake of the colonial Education Acts. Apart from Catholic schools, only a few church schools remained after the abolition of state aid. Catholic resistance and resolve to establish, support and operate their own schools ensured that their schools were the only significant non-government form of schooling in Australia for almost the next 100 years. At the time of opposition to the Acts, themes emerged that would shape the development and nature of the schools for the next century.

Most of the leadership for the establishment of separate schools came from the Roman Catholic bishops. While few of these men had training in education, they pursued the demands of Vatican edicts, which had become increasingly hardline under the papacy of Pius IX, who distrusted the radical ideas gaining currency in Europe. Roman Catholic church members effectively had no option but to follow the demands of the bishops. As Father William Slattery explained to the Victorian Royal Commission into Education in 1883: 'The laity are obliged to concur in the present State system being a grievance, otherwise they would not be Catholics.' Attendance at a Catholic school, once considered to be an assistance to Catholic faith, was also to be a condition of orthodoxy as well.

Catholic schools followed more or less the same curriculum as the government schools. In doing so, they shared a similar concern to the liberal secularists in the acquisition of useful knowledge that would enable the child to prosper in the colony. The Catholics' dispute with the state over the provision of schooling was at base religious, not educational; the belief in the relation of religion to life was at the heart of the Catholic community's dispute with the State over schools.

Catholic schools after 1872 maintained economies of operation in the first instance by contributions from their parishioners. Increasingly, especially after the turn of the century, the importation of members of religious congregations from Catholic Europe meant that schools could be operated economically by women and men who had taken vows of poverty in the service of their church. Lay teachers were employed in schools throughout the country and ensured an economic operation by working for lower salaries than state school teachers (Fogarty 1959: 279–86). The major source of funds came from the laity, who energetically raised money through fetes and dances, as well as making direct contributions.

With the arrival of the religious orders, Catholic schools increased in number, and the majority of Catholic children were able to attend a Catholic school. A uniform system of parochial elementary schools developed under the auspices of parish or religious congregation. The schools were poorly resourced, yet enjoyed great autonomy and freedom from centralised control by church authorities because of the inability to construct a centralised bureaucracy. In time, secondary schools were developed in larger numbers as the demand for them grew in relation to the aspirations of Catholics to join the professions and the universities.

1960–present: a partnership renewed

Major challenges confronted Australian schools in the 1950s and 1960s and had a serious impact on the provision of schooling in the non-government sector. The costs of operating schools escalated. Large numbers of immigrant children entered schools, along with children of the post-war baby boom. For Roman Catholic schools, membership of the religious orders that staffed the schools declined markedly. This had an immediate impact on the staffing of schools. In order to maintain Catholic schools, more lay staff were hired and costs increased accordingly, forcing economies such as larger class sizes and declining conditions. The perception grew that the Catholic school system was at the point of collapse.

Catholic communities began a campaign of political action to focus attention on their situation. The town of Goulburn, in New South Wales, was the site of a demonstration of the political will of Catholics in the pursuit of government funding for their schools. After a series of requests from state government authorities to renovate existing facilities, church authorities moved to close all schools of the Archdiocese of Canberrra–Goulburn and to enrol their students in government schools. At issue was a test of whether it would cost the government more to absorb Catholic school children into its own schools than it would to give the church schools sufficient funds to enable them to carry on. On Monday 16 July 1962, Goulburn's Catholic schools closed and the government schools enrolled 640 of the town's 1350 Catholic school students. The state government minister promised correspondence education for those who were not able to be enrolled in Goulburn's suddenly crowded classrooms. After one week, the strike was called off; Catholic students returned to their own schools, and the attention of the nation's media turned to other matters. The point had been made.

The Goulburn school strike most closely marks the shift in government attitudes to the funding of non-government schools. The relation between the non-government schools and the public administration was to alter dramatically from this time. In 1964 the Menzies federal government approved finance for science blocks in non-government schools, and later, direct funding for libraries and book stocks was approved. Most state governments introduced some form of interest support schemes for schools. This period marks a turning point in the provision of non-government schools.

The culmination of the shift in government attitudes was the so-called Karmel Report, an instrument of the Whitlam government-directed Australian Schools Commission. The 1973 report examined the position of government and non-government primary and secondary schools, and made recommendations on their financial needs and the measures appropriate to assist in meeting them.

The Karmel Report reversed a century of government non-involvement with private schools. The twin reasons for intervention and inclusion were democracy and economy. The Karmel committee reported that it valued 'the right of parents to educate their children outside government schools. It appreciates the high standard which some non-government schools have reached often after years of effort' (Karmel 1973: 12). The terms of reference given to the Karmel committee stressed equality of opportunity and access to education for all Australian children. The main cause of exclusion of private schools from the public purse a century earlier, economic efficiency, was now seen as the major reason for funding non-government schools. Increased funding was required to assist schools that 'lack sufficient resources, both human and material, to provide educational experiences appropriate to the young in a modern democratic industrial society' (Karmel *1973: 139*). All Australian schools once again, according to government views, had a role to play in the development of free, equal and democratic institutions.

For Catholic schools, the funding that flowed to them acted as a catalyst to hasten the development of centralised bureaucracies, which aimed to place Catholic schools on an efficient and strong footing. The growth of Catholic Education Offices, especially in the large metropolitan centres, was rapid and comprehensive. Development of these centralised offices had an impact on all aspects of Catholic schools and changed them from a relatively autonomous, self-supporting loose network under the control of parish priests and religious congregations, into a system of schools with a professional educational outlook.

If it can be stated accurately that the present relation between non-government schools and state and federal governments is a renewed partnership, then some description of the present shape of the non-government school sector will be useful in determining possible directions for this partnership. Most significantly, the non-government school sector is a pre-dominantly Catholic one—there are nearly three times as many students in Catholic schools as in all other non-government schools combined (Ashenden 1989: 13). Most Catholic schools are systemic, coming under the governance of bureaucracies based on diocesan divisions. A limited number of Catholic schools are independent of these systemic schools and are usually owned and governed by religious congregations.

A second tier of non-government schools under the sponsorship of other religious groups has expanded in the past generation. The most prominent schools in this group are under the authority of the Anglican and Uniting Church communities. Also significant in this group are the schools belonging to the Presbyterian, Baptist, Seventh Day Adventist and Jewish communities. Some other independent schools in this group are inter- or non-denominational.

A third group of schools makes up a small, though significant proportion of the 2400 non-government schools in Australia. These are often referred to as alternative schools and are usually founded by groups who have rejected the mainstream schools. These schools are typically controlled by local communities, who have a high degree of involvement in their governance.

The expansion in the number and kind of schools in the non-government sector has resulted in a drift in the number of students away from the public schools and towards the non-government schools. This is especially so of the Catholic schools, in which the growth in enrollments has been the largest. At present, about one-quarter of Australia's children are enrolled in non-government schools. The shift towards non-government schools poses intriguing problems and possibilities for the future of all Australian schools.

Prospects for non-government schools

Although the period since the 1970s has witnessed cooperation between public administrations and non-government schools not seen in Australia for more than a century, the question of survival as distinctive organisations has inevitably come to the fore. Non-government schools now face challenges that go to the heart of their identity and survival as distinct organisations. Their administrators are increasingly confronted with the need to establish a style of governance that promotes the identity of the school and ensures its survival.

To achieve this, school administrators must be proficient in three disciplines. First, they need a sense of history. While those administrators who do not know their history may be condemned to repeat the worst of it, ignorance of the past can mean neglect of the wisdom of colleagues who have dealt with similar foundational questions in diverse settings. History is a source for knowing what is possible, as well as a guide to what might be avoided. Second, administrators must have some understanding of organisations and the ways in which organisational identity is formed and nurtured. With a theoretical perspective, administrators will be better placed to build and sustain the organisational identity of the school. Third, they need practical strategies and techniques that give shape to their organisational interventions. To bring about organisational change, administrators need access to a repertoire of forms for action that can be applied according to need. The second and third of these disciplines will now be addressed.

Organisational identity

Organisational identity crisis reveals itself in a variety of ways. It may be evident in a school in which there is no clear set of expectations; or a clear set of expectations but no agreed priority among them; disorganisation in the day-to-day school life, with everybody either doing their own thing or working at cross-purposes; an overemphasis on internal budgets and financial analysis, with little or no talk about students or parents or educational trends; too much time spent serving internal matters (politics and apple-polishing) and joking about what does or does not go on in the administration. If none of these symptoms is present, then perhaps the question of identity is less pressing than many would believe.

The people in schools, the roles they play, the educational programs they offer, the values they espouse and symbolise in artefacts, are only one dimension of organisational identity. This can be described as the material dimension, that which can be seen, touched and heard. This is the dimension in which sets of organisational expectations are embodied, stored and made accessible. As well as the material dimension, two other equally important dimensions of organisational identity are identified in the literature: the temporal and the social (Luhmann 1985).

The temporal describes the dimension of organisational identity that endures over time. There are many great Australian non-government schools that have passed the century mark and yet still endure as they had become within a few years of opening their doors. How does a school sustain its identity over one and, sometimes many, centuries, when so many generations of staff and students have come and gone? It cannot depend solely, or even significantly, on the people who once taught there, or the roles they once played, or the policies and programs that guided their actions, because these too have changed many times. A perspective that views schools as living systems helps to explain the consistent maintenance of organisational identity. As living systems, schools exhibit a basic thrust for life, for survival.

Any organisation that has a distinctive identity must not only endure over time, it must also be seen as one distinctive organisation, despite the disparate and often conflicting interests of those who belong to it. An organisation with a distinctive identity is socially cohesive. While, in fact, consensus is not possible in organisations, a presumed consensus is achievable, wherein nearly everyone presumes that nearly everyone agrees that what is actually happening ought to be happening. This presumed consensus helps to ensure a socially cohesive organisation, which endures across social space as well as over time.

Strategies for promoting a distinctive organisational identity

The role of governance is to promote survival by creating a distinctive identity. In this section of the chapter, we look at a selection of temporal, social and material strategies for administrators who wish to intervene in their schools to promote a distinctive identity. They are a foundation on which administrators can build a repertoire of strategies for intervention in their schools.

Strategy I: Clarify expectations

School administrators might find it useful to begin by identifying what is expected and enthusiastically conveying these expectations to all interested people as a challenge calling for commitment. The expectations, central to the distinctiveness of the school, can be clarified by means of specific strategies. Administrators can name the expectations in a few key phrases and reinforce them continually in policy documents, school magazines, newsletters, speech day reports, prospectuses, other public relations material and school histories. They will find it important to check all this material regularly to ensure that the expectations expressed in them are consistent. They can track statements of these expectations over time and check how often a particular expectation is expressed. One possibility is for administrators to telephone their own school when they are away for the day and test the expectations conveyed. Also, administrators could talk to their school's visitors about the visitors' reactions on their arrival at the school.

Strategy II: Tell the myths and saving stories

Administrators can engage narrative forms to identify the guiding myths and stories that shape the life of the school. The following ideas about storytelling are drawn from Dick and Dalmau (1991: 33–61), who suggest ways for participants to narrate the myths and saving stories. Participants are given simple instructions, such as: 'Make up a fairy story about our school. You need remember only two things: the way fairy stories begin, which is "Once upon a time . . . " and the way they end: " . . . and they all lived happily ever after".'

Dick and Dalmau (1991) also suggest a history trip. Participants arrange themselves in a semi-circle, with those who have been longest in the school at one end and those who have come to it most recently at the other. Beginning with those who have been at the school the longest, each participant tells the story of something that happened at the school not long after their arrival. Participants are given time to prepare their stories and invited to be brief—no more than two or three sentences for each story—what the incident meant to them at the time, and what it means now. The leader does not record anything but lets people converse about the incident if they wish, before moving on to the next person.

A further variation is to invite people to recall two critical incidents: one that occurred not long after they came to the school, and (when all those stories have been told) one that has occurred at any time since their arrival. Critical incidents are important, because they have meant surprise or disappointment for the person involved. Stories belonging to people's early days at a school reveal their own expectations, brought with them to the school, about what ought to have been happening; and the way they made sense of the incidents likewise reflects the set of expectations they had then. How they make sense of critical incidents should reveal the saving myths that now allow them to be comfortable with the surprise or disappointment such critical incidents bring.

Strategy III: Create relevant rituals

Ritual is found in all communities. Among its many functions, ritual is one of the main ways a community expresses and passes on its values. For school communities, ritual can be as simple and as profound as a sharing of food and drink. In every school there is contest—in the classroom, on the sports field, between the sexes, among staff and students and parents—but ritual can ameliorate any disappointment of this reality. One possibility open to administrators is to plan a week of special activities following a theme chosen by students and teachers. Students can choose songs, texts and ritual actions for celebrations focused on this theme. They can create appropriate decorations, prepare skits, stage a dance or organise a picnic with relay races, tug-of-war, and cheering contests. Students divided from staff by status, and students divided among themselves by different academic programs, different ideas of success and different degrees of power over their circumstances in the school, can temporarily be one in the enjoyment of laughing at teachers, booing at students and urging their team to pull even harder.

Strategy IV: Use sanctions and rewards

The imposition of sanctions is a familiar strategy for dealing with disappointing behaviour in schools, at least where students are concerned. Corporal punishment may be a thing of the past, but detentions, suspensions and even expulsions are ways of maintaining sets of expectations. Creative ways of rewarding those who do measure up to expectations should be a top priority for administrators.

The reward system operating in the school needs to be thoroughly checked as well, to make sure that it is really consistent with the expectations the school has set itself. Administrators could attend to a checklist of questions such as: who is successful in the school? who is feted? who is marginalised? who are the heroes? who are the villains?

Identifying the opportunities for reward through task enrichment, new assignments, trips away, representing the school, giving talks, attending special meetings, designing tasks and training for others, are examples of rewards that are likely to be received equally well by staff and students. Such rewards will underpin sets of expectations even more strongly than punishments, provided they are clearly tied to the fulfilment of those expectations to which the school attaches great significance.

Strategy V: Identify stakeholders

It will be important for the school administrator to identify the school's stakeholders and understand what their stake in the school comprises. These stakeholders can be invited to demonstrate a solidarity of effort to promote not merely what they stand for, but what the school stands for.

In situations of conflict between stakeholders, the administrator strives to increase the area of agreement between the two. This can be done using either consensual or dialectical processes (Dick and Dalmau 1991: 51–5). Consensual processes are those that seek to identify issues about which, potentially, the parties could be agreed. Dialectical processes involve, not position-taking, but dialogue, in an attempt to identify some area of agreement, which can then be expanded.

Sometimes a process by which a group develops a collective view about ends can assist in resolving interest-based conflict. One such process begins with an attempt to identify major external changes likely to affect the organisation and then envisions an ideal future for the organisation; the next step is to suggest how the organisation might move towards that future, and finally to decide on action plans for implementating those suggestions.

Strategy VI: Prepare an organisational audit

An organisational audit can help to identify the shared expectations of staff about 'what ought to be going on round here'. Administrators must look carefully at where and how these expectations are articulated. Deal and Kennedy's (1982) work on corporate cultures suggests that the assessment of prevailing sets of expectations should begin at the surface and proceed inwards. An appropriate place to begin an organisational audit would be the physical plant and equipment and then proceed to the less tangible dimensions of the school's life. An accurate audit should outdo almost any other barometer. It might reveal that the school must change in order to be truly distinctive. The following checklist could comprise an administrator's audit of the school.

Organisational Checklist

Study the physical setting Administrators concerned with the school's identity could start the checklist with an observation of the school's physical setting. However seemingly irrelevant to the conduct of schooling, the investment in bricks and mortar—the buildings and grounds—

inevitably indicates something of the school's sets of expectations. A school that is proud of itself and its culture will reflect this pride through its environment.

Read what the school says about its expectations The school's own statements reveal more than one would expect. All policy documents, school magazines, newsletters, speech day reports, prospectuses, other public relations material, and school histories can be read, and the school's statements in them carefully monitored for consistency. It is often possible to track school statements over time and watch how the sets of expectations evolve; this can be done by tabulating the number of times a particular phrase or belief is articulated in school publications. A warning: published statements are an inconclusive clue to sets of expectations, because administrators' public statements of belief sometimes can be revealed as little more than lip service.

Test how the school greets strangers In testing a culture, consultants usually strike up a conversation with the receptionist; they ask what the school is like and whether it's a good place to work. The responses indicate school values. Likewise, an inspection of the reception area's physical setting provides indications of the school's character. Is the reception area formal or informal? elegant or nondescript?

Interview school personnel It is important that administrators speak periodically and informally with staff, although an incoming administrator might wish to engage in more formal interviews. In talking to staff, administrators should look for consensual and conflicting perceptions. Some questions able to be asked are:

1. Tell me about the history of the school—what were its beginnings? This is a strategy for discovering the temporal and material underpinnings of the school's sets of expectations.
2. In what areas is the school successful? This is another way to discover the sets of expectations, because the satisfaction expressed will highlight what is expected.
3. What explains its growth? People may not be substantively correct, but they are reflecting their impressions of what the school values.
4. What kind of people work here? Who really gets ahead in the long term? The latter question uncovers reward expectations and may reveal how people deal with their disappointment when the real does not match the ideal.
5. What kind of place is this to work in? What is the average day like? How do things get done? The answers will typically characterise the important temporal factors, such as rituals, or the socio-political factors such as meetings and bureaucratic procedures.

Observe how people spend their time What people do is what they value; organisational choices reflect people's expectations. Administrators can compare what people say and what they really do. How they deal with any dissonance is a good indicator of their sets of expectations.

Check your objectivity as an observer Deal and Kennedy (1982) believe that an insider can go much deeper into organisational diagnosis, but they also warn of the pitfalls in achieving an accurate reading of one's own school. Any administrator can easily analyse the shortcomings and strengths of a competitor, but to understand their own school's sets of expectations, administrators must make one important distinction: to forget that they believe 'X' is the right way to make educational decisions. Instead, they must concentrate on how they and their colleagues typically make these decisions. To be an effective observer of one's own school, the administrator must avoid making value judgments about what is important and what is not. Administrators should observe what is—not what they think should be—and must remember that the patterns are subtle.

Understand the career path progression of staff Administrators need to take time to discover expectations and their affirmation by looking at who gets ahead in the school. If all important positions are filled by a certain type of person, it is reasonably clear what the school believes and values. Administrators can look for answers to the following questions: What does an employee have to do to get promoted? Does the school reward competence in key skills, or performance against objective criteria, tenure, and loyalty? Sets of expectations are primarily shaped by people's perceptions of what it takes to get ahead, and so a knowledge of these perceptions is critical for the observer. It is also important to consider how long people stay in jobs, particularly middle management jobs, since tenure is critical in any audit.

Look at the content of what is being discussed or written about A review of the content of formal discussions and other communications highlights the organisational choices, which reveal identity. People in management often spend an enormous amount of time reading and writing memos; administrators could take their in-box some week and simply tabulate it by subject matter. Similarly, during meetings, administrators might do well to sometimes forget the stated purpose of the meeting and keep track instead of what is actually discussed, who does the talking, and to whom; they might also track how much time is spent on each subject. However surprising the result, they will nonetheless discover that the school spends its time on what it values most, on what the school really stands for, which may be different from its publicly professed values. In looking at the content of discussions, administrators should pay attention to anecdotes and stories that pass through the cultural network, because these will give the administrator insight into how expectations persist over time in spite of the disappointment that people feel when expectations are not met. The stories are one way of dealing with disappointment.

Strategy VII: Initiate small changes

If change is needed, the administrator makes many swift, small starts with like-minded people who are committed to the success of these changes. Any administrator who wishes to change a school so that it will become more distinctive must realise that new staff, new roles, new programs and newly espoused values will not, in themselves, achieve the desired transformation. To deal only with such matters is to pay attention to just one dimension of organisational identity; but the more difficult temporal and social dimensions must also be tackled. Once again, sets of expectations must be clear. Not all members of staff need to share the leader's sets of expectations initially, but all must very soon be able to see that choices oriented by these sets of expectations do have desirable outcomes.

Strategy VIII: Publicise successful changes

It will probably be the case that no one in the school will disagree with the administrator's strategy; just as likely, most staff will have little or no faith in the strategy or in themselves. It will fall to the administrator to ensure that things are happening as they ought to be, at least until interventions begin to take effect and staff begin to see that the school is changing for the better. The administrator needs to make the school community aware of the success of the small starts.

Strategy IX: Create new myths and stories

Having assured the success of becoming and being more distinctive in some small ways, administrators must create new myths, invent new rituals and devise new sanctions to underpin the positive experience of a school's becoming more loving, more just, more forgiving, more compassionate, more committed to service, more peaceful, more hopeful or whatever the small start might have been.

Strategy X: Legitimise change

Finally, administrators need to pay attention to how the legitimacy of the new sets of expectations is to be achieved if the new sets of expectations are to be the subject of challenge.

Conclusion

Non-government schools in Australia have contributed greatly to the schooling of Australian children over the past two centuries. They have survived and flourished. But they are again at the crossroads, when failure to promote a distinctive identity for non-government schools could lead to a continued questioning of the rationale for their separateness, a decline in their popularity and perhaps the demise of these schools.

This chapter has offered three complementary tasks in which school administrators can engage to respond to this challenge. First, an administrator requires an understanding of history to gain perspective and assess possibilities for the present and future. Second, they must have an appreciation of contemporary ideas about organisational identity to assist in understanding their own school. Third, administrators require strategies that can be used to promote a distinctive school identity. These three tasks suggest an agenda for the preparation and selection of administrators in non-government schools. University departments of educational administration and professional associations have a share in the promotion of these disciplines. Selection panels can be alert to the capacity of a would-be administrator to understand their school's tradition and their determination to contribute to its distinctive depth and richness.

11 The Provision of Education and the Allocation of Resources

Brian J. Caldwell

Themes on the allocation of resources have moved to centre stage in the unfolding drama of public and private education in Australia. The drama is about restructuring in the design and delivery of the gamut of human services—education, health, law enforcement, transport, utilities and welfare—in a decade of societal transformation. As far as schools are concerned, these themes are defined by questions such as:

- What should be the roles of government at different levels and of parents and others in providing resources for education?
- How should resources be allocated to schools in systems of public and private education?
- At the school level, how should resources be acquired, deployed and accounted for, especially in systems where there has been significant decentralisation of responsibility, authority and accountability?

Such themes are contentious, because resources are scarce and there is much debate about the ends and means of schooling. They are especially so in the political and economic environment of the 1990s, with the first half of the decade characterised by slow recovery from extended recession, debt crises in public and private sectors, the emergence of a global economy, and the imperative to halt a slide through the ranks of nations as far as economic well-being is concerned.

Using the metaphor of drama taken up by Starratt (1993) in his analysis of leadership in education, the purpose of this chapter is to provide a descriptive and critical commentary on the unfolding drama of resource allocation in education. The starting point is a brief account of the manner in which education in Australia is currently resourced, noting in particular the roles and contributions of the public and private sectors. A framework of values seems to shape the drama, whatever the age, whatever the setting, and this is described before an historical account is provided of how that drama has unfolded in the last quarter of the twentieth century. Changes to roles and scripts are examined; the need for improvisation is noted. Offered next are outlines for scripts to address the themes set out above, essentially offering normative models to guide decisions in response to two key questions: 'How shall resources be allocated to schools?' and 'How shall resources be allocated within schools?' The evidence for a plot of 'economic rationalism' is tested and found wanting in some important respects. The chapter concludes by placing the themes on resource allocation in the larger drama of efforts to restructure schooling as the century draws to a close.

Tableau

School education is constitutionally the responsibility of states through their ministers of education, who are responsible for the provision of schooling to all students of school age. This responsibility is exercised through government departments. States provide public funds for government and non-government schools, with the former dependent to some extent on further contributions from their communities and the latter dependent to a much larger extent on student fees and other contributions from their communities. Staff in government schools are employed by the state. Each state has its own scheme of grants to address issues of equity.

Despite the constitutional role of states, the Commonwealth of Australia has an important role to play in the resourcing of school education through grants to state governments, systems of non-government schools and independent schools. For government schools, these arrangements are often made by agreement among ministers for education who meet as the Australian Education Council. As with the states, many of the resource arrangements involving the Commonwealth involve grants to address issues of equity.

It is beyond the scope of this chapter to provide details of financial arrangements, which change from year to year. Up-to-date reports are provided by the Australian Education Council, and these are readily available (see, for example, Australian Education Council 1992).

A conceptual framework for the allocation of resources

It is helpful to have a framework to describe and analyse the unfolding drama in the allocation of resources for schools. A starting point is to set that drama in the theatre of politics and economics along the lines proposed by Swanson and King (1991: 5), with politics 'the process by which *values* are allocated within society' and economics concerned with 'the allocation of *scarce resources* within society'. The objective is *efficiency*, defined as 'securing the highest level of societal satisfaction at the least cost of scarce resources'.

Schooling yields benefits for society and the individual. To use the language of the economist, it is both a public and private good, with decisions made in the public and private sectors.

> To ensure that both individual and societal demands for schooling are met, decisions about the provision of education are made in both the public and private sectors. Decisions in the public sector are made through political processes by governments, whereas decisions in the private sector are made by individuals using market mechanisms. (Swanson and King 1991: 5)

Framing education in politics and economics

Traditionally, educationists have been uncomfortable with the adoption of such a framework to describe their work and the manner in which resources should be allocated to support their efforts. Indeed, the negative connotation of 'economic rationalism' became associated with almost any effort to address economics and efficiency in education. It is therefore necessary to 'rescue' an honourable application of these concepts. At the same time, however, it is important to acknowledge that politics and economics are two of many frames for analysis. Bolman and Deal (1991) offer four frames for making sense of organisations: structural, human resource, political, and symbolic or cultural. Structural and symbolic or cultural frames are considered in other chapters. There will be distortion if an organisation such as a school or a system of schools is viewed through one or a small number of frames. There will be dysfunction if action is guided by a similarly narrow perspective. Using many frames is part of the artistry of leadership (Bolman and Deal 1991).

That the allocation of resources is a political activity, is surely beyond doubt. For the most part, it is an honourable activity, despite its complexity and conflict-ridden nature. The resourcing of systems of public education, the extending of state aid to private schooling, the introduction of grant schemes to redress disadvantage, and mobilisation for universal success to the end of secondary schooling are matters that were settled through political processes. In each instance, consistent with the definition of politics, the settlement involved the allocation of values, particularly the values of equity or equality and choice or liberty.

That the allocation of resources is also an economic activity is also beyond doubt, since resources are scarce. Such activity is neither intrinsically bad nor intrinsically good, but, like politics, it is complex and subject to conflict. If it is a science, it is not an exact science, because it involves the short- and long-term estimation of demand and resource availability, each of which is subject to fluctuation in a range of variables, not least of which is human motivation, as reflected in the desire for schooling and the willingness to pay for it, either personally or through contributions to public revenue.

That efficiency should be a central consideration is also understandable when viewed as 'securing the highest level of societal satisfaction at the least cost of scarce resources'. The arrangements among governments for resourcing schools (set out earlier in the chapter) reflect a settlement, at a particular time, of efforts to achieve this end through political processes in the face of scarce resources. On a broader scale, the allocation of resources across the public sector in the 1990s has been characterised by considerations of efficiency to a greater extent than in the 1980s. The securing of societal satisfaction is arguably a more difficult assignment than ever before, given goals for universal success to the end of secondary school; expectations for the best health care, including the full range of elective surgery, without waiting and in one's own neighbourhood; concern for better law enforcement in the face of rising crime; and higher demand for child care and welfare services with the increase in single-parent families. The difficulty is acute with an aging population, less willing to pay higher taxes, especially to support education; and when the economy is in such parlous state that revenue from the existing regime of taxes and other forms of state revenue to support the public sector are in decline. The task of setting priorities among competing calls on the public purse is an exacting one, which exposes the values that are allocated in the outcome.

Values in the allocation of resources

Efficiency is, at the same time, an objective and a value in the allocation of resources. Indeed, it is one of a number of values that underpin the politics and economics of education. There are five according to Swanson and King:

> Five values or objects of policy that have been historically prominent in shaping Western societies and are also particularly relevant to making decisions about the provision and consumption of educational services are liberty, equality, fraternity, efficiency and economic growth. Each has experienced ascendence and descendence in priority with changing societal circumstances, but none has ever lost its relevance entirely. The current shift in priorities placed on these five values underlies much of the controversy surrounding education today. (Swanson and King 1991: 22–3)

Garms, Guthrie and Pierce (1978: 18–19) identified equality, efficiency and liberty as three strongly held values that significantly influenced public policy in the United States and suggested that education is 'one of the prime instruments through which society attempts to promote all three values' (p. 19).

The five values identified by Swanson and King are evident in the Australian setting, and the view of Garms, Guthrie and Pierce also seems applicable in terms of expectations for schools. The value of efficiency has been clearly dominant for much of the decade, with liberty and equality evident in policies that foster parental choice and encourage universal success to the end of secondary school. The press for a return to economic growth has been constant.

The tensions among these values underlie much contention in policy-making in education. For example, a concern for efficiency in the face of a plateau or decline in economic growth has led in some states to the closing of schools or the curtailment of services to support special needs, thus challenging a commitment to equality in provision. The requirement that students attend their nearest school has been waived in most states in favour of a policy of de-zoning and parental and student choice. When combined with school grants of increasing size that follow the student according to the exercise of that choice, a market condition has been created, which challenges the value of fraternity that traditionally characterised the relationships among government schools.

The range of values allocated through the political process may reassure educators who are uncomfortable with the adoption of a framework in politics and economics. For example, the value of equality in the political frame is a value that underpins the culture of our society and our commitment to a system of public schools. The creation of a market condition is being tested, indeed challenged, by those who see a threat to this value. Expressed another way, the framework in political economy is a robust one if account is taken of the range of values that are at stake.

The unfolding drama

The balance of contention among these values is evident in the themes outlined at the start of the chapter, especially those that concern the allocation of resources *to* schools and *within* schools. It is worthwhile exploring how the drama has unfolded, briefly from the foundation of public education in Australia and more expansively for the last quarter of the century.

Foundations

An understanding of current and emerging patterns of resource allocation is best gained by setting events in an historical perspective. Public education, constitutionally a state responsibility in Australia, has been traditionally provided through a relatively centralised arrangement, wherein an education department, along with other agencies with particular responsibilities for personnel or curriculum, have made most of the important decisions affecting the allocation of resources. Apart from the public service traditions of government schooling, this approach was understandable, given the needs of a geographically dispersed population and assumptions about the desired uniformity of curriculum and approaches to teaching, each of which was monitored by a district inspector (primary) or teams of inspectors (secondary). Staff were allocated to schools according to a simple formula based on size and level of schooling; and supplies and equipment were allocated or requisitioned along similar lines. The value of equality was allocated uniformly. This pattern served Australia well, for it brought public education to virtually every student and every home in the nation. The achievements of government school systems throughout this era are to be cherished and celebrated.

The approach was not without its critics however. Visitors from overseas were often trenchant in their criticism, as in the case of Peter Goyen, Inspector of Schools for the Otago Education Board in New Zealand, who visited Australia in 1902. In Australia, he observed, 'the Department is everything and its influence everywhere, and every school is regarded not as a local institution in which every resident has a living interest, but as part and parcel of a huge machine controlled from the capital city'. In contrast, in New Zealand, 'everybody is interested, because everybody shares in its management' (cited in Phillips 1985: 84–5). In more recent times, the most widely-read questioning of approaches in Australia was offered by Professor Freeman Butts of Columbia University, New York, in his view of assumptions underlying Australian education. Butts (1961) offered essentially the same critique. What was being challenged was the ascendence of equality as uniformity and the absence of liberty (choice) and fraternity (community empowerment).

A new alignment of values

The major impetus for change came in the 1960s and early 1970s when a variety of political and social forces led to the intervention of the Commonwealth government in school education. Until this time, the involvement of the Commonwealth was largely limited to universities. The chief constraint, of course, was that constitutional power on matters related to education resided with the states. The first wave of involvement came with the great state-aid debates and concern about the provision of facilities for science. The provision of special Commonwealth grants for school education began. However, the major thrust came with the Report of the Interim Committee of the Australian Schools Commission (Karmel 1973) commissioned by the recently elected Labor government of Gough Whitlam, which led, in turn, to the creation of the Australian (later Commonwealth) Schools Commission. The major themes of the Karmel Report, and subsequent programs of the Commission, reflected a new alignment of values, especially in respect to equality, with a shift from uniformity to differential allocation of resources to redress disadvantage, and to fraternity in decision-making on resource allocation through the empowerment of communities. The following excerpts illustrate how these values resonate over the intervening years:

> The Commission favours less rather than more centralised control over the operation of schools. Responsibility should be devolved as far as possible upon the people involved in the actual task of schooling, in consultation with the parents of the pupils whom they teach and, at senior levels, with the students themselves. (Karmel 1973: 10)
>
> No single pattern is necessarily the best; diversified forms of schooling are an important part of the search for solutions. Increased resources made available to the schools will not necessarily result in children either learning better or being happier in them . . . This is an important reason for bringing responsibility back to the school . . . All-round improvements are more likely to emerge from experimentation with different approaches than from centralised administration of change. (Karmel 1973: 11–12)

The outcome was a series of special-purpose grants to states, many to be disbursed to schools on the basis of submissions prepared with staff and community input. The number of such grants increased rapidly, supplemented by others at the initiative of state governments. This pattern continued until well into the 1980s, with the demise of the Commonwealth Schools Commission not affecting the general pattern to any large extent.

These developments had two important legacies that are critically important to our understanding of subsequent events, as far as approaches to resource allocation are concerned. The first was the extraordinary growth in the size of state education departments. What were relatively simple centralised structures in the 1960s became complex, expanding bureaucracies in the 1970s and 1980s, as divisions and units were created to administer each of the special arrangements associated with these grants. Expanding enrolments, especially at the secondary level, contributed to complexity. One response was to create regional units of administration. Deconcentration of centralised arrangements rather than decentralisation of authority is the best descriptor of regionalisation. The size of the centre numbered in the thousands for the larger states.

Another development arose from the requirement of the Commonwealth Schools Commission and many state education departments that teachers and parents be involved in school-based decision-making in the preparation of school plans and submissions, and with the implementation of some programs. Against a social background of individual and community empowerment, the result was a range of structures for local decision-making, which in some instances led to the system-wide mandating of school councils or boards, notably in the Australian Capital Territory, South Australia and Victoria. Elsewhere, such structures were created on a voluntary basis.

These developments set the stage for the restructuring of large education departments, which was to gather momentum in the 1980s. Among a range of factors, the increasing cost of public education led to concerns about efficiency in the delivery of service. The large education departments and their heads were increasingly perceived as constrained in their capacity to respond to needs for change. The outcome was a steadily increasing stream of reports, commencing with a White Paper in Victoria in 1980 (Hunt and Lacy 1980) and the Hughes Report in Tasmania in 1982 (Hughes 1982). Restructuring, with reductions in the size of central arrangements, occurred in every state (see Harman, Beare and Berkeley 1991, for a comprehensive account). Gone was the concept of a permanent head and appointments of Directors-General from the ranks of educationists. Emerging was an interest in or mandating of school councils or some other form of school-based decision-making group. Decisions on selection for some categories of staff as well as authority and responsibility for an increased level of resourcing in school budgets also made their appearance.

Efforts to reduce the complexity of Commonwealth and state grant arrangements were made in the early 1990s, with the phrase 'broadbanded equity programs' being coined to describe the consolidation in a single grant (National Equity Program Scheme) of what were formerly a range of separate arrangements.

The Schools Council of the National Board of Employment, Education and Training has pressed the case for the decentralisation of decisions in respect to the allocation of resources, as reflected in the following excerpts from three reports in the early 1990s:

> Some fundamental delivery-system changes are required in Australian schooling. The success of the reforms currently in train will depend on two steps of faith. The first, emanating from governments and system administrators, will be the willingness to devolve genuine power to schools along with accountability for outcomes. The second, willingness to change stable patterns of behaviour and expectations, will have to

come from teachers themselves. (Schools Council 1990, *Australia's Teachers: An Agenda for the Next Decade*, p. 81)

... adopting more flexible approaches to the structures, organisation and procedures in the early years of schooling, is perceived as a constructive step towards achieving the full potential of the self-managing school. (Schools Council 1992, *Developing Flexible Strategies in the Early Years of Schooling: Purposes and Possibilities*, p. iii)

School communities should be able to demonstrate sufficient flexibility to respond positively and swiftly to changing needs and circumstances. If the goal of the self-managing school is to be realised, then schools should have the capacity to modify their resourcing arrangements to increase learning opportunities for all young adolescents. (Schools Council 1993, *In the Middle: Schooling for Young Adolescents*, p. 100)

The Report of the Interim Committee of the Australian Schools Commission (Karmel 1973) and the report of the Schools Council (1993) neatly span two decades of advice to the Commonwealth on matters related to the allocation of resources *to* schools and *within* schools. With the emerging interest in tighter centrally-determined frameworks for curriculum at the state (and territory) level and the possibility of a national curriculum framework, it is apparent that the value of equality has become much more complex, recapturing to an extent a measure of equality as uniformity as far as broad curriculum is concerned, but extending the view that there must be differential allocation of resources to support differential approaches to learning and teaching as the pressure continues for universal success in secondary schooling.

This historical perspective is incomplete without reference to the framework for industrial relations and the role of teacher unions. Centralised approaches have, until recently, characterised the Australian scene in almost every field of public and private enterprise, including education. It is understandable that the determination of awards has been the outcome of negotiations and the settlement of disputes between the parties at the peak level, between governments through their education departments and the teachers through their unions. Almost every aspect of working conditions has been determined on a more or less uniform basis, including key aspects of school and classroom organisation, such as maximum class size, length of the school day and school year, hours of teaching and areas of demarcation in relation to the work of others. In some instances, notably Victoria, the consistent application of these conditions has been secured through the involvement of the teacher unions through their representatives on Local Administrative Committees with whom principals must consult as decisions are made at the school level. This framework was reshaped in 1993, with aspects of individual contracts being addressed at the school level under the industrial relations reforms in Victoria (decentralisation), and the creation of the Australian Teaching Council (centralisation).

Outlines for scripts on key themes

The general shape of approaches to the delivery of public education in Australia became clear in the first years of the 1990s—essentially self-managing schools within a framework of centrally-determined goals, priorities, curriculum, standards and accountability. While the pattern varies from state to state, self-management has involved the allocation of a larger grant to schools, more involvement of the school in the selection of staff and the empowerment of the community through some form of school-based decision-making. If events over twenty or more years are taken into account, the trends have been evolutionary rather than revolutionary, with instances where major steps have been taken. The latter include the empowerment of school councils in Victoria in 1983 to determine the educational policies of the school within guidelines provided by the minister and to approve the budget of the school. In New South Wales, the recommendations in the Scott Report (Scott 1990) led to the introduction of global budgeting for schools. More recently in Victoria, the Schools of the Future reform announced in early 1993 (Hayward 1993) will lead to the most extensive decentralisation of school management in Australia, with schools responsible for planning the deployment of approximately 95 per cent of funds for school operations, the selection of staff and portion of employee agreements negotiated at the school level, and a school charter to guide the allocation of resources to schools and approaches to accountability.

It is beyond the scope of this chapter to note the parallels between these trends in Australia and developments in other nations, notably Britain, Canada, New Zealand and the United States (for accounts and critiques, see Beare and Boyd 1993; Caldwell 1993a; Caldwell and Spinks 1992; and Smyth 1993). Two matters are noteworthy. First, that trends in Australia differ significantly from developments in Britain and New Zealand in an important respect, namely that schools are self-managing rather than self-governing; they are not encouraged to 'opt out' and become grant-maintained schools, as in Britain, and teachers remain employed by the central authority, in contrast to grant-maintained schools in Britain or in the 'bulk-funded' schools that have been encouraged in New Zealand, where teachers are employed by their governing bodies. The distinction is critical as far as resource allocation is concerned.

The second matter concerns the way in which large-scale changes such as those in New South Wales and Victoria have occurred. Guthrie and Koppich (1993) propose a model of education reform that accounts for these and similar large-scale changes in other nations. The model proposes that three conditions coincide when major reform occurs: alignment, initiative and mobilisation. Alignment, or re-alignment, occurs when there is a conjunction of policy preferences, political problems, availability of alternatives and favourable politics. Initiative and mobilisation must then occur:

> Some individual or group or individuals must mobilize existing resources to take advantage of the window of opportunity . . . reform begs for 'policy entrepreneurs'. These are mobilizing individuals, or cohesive groups, who have at least two qualities. First, they want reform—in some manner they are advocates for change. In addition, they must be savvy politically to recognize a window of opportunity when it presents itself. (Guthrie and Koppich 1993: 24–5)

Events in New South Wales and Victoria have followed this script to a large extent. In Victoria, conditions did not coincide when the Labor government retreated from a proposal (Victoria, Ministry Structures Project Team 1986) to further decentralise the management of government schools in 1987; the politics were not favourable, with parent and teacher groups opposed. The window of opportunity was presented next with the change of government in 1992; but the incoming government had powerful majorities in both houses, and the state was beset with financial problems. New South Wales did not proceed with a proposal for the local selection of and budgeting for teachers (NSW Department of School Education 1992). The window of opportunity that may have been open to such a reform in the early years after the Scott Report (Scott 1990) was closed when the Greiner and Fahey governments found themselves on a political knife edge by 1993. Agreement not to proceed was reached with the New South Wales Teachers Federation.

A model for allocating resources to schools

To some extent, the failure to achieve coincidence in the Guthrie and Koppich scenario was a failure to reach settlement on a key value in politics: equality. The critics of reform in Victoria in 1987 and New South Wales in 1992 charged that the decentralisation of decisions related to resources, notably the staff resource, would lead to inequity in the allocation of resources to schools. It seemed to be assumed that the proposed approach would revert to uniform allocation rather than extend the trend in recent years to differential resourcing in response to different needs among students. Moreover, instances were cited of failure to address the equality or equity issue in Britain and New Zealand.

Governments in New South Wales and Victoria were unable to demonstrate how these concerns could be addressed. The same concerns

THE PROVISION OF EDUCATION AND THE ALLOCATION OF RESOURCES

Table 11.1 Student-centred resource allocation to schools in Edmonton Public School District, Alberta, Canada, for 1993–1994

Level	Ratio	Allocation per student ($C)	Illustration of learning needs to be satisfied at this level of resourcing
1	1.00	$3 161	Students in regular kindergarten, primary, junior high or senior high programs
2	1.27	$4 025	Students enrolled in primary or junior high who require differentiated programs of instruction; senior high other than learning needs at Level 1; English as a Second Language
3	1.42	$4 477	Students in trades and services programs
4	1.67	$5 268	Students with serious difficulties in academic learning who require special assistance
5	2.46	$7 791	Students enrolled in specialist facilities for the learning disabled.
6	2.74	$8 652	Students of primary, junior high and senior high age who are moderately mentally or physically handicapped
7	4.24	$13 417	Students who are behaviour disordered, dependent handicapped, hearing impaired, multihandicapped, physically handicapped, or visually impaired
8	6.34	$20 034	Students who are hearing impaired, visually impaired, autistic, deaf and blind, or physically handicapped requiring resourcing at levels higher than Level 7

were raised with the unveiling of the Schools of the Future reform in Victoria in 1993. On this occasion, however, policy-makers were aware of other models for allocating resources to schools which addressed the equity issue. These derived from practice in the Edmonton Public School District in Alberta, Canada, which has had the longest continuing experience with school-based management in North America. The major features are illustrated in Table 11.1, with allocations (per student) for 1993/94 reflecting the relative costs of meeting the educational needs of students enrolled in different educational programs (for details, see Edmonton Public Schools 1993).

Allocations in Edmonton range from a basic $3161 for students involved in regular programs in kindergarten, elementary, junior high and senior high to $20 034 for students who are autistic, or have the highest level of learning or physical handicap. The eight levels of funding reflect the known differential costs of providing schooling for children with a range of educational needs, including those with learning difficulty as well as those who are academically gifted. The total allocation for a school consists of the total of per student allocations based on the student learning need profile to which are added special amounts reflecting community use of schools, participation by some in a pilot program for the purchase of consulting services, designation as a community school, rapid enrolment growth, start-up costs of new programs, higher needs reflecting the characteristics of a school's student community, and additional costs incurred by small schools. Special education schools are funded on a school-by-school basis.

The total allocation provides a frame for school planning, including the mix of staff and non-staff resources. Of special importance in the light of critical commentary in the international setting is the manner in which schools are charged for staff—namely, on the basis of average salary costs for different categories of staff across the system. In a sense, schools are allocated resources and are charged for staff on the basis of system average staff costs. This differs from situations in some parts of Britain, where the total grant to a school is based on system average staff costs but the school is charged real costs of staff deployed at the school. The British experience has led to situations where some schools have had to dramatically restructure staff profiles to manage their budgets.

Table 11.2 contains the allocation of resources to an elementary–junior high school (K–9) in Edmonton. It is noteworthy that these amounts were advised on 27 January 1993 for the commencement of the next academic year in September 1993, based on the projected profile of student enrolment and program, thus allowing adequate time for the principal and staff of the school to plan for 1993/94. The example furnishes evidence that equity can be addressed to a higher level than has hitherto been the case in Australia, for it is a far cry from the uniformity of allocation that prevailed for much of this century in most systems. In other words, it moves the value of equality further from uniformity towards resourcing that matches individual learning needs.

There has been progress toward an Edmonton-style model in a number of Australian states, notably Tasmania, which has led the nation in school-based budgeting since the mid-1970s. Tasmania takes account of the needs of remote and isolated schools in determining allocations to schools. Extension of this approach was recommended in 1993 (Caldwell 1993b). The groundwork for an Edmonton-style model was also laid in Victoria in early 1993, with a report recommending differential per student funding to address special education needs (Pickering 1993).

An indicator of the acceptability of the Edmonton approach is offered by the responses to surveys of principals, teachers, parents and students, conducted annually since the early 1980s. Views on equity in resource allocation have been sought. Brown's independent appraisal of the findings is striking:

> The Edmonton surveys reveal an increase in outcomes in the form of satisfactions registered by large numbers of parents, students and person-

Table 11.2: Edmonton Public School District's allocation forecast 1993/94 to one school, an elementary-junior high*

Students	Programs	Amount ($C)
10	Regular kindergarten	15 806
38	Regular elementary (1–6)	120 126
70	Bilingual-German (J-H)	221 285
3	Home schooling (J-H)	9 484
76	Regular junior high	240 252
4	Academic challenge (J-H)	16 100
1	Academic assistance	5 268
5	Adaptation	26 339
2	Behaviour disordered	26 833
1	Dependent handicapped	13 417
1	ESL elementary	4 025
1	ESL junior high	4 025
4	Multi-handicapped Level 7	53 667
19	Multi-handicapped Level 8	380 646
	1st program	89 885
	2nd program	58 844
	3rd program	50 344
	Community use of schools	3 298
	Consulting services project	22 049
	High needs	16 795
	Multiple program adjustment	-20 138
	Secondary learning resources	2 475
	Utilities	46 266
235	Total resource allocation	$1 407 091

* Advice to school on 27 January 1993, for next academic year commencing September 1993.

nel working in schools and the district office. These results appear stable, significant, and superior to those observed in general surveys conducted in the rest of Canada and the United States. (Brown 1990: 347)

The challenge in Australia is to determine an equitable approach to the allocation of resources to schools, which takes account of different costs for various programs. It is dismaying that these costs are not known as a matter of course; in most places, the data base does not exist and must now be established.

A model for allocating resources within schools

There can be no standard script for allocating resources to schools but there are models for the process. Such a model was proposed by Caldwell and Spinks (1988) in *The Self-Managing School*. An updated model, which takes account of the context for the 1990s, was set out in *Leading the Self-Managing School* (Caldwell and Spinks 1992) and is illustrated in Figure 11.1.

The annual management cycle in the lower half of Figure 11.1 is similar to others in general texts on management and administration, but it makes a special contribution in three ways: (1) it specifies the phases that are the concern of the group responsible for policy-making in the school (the policy group) and of other phases that are the concern of groups responsible for implementing policy (program teams); (2) it defines policy that goes beyond a statement of general aims or purposes but is not so detailed as to specify action—it provides a brief statement of purpose and a set of broad guidelines; and (3) it organises planning activities around programs that correspond to the normal patterns of work in the school.

The distinction between 'policy group' and 'program teams' provides the framework for a collaborative approach to the school management, hence its original designation as the Collaborative School Management Cycle. The people who constitute the policy group vary according to the setting. Where the wider community is not involved, the policy group may be the principal alone, or the principal and senior teachers, or the principal and senior teachers with advice from other teachers and members of the school community. There may, in some instances, be different policy groups in the school, each addressing different sets of issues.

The school's activities associated with learning and teaching and which support learning and teaching are divided into programs. The policies and priorities set by the policy group shape the planning of these programs by members of the program teams, who in most instances will be teachers. Program teams are responsible for preparing a plan for implementation of policies related to their programs and for identifying the resources required to support that plan. A program plan and the proposed pattern for resource allocation together constitute a program budget.

While program budgets are prepared by program teams, they must be approved by the policy group; they must reflect the policies and priorities established earlier by that group. Following implementation by program teams, the evaluating phase is again a shared responsibility—the program teams gathering information for program evaluation, and the policy group gathering further information as appropriate to make judgements on the effectiveness of policies and programs.

In general, then, referring again to Figure 11.1, the policy group has responsibility for phases emphasised with black borders, while program teams work within a framework of policy to take responsibility for the remaining phases. It is important to note that while a clear distinction is made between the responsibilities of the policy group and program teams, there will, in fact, be a high degree of overlap as far as personnel are concerned, and a continuing high level of formal and informal communication. The principal and some teachers will, for example, be members of the policy group and program teams where the policy group is a school council that includes representatives of teachers. The policy group may frequently depend on the principal and program team for the development of policy options. Illustrations and guidelines for each phase of the model, as outlined thus far, are contained in *The Self-Managing School* (Caldwell and Spinks 1988).

Figure 11.1 A model for the allocation of resources within schools

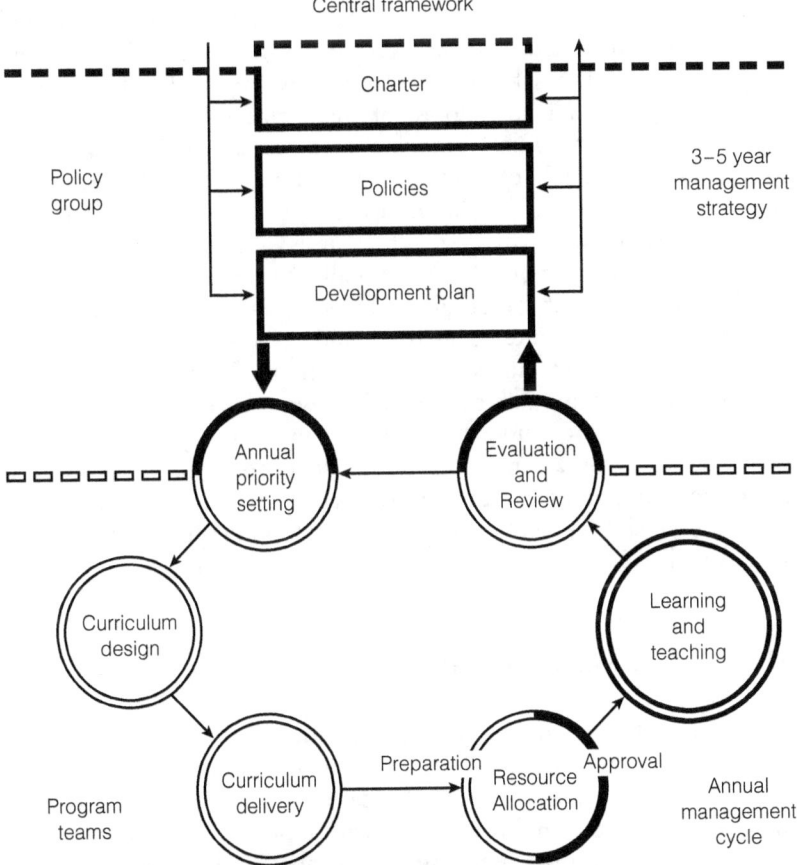

Source: B.J. Caldwell and J.M. Spinks (1992) *Leading the Self-Managing School*, London and Washington DC: The Falmer Press

The upper half of Figure 11.1 highlights the importance for schools in the 1990s to work within a three- to five-year management plan. A school charter is proposed, this being a document to which both government and school policy group (council, board) have given their assent, containing a summary of the centrally-determined framework of priorities and standards; an outline of the means by which the school will address this framework; an account of the school's mission, vision, priorities, needs and programs, together with an overview of strategies that will be followed in addressing them; reference to key decision-making processes and approaches to program evaluation; all reflecting the culture of the school and an intended pattern of action in the medium to longer term. Once approved, the charter becomes the basis for allocating resources and monitoring outcomes. The charter is a key element in the Schools of the Future reform in Victoria.

The development plan, often described as an improvement plan or strategic plan or corporate plan, is a specification in general terms of priorities to be addressed, and of strategies to be employed in addressing those priorities, as the school seeks to achieve multiple objectives over a number of years. The development plan, along with the charter and policies of the school, is an outcome of a three- to five-year strategic management plan. Each of these features illustrated in the top half of Figure 11.1 is important for the allocation of resources in the school.

Returning to the drama metaphor, it is important that the model does not become the script. One should also be mindful of the limitations of models in the spirit of Sergiovanni and Starratt, who asserted that 'when proposed and marketed as truth and prescribed . . . as a one best way to achieve, they are likely to be ill-fitting to the realities of practice'. They proposed that models be viewed as ways to think about practice, providing 'frames for understanding the problems professionals face'. Models, they believe 'are not true with respect to telling the professional what to do but are useful for informing the professional's judgement, guiding the decision-making process, and making professional practice more rational'. (Sergiovanni and Starratt 1988: 40–4)

Is there an economic rationalist plot?

There has been much debate about the extent to which the allocation of resources in education has been shaped by economic rationalism. As far as the themes canvassed in this chapter are concerned, an examination of the evidence would indicate only partial support for the charge. Much depends, of course, on the meaning one ascribes to economic rationalism. If it is synonymous with economics, then all matters related to the allocation of scarce resources would be instances of economic rationalism.

So, too, with the efforts of governments to achieve efficiency in the public sector under conditions prevailing in some states, as in Tasmania and Victoria in the early 1990s. These views of economic rationalism are too broad. That observation made, a case can be mounted about excessive zeal or haste in efforts to achieve greater efficiency. Some would place in this category the adoption of national averages as national norms on key indicators such as student–teacher ratios. This was the case with the Cresap Review in Tasmania (see Caldwell 1991) and the activities of the Victorian Commission of Audit (1993), each of which treated national averages in data provided by the Commonwealth Grants Commission as a norm for resource allocation for schools in their respective states.

Pusey (1991: 210) provided a helpful view of economic rationalism with his description of an economically rational system as one that attempts to achieve the tightest possible linkage between four systems: the world economic system, the national economic system, the political administrative system and the socio-cultural system. In the case of education, the critique may apply in efforts to tightly link education and training to the economic needs of the nation (see the critique of economic rationalism in education of Marginson 1993, and of 'economic essentialism' in the competency movement offered by Porter et al. 1992).

Except where it is inextricably linked with excessively zealous efforts to achieve greater efficiency, it is difficult to see the trend to self-managing schools as an economic rationalist plot, given the manner in which the drama has unfolded in recent decades. The intention has been to sustain but refocus the value of equality to ensure the allocation of resources to meet, as far as possible under conditions of scarcity, the educational needs of all students.

In the final analysis, however, one is confronted by the narrowness of a purely economic view of humankind. As Harper (1993: 41) has expressed it, 'Economics is the study of the *material* condition of humankind; it has nothing to tell us about the *spiritual* condition of humankind, a task which properly belongs to theology.'

The big drama

While trends and issues in resource allocation for schools in Australia may be significant, they should be seen against the larger drama that is unfolding, as far as societal transformation is concerned. Drucker casts this drama in epic terms:

> Every few hundred years in Western history there occurs a sharp transformation . . . Within a few short decades, society rearranges itself—its worldview; its basic values; its social and political structures; its arts; its

key institutions. Fifty years later, there is a new world . . . We are currently living through such a transformation. (Drucker 1993: 1)

According to Drucker, knowledge as a resource lies at the heart of such transformations over the past three centuries. Until the Industrial Revolution, knowledge had been seen as applying to *being*, a private good. It then became a resource for *doing*; it also became a public good. After the Industrial Revolution and until about the Second World War, knowledge was applied to *improving the doing*. These transformations characterised a capitalist society in which the factors of production were capital and labor. Since the Second World War, however, knowledge is being applied to *knowledge* itself, so that 'knowledge is fast becoming the sole factor of production, sidelining both capital and labor' (Drucker 1993: 19). It is now a post-capitalist society. The implications for schools are profound:

> As knowledge becomes the resource of post-capitalist society, the social position of school as 'producer' and 'distributive channel' of knowledge, and its monopoly, are both bound to be challenged. And some of the competitors are bound to succeed . . . Indeed, no other institution faces challenges as radical as those that will transform the school. (Drucker 1993: 209)

If Drucker is correct, and his analyses in recent years have been penetratingly accurate, then the implications for resourcing Australia's schools are profound. It should become the pre-eminent priority in the national agenda, publicly and privately. But it will be a commitment to a transformation of schooling. It would appear that this transformation has only just begun.

12 The Statutory Framework of Education and Legal Issues of Concern for Administrators*

Ann R. Shorten

Educational administrators are becoming increasingly aware of the interface of education and the law. The chapter provides a brief outline of *some* aspects of statute law and case law as they relate to education. Such an outline survey is necessarily selective, and many issues (for example, issues relating to criminal law and contract law) are either not canvassed or are mentioned only very briefly. Nevertheless this survey highlights a number of basic issues for educational administrators and teachers. The first of these issues is that they need to be aware that the law changes constantly. The second issue is that they need to be aware of their statutory responsibilities and to develop appropriate policies and procedures to meet these responsibilities. The third issue is that there should be awareness of the responsibilities of educators and educational administrators at common law. Finally, educational administrators and teachers do need to be aware that, whatever the changes that may occur in the future, these basic issues will remain.

The law relating to education is found in statute law, in subordinate legislation (that is, statutory rules and regulations) and in case law (that is, law derived from the decisions of the courts). The executive arm of government may also make laws in the form of orders of the governor-

---

* The author wishes to acknowledge the kindness of Ms J. Blakie, barrister-at-law, Victoria, and Mr K. Dare, barrister and solicitor, Victoria, in critically reviewing the drafts of this chapter, but stresses that responsibility for the selection of the material and the views expressed in the chapter lies with the author.

Every effort has been made to ensure that the material in this chapter is as accurate as possible. However, the author, editors and publisher are not responsible for any error or omission in the contents of the chapter. The author, editors and publisher do not provide professional legal advice and expressly disclaim any liability and responsibility to any person placing any reliance on any part of the contents of this chapter.

Reference numbers in this chapter refer to notes on p. 203.

in-council, ministerial orders and proclamations.[1] It is useful to keep in mind that statute law made by parliaments may override the common law, and also that subordinate legislation can only be made according to powers set out in the specific act of parliament. Because there is a considerable volume of law relevant to the administration of education, and aspects of that law change constantly, it is essential that the accuracy of legal information at any given time be ascertained. Although educational administrators should take every opportunity to keep their general knowledge of legal issues in education up-to-date, in practice when dealing with specific matters they should seek legal advice from an appropriately qualified practitioner. However, it must be realised that it is not possible for expert advisers to offer immediate advice for every situation that may arise.

The statutory framework of education in the Australian states and territories

The importance of the statutory framework of education in Australia cannot be overemphasised. It determines how education is organised and financed, and the powers and responsibilities of the participants in the educational process for the development and implementation of educational policy.

Commonwealth involvement in education

In recent decades one of the most important legal issues in education has been the increasing involvement of the Commonwealth government in education.[2] At Federation in 1901, education was a power that remained with the states, and the *Commonwealth Constitution* did not give any direct power over education to the Commonwealth government. However, during the decades since Federation, there has been increasing Commonwealth involvement in the funding of all levels of education.[3] There has been a concomitant growth of Commonwealth legislation concerning education. A current major act is the *Employment Education and Training Act* 1988, which *inter alia* established the National Board of Employment, Education and Training, and four other councils, the Schools Council, the Higher Education Council, the Employment and Skills Formation Council and the Australian Research Council, to provide information and advice to the Minister concerning the development of policies relating to education and the funding of education by the Commonwealth. The Commonwealth has also taken a strong interest in Aboriginal and Torres Strait Islander education.[4] Specific funding legislation is passed for grants to the states for schools, for the technical and further education (TAFE) sector, and for higher education.[5] Commonwealth legislation also provides for charges for students, both local and overseas,[6] and for financial assistance to students,[7] and for the regulation of providers of education to overseas students.[8] This Commonwealth legislation has given rise to some cases brought by non-government school authorities relating to its interpretation[9] and to some cases where judicial review has been sought of administrative action taken under the legislation.[10]

State and territory legislation for school education

The state and territory Education Acts are of prime importance and generally provide for primary and secondary education, and in some jurisdictions for preschool education.[11] The Acts provide for the establishment and operation of the administrative infrastructure for the provision of education. They also define parental duties and rights as far as compulsory education is concerned.[12] In most jurisdictions they provide for the registration of non-government schools,[13] and in some jurisdictions for the registration of teachers.[14] Further, in several jurisdictions there are one or more additional Acts dealing with matters that may not be included in the principal Act. These supplementary Acts may deal with matters such as the structure of the relevant education authority, the organisation of the teaching service, the organisation and powers of school councils, or the establishment of curriculum and assessment authorities and advisory boards.[15] It does not put the matter too highly to say that the legislative schemes of the principal Acts, and of the relevant supplementary Acts, result in the effective centralisation of the control of education in each jurisdiction.

The provision of primary and secondary education

In general, the parliaments have given broad discretionary powers to the relevant minister as far as the provision of education in each jurisdiction is concerned,[16] although in most jurisdictions there is express legislative provision for the appointment of councils or boards to provide advice to the ministers.[17] There are also certain specific powers conferred on the chief administrators of the ministries or departments. The Education Acts also usually provide for the ministers and chief administrators to delegate their powers.[18] School councils are statutory bodies and derive their powers and responsibilities for the management of government schools solely from legislation and subordinate legislation, although these powers and responsibilities are also generally limited by ministerial direction. Members of school councils are generally parents and teachers.[19] The law regulating the management of schools is also to be found in the statutory rules—that is, the regulations made under the Acts—as well as in ministerial orders and departmental rules.[20] Administrative guidelines will also be issued to assist the implementation of educational policy.

The state and territory parliaments have not generally imposed an express statutory duty upon the state and territory education authorities to provide education for every child according to that child's needs as an individual, although the New South Wales *Education Reform Act* 1990 does include in the principles upon which the Act is based the provision that 'the principal responsibility of the State in the education of children is the provision of public education.'[21] The Acts in the Australian Capital Territory, the Northern Territory and Queensland do seem to go further than the Acts in the other jurisdictions in defining ministerial responsibilities in the provision of educational facilities.[22] Save in the Australian Capital Territory, the principal Acts provide for special education, although at the time of writing no Act contains express reference to the integration of special education students in mainstream schools, although this is a widely adopted policy.[23]

The principal Acts in New South Wales, Queensland and Tasmania expressly state that instruction provided in state schools is to be free.[24] The Victorian Act provides that instruction in certain subjects is to be free to all pupils at government schools, except for overseas students.[25] The Western Australian Act provides that instruction in pre-primary and primary schools is to be free, but that the Minister may authorise the payment of fees for instruction in any other government school.[26] The legislation in the Northern Territory and South Australia is silent on the matter of fees although in South Australia fees may be charged to overseas students, and in the Australian Capital Territory express provision is made for charging fees in preschools.[27] Consequently, whether or not fees are charged may, in some jurisdictions, be a matter of policy rather than of law.

Parental duties and rights
All the principal Acts make it a parental duty to see that children of compulsory school age are enrolled in and attend school. This duty may be satisfied by attendance at a non-government school.[28] There are also statutory provisions for exemptions from compulsory attendance in certain circumstances, which include the situation where the child is under efficient and regular instruction in some other manner, which may include home tuition, and for the exclusion of children from school in certain circumstances.[29] The New South Wales *Education Reform Act* 1990 provides for statutory registration for children for home schooling and also for conscientious objection on religious grounds to such registration.[30]

The Australian parliaments have not generally seen fit to place any duty on state education authorities to take account of parental wishes in the education provided for children. The New South Wales *Education Reform Act* 1990 does include the proposition that 'the education of the child is primarily the responsibility of the child's parents' in the principles upon which the Act is based, but it is presently unclear what might be the practical legal effect of the inclusion of this principle in determining how far parental wishes are to be taken into account.[31] The compulsory education provisions of the principal Acts do provide for parents the right to choose that a child attend a non-government school or alternatively satisfy the educational authority that their children are receiving efficient instruction.[32] However, parents do not necessarily have a right to send a child to the government school of their choice, and the principal Acts are generally silent as to parental choice of government schools.[33] Generally, the principal Acts that make provision for religious instruction to be given in schools in certain circumstances expressly provide that parents can withdraw their children from religious instruction classes, and in the Northern Territory and South Australia there is express provision for the right of withdrawal from other specified classes. However, policy provision may be made in other jurisdictions for such conscientious withdrawal from specified classes.[34]

The registration of non-government schools
In all jurisdictions apart from Queensland, the Education Acts provide that non-government primary and secondary schools must be registered, and the establishment, maintenance and conduct of unregistered schools is proscribed by the Acts.[35] In South Australia, Tasmania and Victoria statutory boards are given the task of determining matters relating to the registrations of schools. In the Australian Capital Territory and Western Australia that power is given to the Minister, and in the Northern Territory it rests with the Secretary to the Department of Education. In New South Wales also the power rests with the Minister, who is to take into account the recommendation of the Board of Studies. As a general rule, non-government schools seeking initial registration or maintenance of registration are required to satisfy the registering authority as to a number of matters, which include curriculum, the qualifications of teaching staff and the physical condition of the school property.[36] In Tasmania and South Australia, there is provision for decisions of the registration authority to be subject to review by a court, and in the Australian Capital Territory, by the ACT Administrative Appeals Tribunal.[37] In the Northern Territory and in Victoria there is statutory provision for appeal to the Minister, and in New South Wales the Minister in dealing with appeals relating to the registration of schools is required to take into account the outcome of any appeal to the Schools Appeals Tribunal.[38] Educational authorities dealing with matters of school

registration will also fall within the purview of the law in the relevant jurisdiction as it relates to judicial review of administrative actions.

The New South Wales *Education Reform Act* 1990 provides for conscientious objection to the registration of a non-government school, and the discretion to recognise such conscientious objection resides in the Minister, who has however to consider a report made by the Board of Studies, and any decision of the Schools Appeal Tribunal if an appeal is made to that body.[39] It should also be noted that although the Queensland *Education (General Provisions) Act* 1989 does not provide for the registration of non-government schools, it does provide that the Minister may authorise an inspection of a non-government school, attended by children whose parents have received a dispensation from compliance with the compulsory attendance provisions of the Act, where a complaint is received of a matter that may threaten or interfere with the education of students in a non-government school, and the Minister considers the complaint is not vexatious or frivolous.[40]

Legislation relating to post-secondary education

In all jurisdictions, legislation relating to post-secondary education generally covers technical and further education, vocational education and higher education, and in some jurisdictions, such as New South Wales and Victoria, there is legislation dedicated to adult education.[41] However, in other jurisdictions adult education is provided for in the principal Education Act or in the legislation relating to technical and further education.[42]

TAFE and vocational education

The *Australian National Training Authority Act* 1992 established the Australian National Training Authority. The state and territory legislation relating to technical and further education generally provides for broad discretionary powers for the relevant minister, and for a relatively complex structure of statutory advisory boards and committees and institutional councils for the governance of TAFE colleges.[43] There may also be separate legislation providing for vocational education—that is for the conditions governing apprenticeships and traineeships. There is similar provision for broad discretionary powers for the relevant minister, for the establishment of statutory boards for vocational education, and for the involvement of representatives of industry and commerce on advisory boards and committees. Legislative provision is usually made for accreditation of programs of vocational education and training.[44]

Higher education

There has been much change in higher education in recent years. A current issue is the extent to which institutional autonomy remains a significant characteristic of public universities given their reliance on federal and state government funding, and the increasing involvement of the Commonwealth in the formation of policies relating to the provision of higher education. The Commonwealth *Employment, Education and Training Act* 1988 provided that all institutions of higher education would become universities. Historically, universities as institutions of learning had certain distinctive attributes, which included being engaged in the higher branches of learning, such as theology, law, philosophy and medicine, and having certain rights and privileges including the right to confer degrees. However, an essential criterion of a university was that it was, as an institution of learning, a body incorporated by the sovereign power of the state. Consequently, today each university, whether public or private, is incorporated by its own founding statute, which provides for its constitution and governance.

Generally, there is a council or senate, which has the power to make statutes and regulations for the university with respect to all matters, including the appointment of staff, the matriculation of students, the granting of degrees, and the establishment and affiliation of colleges of the university. Universities have extensive powers relating to financial matters and the acquisition and disposition of property.[45] Most, but not all university statutes,[46] provide that the Governor in the relevant jurisdiction is to be the Visitor to the university. The Visitor has the jurisdiction to resolve disputes that arise within a university and to grant relief if this is in the best interests of the university. The Visitor's jurisdiction is usually held to be an exclusive jurisdiction.[47] It may also be noted that it has been a traditional feature of the founding statutes of Australian universities to proscribe religious and political tests, and in some of the more recent statutes other forms of discrimination are also proscribed.[48]

Statutory responsibilities of educational authorities

Statutes specifically relating to education are not the only legislation of significance for educational administrators. Educational authorities have a number of responsibilities cast upon them by other statutes. This is not necessarily an onerous burden if appropriate legal advice is sought. What educational administrators must undertake, after consultation with their legal advisers, is the development and implementation of appropriate administrative policies and procedures. This necessarily requires that all staff are properly informed of the significance of the policies and procedures they are required to follow. Some of these legislative responsibilities may fall on educational authorities in their capacity as employers, but others will arise in the course of their specifically educational activities.

Some general statutory responsibilities of educational authorities as employers

A range of both state and Commonwealth legislation relating to employees and their conditions of employment raises responsibilities for educational authorities. Workers' compensation legislation, occupational health and safety legislation, anti-discrimination law, affirmative action legislation, taxation and superannuation law, and industrial law are obvious examples. It is not possible within the scope of the chapter to describe in any worthwhile detail the obligations imposed by these laws on educational authorities as employers, but it must be emphasised that educational authorities must be fully aware of their responsibilities and must develop sound policies and administrative procedures to ensure compliance with the legislation.

Some statutory responsibilities that relate to educational activities

In certain jurisdictions public educational authorities may fall within the operation of Freedom of Information legislation.[49] Briefly, the purpose of this legislation is to give people rights to obtain information held by government authorities and to see documents relating to them personally and to correct these documents if they are inaccurate. Certain materials may, however, be exempt from disclosure under the legislation.[50] It is not possible within the scope of this chapter to provide a detailed account of these Acts, but for educational administrators the major issue is the very practical one of seeking expert advice as to the requirements of the legislation relevant to them, and ensuring that procedures are in place for handling any inquiries made under the legislation.

Another law that raises responsibilities for educational administrators is the Commonwealth *Copyright Act* 1968. The scheme of the *Copyright Act* 1968 is too complex to describe within the limits of this chapter, but educators and educational administrators should be aware that the Australian Copyright Council is an excellent source of information about this Act.[51] Educational authorities will be aware that the Act provides for certain exceptions and statutory licences to enable the use of works for educational purposes. However, the statutory conditions governing the use of all copyright materials must be strictly observed. Educational administrators do need to have in place administrative procedures which comply appropriately with the recording and reporting requirements of the copyright agencies. Some umbrella agreements have been made between educational authorities and agencies such as the Copyright

Agency Limited, which prevent or reduce the risk of staff and students breaching copyright ownership or licences. It may also be noted that the staff and students may themselves be owners of copyright material, although there can be exceptions to this rule relating to materials created in the course of employment. Further difficult questions can arise where there may be joint owners of copyright interests. In addition, there is legislation relating to patents, trademarks and designs, which can be relevant to the work of educational institutions where research is undertaken. This law relating to intellectual property rights is a complex area, and educational authorities and institutions should seek legal advice concerning issues in this field.

Educational authorities are undoubtedly well aware of their responsibilities as employers under the anti-discrimination legislation, but they need to be aware also of the impact of that legislation upon their educational activities. At the time of writing there is anti-discrimination law in the federal jurisdiction,[52] and in every state and territory except Tasmania.[53] This legislation proscribes direct and indirect discrimination against persons on certain grounds, which may include, depending upon the particular Act, race, colour, sex, religion, political views, marital status, pregnancy, mental, intellectual and physical disability, and sexuality, in certain areas of activity. Generally, education is one of the areas of activity covered by the Acts, which typically proscribe discrimination against students in their admission to educational institutions and in their access to the benefits provided by the institutions. However, some private educational institutions may be excluded from the operation of this legislation, and certain activities may come within the statutory exceptions provided for in the legislation. Educational administrators must, however, seek advice as to the detail of the provisions of the legislation relevant to the jurisdiction in which they live.

It is also necessary to be aware of the need to develop effective equal opportunity policies, not only in relation to employment matters but also in relation to educational matters. The need to avoid discriminatory policies and practices in the provision of education has been highlighted by the decisions in *Haines* v. *Leves*[54] where the New South Wales Court of Appeal upheld the determination of the New South Wales Equal Opportunity Tribunal, which had found discrimination on the ground of sex in the failure of the Minister of Education, who was held to be the responsible 'educational authority', to provide for a student at a girls' high school the same range of subjects as those made available to students at a nearby boys' high school.

Generally, the anti-discrimination Acts proscribe sexual harassment. The Acts define what constitutes sexual harassment, and although those definitions are similar but not identical, sexual harassment may be described as being the kinds of behaviours in which there is unwelcome making of sexual advances, or unwelcome requesting of sexual favours, or the making of verbal or written statements of a sexual nature, so that another person reasonably feels offended, humiliated or intimidated and is threatened with disadvantage in employment or education if he or she resists these advances.[55] Educational administrators should be aware that behaviour that constitutes sexual harassment may occur in educational institutions, and the development of clear policies discouraging such behaviours and providing procedures for the reporting of alleged incidents should be a matter of the highest importance.

School educators and the *Family Law Act* 1975

The Commonwealth *Family Law Act* 1975 is not an Act concerned with education, but sometimes matters arising under this Act can impinge on the relationship between schools and their clients. This Act deals, *inter alia*, with the legal issues relating to the welfare and custody of children of a marriage that has broken down. It should be remembered that unless a court order is made, or a child agreement to the contrary is registered, both parents are joint guardians and custodians of their child.[56] A person who has guardianship of a child has responsibility for the long-term welfare of the child, other than the right to have the daily care and control of the child. The right and responsibility to make decisions concerning the daily care and control of the child belongs to the custodial parent.[57] Access is not defined by the Act but is regarded by the Family Court as the *right of the child* to develop an on-going relationship with the non-custodial parent. Educational authorities should require that records for all pupils include information about the guardianship and custody of each child, and, where it is relevant, information relating to Family Court orders. A guardian should not be prevented from receiving any report or talking with any school staff on any matter that reflects on the long-term welfare of the child. However, guardianship does not automatically bring with it a right to access to the child. If the parent with guardianship is granted access to the child, the access will be the subject of a court order, or child agreement, which, however, may or may not specify the details of the access granted.

Principals and teachers should not try to usurp the powers of the Family Court by trying to settle parental disputes. Parents must be advised to seek their own legal representation, as court orders can be obtained very quickly by a parent if it is necessary for the welfare of the child to do so. Teachers should not take sides in a dispute between parents before a court. Where a parent in a dispute requests the making of a special report, or the swearing of an affidavit, great care must be taken. Affidavits are sworn testimony, and teachers should not agree to make such depositions unless they can attest to the trust of the matters sworn. Legal advice should be sought, as it is preferable only to describe events that have actually happened and to avoid drawing conclusions from those facts. Where opinion in a professional capacity is called for, it should be limited to a professional opinion clearly within the teacher's qualifications and experience. Teachers should be aware that it is essential that they comply with all court orders including subpoenas.

Schools should have in place appropriate security procedures against the abduction of students, not only by strangers but also by a parent whom the school authority knows does not have a legal right to have custody or even any kind of access. There are sanctions in the *Family Law Act* for breach of orders of the Family Court, but unfortunately the Act does not provide specific guidance to educational administrators and teachers who may have to make critical on-the-spot decisions such as whether a parent has a right to immediate access or whether there is likely to be an abduction.

Professional negligence in education

A legal issue of considerable importance for educators arises from the common law tort of negligence. The tort of negligence has been extended during the twentieth century to enable compensation to be gained not only for the negligent infliction of physical injury and nervous shock, and damage to property, but also for economic loss arising from negligent advice. The complexities of this tort, as it has been developed by the courts during the twentieth century, are many, and brief descriptions (such as that which follows) must necessarily be treated with caution because it is not possible to deal with the scope and subtleties of the tort in a few words. For negligence to arise there must be a duty of care recognised by law as being required from one person to another in the given circumstances. If the behaviour of the person on whom that duty lies is such that it breaches that duty of care, and there is, flowing from the breach of duty, reasonably foreseeable injury to the other person, then negligence may be established. However, the causative link between the breach and the damage must be shown, and the test for causation must be met. In some circumstances, defences to allegations of negligence are available. However, negligence is always a question of fact, and consequently what has been found either to be or not to be negligent in a particular set of circumstances can be no more than a guideline, for factual situations are rarely if ever identical.[58]

The duty of physical care of children at school

As far as teachers and schools are concerned, there is no doubt that the law recognises that there is a duty of the physical care of pupils. At common law the traditional view of this duty was that the teacher should take such care as a reasonably prudent parent would take, but the High Court of Australia has indicated that the standard of care required of teachers may be a higher standard than this.[59] The teacher—pupil relationship is the foundation of the duty, and consequently it may not be confined to school hours, if the school has taken responsibility for the pupil.[60] This duty of care requires that teachers adequately supervise pupils, and that safe premises and equipment are provided for pupils. Factors that may be taken into account in deciding whether the duty of care has been breached include the standard of care required, the foreseeability of injury,[61] the gravity of the risk and the practicability of removing it, and the capacity and maturity of the pupil.[62] Teachers and educational administrators may follow common practice and relevant administrative guidelines, but even if this is done, these may be held to be inadequate and therefore not support the absence of negligent behaviour.

The duty of the physical care of pupils falls on individual teachers, principals, educational administrators and the educational authority itself,[63] but the duty is not one of insuring the absolute safety of pupils.[64] As employers, educational authorities may also be liable for the negligence of their employees, under the usual principles of vicarious liability. If there is a failure to provide safe premises and equipment, occupier's liability may arise either at common law or under the relevant statutory codification of those common law principles in jurisdictions where such statutes apply.[65] It may be noted that a 'stranger' or third party in the school situation—for example, a fellow pupil,[66] or a manufacturer of school equipment—will also owe a duty of care to pupils. Finally, a word of caution must be given about an educational authority seeking to rely on parental agreement to exclude the school and teachers from liability, or to indemnify the school or teachers against liability. A parent cannot abrogate the right of the child to sue, and attempts to exclude liability will tend to be construed by the courts against the person seeking the exclusion. Further, promises to indemnify another person or body may not prove to be of value when enforcement is sought.

Educational authorities can lessen the likelihood of negligence claims for failure in the duty of the physical care of children by implementing school management policies to prevent inadequate supervision in the classroom, in the schoolyard, in sporting activities and on school camps and excursions. Schools also need to have clear policies relating to the daily arrival and departure of pupils. There should also be safety policies established not only for school activities involving the use of laboratory equipment, machinery or tools, but also for the storage and use of dangerous substances and the state of the school buildings and premises generally. The recognition of potential dangers is important, and safety policies should provide for prompt reporting of a warning about potential dangers in equipment, and in the school buildings and schoolyard, and for the prompt undertaking of repairs. School car access and parking areas need to be identified and kept 'pupil-free'. Staff must be informed of these policies and the reasons for them. Educational administrators and teachers do need to understand that if the teacher–pupil relationship is brought into existence, then the duty of the physical care of pupils will arise. Prudent administrators will not permit the undertaking of any activities on or off the school campus for which appropriate supervision cannot be provided by the school.[67]

Educational malpractice

Educational malpractice is a term used to refer to acts or omissions that lead to a failure to educate a pupil appropriately. During the past twenty years educational malpractice has been alleged in a number of cases in the United States of America, where educational authorities have been sued for damages for negligence in the education of the plaintiffs.[68] In Australia there has so far been no reported decision dealing with educational malpractice. However, is such an action were to be brought within the rubric of tortious liability for negligence, then certain issues would have to be addressed. It would have to be established that the law recognised a general duty of care on the part of teachers to educate their pupils appropriately. The scope of that duty would have to be defined, as would the appropriate standard of care. The causal connection between the behaviour of the teacher or of the educational authority, which would be alleged to have breached such a duty, and the injury to the pupil would have to be shown. The criteria for the recognition of the kinds of harm suffered and for the assessment of damages would also have to be established.

These are not simple matters to resolve, as the decisions of the American courts reveal. Although there have been dissenting judgments in the American cases, they nevertheless show that the courts in the United States have been reluctant to recognise a general duty to educate for reasons of public policy—that is, because of the burden it would place on teachers and educational authorities. Further, the American courts have said that because teaching is such a complex process, it would be difficult to develop a measurable standard of care, and that there would be difficulty in proving the causative link, for example, between the acts and omissions of educators and a plaintiff's illiteracy.[69] However, in circumstances where there is a specific act with specific consequences, such as a misdiagnosis of a child's ability and a consequent educational misplacement which retards the child's progress, then proving the causative link between the breach of a duty to educate and the injury to the pupil would possibly be easier.[70]

In the Australian context the concept of educational malpractice as a cause of action remains untested. This is not to say that the issue could not come before the courts. It is to say that the outcome of any such claim would be uncertain. Consequently, it remains to be seen whether the Australian courts would recognise a general duty to educate, or whether the public policy issues would prevent the recognition of such a duty. It also remains to be seen whether or not the evidentiary problems in establishing causation could be overcome even if a duty to educate were recognised.

Conclusion

It is likely that in the foreseeable future legal issues will remain of concern for educational administrators. Regrettably some problems will continue to arise. Some may relate to the criminal law—for example, assaults. Others may relate to administrative law and concern for natural justice—for example, in disciplinary matters. Whether the importance of legal issues will grow is necessarily a matter of speculation, but teachers and educational administrators should be trained to be aware of the legal interface of their professional tasks.

The current awareness of educational administrators of legal issues in education is not infrequently accompanied by a sense of unease that litigation in education is increasing. An unequivocal answer to this question cannot be given in the absence of historical and contemporary empirical analysis of the litigation involving educational authorities. However, it is useful to remember that in Australian society there do seem to be certain factors that may well inhibit a significant growth of educational litigation. One factor is the relative absence of statutorily guaranteed human rights referable to education. Another is the centralised rather than local control of education, which has led to a tradition of internal (albeit, often bureaucratic) resolution of disputes. A third factor is, of course, the cost of litigation. Other common law jurisdictions that appear to have more educational litigation differ from Australia in one or more of these factors. However, it should be remembered that even if any one or more of these factors changes in Australia, there is no reason why Australian legislatures in replacing and amending educational legislation could not provide for the use of alternative dispute resolution, such as conciliation, negotiation, mediation and arbitration, in the resolution of disputes arising between educators and their clients.

The future influence of international law is of interest as far as the issue of 'rights' for participants in the educational process is concerned. Certainly international law, which during the second half of the twentieth century has reflected the growth of human rights jurisprudence, has influenced the development of certain Australian legislation—for example, that relating to the proscription of discrimination—which is relevant to the provision of education. However, it does need to be understood that particular instruments of international law, although signed by Australia as a member of the United Nations, do not become part of Australian law except by the express will of the Australian Parliament. Consequently, whether the influence of international law will grow in the provision and governance of education in Australia remains a question for the future for the Australian people and their elected representatives. What must be understood is that it is the legislative policy expressed in the statutes and subordinate legislation that determines the contemporary balance of power and responsibilities among participants in education. If change is desired, then new laws reflecting different legislative policies will be required. However, if there is change, the task for educational administrators will not alter. It will still be the administrators' task to be aware of what the law requires and to implement policies and procedures conforming to those requirements.

Notes

Readers should be aware that the amendment or repeal of legislation may overtake the statutory references given in these notes.

1. D.C. Pearce and R.S. Geddes (1988), *Statutory Interpretation in Australia*, third edition, Butterworths, Sydney, p.2. Note that the distinction between legislative and executive instruments is a fine one where gubernatorial proclamations, ministerial orders and departmental rules are concerned.
2. See I.K.F. Birch (1975), *Constitutional Responsibility for Education in Australia*, ANU Press, Canberra, and 'Implications for the governance of Australian schools', *Australian Journal of Education*, vol. 27, no. 3, pp. 234–8.
3. In *Attorney-General (Victoria): ex rel Black* v. *The Commonwealth* (1981) 146 CLR 559; [1981] 55 ALJR 155, the High Court held that Commonwealth grants to the states for financial aid to non-government schools did not contravene s. 116 of the *Commonwealth Constitution*.
4. See, for example, (CTH) *Australian Institute of Aboriginal and Torres Strait Islander Studies Act* 1989.
5. See, for example, (CTH) *States Grants (Schools Assistance) Act* 1988, as amended; *States Grants (Technical and Further Education Assistance) Act* 1989,

as amended; and the (CTH) *Higher Education Funding Act* 1988, as amended. The (CTH) *Vocational Education and Training Funding Act* 1992 provides for the funding of vocational education and training through the Australian National Training Authority established by the (CTH) *Australian National Training Authority Act* 1992.

6. See (CTH) *Higher Education Funding Act* 1988, as amended, and the (CTH) *Overseas Students Charge Act* 1979, as amended.
7. The principal act is the (CTH) *Student Assistance Act* 1973.
8. See (CTH) *Education Services for Overseas Students (Registration of Providers and Financial Regulation) Act* 1991, and complementary state legislation, for example, (TAS) *Education Providers Registration (Overseas Students) Act* 1991.
9. Some examples of cases involving the interpretation of the Commonwealth statutes have been the following: *Santa Sabina College v. Minister for Education* (1985) 58 ALR 527 (Federal Court of Australia, Beaumont J) and *The Uniting Church in Australia Property Trust (Vic) v. The Honourable John Sidney Dawkins and Anor* (1990) 94 ALR 594 (Federal Court of Australia, Jenkinson, J.) where it was held that an amalgamated non-systemic school was a single entity for funding purposes under the then operative *States Grants (Schools Assistance) Acts*; *Peninsula Anglican Boys School v. Ryan and Anor* (1985) (1985) 7 FCR 415; (1985) 69 ALR 555 (Federal Court of Australia, Wilcox J) where it was held that the Minister's discretion to authorise payments to schools under the same *States Grants (School Assistance) Acts* must be exercised fairly, but the Minister had not acted unfairly in not giving notice of the change in government policy guidelines.
10. Some cases where judicial review of administrative decisions relating to the HECS has been sought include: *Re Moran and Department of Employment, Education and Training* (1990) 13 AAT 5 (CTH AAT); *Re Rodriguez and Secretary, Department of Education* (1991) 22 ALD 692 (CTH AAT); and *Re Teik Hok Lim and Department of Employment, Education and Training* (1991) 22 ALD 201 (CTH AAT). Cases relating to judicial review of administrative decisions about financial assistance to students include: *Re McTier and Secretary, Department of Education* (1987) 8 AAR 128 (CTH AAT); *Re McLoughlin and Department of Education* (1988) 9 AAR 81 (CTH AAT); *Re Clift and Department of Employment, Education and Training* (1991) 13 AAR 371 (CTH AAT); and *Secretary, Department of Employment, Education and Training v. Stewart* (1991) 13 AAR 529 (Federal Court of Australia, Gray J).
11. For statutory provision for preschool education, see: (ACT) *Schools Authority Act* 1976 ss. 6(1)(a), 7B–7C and 50; (NT) *Education Act* (1979 s. 6(4)(a)(ii); (QLD) *Education (General Provisions) Act* 1989 ss. 3(1) and 31; (SA) *Education Act* 1972 ss. 5(1) and 9(1)(b); (WA) *Education Act* 1928 ss. 3 and 27A–27D. In Tasmania there is no express reference in the *Education Act* 1932 to preschools, but they do fall within the aegis of the state Department of Education.

12. At the time of writing the following are the principal Acts: (ACT) *Education Act* 1937; (NT) *Education Act* 1979; (NSW) *Education Reform Act* 1990; (QLD) *Education (General Provisions) Act* 1989; (SA) *Education Act* 1972; (TAS) *Education Act* 1932; (VIC) *Education Act* 1958; see also *Community Services Act* 1970, ss. 74A–74F; (WA) *Education Act* 1928.
13. As to the registration of schools, see, for example: (ACT) *Education Act* 1937 ss. 21–30A; (NT) *Education Act* 1979 ss. 62–68C; (NSW) *Education Reform Act* 1990 ss. 37–69; (SA) *Education Act* 1972 ss. 72a–72p; (TAS) *Education Act* 1932 ss. 33–46AA; (Vic) *Education Act* 1958 ss. 34(1A)–52.
14. As to teacher registration, see, for example: (QLD) *Education (Teacher Registration) Act* 1988 ss. 5–31 and 33–46; (SA) *Education Act* 1927 ss. 55–68; (TAS) *Education Act* 1932 ss. 34–35, 37, 40–41 and 46 and regulations made under the Act; and (VIC) *Education Act* 1958 ss. 36–39, 41, 44(2)–(3), and regulations made under the Act.
15. At the time of writing the following are examples of supplementary education legislation: (ACT) *Schools Authority Act* 1976; (NSW) *Teaching Services Act* 1980; (QLD) *Education (Student Work Experience) Act* 1978; *Education (Teacher Registration) Act* 1988; (SA) *(Senior Secondary Assessment Board of South Australia) Act* 1983; (VIC) *Teaching Service Act* 1981; (WA) *Secondary Education Authority Act* 1984.
16. See, for example: (ACT) *Schools Authority Act* 1976 s. 6(3); (NT) *Education Act* 1979 ss. 5–6; (NSW) *Education Reform Act* 1990 ss. 19, 27–28 and 125; (QLD) *Education (General Provisions) Act* 1989 ss. 13–20; (SA) *Education Act* 1972 22. 60–9, 12(b) and 13; (TAS) *Education Act* 1932 ss. 5 and 17; (VIC) *Education Act* 1958 ss. 16–21, 30–31 and 64A–64H; (WA) *Education Act* 1928 ss. 4–5 and 9. In *Durant v. Greiner* (1990) 21 NSWLR 119 it was held that s. 8(3) of the now repealed *Education and Public Instruction Act* 1987, which provided that the Minister had the power to close a state school, meant that there was no legitimate expectation that schools would not be closed where such a power existed.
17. See, for example: (ACT) *Schools Authority Act* 1976 ss. 15–22; (NT) *Education Act* 1979 ss. 11–14 and 19–20; (NSW) *Education Reform Act* 1990 s. 9; (SA) *Education Act* 1972 ss. 10 and 82; (TAS) *Education Act* 1932 s. 4A. In Western Australia the *Education Act* 1928 does not make express provision for the establishment of advisory councils.
18. As to the powers of Chief Executives or Directors-General see, for example: (ACT) *Education Act* 1937 s. 16(1); *School Authority Act* 1976 ss. 8–11 and 55; (NT) *Education Act* 1979 ss. 8–10, 10N, 26, 64–67, 68B and 69; (NSW) *Teaching Services Act* 1980 ss. 23A–28A, 37–38, 41 and 100; (QLD) *Education (General Provisions) Act* 1989 ss. 3(1), 21, 24–25; (SA) *Education Act* 1972 ss. 1(1)–(2), 12–14(1), 17(1), (1a), (1b), 26–28, 75(2)–(3) and 75a; (TAS) *Education Act* 1932 ss. 4(1)–(5) and 7A; (VIC) *Education Act* 1958 ss. 4(2)–(7), (11)–(12), 5–5A, 6(1), 7 and 25a; (WA) *Education Act* 1928 ss. 7, 7A–7E, 8 20G(4) and 27B(3)–(4).

19. As to the scope of powers and responsibilities of school councils and/or parents and citizens associations, see, for example: (ACT) *Schools Authority Act* 1976 ss. 36–49 and *Schools Authority Regulations* 1978 and 1979 regs. 1–63; (NT) *Education Act* 1979 ss. 70–71K and *Education (Schools Councils) Regulations* 1988; (NSW) *Education Reform Act* 1990 ss. 36, 114–117 and *Education Reform Regulation* 1990 regs. 8–9; (QLD) *Education (General Provisions) Regulations* 1989 ss. 31–32 and *Education (General Provisions) Regulations* 1989 regs. 33–34 and 37–54; (SA) *Education Act* 1972 ss. 83–90, 107(a), (sa)–(sb) and *Education Regulations* 1976 regs. 201–214; (TAS) *Education Act* 1932 ss. 14–15; (VIC) *Education Act* 1958 ss. 14–15AA, 15B–15H and *Education Regulations* 1988, regs. 8.18–.26 and 9.1–9.10.2; (WA) *Education Act* 1928 ss. 22–34 and 26–27 and *Education Regulations* 1960 regs. 263–275.

20. At the time of writing the following, as amended, are examples of subordinate legislation governing education: (ACT) *Schools Authority Regulations* 1978; (NT) *Education (Schools Councils) Regulations* 1988; (NSW) *Education Reform Regulations* 1990; (QLD) *Education (General Provisions) Regulations* 1989; (SA) *Education Regulations* 1976; (TAS) *Education Regulations* 1971; (VIC) *Education Regulations* 1988; (WA) *Education Regulations* 1960.

21. (NSW) *Education Reform Act* 1990 s. 4.

22. ACT *Schools Authority Act* 1976 s. 6; (NT) *Education Act* 1979 ss. 6(1), (2) and (4); (QLD) *Education (General Provisions) Act* 1989 ss. 12–14.

23. Statutory provision for special education is as follows: (NT) *Education Act* 1979 ss. 33 and 35(3); (NSW) *Education Reform Act* 1990 s. 20; (QLD) *Education (General Provisions) Act* 1989 ss. 3(1), 12(2)–(4); (SA) *Education Act* 1972 s. 5(1); (TAS) *Education Act* 1932 s. 3(1); (VIC) *Education Act* 1958 ss. 3(1) and 64A; (WA) *Education Act* 1928 s. 20A(1).

24. (NSW) *Education Reform Act* 1990 s. 31; (QLD) *Education (General Provisions) Act* 1989 s. 23; (TAS) *Education Act* 1932, s. 7, but s. 7(2) provides for the charging of fees in technical colleges.

25. (VIC) *Education Act* 1958 ss. 22(2), 25A Sch. 2.

26. (WA) *Education Act* 1928 ss. 11–12.

27. (ACT) *Schools Authority Act* 1976 ss. 7B–7C; (5A) *Education Act* 1972, ss. 72i, 72ia, 72ib.

28. (ACT) *Education Act* 1937 s. 8(1); (NT) *Education Act* 1979 s. 21(1); (NSW) *Education Reform Act* 1990 s. 22; (QLD) *Education (General Provisions) Act* 1989 s. 57; (SA) *Education Act* 1972 s. 75; (TAS) *Education Act* 1932, s. 7A; (VIC) *Education Act* 1958 s. 53(1); WA *Education Act* 1928 s. 13(1). In *Cunningham* v. *Cannon* [1983] VR 641 it was held that only the parents of a child of compulsory school age can be guilty of a breach of the statutory requirement of ensuring that the child attend school.

29. See (NT) *Education Act* 1979 s. 24 and (QLD) *Education (General Provisions) Act* 1989 ss. 58–59 for typical examples of statutory provisions relating to exemption from school attendance, and (NSW) *Education Reform Act* 1990

ss. 34–35 and (WA) *Education Act* 1928 s. 18(5) for typical examples of statutory provisions relating to the exclusion of children from school.
30. (NSW) *Education Reform Act* 1990 ss. 70–83.
31. (NSW) *Education Reform Act* 1990 s. 4(b).
32. See notes 28 and 29 above.
33. Statutory provisions as to choice of government schools are to be found in (NSW) *Education Reform Act* 1990 s. 34 and (SA) *Education Act* 1972 s. 75. However, in *Ex parte Wilkes; Re Minister for Education* (1961) NSWR 989 and *Ex parte Cornford; Re Minister for Education* (1962) SR (NSW) 220 it was held that there was no right given to parents of unfettered selection of schools, nor any right of continued attendance at a school under the former *Public Instruction Act* 1880 and the *Public Instruction (Amendment) Act* 1916, and in *Pannifex v. Minister for Education* (1976) 1 NSWR 449, Bowen C.J. held that there was under those same Acts no principle of proximity to enable a child necessarily to attend the public school nearest his or her home.
34. See, for example: (NT) *Education Act* 1979 ss. 23 and 73; (NSW) *Education Reform Act* 1990 ss. 30, 32–33; (QLD) *Education (General Provisions) Act* 1989 s. 30; (SA) *Education Act* 1972 s. 102; (VIC) *Education Act* 1958 s. 23; (WA) *Education Act* 1928 ss. 29–30.
35. (ACT) *Education Act* 1937 ss. 21–30A; (NSW) *Education Act* 1979 ss. 61–68C; (NSW) *Education Reform Act* 1990 ss. 37–69 and 84–93; (SA) *Education Act* 1972 ss. 72–73; (TAS) *Education Act* 1932 ss. 33–36, 38, 41, 43–44, 45(d), 46(b) and 46AA; (VIC) *Education Act* 1958 ss. 34ia–37, 42–43, 44(1)–(3), 45–48, 49(1)–(3) and (5), 51–52(a); (WA) *Education Act* 1928 ss. 32A–32B, 33–34. In *Grace Bible Church Inc v. Reedman* (1984) 36 SASR 376, an appeal against a conviction for conducting an unregistered school under the *Education Act* 1972 s. 72f, the South Australia Supreme Court held that the common law had never guaranteed the inalienable right of religious freedom and expression, nor had such a right ever been established in South Australia, and even if such a right had existed it could have been overridden by the Parliament.
36. In *Regional Director of Education, Metropolitan East, Department of Education, NSW v. International Grammar School Sydney Ltd* (1986) 7 NSWLR 302, where the issue was one of provisional registration under the now-repealed *Public Instruction (Amendment) Act* 1916, it was held that Ministerial satisfaction as to the condition of the premises and the provision of regular and efficient instruction was required for the provisional registration of a non-government school which was not currently certified. In *R v. Ligertwood: ex parte Darwin* (1982) 30 SASR 328 the Court held that the Registration Board did not have the power under the *Education Act* 1972 s. 72g to grant registration for a limited period only, but it did have the power to grant registration on condition that a school did not offer secondary education. In *Fountain Centre Christian School Incorporated* v.

Harrington (1990) 53 SASR 361 the Court held *inter alia* that a decision of the SA Registration Board to cancel the registration of a school because of a small enrolment and perceived inadequacy of social and educational interaction was invalid.

37. (TAS) *Education Act* 1932 s. 41; (SA) *Education Act* 1972 s. 72m; (ACT) *Education Act* 1937 ss. 30–30A.
38. (NT) *Education Act* 1979 s. 68; (VIC) *Education Act* 1958 ss. 42(2)–3); (NSW) *Education Reform Act* 1990 ss. 51–59.
39. (NSW) *Education Reform Act* 1990 ss. 75–83.
40. (QLD) *Education (General Provisions) Act* 1989 s. 74.
41. (NSW) *Board of Adult and Community Education Act* 1990; (VIC) *Council of Adult Education Act* 1981, as amended by the *Adult, Community and Further Education Act* 1991.
42. See, for example: (NT) *Northern Territory University Act* 1988 s. 20(4); *Education Amendment Act* 1989 s. 4(1)(b); (QLD) *Vocational Education, Training and Employment Act* 1991 s. 2.28(1)(d)–(e); (SA) *Technical and Further education Act* 1975 ss. 4(1) and (5); Tas *Education Act* 1932 19N– 19ZA; (WA) *Colleges Act* 1978 s. 11(b)(vii).
43. (ACT) *ACT Institute of Technical and Further Education Act* 1987; (NT) *Education Act* 1979, as amended by the *Education Amendment Act* 1989 ss. 40–60M; (NSW) *Technical and Further Education Commission Act* 1990; (QLD) *Vocational Education, Training and Employment Act* 1991; (SA) *Technical and Further Education Act* 1975; (TAS) *Industrial and Commercial Training Act* 1985; (VIC) *Tertiary Education Act* 1992; *(WA) Colleges Act* 1978.
44. (ACT) *Vocational Training Act* 1989; (NT) *Northern Territory Employment and Training Authority Act* 1991; (NSW) *Industrial and Commercial Training Act* 1989; *Vocational Education and Training Accreditation Act* 1990; (QLD) *Vocational Education, Training and Employment Act* 1991; (SA) *Industrial and Commercial Training Act* 1981; (TAS) *Industrial and Commercial Training Act* 1985; (VIC) *Vocational Education and Training Act* 1990. Western Australia does not at the time of writing have comparable legislation governing apprenticeship, which falls within the rubric of employment law.
45. At the time of writing there are well over sixty statutory instruments relating to Australian universities. The following list notes only one Act relating to a public university in each jurisdiction, although it should be remembered that the number of acts varies from jurisdiction to jurisdiction: (ACT) *Australian National University Act* 1991 (CTH); (NT) *Northern Territory University* Act 1988; (NSW) *University of Sydney Act* 1989; (QLD) *University of Queensland Act* 1965; (SA) *The University of Adelaide Act* 1971; (TAS) *Higher Education Amalgamation Act* 1990; (VIC) *Monash University Act* 1958; (WA) *University of Western Australia Act* 1911. For legislation relating to private universities, see for example: (QLD) *Bond University Act* 1987.
46. See, for example, the *Australian National University Act* 1991, the *Northern*

47. See *Patel v. University of Bradford* [1978] 1 WLR 1488, which has been followed in a number of Australian cases including *Murdoch University v. Bloom and Kyle* [1980] WAR 193 (WA Sup. Ct. FC). However, in Victoria the *Administrative Law (University Visitor) Act* 1986 provides that certain matters previously within the exclusive jurisdiction of the Visitor of universities specified in the Act may be reviewed under the *Administrative Law Act* 1958.

Territory University Act 1988, and the statutes of several Queensland universities including the *University of Queensland Act* 1965.

48. See, for example: (NT) *Northern Territory University Act* 1988 s. 48; (NSW) *University of New South Wales Act* 1989 s. 23; *Australian William E Simon University Act* 1988 s. 8; (QLD) *Griffith University Act* 1971 s. 40; (SA *The Flinders University Act* 1966 s. 5; (VIC) *Melbourne University Act* 1958 s. 42; *Australian Catholic University (Victoria) Act* 1991 s. 7.
49. (CTH) *Freedom of Information Act* 1982; (NSW) *Freedom of Information Act* 1989; (SA) *Freedom of Information Act* 1991; (TAS) *Freedom of Information Act* 1991; (VIC) *Freedom of Information Act* 1982.
50. See, for example: *Re Barkhorder and Australian Capital Territory Schools Authority* (1987) 12 ALD 332—papers relating to successful applicants for promotion in a teaching service held to be exempt (CTH AAT); *Baueris v. Commonwealth of Australia* (1987) 75 ALR 327—information relating to an application to the Commonwealth Schools Commission for funding for the establishment of a school held to be exempt (Fed. Ct. of Aust., Beaumont J).
51. The Australian Copyright Council is located at Suite 3, 245 Chalmers Street, Redfern, NSW 2016. It publishes an excellent series of bulletins, which provide clear guidance about copyright.
52. (CTH) *Racial Discrimination Act* 1975; *Sex Discrimination Act* 1984; *Human Rights and Equal Opportunity Commission Act* 1986.
53. (ACT) *Discrimination Act* 1991; (NSW) *Anti-Discrimination Act* 1977; (QLD) *Anti-Discrimination Act* 1991; (SA) *Equal Opportunity Act* 1984; (VIC) *Equal Opportunities Act* 1984; (WA) *Equal Opportunities Act* 1984; (NT) *Anti-Discrimination Act* 1992.
54. (1987) EOC 92–192.
55. (CTH) *Sex Discrimination Act* 1984 ss. 28–29; (ACT) *Discrimination Act* 1991 ss. 58–64; (QLD) *Anti-Discrimination Act* 1991 ss. 117–119; (SA) *Equal Opportunity Act* 1984 s. 87; (VIC) *Equal Opportunity Act* 1984 ss. 19–20; (WA) *Equal Opportunity Act* 1984 ss. 24–26. The New South Wales *Anti-Discrimination Act* 1977 does not contain provisions expressly proscribing sexual harassment, but in *O'Callaghan v. Loder* (1984) EOC 92–203, the New South Wales Equal Opportunity Tribunal held that sexual harassment amounted to discrimination on the ground of sex within the meaning of the Act.
56. (CTH) *Family Law Act* 1975 s. 63F(1).

57. *Ibid.*, s. 63E(1) and (2).
58. See P.G. Heffey, 'The duty of schools and teachers to protect pupils from injury', (1985) 11 *Monash Law Review* pp. 1–66 for a comprehensive analysis of the issues relating to teacher negligence.
59. *The Commonwealth* v. *Introvigne* (1982) 56 ALJR 749, *per* Murphy J at p. 757.
60. *Richards* v. *State of Victoria* [1969] VR 136; *Geyer* v. *Downs* (1978) 52 ALJR 142, *per* Stephen J at p. 144.
61. See, for example: *Richards* v. *State of Victoria* [1969] VR 136, where a teacher who ignored misbehaviour in a classroom should reasonably have foreseen that a fight might occur; *Bills* v. *State of South Australia* (1985) 38 SASR 80, where the evidence did not show that the teacher should have expected disobedience when she moved away from a trampoline at the end of a class.
62. See, for example: *Richards* v. *State of Victoria* [1969] VR 136, where a teacher was considered to hold a duty of care towards a sixteen-year-old boy; *Miller* v. *State of South Australia* (1981) 24 SASR 416, where it was considered that a high standard was required when caring for very young children.
63. See, for example: *Watson* v. *Haines* (1987) Aust. Torts Reports 80-094, where the educational authority failed to warn teachers of the risks run by pupils of a certain kind of build in playing in the front or second row of scrum in rugby league football.
64. See, for example: *Kretschmar* v. *State of Queensland* (1989) Aust. Torts Reports 80-272, where the facts of the case concerned injury sustained by an intellectually disabled boy in an indoor game, and the Full Court of the Queensland Supreme Court said that the standard of care was that of the reasonable parent and certainly not that of an insurer.
65. For examples of statutory codification of the principles of occupier's liability, see: (SA) *Wrongs Act* 1936, ss. 17a–17e; and (VIC) *Wrongs Act* 1958 s. 14B.
66. See, for example: *Harvey* v. *Pennell* (1987) Aust. Torts Reports 80-112, where the liability for a student's injury was held to rest on the fellow pupil.
67. *Geyer* v. *Downs* (1978) 52ALJR 242, *per* Stephen J at p. 144.
68. Useful analysis of the concept and its operation is to be found in: B. Thompson (1985), 'In a class apart? Educational negligence claims against teachers', 1. *Queensland Institute of Technology Law Journal* 85; T.E. Loscalzo (1985), 'Liability for Malpractice in Education', 14 *Journal of Law and Education* 595; J.W. Nelson (1987), 'A new dimension to accountability? Educational negligence claims against teachers', *Australian Journal of Education*, vol. 31, no. 3. p. 219; A. Wolfgarten (1990), 'Educational malpractice: A potential problem for LEAs or teachers?', *Education and the Law*, vol. 2, no. 4, p. 157; and G. Parry (1990), 'Teacher incompetence and the courts: the American experience', *Education and the Law*, vol. 3, no. 2, p. 71.

69. See, for example, the judgments in the following American cases: *Peter W. v. San Francisco Unified School District* (1976) 60 Cal. App. 3d. 814; 131 Cal. Rptr. 854; *Donahue v. Copaigue Union Free School District* (1977) (408 NYS 2d. 584; *Hoffman v. Board of Education of City of New York* (1978) 41 NYS 2d.; (1979) 49 NYS 2d. 121; *Smith v. Alameda Country Social Services Agency* (1978) 90 Cal. App. 3d. 929; (1979) 153 Cal. Rptr. 712; *Loughron v. Fairbanks North Star Borough School District* (1981) 628 P. 2d. 554. It should be noted that the plaintiff in Hoffman's Case (1978) did succeed at first instance and on the first appeal, although the quantum of damages was reduced on the first appeal, but the New York Court of Appeals by a majority of four to three reversed the earlier decision.
70. See *Snow v. State of New York* (1983) 98 AD 2d. 442; (1984) 469 NYS 2d. 959; (1986) 485 NYS 2d. 210, which concerned the misdiagnosis of a child as retarded. The plaintiff was successful on a plea of medical malpractice; but compare *Torres v. Little Flower Children's Services* (1984) 485 NYS 2d. 15, where there was also an inaccurate evaluation of a child's abilities, and the plaintiff was not successful.

13 Management of the Curriculum: Stability vs Change, Evolution vs Destabilisation

Brian J. Spicer

The prospect and challenge of change liberates some people, transfixes others, and alienates still others. While probably all of us expect to be subject to frequent change in many aspects of our lives, we basically expect most of these changes to be of very small magnitude, at times unsettling but rarely so dramatic that we are unable to cope. Hence, when dramatic changes are forthcoming we often find ourselves fearful of the prospect, unable to respond easily to the almost inevitable paradox of the situation. For change is a paradox. On the one hand, it threatens to do away with many of the things we have come to trust and rely on in our personal, occupational and organisational lives, while, on the other hand, it tempts and challenges with the prospect of new opportunities.

There is no doubt that many people perceive change itself as being the major purpose of much of what is undertaken by governments and by organisations. While we may all feel this way at times, it is not an easily sustained position because it suggests that much change is instigated for no better reason than to be different. At the organisational level this view is almost always incorrect. It ignores the reality that in a more or less rational world 'change is not the goal of change'. It is instead a process—a process through which individuals, organisations and countries seek to reach a new point of order, a better state than the one previously attained (Kovach 1989).

Understandably, when judging any change, we often focus (especially in the short-term) on the process experienced to gain the desired end. Although not wishing to adopt the view that 'the ends justify the means', it is probably desirable in most cases that our ultimate judgement centres on the nature and quality of the point reached as a result of that process, rather than on the process itself. Of course, while many changes are planned and desired, many others are forced upon us, and it is these changes that tend to cause the greatest negative response. At no time is this sort of impact more obvious than when government decisions set the scene for major alterations and upheaval for the key services that we expect governments to provide and/or for the areas in which we ourselves are employed. However, the nature of democracy is such that very frequently the minority will have to accept the products resulting from the change processes established through the exercise of the will of the majority.

Education, as one of the cornerstones of society, and one of the most expensive of its services, is frequently the subject of change; and in countries where the state accepts the major responsibility for education, much of that change will reflect the differing ideologies and educational philosophies of different governments and the strong impact of special interest and pressure groups. It can also, as in recent times in many Western countries, reflect economic pressures and the tendency for many within a community to blame the education system for a country's economic woes. The education scene in Australia is no exception, and within its broad parameters the curriculum and its organisation and management structures have been a growing focus for change.

Since the 1950s, Australian education has seen many changes, changes that have embraced virtually all dimensions of the educational scene—changes to the general structure and administration of schools and systems, changes to funding and resourcing, changes to broad and specific goals, changes to staffing structures and requirements, and changes to curriculum, its content, delivery, organisation and management. This is neither an exhaustive list, nor does it represent the end of major change for the twentieth century. Indeed, there is much to suggest that the next few years will be equally as demanding and as tumultuous for teachers and students and for all other educational stakeholders as the past two decades have been.

What we are observing is a major shift in the orientation of education systems and of schools, in terms of both their orientation to each other and their orientation to the external world. This refocusing revolves around the responsibility and accountability dimensions, as the system devolves more and more management responsibility to the schools with the purpose of making them into significant decision-making centres and a better role model for students in a democratic community and, at the same time, making them increasingly accountable for their actions and performance. The schools, in their turn, have been defining much closer relationships with their own communities. Yet there are paradoxes to be observed in these new practices. For example, the move towards greater decentralisation and devolution of decision-making and responsibility seems in opposition, at least in part, to the burgeoning concern for common national curricula, key competencies and national standards. Likewise, in the government sector, while schools and school councils have had an important role to play in the selection of school principals, they have had a much lesser role in determining which staff are to be employed to ensure that government as well as school policies and goals are pursued with real effectiveness. Many other resourcing decisions, all with great significance for the effective operation of schools and for the improvement of school performance, still remain under central control. The tension between centralisation and devolution in education still remains as a major issue in the school system evolving in Australia today.

Indeed, while the traditional hierarchical view of education, with its focus on meeting the needs of the society, gave way in the late 1960s to much more of a *laissez faire* approach, in which acceptance of the doctrine of professional autonomy gave educators almost free rein with little or no concern for the totality of the product. In the 1990s we can recognise a return to a more societal focus, albeit while maintaining the central tenet of decentralisation and devolution. This aspect of change, combined with the impact of those other forces outlined previously, has enormous potential repercussions for schooling in Australia over the next decade.

The curriculum and its management

The curriculum domain can rightfully be argued to be the most important operational dimension in education. Unfortunately, however, at the school or institutional level, concern for its effective management has been traditionally subsumed within the broader spectrum of school management and school leadership or, alternatively, placed within the realm of the teacher's day-to-day operations. Curriculum itself is perhaps best defined as 'all the planned opportunities offered to learners in an educational institution and the experiences learners encounter when the curriculum is implemented' (Pring 1989: 4). This definition accords with the general consensus of meaning that one gains from a review of the literature over a long period of time, from Tyler (1949) to Taba (1962) and on through the work of writers such as Popham and Baker (1970), Stenhouse (1975), and others.

Management is central to curriculum because of its concern with the planning and action processes through which the goals are determined, the substantive and conceptual elements structured and presented, and the available resources utilised efficiently, effectively and equitably in the pursuit of those goals. A definition for 'curriculum management' thus encompasses:

> the process through which curriculum goals, structures and plans are determined, and the plans for their implementation, development, and evaluation are operationalised, so as to make the best and fullest use of all the available resources—human, financial and capital—in pursuit of

the highest level of excellence that can be attained in the achievement of those goals.

Figure 13.1 provides a diagrammatic representation of the process of curriculum management, as conceptualised within this definition.

Aims of the chapter

This chapter seeks to provide a broad perspective of curriculum management in Australian education at the system and school levels, identifying the general structures, networks and processes, the roles and responsibilities of the various actors in the curriculum management process, and directing attention towards models of the process and their interaction with societal directions. The concern overall is therefore with management issues rather than specific curriculum issues such as development, innovation, dissemination, adoption or evaluation. While these are all vital to the curriculum process, it is not the purpose of this chapter to examine them *per se,* but only to the degree that any such examination helps us to understand the management process.

Strategic and operational dimensions of curriculum management

Like all management functions, curriculum management has both a strategic dimension and an operational dimension, and like the majority of management domains it is concerned with different levels of operation: the macro (which may include national as well as state authorities and concerns), the regional and district, and the micro (local and school) levels. In some countries this organisational structure is a very formal hierarchy, but throughout Australia the process of devolution has now changed the hierarchical relationships and created numerous, autonomous curriculum units.

To a great extent, the pyramid of power in curriculum management has been flattened and, in some ways, even inverted in the changes that have affected Australian education since the late 1960s. It is similar to what is happening in many large corporations where strong vertical hierarchies have given way to flatter, more participatory structures in which small centres operate almost autonomously, seeking to run at a profit and thereby contribute to the overall health of the enterprise.

The strategic phase of the management process emphasises the concern that each enterprise, public or private, has with determining its primary role or mission, determining the specific goals that flow from that mission, making a thorough and objective assessment of all critical areas with

Figure 13.1 A strategic approach to curriculum management

The curriculum management process for the government school in a devolved management structure: this model can be readily modified to describe the curriculum management process at the macro level of the system or state. The resource management dimension is separated, at least in part, because some resource needs, acquisition and allocation decisions do not always take place in a logical chronological sequence. The model is equally applicable to curriculum management in non-government schools and systems.

	1. *Situation analysis* • What sort of world is it? • What sort of school do we want to be? • What should be our mission and/or policy? • Resource appraisal	
	2. *Goal identification* • Government policy—state and federal • Education Department guidelines • Community interests and concerns • Staff, parents • Students	
Strategic planning	3. *Statement of goals* • General and specific (i.e. subject areas)	*Determination of resource needs Stage 1: General*
	4. *Assessment of critical areas* • Strengths, weaknesses opportunities, threats 'SWOT'	• Buildings • Other capital resources and equipment • Teachers and support staff • Other resources
	5. *Objectives* • To achieve goals • To eliminate problems • To use opportunities	
Critical linkage	6. *Strategic plans to meet objectives* • Develop school and subject programs • Program budgets	*Determination of resource needs Stage 2: Specific (program-related)*
	7. *Analysis of plans by school committees* • Budgets • Priorities/resource implications • Decisions	*Resource acquisition (This will often be a long-term process continuing over months)*
	8. *Resource allocation*	
Operational Planning	9. *Development of action plans* • Syllabuses and work programs	
	10. *Implementation* • Class, laboratory, field and other learning experiences	
	11. *Monitoring and evaluation* • Student testing • Curriculum evaluation • Teacher performance appraisal • Other performance indicators	
	12. *Review and feedback* • Reporting to school council and/or ministry	

concern for strengths, weaknesses, opportunities and threats ('SWOT'), and identifying the broad strategies that should be used to seek the achievement of those goals. It is a reflective, analytic and forward-thinking phase, which puts great emphasis on the notion of the team, on working together, and on communicating ideas to create a pathway towards particular and accepted goals.

The operational phase, in constrast, is very much focused on putting the strategies to work and embraces a full analysis of possible plans and their resource implications, the development of specific action plans for the ensuing period, the implementation, monitoring and evaluation stages, and the final review and feedback leading to reassessment of the original goals and even of the mission itself. Whereas the strategic phase is concerned with determining the right things to do, the operational phase is concerned with ensuring that things are being done appropriately.

While the terminology employed by educators may be different from that of the corporate planners, the essence of curriculum management is the same as for all other areas of management. Curriculum planners, at whatever level, are indeed being called on to develop a mission or policy for their sphere of responsibility (whether for system, school or subject department) and from that mission determine goals and strategies, and develop, resource, implement, and evaluate plans to achieve those goals and fulfil that mission.

Of course, the degrees of freedom for the curriculum planner at the school, subject or grade level, are much less than for those holding major responsibility for curriculum at the system or national level. The development of national curriculum statements for the key learning areas —Mathematics, English, Science, Technology, Studies of Society and Environment, Health, LOTE (languages other than English) and the Arts—will certainly impose quite serious limitations on curriculum autonomy at the micro level.

Increasingly, too, in the same way as the business centre is called to account for its success or otherwise in the pursuit of its mission, so are the various units of the education system being asked to 'perform' in respect of their policies. The smallest such units, the grade or subject class, are just as subject to these pressures as are whole schools, larger specialist units and educational systems. Accountability is a key issue at all levels.

Structures and networks

Before the 1960s the formal curriculum management structures were extremely hierarchical, and the classroom teacher had only limited autonomy in his or her selection of teaching strategies and very little control over the substantive and conceptual content of courses and lessons. The area of decision-making available to classroom teachers was generally related to the way(s) in which the experience of the child could be integrated into the study unit. In larger schools, even this was a subject department's or year-level teachers' decision, rather than that of the individual teacher.

At the non-examination levels of secondary school and all the levels of primary school, the state departments of education held a monopoly of the curriculum decision-making power. Courses of Study were produced and published centrally, and teachers wrote their syllabuses and work programs to accord with those course outlines. Across Australia, state education departments published and presented curriculum materials. Typically there was a class Reader for each year-level, and this was supplemented by other materials; in Victoria, for example, these included graded spelling lists and a School Paper, which was cross-curricular in orientation.

By the late 1960s the publishing role of the state departments had diminished, and syllabuses were supported by materials from commercial publishing houses. Companies chose authors with appropriate experience and credibility to produce texts to support the centrally determined courses. While teachers and schools could choose the text(s) they believed would best suit their needs, even that choice still meant the maintenance of overall state-wide consistency of programs. The inspectorial system further enforced a pattern of conformity and minimised intra-state differences between schools, although there were significant interstate differences in some curriculum areas—such as language studies (reading and writing especially) and mathematics (Mackay and Spicer 1975).

The management process was conducted through officially appointed curriculum committees, the members of which had been selected centrally usually on the basis of inspectorial recommendation. These committees determined goals and priorities and the essential substance of the curriculum and its various entities, and even indicated their support for a preferred approach to teaching. This was bulwarked by a very centralised support service, by course-focused textbooks, and by head teachers and subject and class teachers who were aware of the power of the inspectorate, and who had themselves been trained in a highly conformist situation neither conducive to creativity nor inclined towards revolution. They saw themselves as accountable to the central administration and the inspectorate and, through that channel, to the education minister. In that situation, the discretionary management of the curriculum at the classroom level was generally concerned only with the management of time, as other crucial issues had been resolved at higher levels.

At the examination levels of the secondary school, the situation for the average class or subject teacher was just as controlled. Courses of study were determined by committees appointed by and reporting to key agencies such as Examination Boards, on which the universities of the time played a most significant and powerful role. Examinations were set by panels also appointed by the boards and were based on the published course, while the key text resources were written by well-known and successful teachers who were believed best able to write materials that reflected the course requirements.

Successful performance by students in the examinations was regarded as a very efficient way of judging the quality of student learning as well as the quality of teacher and school performance. While teachers at these levels did not have imposed quite the same operational controls as their primary peers—in that there was no requirement to prepare highly detailed weekly work programs—it was expected that there would be a detailed syllabus, which would indicate clear and comprehensive coverage of the course and provide indications of teaching methods and resources to be used. The examination-level teacher, like his or her non-examination counterpart, was even more 'a manager of time' as the examinations clock ticked rigorously and the uncertainties of the examinations meant that there was little room for individual manoeuvre or difference, topics being omitted from the syllabus only at some peril to one's students and to one's reputation as a teacher.

Although the examination system dictated curriculum and its implementation for both government and non government schools, it should be noted that, even at the primary level, there was no essential difference between the management structures controlling curriculum in the government education sector and those operating in the non-government sector. The non-government sector simply did all that the government schools did, and more, and tried to do it better. In all the corresponding areas of the curriculum there was virtually no discernible difference in what was taught and how it was taught. Effectively, in all areas of the curriculum, with the exception of religious education, the non-government school sector exercised its independence to adopt and follow the courses of study prepared by the state education departments.

Administration and implementation

The classroom teacher's role as a curriculum timekeeper within a highly structured syllabus and examinations framework gave way in the late 1960s and 1970s to what was regarded by the curriculum architects of the time (for example, Reed and Hannan in Victoria) to be a liberation of teachers from unreasonable curriculum shackles. At last, and appropriately, it was argued, teachers would be free to make curricular decisions of relevance to their own students' needs and contexts.

On reflection, the role and importance of external control in managing the curriculum at the school level could only be assessed when these ideas about the appropriate locus of curriculum management filtered down to the school level. When, towards the end of the 1960s and the beginning of the 1970s, teachers were confronted with a dramatic reduction in their safe and comfortable curriculum controls—when the focus began to shift towards the individual teacher as curriculum manager—deficiencies, even voids, began to appear in curriculum management structures and processes. Teachers were uncertain about the range and implications of their new curriculum responsibilities. For many, far from being delighted with the freedoms and opportunities afforded them to create appropriate and relevant curricula, including assessment and evaluation for their students, the new responsibilities occasioned resentment.

The 1980s school review process that replaced the inspectorial system in Victoria, for example, highlighted some of the problems emanating from this autonomy, with many teachers, even at the same year-level in the same subject at the same school, feeling that they were curriculum isolates. In some cases the result was that students would progress to the next level with very different experiences from other students who had taken the same subject the previous year, thus creating problems for teachers and students alike.

Yet the devolution process proved to be inexorable, so that what has occurred in the past two decades (and in some ways, at an even faster pace more recently) has been a dramatic shifting of the responsibility for managing the curriculum away from the centralised state authorities towards, on the one hand, the school and the teachers, and on the other hand, towards the new centre—the Federal authorities and nationally oriented committees and groups. In brief, the state central bodies have relinquished a great deal of management control over the curriculum, firstly to the schools and to the teachers, and secondly to Canberra and to certain 'critical' groups. The hierarchy of management control has been shattered forever at the state level.

The new management philosophy that emerged was that teachers, as well-trained professionals, are the people best able to determine the actuality of the curriculum in the context of official policy and course guidelines, the nature of the school itself, the local environment, as well as the background, needs and aspirations of the students and the community, and with due regard to their own personal expertise, skills and interests. Thus teachers were freed from the need to conform rigidly to externally determined programs and instead were encouraged to 'customise' their curricula to the context of their students and classrooms. The gradual removal of the inspectorial system and reduced concern for the formal evaluation of classroom teachers, except in the context of promotion, added momentum to this move to professional autonomy. In a very short period, teachers at all levels, with the exception of those engaged in teaching the examination forms of the secondary school, were for the first time decision makers, and *real managers* of curriculum.

However, this shift in managerial power from the central curriculum bodies to the schools and the teachers was not accomplished without tension, considerable difficulty and frequent failure. Many schools and very many teachers were not ready to take on such important new responsibilities. For example, in Victorian secondary schools, when detailed Courses of Study in subjects such as Geography and History were no longer published, it did not lead all teachers of these subjects to immediately embark on creating new programs designed especially for the needs of their particular circumstances. In fact, it was rather that many (if not most) simply eschewed the opportunity and kept doing exactly what they had been doing previously. There was a marked inertia to change; many just followed the 'old courses'.

Several key external groups moved to fill the emerging void. Firstly, there were the publishing companies who saw the opportunity to seek appropriate and innovative writings in all curriculum areas—writings that reflected the very latest in academic and pedagogical thought and which could provide appropriate signposts and pathways for those now seemingly lost without the support of the formal central curriculum. In a very short time the new texts, and there were many of them, became the *de facto* Courses of Study and the authors were, at least for a time, the new 'change agents' in the education system.

Secondly, there were the professional associations—the English, geography, history and mathematics teachers' associations—anxious to support their colleagues and recognising that their own future as professional groups depended on their ability to meet these emergent needs, and to do so without taking from members the independence afforded by the changes. Some, like the Geography Teachers Association of Victoria (GTAV), became, over a period, *de facto* curriculum bodies and exercised considerable informal power over what was taught in secondary classes in their state. These associations not only provided their members with detailed course guidelines; they also offered a mass of information about alternative approaches to teaching and about the efficacy of various classroom and fieldwork strategies, and were soon major publishers of materials, text and audio-visual, to support their guidelines. The Secondary Geography and Secondary History projects were major examples of new post-primary curricula emerging from the work of these associations.

Thirdly, there were the curriculum committees and curriculum support services of the education departments, which found suddenly a new role, not of direction, but of facilitation, guidance and support.

While there has been only limited research into the role of particular individuals in all three of these areas, it was certainly true that in a number of cases the same people were key parties in all three operations. The practice of the 'interlocking directorate' had arrived in education. Curriculum control had shifted, theoretically to *all* the teachers, but in practice the shift had never been completely accomplished. Many, perhaps a majority of teachers, were now working under the direction of new control groups; the management of the broad curriculum scene had passed to a new group of leaders, who were destined to be the 'change agents' and curriculum 'power brokers' of the period.

A further element in this era of change was the widespread adoption in Australia of the Brunerian concern for concept development and the acceptance of the notion that central curriculum bodies should be more concerned with defining the key learnings—concepts, reasoning abilities, basic skills, theories, principles, attitudes, etc.—to be achieved at particular grade levels, rather than with the detail of content.

The operation of all these aspects of change created considerable curriculum diversity within schools, apparent within small regions within states as well as between states. This led in the 1980s to the introduction in some states of curriculum statements produced by the state education departments and covering a range of curriculum areas, (for example, Language, the Study of Society, Mathematics, Science and Technology, the Arts, Physical and Personal Development, etc.).

In Victoria these documents, known as *Frameworks*, were a clear attempt to bring some greater degree of centralised control to curriculum and to ensure an acceptable level of congruence both in the scope of the curriculum offered across the state and within the various subjects themselves. The Frameworks approach was also designed to ensure that schools paid greater attention to areas of study (LOTE, Technology, Music, etc.), which may not otherwise have been given high priority. The schools then had the management responsibility to ensure that the policies and educational goals presented in these documents and other departmental and ministerial papers were reflected in the policy documents and curriculum programs developed by teachers, administrators and parents working collaboratively.

The effect of these changes was to devolve power and control to the schools, the teachers and the community, to build a foundation for the self-governing state school, and return to the centre the power to determine the focus and broad structure of the curriculum and various other operational aspects of the school system.

Another change that seeks to create greater national portability of qualifications, but which also adds stimulus to a centralised curriculum focus, is the movement towards identification and inclusion in the curriculum of *key competencies* or skills and abilities. These key competencies, it is argued, should be possessed, albeit to differing degrees, by all students leaving secondary school whether they follow the pathway to university or to a TAFE (Technical and Further Education) college or to employment. Mayer (1992) suggested seven key competency strands:

- Collecting, analysing and organising ideas and information
- Communicating ideas and information
- Planning and organising activities
- Working with others and in teams
- Using mathematical ideas and techniques
- Solving problems
- Using technology

All of these are embodied in the current school curriculum, although perhaps not as clearly in the frontline as the advocates of the competency approach would wish. The competency approach, of course, is not just an Australian phenomena. As Figure 13.2 demonstrates, it is also important in both the UK and the USA. However, in the context of this chapter, the vitally significant aspect of these proposed changes in curriculum is that they have emanated from the impetus of non-professional educators.

The key people, the advocates of the competency approach, represent a mixture of Australian corporate and union leaders, who argue that deficiencies in the product of our schools are damaging Australia's ability to be a world economic power and be competitive with other countries. They see the introduction of non-subject-based competencies and appropriate testing of their achievement as a way of building a more effective interface between schools and the world of work. The danger is that, having removed the content prescriptions, we are now moving towards the prescription of competencies. Furthermore, the drive to have these competencies included as requirements for all secondary students is a powerful push indeed and suggests that the locus of curriculum decision-making is shifting quite dramatically away from the professionals in education towards leading entrepreneurs and chief executive officers (CEOs) in key manufacturing and commercial enterprise.

In part, this reflects the desire of Australian leaders, including government, to find a way out of the economic recession of the past five years and, in part, the fact that educators generally are not held in very high esteem within the society and are to some extent to be blamed for the troubles that have beset the country. The shift of control over the enginehouse of curriculum change, from the professionals to the outside, means effectively that the new change agents are the barons of industry. Their informal yet highly significant 'expert' power (Hunt 1979) is based on their credibility with, and high profile in, the Australian community as successful businessmen and leaders.

This movement is not without its critics, especially from educators (Porter et al. 1992) who would prefer an enhanced concern for social literacy (Apple 1987) rather than for specific workplace competencies. However, criticism alone is not enough. 'What is necessary is a creative and vigorous engagement with the thrust of Mayer, Carmichael, et al., rather than an academic retreat to what is essentially intellectual marginalisation. Whether we like it or not, our education system has to become more responsive to the economic needs of this country' (O'Brien 1992: 16).

It is important to note that this movement towards competencies is strongly supported by governments at both state and federal level. 'At their meeting in Auckland (September 1992), the Australian Education Council and Ministers of Vocational Education, Employment and Training adopted a number of resolutions in response to the Mayer Committee's report. The first of these underlined the place of Key Competencies in reinforcing the role of general education as a foundation for vocational education and training' (Borthwick 1992: 7).

The Australian Education Council (AEC), a forum of state ministers of education, is also the key player in another crucial development in the curriculum debate. Increasingly, the AEC, in working to reduce interstate differences in education through the development of national curriculum statements and profiles in eight learning areas, has added another force strengthening the centralised management of curriculum.

The curriculum statements referred to earlier in this chapter, all of

Figure 13.2 Key competencies: an international comparison

Australia *Key Competencies*	UK *Core Skills*	USA *Workplace Knowhow*
• Collecting, analysing and organising information	• Communication	• Information • Foundation skills: basic skills
• Communicating ideas and information	• Communication • Personal skills: improving own learning and performance	• Information • Foundation skills: basic skills
• Planning and organising activities	• Personal skills: improving own learning and performance	• Resources • Foundation skills: personal qualities
• Working with others and in teams	• Personal skills: working with others	• Interpersonal skills
• Using mathematical ideas and techniques	• Numeracy: application of number	• Foundation skills: basic skills
• Solving problems	• Problem-solving	• Foundation skills: thinking skills
• Using technology	• Information technology • Modern foreign language	• Technology • Systems

which should be completed during 1993, will outline the main knowledge and skills distinctive to a given area but will not deal with the detail of learning. 'They are intended for use mainly by curriculum developers, not directly by classroom teachers' and 'will be a point of reference for state curriculum documents and courses which schools develop' (Hannan and Wilson 1992: 2). While not possessing the rigid conformity of the British national curriculum, and not seeking to eliminate local and regional differences in curriculum, the statements and profiles are part of an attempt by the AEC to develop 'a more common view of the purpose of schooling and of the shape of the curriculum' (Hannan and Wilson 1992: 2).

Clearly, at the policy level there are strong centralist forces which are now threatening to break the state monopoly on school education. What we have observed over the past thirty or more years have been a number of dramatic shifts in the locus of control over curriculum and concomitant dramatic shifts in curriculum management structures and networking processes. The process of change continues unabated.

Resource and effectiveness issues

Over a period of thirty years the formal hierarchy has given way to a very large number of significant curriculum units, each seeking to optimise their use of resources in the attainment of top priority goals, for the total benefit of the Australian community. While the vast majority of these units are school-based, there are others that have been directly created by state education authorities, others that have a national genesis, and some that reflect the professional interests of teachers. It is certainly possible to view and discuss the management structures and processes of these units as separate entities within the curriculum domain, but it is important to focus directly on the decision-making structures and relationships, including aspects of power, authority, leadership and responsibility, within these units, as well as on the formal structures and processes of the units themselves.

Certainly, it took considerable time for the majority of teachers, in both primary and secondary schools, to exercise their new-found independence and personal autonomy over what was to be taught and consequently over the resourcing decisions that flowed from the exercising of that control. Of course, while the education departments had provided the freedom for the shift of control, they had not provided any major shift in the control of resources. Staffing decisions were still centralised, and effective interfacing between school curriculum decisions and central office staffing decisions was still some distance down the devolution pathway. At the senior secondary levels there was greater freedom than previously given to teachers to select components for study, but the controlling power of the external examinations meant that choices were always confined within very tight and well-defined parameters.

The 1980s saw even more shifts in the decision-making powers as they affected curriculum. The widespread introduction of program budgeting as a means of bringing curriculum decisions and resource decisions together to ensure that goals and strategies were matched by appropriate resource allocations was a major move towards realisation of the self-governing government school in Australia. Program budgeting was not confined to the curriculum areas, but it provided a new dimension to the management powers of the school council and school administration over the school curriculum, and a new dimension of formal management responsibility to the work and responsibilities of subject heads or coordinators.

Program budgeting gave school councils much closer control over curriculum priorities and resource allocation decisions and hence meant that council ideas (and presumably community ideas) about priorities would receive more favoured treatment in decision-making. It also meant that where the professional view (the view of the school and subject leaders) was at variance with the views of the council, the onus was on the former to convince the latter as to the importance and soundness of their plans and requests.

In these emerging circumstances it became important for the subject or program leaders to prepare and present plans that were clear and visionary and yet catered for the perceived needs of the community. Within each school, special committees of teachers and school leaders met to consider the various program requests and make priority decisions before the program budgets were submitted to council. The program leader had first to convince his or her peers and then to convince the council. Program budgeting also reflected the general move towards strategic management in both government and private enterprise and has been significant in creating a new awareness of the need for schools—and units/departments within schools—to plan on a much fuller and longer-term basis than before. The nature of this planning process is reflected in Figure 13.3.

This approach to curriculum management also gave great impetus to the use of collaborative and participatory strategies in school decision-making. The hierarchical approach to management within the school, an established tradition for virtually the entire history of Australian education, gave way to a flatter management structure in which more people were given responsibility; in many schools, for the first time, staff had the opportunity to be involved in the decision-making if they so wished.

The irony of the situation is that not all teachers, trained professionals as they are, have shown the total commitment to this approach that might have been expected. Many have chosen not to be any more involved than before. Others have indicated concern that the new approach has added unreasonable new burdens to the normal duties of teaching and supervision and has therefore been counterproductive by creating a negative view of the changes for many teachers.

Managing change through evolution rather than destabilisation

In any system as complex as education, no matter how devolved, there are levels of management, levels of communication and, hence, inevitably levels of power. Devolution does not necessarily connote a totally democratic system. Hence, the researcher into curriculum practice can observe a system—say, the school-based assessment system that has operated in Queensland since the 1970s—and make the observation that the power is truly in the hands of the classroom teacher. But, if one samples a group of teachers across the vast distances of Queensland regarding their perceptions of their curriculum power, then a range of answers will emerge.

These answers will depend very much on the teacher's sense of communication and of being valued by the system. Many country-based teachers whose work programs are returned for resubmission feel that their work is unappreciated, that they are unclear about requirements, and that they are powerless to make an impact on the system. These teachers do not see, as does the observer, that processes of reviewing work programs are providing teachers with professional development opportunities and creating a teacher-owned system.

Curriculum management structures can never be conceived of as static; by nature they are in flux as they respond to societal changes and directions. Yet while the structures are at once paradoxically stable and fluid, it is both possible and useful to conceive of them as a series of snapshot models, which at a particular moment of time reflect stages in the process of change between centralised and devolved control and power.

The history of curriculum management in Australia affords us the opportunity to sample a number of models of the process, although it is important to realise that at any given moment several or all models may be present in an education system at least to some degree. In the explication of the models which follows, the major parameters are indicated:

Model A *Centralised control and management: the hierarchy*

This is the most hierarchical model, which clearly establishes decision-making power at the centre of the education bureaucracy. Reflecting the traditional compliance model for organisational control and management, it leaves little space for the classroom teacher's initiative and creativity. Even new teaching and learning strategies tend to evolve centrally and follow a centrally determined pattern of dissemination. External examinations and inspectors act as the enforcement agencies in this model. This is certainly not a model of 'professional' responsibility. The key characteristics of this model are:

- Limited participation by teachers in the decision-making processes affecting curriculum.
- Subject heads and year-level coordinators given basic management tasks to ensure that syllabuses and work programs are appropriately prepared and that texts and class set materials are ordered and obtained.
- School community has little or no role in curriculum decision-making or management; its major function is raising funds for specific projects.
- Very little curriculum evaluation; the major emphasis is on student testing.
- Senior secondary levels dominated by external examinations testing rigid and prescribed syllabuses.

Figure 13.3 An example of the program budgeting process for a department in an Australian primary school

The following is a typical structure for the program budgeting process in a school subject department. Compare the process shown here with that in Figure 13.1; while the process outlined here is somewhat simpler, the inherent logic is identical.

1. *Program title and responsibility*
2. *Year–level applicability* (eg Grades 1 to 6)
3. *Program narratives*, ideally describing:
   - Current situation in institution in relation to this area of responsibility (strengths and weaknesses)
   - Goals for this area of responsibility
   - Objectives of program (short-term and medium-term)
   - Plans for implementation
4. *Resource requirements* (preferably in monetary units and with a clear indication of priority needs)
   - Staffing (teaching and non-teaching personnel)—in the case of government school systems where staffing is determined centrally and paid centrally, the level of staffing required may only be stated as 'effective fulltime staff' (EFTS)
   - Curriculum needs (space, references and texts, equipment, field trips, etc.)
   - Pupils' requisites (if appropriate)
5. *Plans for monitoring and evaluation*

- Inspectorial system used to ensure general compliance with prescribed courses and to reinforce general patterns of organisation and presentation.
- All staffing and major resource decisions made at the centre, with only marginal concern for school perceptions of needs.
- Professional associations of teachers involved in only a minor way with curriculum decisions at the state level.
- Most texts and other published materials specifically designed to meet needs of syllabus.

Model B First-wave devolution of curriculum management: freedom and power

In Model B the hierarchical organisation begins to break down into a flatter, more participative structure. Central planning and control is dramatically reduced in favour of teacher control of curriculum, either individually or through professional associations. Resource management is still centralised, but the organisational rhetoric is increasingly concerned with decentralisation and devolution. The key characteristics of this far more professionally oriented model are:

- Rise of teacher professionalism.
- Some central involvement in curriculum development but not rigidly binding on teachers.
- Teachers at all levels, primary and post-primary, given greater freedom to define, plan and introduce their own courses reflecting needs of students. But teachers respond variably.
- Hierarchy of external control is replaced by the discipline of personal control.
- Guidelines replace detailed course prescriptions.
- Inspectorial system fades away, reducing pressures on teachers.
- Curriculum void created; filled by texts commissioned by major publishers, by subject teacher associations, and by consultants; these become the new elite of management power players.
- Era of teacher-association-based curriculum development projects designed for major impact in the schools.
- Role of teacher still mainly focused on classroom and time management.
- At senior secondary levels, curriculum managers are still the external examination boards, with little autonomy and/or freedom for teachers.
- Devolution in curriculum control and management in its infancy, moving towards mature concept of the self-managing school.

Model C Second-wave devolution: total school management and empowerment

Model C reflects a strong and concerted policy move by governments to give more power to schools and teachers. The key goals are to encourage workplace participation and collaboration, to develop stronger linkages between schools and communities, and to encourage greater educational and resource responsibility and accountability by introducing program budgeting. While most of the major resource decisions are still centralised, we can detect real shifts at this stage towards a 'commitment' model of educational management and towards far greater school site management of all aspects of schooling. The characteristics of this model include:

- Schools gain significant control over content and resource allocation.
- Total school administration involvement in all aspects of curriculum management.
- Maturation of the teacher as curriculum manager.
- More even partnership between schools and central offices of the state education departments in staffing and resourcing decisions.
- The school community (teachers, administrators, parents and students) has the major role in determining implementation and integration of central policy.
- School council involvement in selecting school principals and staff.
- Considerable reductions in the power of central examining bodies and universities concerning the curriculum.
- Subject teacher associations' role as change agents and in curriculum has declined in significance.

Model D Internal autonomy vs external control: paradox and tension

In Model D the nearly autonomous government school emerges, with immense local power over all aspects of schooling—including control of human and financial resources—but within the parameters of national curriculum policy. Commitment is the dominant organisational focus for all staff, and there is a concomitant concern for responsibility and accountability. Some of the major characteristics of this model are:

- The meeting of minds of government, industry and commerce creates forces that transcend state and regional interests to create a new centralism.
- Key people from non-educational domains make an impact on school curriculum, most obviously at senior post-primary levels, but indirectly at other levels also.
- Transfer of resources and power to school management so that the

school will have the opportunity to match staffing requirements with curriculum needs perceived at the local level.
- School administrators, teachers and community given greater responsibility in the management of the financial and capital resources, including the nature and extent of professional development activities of the staff.
- Increased accountability to, and increasing expectations from the community.
- Use of measures such as performance indicators and performance appraisal.
- Nexus between curriculum management process and strategic management plan/operations at the school level.
- Strong links between success and funding.
- The development of strategies such as 'district provision' to improve resource usage and efficiency.
- A reduction in the role of external examinations and hence the influence of the universities over the schools and the curriculum.
- Increasing retention rates escalate pressures for schools to ensure efficient and effective transition to higher and further education and to the workplace.
- Marketing of schools increasingly important in the competitive struggle for a share of the education 'cake'.
- The emergence of the autonomous government school.

The economic basis for educational rationalism

An alternative way of viewing these models is to relate the key or central focus of the management structure and human-resource orientation of each model with the societal predisposition which appears to have been in dominant coexistence with each model (Figure 13.4). Societal predisposition, in this context, refers to the dominant economic imperative of the day which suggests the state of economic health and economic direction for the society at the time. The assumption is that more than any other single factor, the economic imperative drives education. In essence, the need to achieve wellbeing for the people and the country has an enormous impact on the nature of the education we desire and seek and on the nature of the education we can afford.

In an era of *predictable production* when the predominant imperative is growth, a hierarchical structure for curriculum management works effectively, as does the practice of central control over the human resource. In a growth phase, the emphasis is more on getting things done; the centralist and hierarchical approach is successful because fundamentally we all are in agreement about the goals. In this era the demands for curriculum change are minimal, and the role of the curriculum manager is to ensure that teachers keep on doing what is considered necessary for the growth phase to continue.

The era of *economic security* represents the settling down after the previous burgeoning growth phase. People feel secure and become more concerned with issues of participation and democracy in school and educational management. At this time the schools are being run by well-qualified people who, with some justification, can argue for a decision-making role. This is the time when we experience the first wave of devolution and the era when the orientation is towards giving teachers far greater freedom and power. Central control is on the wane during this era.

The stage of *second-wave devolution* signifies a movement towards total school empowerment and coincides with a societal sense of fiscal euphoria—a general belief that all will remain well with the economy, and hence it is reasonable to maintain spending levels and let the future take care of itself. In many ways it is an era of resource and financial irresponsibility. Control in many areas, including that of curriculum management, moves further from the centre towards the schools and towards the teachers.

As economic insecurity sets in with an emerging context of escalating unemployment and national debt, this state of euphoria gives way to and is ultimately replaced by a growing concern for *fundamental accountability*. The public focuses attention on the obvious failings of the economy, and governments and their ministries are regarded as culpable. People begin to demand and expect quality performance. There are moves towards the use of performance-appraisal systems and performance indicators, including national testing of students in core areas, to ensure that the quality of performance strongly supports the new demands for economic growth.

In the domain of curriculum management there is a situation of internal autonomy, with schools and teachers having very great control over the curriculum, but with external forces demanding strong accountability especially in key areas of learning. It is a time when education is

Figure 13.4 Overview of models in context

Model	Societal predisposition	Management structure	Human resource orientation
A	Predictable production	Hierarchical	Control from centre
B	Economic security	First-wave devolution	Freedom and power
C	Fiscal euphoria	Second-wave devolution	Total school empowerment
D	Fundamental accountability	Internal autonomy vs external control	Paradox and tension

seen 'in some influential quarters primarily as an instrument of national economic purpose' (Campbell et al. 1992: 2); a time when all involved in education, and especially in the curriculum area, are enmeshed in paradox and tension. Australia is in that state as we move towards the twenty-first century.

The implications for school administrators

Perhaps the greatest significance of these changes for school administrators at all levels is that they must come to see themselves as both leaders and managers and they must develop the skills to enable them to act accordingly.

School principals, while not having to take direct responsibility for the day-to-day management of the curriculum, must have the interpersonal and communication skills to enable effective linkages and bonding between all the stakeholders in the school community, and between those stakeholders and the demands of central policy. The strategic management approach outlined earlier in this chapter provides a route towards this goal. They must also have the skills to engender teacher commitment to the mission of the school—a commitment that can only be built on skills and strategies to ensure that all staff have:

- Clarity about the school's goals and values.
- The competencies as teachers, administrators and team members that allow success.
- Real influence in decision-making, both individually and in teams; and that they receive expressed appreciation for their contributions to that success. (Kinlaw 1989)

Yet, it would be an error to demand that the principal's leadership must emphasise curriculum planning skills, up-to-date knowledge of large bodies of curriculum-related literature, and up-to-date understanding of all relevant issues in the curriculum arena. As Griffin suggests, this typical view is unrealistic and far too wide in terms of achieving significant school-level curriculum changes. Instead, 'a principal must be sensitive and skilful in manipulating a complex environment, one part of which is curriculum expertise' (Griffin 1988: 245).

In this sense, the principal should focus on the early stages of the strategic management cycle, especially the determination (in concert with the school council and the wider school community) of the mission and goals of the school, which will in turn clearly establish the curriculum orientation of the school and give direction to all other activities. On the leadership side, this demands that the principal be able to give a vision for the future or at least create the environment in which such a vision might be built. On the managerial side, it demands a firm grasp of a variety of other important areas; these range from understanding the principles and practice of staff selection and human resource management to understanding the principles and practices required for the most efficient use of all available resources. Being able to understand and put in place the strategies for effective and efficient financial and capital resource management are vital to this process. Of major importance are also the strategies, some related to marketing and others to public relations, that will guarantee a high positive profile for the school and build its reputation within the community. The quality of the principal's performance will be assessed very much in terms of performance of these management tasks. In contrast, the delegated responsibilities and performance appraisal of other school leaders, such as curriculum directors and subject co-ordinators, will focus more on the operational planning, implementation and evaluation phases.

In fulfilling their operational tasks, these people will need not only high-level curriculum knowledge but also leadership skills to bring together the disparate interests and abilities of teachers in effective teams that pursue agreed goals. While, in the devolved school, the principal will almost certainly have the ultimate status and responsibility, those who are the operational leaders will be key figures in ensuring success.

14 Managing the Reform of Teachers and their Work: Perspectives, Prospects and Paradox

Terri Seddon

Australian schooling has been going through a period of rapid change in recent years, and in this, teachers have been central. They have been a key focus of policy interventions aimed at changing teachers and their work; and teachers and their organisations have been critical in enacting policy interventions. This chapter examines how the conception of teachers and their work informs these policy interventions. I argue that there are three distinct perspectives, and each has different implications for restructuring teachers and teaching. These perspectives are first outlined theoretically and then illustrated with reference to four different policy interventions in Australia in 1989–90. On the basis of this analysis, I discuss the prospects for the reform of teachers and their work, and point to a major paradox confronting educational administration and management.

Framing the debate about teacher reform

The central focus on teachers in educational restructuring is not a purely local development. The Organization for Economic Cooperation and Development (OECD) is involved in a major project on teachers (OECD 1989a, 1989b, 1989c), and there is a 'critical chorus' about teachers in Europe, Japan, the United States, Britain and New Zealand, as well as Australia (see, for example, Holly 1986; Demaine 1988; Ninomiya and Okata 1990; Hill 1990; Lauder 1987). This chorus is sometimes described as the 'teacher quality' debate, but ironically it is less about celebrating teachers than arguing a case (often on flimsy evidence) for their 'improvement'.

In Britain and the United States, for example, moves to improve teachers and teaching have involved a variety of reform strategies. One 'professionalising' strategy focuses on changing teachers through teacher education, enhancing professional development and the teaching professions' capacity to regulate itself. Another strategy has entailed industrial restructuring, changing the conditions and character of teachers' work. Such restructuring has often offset salary increases against new pay and promotion structures and systems of appraisal (Poppleton and Riseborough 1990). Concern about teacher supply and demand has also legitimated flexible entry into teaching; as well as traditional routes into teaching, there has been a move towards school-based apprenticeships and licensing, in which people qualify by teaching under licence while taking basic training (Hill 1990). These changes are redefining who can become teachers and the practices required of them. Such shifts in what counts as teachers' work is being effected directly, by reshaping teachers, and indirectly, by restructuring the regulatory agencies (curriculum, assessment, policy, funding and teacher education agencies, and industrial relations) that shape teachers and teaching.

These direct and indirect strategies for restructuring teachers and teaching presume that changes in the practice of schooling can be brought about by targeting either the individual teachers or their context. However, there is now a new conception of teachers and their work that is beginning to inform policy interventions. This focuses not on 'individuals in context' but on the teaching labour process; that is, on the practices of teachers' work.

Conceptions of teachers and their work

Seeing teachers and their work as 'individuals in context' presumes a psychological view in which individuals are accepted as simultaneously a unit of biological functioning and a unit of social action; an individual's skin is the boundary that separates the individual from his or her social circumstances and delineates the individual as the source of behaviour (action). This positivistic understanding of individuals has been tempered in recent years by the recognition that individuals always exist and act in a 'context'. This trend to consider context has destabilised the theoretical bases of education, but it has not substantially changed commonsense ways of understanding individuals (Seddon 1994b). Most policy, for instance, still takes the individual for granted as a dermatologically bounded unit of action.

There are two distinct ways of understanding the relationship between the individual and context. In its simplest form, the context is seen to constrain and influence individuals, while individuals respond to contextual stimuli. With this stimulus-response model, policies to enhance teacher quality must institute the appropriate constraints and disciplinary measures so that teachers comply with policy-makers' expectations. These contextual constraints are accompanied by mechanisms for identifying and rejecting deviant individuals who fail to conform to expectations.

A more sophisticated version of the 'individual in context' perspective recognises that individuals are active agents, rather than merely passive responders to stimuli. Context is still accepted as the world beyond the individual, but it also includes the meanings that individuals make as they interpret the world as a basis for action. There is therefore an objective context and a constructed subjective context made up of the meanings and understandings that individuals make in their lived experience. Policy framed by this interpretivist view of the 'individual in context' aims to construct a context that will tend to be interpreted in ways that lead to the desired action. The emphasis is on reshaping teachers' processes of meaning-making and reforming the context out of which teachers make meanings. Such interpretivist policies therefore tend to stress teacher education, professional development and school improvement.

However, in the late 1980s another kind of policy intervention emerged in Australia. It did not conceptualise teachers and teaching as 'individuals in context'. Rather, it focused on work as a social process. The key unit of analysis was not the individual, but practice. There is now a growing body of research on what is known as the teachers' work perspective (Connell 1985; Seddon 1994a). It recognises that teachers are workers engaged in a labour process in classrooms, schools and school systems—their workplaces—and that their work involves them, either consciously or unconsciously, in social and political projects that have effects within and beyond the walls of the classroom and the lives of individuals.

This way of understanding teachers and teaching does not accept that there is some intrinsic, essential individual, the source of behaviour and separable from the conditions in which these people live. Rather it is the integration of biological individuals with historically specific social conditions which constitute social action (that is, practice). What counts as the 'individual' and his or her 'context' are social products, which are made and remade through practices that are constituted, shaped and constrained by historically embedded and socially situated relations of gender, class, race, age and other social divisions. These relations of power are experienced practically as relations of advantage/disadvantage and possession/dispossession. They are conflictual and contradictory, and it is these tensions that provide the dynamics of social change and the generative mechanisms of social action. Given the goal of teacher quality, the challenge is to intervene in the social processes that form and reform teachers as workers, their workplaces and their integration in an historically specific teaching labour process.

The teachers' work perspective rests upon an epistemological shift away from a categorical or essentialist perspective to a practice-based relational perspective. Where the former accepts the world of experience as an unproblematic source of conceptual categories, the latter attends to the social practices and processes that produce the world of experience and the categories by which we understand it. Categorical approaches are useful as a preliminary way of understanding social life and are central to sloganising in political mobilisations, but as Connell (1987: 57) notes:

> The trouble starts when the first approximation becomes the end of the analysis; when the categories 'women' and 'men' are taken as absolutes, in no need of further examination or finer differentiation. For there are problem areas where this will not work at all, and others where the approach rapidly becomes misleading.

In summary, the categorical 'individual in context' and relational 'teachers' work' perspectives are distinct ways of seeing teachers and teaching. They each offer different ways of understanding the problem of teacher quality and identifying different solutions. Between 1989 and 1990 there were four major interventions aimed at reconstructing teachers and teaching, which illustrate very clearly these different approaches to reform. Let us consider them in turn.

A professionalising managerial intervention

In 1989 the Schools Council published a report entitled *Teacher Quality: An Issues Paper*. It seeks to improve teaching by extending professional development oriented to the preparation of a preferred 'professional'— one showing 'teacherly' and managerial capacities. In passing, it also suggests a 'partnership' model for the management of teacher education.

The Schools Council is one of four Councils of the National Board of Employment, Education and Training (NBEET). It was established to provide independent advice to the federal minister on matters related to the development of primary and secondary schooling. Its chair was a former commissioner of the Commonwealth Schools Commission, and many of its members were drawn from an educational constituency dating back to the 1970s.

Schools Council focuses its discussion on what it terms a 'value-added approach' (Schools Council 1989: 2), exploring 'what opportunities are and should be provided [for] teachers to increase their skills and knowledge at various stages throughout their career'. The 'value-added teacher' (VAT) has a number of characteristics. VATs have been through structured training activities, which increase knowledge and skills relevant to schools and classrooms. Breadth of prior experience is recognised, but the emphasis is on educational knowledge and skills and/or experience in private industry. They show personal characteristics such as confidence, patience, persistence, imagination, flexibility, adaptability and cooperation. They are good teamworkers, skilled at conflict resolution and mediation, able communicators with human relations skills, diligent in preparation and using imaginative teaching strategies, and show open attitudes of inquiry to teaching and learning. They are 'reflective practitioners' with 'demonstrated excellence in the classroom', and are industrially conscious professionals, aware of industrial relations, the legitimate place of employer and union, and the interrelatedness of education and industry.

The VATs' role involves 'helping students to learn'. It stresses teachers' teaching function and de-emphasises more recent expectations of teachers' work. Their site and scope of operation are defined by 'the school'—signifying the school organisation, its climate and ethos, the processes and procedures of administration school policy, the relationship with parents and the outside community, and the activities of the union and the employer (Schools Council 1989: 30). Their primary focus is fixed on the students in their classrooms, with special provision to help them understand and work with different types of students. Socio-cultural differences are recognised, at least among students, but the concern is with enhancing the delivery of education rather than questions about understanding student diversity in a broader context.

The tasks of training are to produce reflective practitioners; to enhance teaching skills and knowledge, including the skills of teaching special groups of students; and to prepare teachers for employment in different educational sectors with distinctive culture and corporate approaches.

The notion of the VAT rests upon an 'individual in context' perspective. The teacher is defined behaviourally, in terms of individual attributes, capacities and orientations. The individual is defined as a 'professional', focused on the act of teaching but showing the personal characteristics of a good manager. The 'professional' is no longer to be simply a loyal teacher of students, but a manager of a learning context.

This designation of a preferred professional defines a norm that indicates what is, and is not, a good teacher. But the specification implies fluidity, rather than tight definition. It recognises that, in practice, teachers do not simply play roles but are active agents who engage with and interpret their worlds and act according to those understandings. This normative openness gives legitimacy to professionalism that shows intellectuality and independent integrity.

But these positive aspects of the *Teacher Quality* report are undermined by what is not said in the report. Teachers are to develop knowledge as well as skills, but what knowledge remains unspecified. Questions of control are little discussed. The report proposes 'partnership', noting the importance of employing agencies participating in the specification of training programs. In line with its advocacy of professional flexibility and integrity, the report notes administrative, financial and attitudinal constraints on partnership and justifies the critical stance of higher education institutes (HEIs) in professional preparation. But it also suggests that partnership would entail HEIs being 'brought in' to the process of teacher education. The implication is that 'partnership' is not equal participation but entails a subordination of the HEIs and what they stand for. Finally, the context is addressed only through recent teacher reports, which means that *Teacher Quality* accepts prevailing definitions of the 'problem' of teachers and teaching. It makes the report's preferred professional seem abstract and divorced from the everyday world, and it excludes a basis for social judgements which results in lead to technical ways of seeing and solving problems.

A regulatory managerial intervention

In 1990 a report commissioned by the Australian Education Council (AEC), entitled *Teacher Education in Australia* (better known as the Ebbeck Report), was released. This report builds on the Schools Council document, but with significant elaborations and omissions. It clarifies the preferred professional and spells out a partnership that prepares (but does not include) teachers.

The working party that prepared the report included substantial representation of large teacher-employing and funding agencies. It reported directly to the AEC, comprising state and federal education ministers and chaired in 1990 by the federal Minister for Employment, Education and Training. Unlike the Schools' Council, the Ebbeck Report feeds into a powerful policy-making (rather than advisory) structure, which has already spearheaded major 'corporate federalist' interventions oriented to the creation of a national system of schooling (Lingard 1991).

The Ebbeck Report presents a model of teacher preparation for primary and early childhood teacher education but then generalises it to most teachers. It proposes a three-year first teaching degree, a BA or BSc (Teaching), taken over seven semesters, followed by a concurrent 'associateship' and part-time BEd over two years. The first degree would prepare students for their first employment contract as an 'assistant teacher'. Primary and early childhood teachers would be offered a general education, plus studies in curriculum, school organisation, human development and teaching methodology. Secondary teachers would receive an intensive preparation in the school subjects to be taught. The BEd degree is to be taken while neophyte teachers are employed on a 50 per cent load as an assistant teacher, allowing time for reading into the 'mainstream educational studies—educational psychology, educational measurement and assessment, contemporary issues in educational thought and practice' (AEC 1990: 30). Secondary teachers' BEd could emphasise teaching methods in the subject discipline (AEC 1990: 35).

Assistant teachers would receive *pro rata* salary and leave, but would have independent classroom teaching duties, full legal status as an employee, including full duty of care, and they could not be employed unless also enrolled in BEd studies (AEC 1990: 31). For the first two years of their career, teachers would receive the equivalent of one year's pay, but with the opportunity to experience whole-school life while on a reduced load with regularised induction.

The Ebbeck Report's model of teacher preparation would give all teachers (early childhood, primary and secondary) double degrees and the equivalent of four years' training and make teaching a fully graduate profession. As with the Schools Council's outline, the preferred professional's task is teaching, servicing students. Effective teaching demands training to improve teaching skills and links between educational 'theory' and practice, but Ebbeck goes beyond the Schools Council in determining the preferred professional's context and content.

The preparation of the preferred professional is targeted to a particular sector of schooling. The Schools Council proposed such differentiation to meet teachers' needs in teaching special groups of students and employers' needs in developing their corporate approach. Ebbeck reweights these issues; the point is not to target different groups of students but to recognise institutional pluralism as a contextual feature. The report notes:

> As the options for taking advantage of non-government schooling expands and as zoning constraints are removed from schools within the government sector, the schools which have the obligation to accept all children wishing to attend from the surrounding community will increasingly require teachers who can cope with a greater concentration of students with poor motivation, lack of parental interest and support, behavioural problems and learning difficulties. (AEC 1990: 9)

The implication is that there is a market in schools and that 'residualisation' (Preston 1984) is simply a feature of our system, requiring the preparation of some teachers for the able, committed and wealthy, and other 'residual' teachers for the residual poor and/or 'less able' and alienated students.

The preferred professional's content is defined by the completion of both degrees and associateship. They would have a general education and some grasp of psychologically based educational theory. There may be some consideration of philosophy of education but not of the historical and social context of schooling. Secondary teachers entering teaching by this route would be focused on the content and teaching method of academic disciplinary knowledge. This valuation of content prioritises 'the school' and classroom, subordinating any consideration of or involvement with the 'outside world' to the demands and problems of the immediate teaching situation. Such an evaluation is encouraged by Ebbeck's notion that school realities are a touchstone for judging other content, such as the higher education institutions' more theoretical offerings (AEC 1990: 30), and by measures (such as reducing contact with non-education HEI staff and students; the privileging of educational issues, while marginalising industrial concerns and teacher unions; limiting the period of studentship during which neophyte teachers can follow their own interests unfettered by an employment contract, while also limiting extensive contact with schools in this period) which would seem to limit the development of teachers' breadth of vision and therefore their capacity to ask questions (AEC 1990: 53–4).

Unlike the Schools Council view that teacher education should build on students' personal qualities and experience to produce a reflective practitioner, the Ebbeck Report presents teacher education as a constrained and passive transfer of knowledge and skills. Student teachers appear as undifferentiated units, or empty vessels, which are filled through the training sequence. Professionals, it seems, are to simply deliver a service defined elsewhere and not be concerned about formulating or questioning policy, nor responding flexibly in practice. Critical inquiry or reflection do not seem to be valued; and the teacher unions, those concerned with the social and historical context and other professionals are delegitimised. On this ground the Ebbeck Report spells out its notion of 'partnership'.

'Partnership' is developed by redefining the roles of major partners: employing agencies, the schools, the federal government and the HEIs. Teachers and teacher unions are not mentioned. The redefined roles consolidate relationships between the first three partners (that is, parts or closely regulated adjuncts of the state) and sets HEIs in a contracted market relationship with them.

Employers of teachers contract with one or more HEIs for teacher education programs that meet their approval, and with HEIs and other public and private providers for inservice training. All this professional development, being 'system provided', is to provide credit towards the HEI awards. The HEIs are also in partnership with schools for program preparation, delivery and student assessment. Supervisors are school-based, and reports on assistant teachers are provided by schools to both HEIs and employers, although it is not clear what happens if their evaluations of the student assessment reports differ. The HEIs are 'expected to accept' (AEC 1990: 32) a school's satisfactory reports as a basis for the award of degrees. Partnership extends, then, to the determination and allocation of student awards.

There is also a partnership between the HEI and federal government based on the institutional profile, which determines funding and student numbers. This mechanism implements the HEI–employing agency contract. It also establishes an implementation partnership between the employing agency and the federal government, which is supplemented by an advisory partnership, enabling employers to convey their concerns in the area of teacher education and inservice training to the funding body.

This network of partnerships promises to reduce HEI autonomy and massively increase employer control of professional development for teachers through the establishment of negotiated and competitive contracts linked to credit transfer and institutional profiles, the associateship, and the new definition of a qualified teacher and its monitoring through a national teacher registration board.

The negotiated contract means that the state, as employing and funding agency, is the 'consumer', choosing from a range of programs for pre- and inservice education, all of which provides participants credit towards award programs. It is also 'the piper who calls the tune'. HEIs will have to compete in this marketplace because their institutional funding depends on it. They will have to offer attractive and marketable products; nothing too dangerous or too far from the defined image of a good teacher or they will risk losing the contract to some other provider.

The associateship provides a means of closely supervising HEI programs and products. Assistant teachers are not students, but probationary employees locked into an employment contract and therefore subject to labour discipline. The HEIs are, by extension, also regulated by this labour discipline. 'Deviance' on the part of the assistant teacher reflects upon the HEI, but more significantly, the HEI is subject to the discipline of the schools' 'practical survival techniques'. With the day-to-day realities of the school as the defined sphere of operation and the touchstone for judging HEI performance, relevance to 'the school' will define important (legitimate) content and process. Assistant teachers, teachers, schools and employers will all be in a position to adjudicate on the validity of HEI programs and to police, regulate and shape HEI programs on a day-to-day basis.

The newly defined 'qualified teacher' means that the only way of becoming qualified is through the proposed model. Higher education institutes cannot stand outside the system and offer alternative teacher education programs because these will neither be funded nor give teacher registration. Nor can employing agencies. Monitoring compliance with this new definition of the qualified teacher is linked to Ebbeck's proposal for a 'voluntary national teacher registration board'; but lacking trust in the profession, the report argues for a voluntary national system under the aegis of the AEC (AEC 1990: 49).

The registration board would recognise teacher qualifications and facilitate intra-national migration to iron out unevenness in teacher supply and demand. It would deregulate the teaching labour market but provide a means of screening entry to, and performance in, teaching. As the report notes, further work on 'important questions' related to the duration of registration, deregistration and the registration of teachers in independent schools is necessary (AEC 1990: 49).

The Ebbeck Report offers a blueprint for teacher education and a coercive managerial strategy for its implementation. Like the Schools Council, it adopts an 'individual in context' perspective but of a far more suspicious, coercive kind. The proposal aims to restructure the context of teaching in order to bind individuals in carrot-and-stick regulatory and contractual arrangements. The preferred professional is defined behaviourally and focused firmly on classroom teaching. But the norm that emerges is far more tightly specified, with less scope for flexibility, independent integrity and intellectuality.

Restructuring work: the principles of award restructuring

Two policy interventions can be identified that target the teaching labour process. These build on the general principles of award restructuring—a non-educational policy intervention emanating from the Australian union movement, based on a broad assessment of Australia's social and economic context.

Rejecting a radical deregulatory response to Australia's economic problems, in which there have been highly conflictual industrial relations and high costs that are disproportionately born by workers, the labour movement and its peak organisation, the Australian Council of Trade Unions (ACTU), has sought consensus through neo-corporatist structures, such as the Accord. But by 1986, pressures on the Accord were mounting, and the Hawke Labor government abandoned full wage indexation linked to the consumer price index. The ACTU responded by proposing a fact-finding mission to Europe to identify principles that could underpin a new accord. The ensuing report, *Australia Reconstructed* (ACTU/TDC 1987), recognised the severity of Australia's balance of payments crisis and vulnerability to the international economy, but sought solutions that produce 'low unemployment, low inflation and economic growth which is more equitably distributed' (ACTU/TDC 1987: xi).

The final report of the ACTU/TDC mission is a complex document, which makes a number of recommendations for macroeconomic and microeconomic reform. It advocates a corporatist consensus-based approach to managing Australia's economic crisis. It involves negotiating and actively pursuing a set of national economic and social objectives, which aim to achieve full employment, low inflation, and equitable increases in living standards. These objectives are to be achieved by maximising economic growth and development through innovative, tripartite management and the removal of impediments to change. Such consensual management rests upon maintaining a stable economic context through a prices and income accord; strategically guided trade and industry policies; measures to encourage productive investment; and industry-restructuring programs. These restructuring programs have two dimensions.

The first is an active labour market program that tackles unemployment not through passive programs of minimalist cash transfer, but through actively promoting skill formation, effective job placement and reduced labour market segmentation. Rather than blaming someone for unemployment, this kind of active program recognises its structural character. As the report notes:

> There is something deeply unfair about the fact that those who are on the contracting side of the structural transformation lose both security of employment, income level and general status in the labour market, while those who are on the expansive side are regarded and rewarded as 'heroes' with good pay trends and secure jobs. Both of these changes are equally necessary. The real heroes should be those who make the changes possible by shouldering the 'work' of changing over to a new job. The least we can do to encourage this highly productive 'work' is to offer generous training opportunities. (Swedish Trade Union Confederation 1986)

The second dimension of industry restructuring entails a reformed practice of work. Firstly, it requires the promotion of a production consciousness and culture which recognises that the 'creation of wealth is a prerequisite of its distribution' (ACTU/TDC 1987: 154)—that there is a basis for cooperation in production, as well as conflict over distribution. Secondly, the reform of production involves changing the interaction of skill formation, technology, work organisation, industrial relations, training and education. No one element can be separated out and privileged as an autonomous good. Technology (or education) cannot be treated as 'cargo cult' (ACTU/TDC 1987: 156). The emphasis is firmly on the integration of these elements of a process in which the active part is played by people. As the managing director of Ford Australia puts it, 'harnessing the human factor to the quality and productivity challenge' (Dix 1985: 6).

Central to the process of restructuring is skills formation, viewed not as a cost but as an investment in people who are productive resources (ACTU/TDC 1987: 155). The use of such productive resources requires radically different management practices, which provide scope for workers' active contribution to production rather than controlling and limiting their contribution to the performance of prespecified tasks. This emphasis on skills formation and industrial democracy places education and training for both workers and managers at the centre of award restructuring.

The mission's proposal for a two-tiered system of wage fixation was accepted by the ACTU in 1986 and submitted to the national wage case in 1987. It proposed flat-rate wage increases and percentage increases linked to improved performance and efficiency. In 1988 the national wage case was linked to award restructuring in line with the Australian Industrial Relations Commission's (AIRC) structural efficiency principle. This stated that employers and unions should cooperate to review their awards in order to improve industry efficiency and workers' career opportunities. These general principles of award restructuring have informed two distinctive interventions into the reconstruction of teachers' work.

Teacher award restructuring: a union intervention

State teacher unions and the national Australian Teachers Union (ATU) have actively grasped the opportunities opened up by award restructuring. In 1986 the High Court set aside the 1929 State School Teachers Case decision (Spaull 1987), enabling education to be defined as an industry for federal industrial relations purposes. In September the following year the ACTU recognised the strategic significance of the teacher unions in the ACTU, and the centrality of education in award restructuring, and agreed to mount a special case for teacher salaries. In 1989 the proposal for teacher award restructuring was submitted to the national wage case and to state industrial jurisdictions. In line with the AIRC's structural efficiency principle, it proposed a national benchmark salary to restore wage relativities with other professional workers and introduced an Advanced Skills Teacher category and salary range. The ATU also launched a national campaign which enabled state unions to coordinate their demands for award restructuring. Agreements followed in all states and territories, although the coincidence of teacher award restructuring with budget cuts and other educational reform programs has led to delays, trade-offs and sometimes the suspension of negotiations.

Teacher award restructuring has focused on a relatively narrow range of general award restructuring principles. It stresses the restoration of relativities because of the AIRC's instruction to 'incorporate all past work value changes' (H9100: 22, quoted by Moloney 1990: 14) as a basis for new fixed relativities. This means that the onus is on teacher unions to make up the decline in teachers' real wages and the increased demands of teachers' work in a new salary scale commensurate with other

professional workers (Division 3 of the engineers award is being used as the standard for the top of the automatic incremental scale). Teacher award restructuring also pursues an improved career structure for teachers, particularly for experienced classroom teachers. Other issues have been addressed, but are less high profile. In Queensland, for example, there have been discussions on inservice, performance review and development, review of teachers duties and detailed examination of role statements for existing and new promotional positions (Molony 1990).

As Moloney argues, the general principles of award restructuring open up an enormous potential agenda, which is limited by timelines and what are practical goals at this stage:

> In the end, award restructuring comes down to practical collective choices about which of the multitude of desirable changes are achievable and have priority. (Moloney 1990: 14)

While this commonsense assessment has a certain validity, strategically assessing what is a 'practical choice' now and in the future depends significantly on teacher union traditions and orientations to educational and industrial issues and on actors besides the union movement. The employing agencies, for example, have been unenthusiastic, showing uncertainty and unwillingness to commit themselves to firm proposals in the face of proactive union action. There have been delays in establishing structures, starting negotiations and reaching agreement (Moloney 1990). Future developments will also depend on the outcomes of the current award restructuring negotiations. All the while, further system changes are proceeding, changing the environment of award restructuring and union, teacher and employer commitments. For example, in Victoria agreement on award restructuring had been reached between unions and the Ministry of Education, and agreement from the federal government about payment, but the ratification of the agreement as an award through the Victorian Industrial Relations Commission was halted by teachers' outrage at the impact of budget cuts.

Restructuring the labour process: a managerial intervention

The second intervention depends on a development of general award restructuring principles, which recognises current education policy concerns with output and accountability, but differentiates between 'efficiency' and 'productivity' in policy and industrial reform (Marginson 1990). 'Efficiency' addresses the relationship of inputs and outputs in monetary terms, describing the cost per unit of a constant level of output. Increasing efficiency aims to reduce the cost of output by cutting labour costs or increasing work demands. By contrast, 'productivity' addresses the relationship between actual inputs and outputs (not their monetary value), describing the volume of actual output for constant levels of input. Increasing productivity aims to increase real outputs, both in quantity and quality, using a constant amount of labour over a constant time. As Marginson argues, increased productivity growth involves changes in the organisation of work:

> [it] . . . is not *intrinsically* exploitative and therefore provides the best basis for management–worker agreement on the expansion of output. (Marginson 1990: 7, emphasis included)

Some aspects of the productivity perspective have been picked up and actively prosecuted by private educational consultant Dean Ashenden (Ashenden 1990a). This intervention jumps off from a critique of award restructuring. He argues, firstly, that current teacher award restructuring offers useful short-term solutions and reform strategies, but ultimately they will fail to solve the problems of teachers and teaching because they neglect the core issues: for teachers, the organisation and management of teachers' work and the nature of student–teacher relations; and for teacher employers, arresting the loss of public faith in schooling and limiting expenditure (Ashenden 1990b: 2–3). Secondly, it has entailed conflictual trade-offs in which it is assumed gains by one party entail losses by the other, and vice versa. Thirdly, teacher award restructuring has taken the model of metal industry award restructuring without recognising the differences between the metals industry and the education industry and therefore the inappropriateness of the reform proposals currently being negotiated. Multiskilling, for example, is appropriate for the metals industry, but not for education, where teachers are already multiskilled and need reduced work demands (Ashenden 1990b: 11). Finally, the teacher unions are taking the problems and solutions of the metals industry when they should be taking 'their mind-set, their problem-solving methods, their willingness to look at the 'industry' as a whole and to question it from the ground, from the work process, up' (Ashenden 1990b: 11).

What is most valuable about Ashenden's starting point is that it focuses attention unequivocally on teachers' actual labour process—the work teachers do and the workplace they do it in—rather than on the agencies that regulate teachers' work or the imputed problems facing teachers and teaching. From this basis he offers a redefinition of the problem of teachers and teaching and a new solution.

Ashenden argues that leaving aside disputes about money and control, teachers and employers have much in common. Above all, educational work is insufficiently rewarding because the 'productivity of learning' has not improved and may have declined. The solution is to seek productivity increases 'not from spending more or from working harder but from working *smarter*' (Ashenden 1990b: 4, emphasis included).

The core problem of teachers' work lies in the conflict between the labour process typical of classrooms and the teachers' professional ideology involving a commitment to educating children. There is a conflict between situation and aspiration, and teachers are torn by the contradiction between the 'real job' of teaching children to think (Ashenden 1990b: 5) and the endless demands of 'baby-sitting', student control, discipline and classroom management in which teachers, rather than students, take responsibility for learning.

This fundamental conflict exists because the classroom organisation of teachers' work is incompatible with real teaching and learning. The 'cottage classroom', the standardised work unit of the 'last of the mass cottage industries' (Ashenden 1990b: 5), has been institutionalised by teachers (through their unions) and employers in industrial agreements and awards. These dictate the kinds of educational workers, access to teaching, hours of work, class contact hours and the standardised educational group (size and character). Industrial relations have 'set in concrete' a standardised labour process and low productivity of learning with which both teachers and employers are dissatisfied.

Ashenden's solution is to propose an unconstrained look at teachers' work in order to identify and reform limitations on the productivity of learning. He argues that the teaching labour process can be improved by offering varied career structures; easy movement in and out of the profession; a more complex division of labour, reducing the range of teachers' tasks while increasing the range of other educational workers to take on the 'non-teacherly' work. Teachers would be 'freed to concentrate on high-level educational work'. Their training would stress 'not multi-skilling but deep-skilling, in both knowledge of curriculum areas and in teaching and learning methods and strategies' (Ashenden 1990b: 11).

The message is that no one and everyone is responsible for the poor organisation of teachers' work because it is an historical development, consolidated by both teachers and employers. But everyone suffers from it and is dissatisfied with it. With blame and suffering generalised to all, the heat can be taken out of teacher industrial relations, and both parties can collaborate to bring about reform satisfactory to all. He proposes a round table, beyond media glare, where the big picture and detail of future schooling can be worked out, and the (managerial) problem of getting schools to own this picture can be tackled.

Ashenden's intervention seems likely to be industrially attractive to educational managers and many teachers, because it bridges educational and industrial strategies but sidesteps current conflict by offering a way of seeing the problems of teachers and teaching beyond either framework. But it is likely to worry teacher unions, which are being asked to reconsider industrial agreements on working conditions as a basis for dialogue, without any guarantees that the protection historically given to teachers by those agreements will be maintained. What is striking, and indeed gives some support to union fears, is the convergence of Ashenden's intervention with conservative specifications. These convergences arise because of the way Ashenden develops his argument.

Firstly, he takes as his unit of analysis the 'cottage classroom', where one teacher confronts the standardised educational group of students. This focus neglects important aspects of teachers' work that occurs in schools and school systems but beyond the classroom. It enables Ashenden to leave aside conflict about money and control (Ashenden 1990b: 4)—that is, the economic and political dimensions of teachers' work—and address 'common' (because abstracted) 'educational' relationships between students and teachers.

Secondly, he usefully focuses on the contradiction between aspiration and situation, noting positive educational developments that have arisen from the creative tension (Ashenden 1990b: 6). But his analysis consistently privileges the ideology of 'education' over the actual practice of teachers' work. He affirms the abstracted discourse of 'education', 'teaching and learning' and 'professionalism', which obscures actual inequality in school provision and conflicts in teachers' work because his touchstone is a traditional notion of education rather than the actual experience of teachers and teaching. His campaign becomes one of making the ideal real, through the reorganisation of teachers' work to allow 'situation' to converge with 'aspiration' for at least some educational workers. Its effect is to reconfirm existing inequality of schooling structured by academic–vocational, mental–manual, educational–instructional divisions.

The Australian teacher debate: perspectives, prospects and paradox

The Schools Council report and the Ebbeck Report are both educational managerial interventions informed by an 'individual in context' perspective. This sees the goal of teacher quality being achieved by strategies of school improvement and teacher professional development, which tend to target the regulatory agencies rather than teachers' work directly. The psychological focus on teachers as individuals and the behaviourist assumption that abstracted individuals are the source of observable activity encourage a 'blame-the-victim' view of teachers. Teachers who do not show particular personal characteristics, teaching delivery skills or subject expertise are seen to require improvement (professional development), closer control or are to be screened out of the profession. The usually implicit assumption is that the crisis of schooling can in some way be linked to teacher deficit. What differentiates the two reports is the Schools

Council's liberal humanism, which sees teachers as people to be managed through benign techniques of education, while the Ebbeck Report takes a hard-nosed view, seeing teachers as simply elements of state capacity, which must be managed like other non-human resources; people are ciphers in an economic game to be managed efficiently and effectively regardless of human cost.

The relational 'teachers' work' perspective offers a different view of teachers and teaching. From this perspective what is at issue in the debate about teacher quality is a political campaign to restructure the historically specific form of the contemporary teaching labour process. The problem cannot therefore be simply a matter of deficient teachers and inadequate school or classroom contexts. It is rather about how the social and historical formation of teachers as workers and the formation of teachers' working conditions can be reformed so that their integration in the teaching labour process has different social effects. The way into this problem is not to target individuals with different educating and disciplinary techniques and schools with school effectiveness strategies, but to intervene in the practices and processes that constitute and constrain 'teachers as workers' and 'teachers' working conditions' and their integration in the teaching labour process.

Reformulating the problem of teacher quality in this way expands the scope of potential restructuring immensely, turning attention away from classrooms, schools and school systems in themselves and focusing on the changing institutional and discursive setting of the teaching labour process. What becomes central is the organisation, regulation and division of labour of the entire education industry and the way that practices (at every level and in every sector) constitute educational regimes: distinct sets of objectives, outcomes and experiences of schooling, particular relations of power and patterns of interaction, mobilisation, conflict and consent. As Holly (1986) suggests, the concern about teacher quality maintains a moral panic about teachers, which legitimises quite fundamental shifts in the social relations of teachers' work and the reconstruction of school system regimes. The teacher debate therefore forms an arena where the modern practice of teachers' work and its place and purpose in the nation state is debated and struggled over.

In the restructuring debate so far, there are convergent qualitative themes emerging. It would seem that Australian teachers' work may increasingly show 'professionalism' as a unity of teacherly and managerial qualities; 'partnership' in the form of apparently neutral mechanisms, which mask patterns of subordination and domination; and 'practicality' as mind-set and practice, which conforms teachers to the immediate 'realities' of their classrooms and subordinates other things to that touchstone. Teachers may well become re-centred on teaching—that is, educational relationships with students in a classroom setting with a reduced role in administrative and curriculum decision-making. Teaching would entail the delivery of a service rather than its formulation. This could be seen as a kind of deskilling, separating conception from execution of task. So what is likely to be stressed is teaching as a skilled specialist activity; teaching as classroom-based craft and management, which is distinct from skilled, specialist non-classroom-based policy, administration and management. Educational work would therefore develop a more complex division of labour, involving a horizontal division between teacher managers and administrative managers and an increased vertical division organised around skills.

However, while it is possible to speculate on the outcomes of the current teacher debate, predictions about the effects of the different policy interventions cannot be made. This is because proposals for reform, policy and its implementation are not simple managerial but intensely political processes.

The interventions in the teacher debate are all instances of active participation by agencies attempting to define an agenda for future schooling. What we don't know is how the interventions will be affected by each other's successes and failures, or by broader social developments. What is at issue is not only the fate of each intervention, but how their interactional effects will shift the balance of social forces and the kinds of new interventions that will be called forth in the process. The potential for interactive effects is magnified if one recognises that education policy is not specific to education but is a particular aspect of an ongoing debate about the organisation and coordination of social life. In its modern form this is a debate between social democracy and radical conservatism, in which the efficacy of states or markets as a means of social regulation is in question. These debates have a major effect on the mechanisms of educational provision (Dale 1989; Ball 1990; Chubb and Moe 1990).

The interventions are also all top-down managerial strategies, in which active managers in states or unions define the terrain for compliant policy-implementers. But teachers are not always compliant. Policy must be seen as an ambit claim, which is preceded, accompanied and followed by actual politics (Beilhartz 1987). Contingency arising from inter-managerial politics is compounded in the politics of translating policy to practice (Ball 1992). While many teachers have gone along with recent educational change, there is no reason to suspect that such resignation will exist indefinitely.

For these reasons, the outcomes of the teacher debate cannot be known theoretically. The debates and practices of restructuring are contingent, complex and contested social and political processes in which we are all implicated, regardless of our will. Whether we live that participation actively or passively is a matter of 'choice', a consequence of our own self-formation and the conditions of our lives.

However, one thing is clear. The interventions outlined here are premised upon distinct ways of seeing the crisis of teachers and teaching, and its solution. The Schools Council and Ebbeck educational managerial interventions target *individuals* and suggest management strategies that stress active leadership by some individuals and passive or compliant following by others (Angus 1993b). Such individualist management is consistent with the individualist reform strategies being proposed. The award restructuring managerial interventions target *work*, proposing a relational reformulation of the teaching labour process, but they veer towards individualist managerial strategies for its implementation. Like the educational managerial strategies, these award restructuring managerial strategies attempt to change individuals and contexts. They end up separating subject and object, actor and system, individual and context, educational and industrial. But conceptually this is not where the work perspective starts, nor where it ends politically. There is a profound and potentially generative contradiction here.

The work perspective offers a basis for new questions about teachers and their work. It begins to offer new strategies for reform, but one need not follow Ashenden in seeing the teaching labour process as restricted to very limited sites (the 'cottage classroom'), socially unconstrained (ignoring the prevailing human–human and human–nature relationships), politically uncontentious (assuming a level playing field) or amenable to uncontradictory 'management' (harmonising the situation–aspiration contradiction by simply stressing the 'educational'). This slide back to traditional management solutions could be resisted. The pressing questions are therefore: Where might the work perspective lead if the contradiction between a relational formulation of the problem of teachers and the individualist practices of effecting and coordinating change could be reconciled in other ways? What might reform interventions, the policies and the practices of effecting and coordinating change informed by a relational perspective look like? What solutions to the problems of teachers and teaching might appear possible? And what might such interventions, policies and practices mean for the practical politics of reforming schools and the work of educational management?

15 Parents, the Community and School Governance

Tony Knight

Towards parental involvement (the Education Act 1872)

Parent opinion was first recognised in the Education Act 1872 (Sections 14 and 16) ruling that each school was to have a Board of Advice, which was to include parents and citizen representation. The powers of the board were varied but included the right to suspend any teacher for misconduct or to summon parents before a Justice if they neglected to send their child to school. These boards of advice were abolished in 1910. School committees were brought in to take their place, and parents were removed from the governance of school policy formation (Collins 1973: 10).

Centralised, bureaucratic control of school decision-making was to remain in place for almost a century. If parents were to exert any influence over school policy at all, it was through the Minister of Public Instruction, not the director-general. This form of hierarchical authority meant a distancing from the local community. Schools operated with a kind of grant of authority from parents, who functioned as clients under an assumption of *loco parentis*. Education came to be seen as something that happens in a classroom, and parents were not encouraged to be actively involved in their childrens' schooling; they saw little reason for being concerned with broader values of an education for the common good.

Towards parent participation

Since the 1970s school systems in Australia have attempted to devolve their control over school decision-making and encourage the participation of parents, teachers and students. A powerful impetus to this governance movement was the Karmel Report (1973), entitled *Schools in Australia*, which was a seminal influence in developing the broader participation of parents and community within local schools. The report reflected changes occurring in the educational community more broadly. For instance, before the 1973 Karmel Report an action research project instigated by La Trobe University's School of Education in 1971 set out to provide a school-based and curriculum-oriented course of teacher education of two years' duration, in an inner-urban girls secondary high school (Claydon 1975). Part of the brief of this task force was to 'involve parents in its decision-making processes and at the same time, to involve itself in the community, to break out of the fortress and meet people where they lived and worked' (Gill 1975: 163). The school principal at Brunswick Girls High School made the following comments about a program of 'home visits' made by the teaching staff:

> So things have changed since 1970. Take home–school relations as they are now. Parents have formed Ethnic Parent Councils whose executives, over this last year, have held ongoing discussions about the school and how it can best serve the community. Meaningful parent involvement is growing as parents are gradually empowered to take a far more central role in the education of their daughters and to change the role of the school according to their needs. A close relationship with the form teacher has been as meaningful for the parent as for the teacher and the student—all parties have become well-trusted friends whatever the need. It makes our artificially home pastoral period of 1971, where parents met some staff stranger for a talk, appear like a weird game. (English 1975: 126)

This parent–school/community program was within the context of legislation contained in a report published in May 1973 by Dr L. Shears, Director-General of the Victorian Department of Education, to the effect that school councils should be larger, with wider powers, and would be divided into two areas:

1. The School Council would comprise 15–17 members, elected or nominated, representing parents, municipalities, community organisations and others. Powers of the council included maintenance, organisation of community use of facilities, administration of grants and Education Department moneys and *advice* to the principal on education policy.
2. The School Education Committee was composed of representatives of staff, parents, the community, the school council and, where appropriate, students. This committee was to *advise* the principal and School Council on matters relating to the school's education program.

This was the first attempt since 1872 to grant parents and members of the community a role in planning school activities. It did not have the hiring-and-firing power of the early legislation but instead had an *advisory* role, with the principal retaining the right of veto.

Despite the advisory nature of its role, this Victorian legislation ought to be considered as a step towards a more serious involvement of parents and community in influencing policy within local schools. As Gill states:

> As a consequence of the announcement of the new Department position, there has been much debate within Victoria about the advantages of parent involvement, the problems and the dangers. Parents are beginning to feel free to assert their rights and some are beginning to realise their responsibilities towards both their children and the school. (1975: 171)

Kirner made a supporting claim at the time:

> If we as parents have a right to participate in the control of education then we have an equal responsibility to communicate with all participants—the administration, the teachers, the student and community.
> Real and effective communication cannot be achieved unless all are partners in school government. (1973: 4)

At the same time a number of teachers 'reacted with a degree of cynicism in relation to this official statement'. In general it was felt that the heavily centralised power of the administration would obstruct any genuine devolution of power over critical issues (Hartshorne 1973; Freeman 1973).

The egalitarian policies of parental involvement set in motion during the 1970s aimed to provide better educational opportunities (across class and gender) through improving parental involvement in school activities. The intended outcome of this newer relationship was to improve the learning outcomes of students. However, experienced teacher practitioners such as Gill were to forecast changes to the 'involvement' mode of parent–school relations:

> The results of the parent councils so far must not be overestimated. Attendances at parent–teacher days in 1973 were no higher than before, and the core of involved parents remains relatively small. We must be aware that there is danger of becoming satisfied with a program that has done no more than scratch the surface. I believe that by parent involvement we should mean *participation* in educational planning—and we have a long way to go before that will occur with more than a handful of parents. I believe also that parents should be involved not merely in an advisory capacity, but in a capacity which gives them some measure of power. The Coordinating Council at BGHS [Brunswick Girls High School] has no real power with regard to the running of the school. It is only working successfully because we have a Principal who wants it to work. Unless it is formally written into the constitution of the school that parents are to play a part in the educational planning and decision making, the parents' councils will remain subject to the whim and fancy

of a Principal who retains the power of veto. If our present Principal were to be replaced tomorrow, there is nothing to say that the councils would continue. It is vital, therefore, that something be done to ensure their survival. (Gill 1975: 180)

Something was to be done, starting in the 1980s. The concept of 'involvement' in school activities was to be replaced by a definition of 'process participation'. The 'involvement' view of parent decision-making was the narrowest view of democratic decision-making; it was essentially an institutional definition of democratic rights that 'sees democracy as a method of choosing and authorising leadership' (Gaze et al. 1990: 18). In the 'involvement' model, parents acted as consumers attempting to package the model in better form, but they were removed from voting and the power to influence collective decisions binding on school curriculum policy. It was never to confirm political responsibility to parents. It was in essence a soft commitment to a meritocratic argument, based on social mobility through educational achievements, that was the informing core to the movement.

Improving the quality of schools became the new direction for the educational agenda being written for the 1980s. The 1973 Karmel Report had set the agenda for parent participation within schools during the 1970s. Considerable pressure from parents and teachers during this decade was to influence the next step toward parent participation. The Schools Commission report was broader in scope:

> To shape relevant and effective programmes, schools must have an understanding of the community needs and the out-of-school experiences of their students . . . The role of the community is vital in assessing schools in this process and schools therefore have a special responsibility not only to set up and support means by which participation is possible, but also to ensure that the process of interaction occurs. (Schools Commission 1981: 1045)

Parent involvement to parent participation

Parental involvement in school activities did change from the beginning of the 1980s. There was a movement from parental duties (parent involvement) to parent participation in school decision-making. Pettit (1980) argued that the underlying reasons for parent participation were to make their children's learning more effective and to develop greater community investment and influence in state-provided institutions. An example of the newer interest in improving the quality of schools was the formation of the Parents and Teachers in Curriculum (PATIC) Project (1980–82 report published in 1983). The original project was a combination of two submissions from the Access Skills Project Team and the Victorian Federation of State Schools Parents Clubs. Their mutual aims were to 'foster and monitor the process of participation and collaboration between school and community'.

Eight primary and secondary schools were selected as starting points, with six of them being finally adopted as project sites. The most significant results were as follows. In each of them 'the parents, in different ways have seen themselves as powerless in areas they wish to be more powerful' (PATIC 1983: 60). Teachers in general reacted against increased participation by parents. Several projects demonstrated how parents had 'grown enormously' in their confidence to contribute to policy formation, and at Princes Hill 'a section of the parent community has demonstrated its capacity to engage with a long-term decision making process, and has done this with determination' (PATIC 1983: 61).

The editor of the PATIC project report wrote that 'no fundamental shifts in the balance of power in school community relationships have taken place and this is particularly true in the curriculum area' (M. Hunt, in PATIC 1983: 60), thus echoing judgements similar to those of Gill on the 1970s BGHS project, that parent involvement should mean participation in educational planning.

Other projects of this era had similar ambitions to PATIC for parent participation in school decision-making (Claydon 1975). For example, one school-based inservice education project with ten primary schools from the western suburbs of Melbourne viewed parents as active participants within the debates for proposed change (Knight 1984: 2). School programs emerging from this process included the following:

1. Action research teams: students as researchers (this included a 'Vandalism' research project, funded by Victorian state government).
2. 'Transition from primary to secondary school'.
3. 'Mathematics across the curriculum: multicultural perspective'.
4. 'Aggressive behaviour: theory and school policy'.

Parental and community involvement was built into every project. An example of this relationship is contained in the following project summary concerning a three-school student research program on 'technology and change':

- A program of excursions presupposes the use of parents. These supervisors as well as those unable to participate actively, become involved in the educational process. The parents are informed and educated through newsletters, personal explanations of the purposes of excursions, questionnaires and surveys to be conducted. The excursions themselves provide parents with information for discussion with their children.

- By actively involving parents not simply as supervisors but as co-educators the effectiveness of the educational processes is heightened.
- Through such excursions which provide personal interaction with the adult community the children have come to see themselves as accepted in the adult world, people with a purpose, able to relate to adults, taken seriously and, when they see their efforts in print, useful members of a society in which they have a role to play.
- The members of the community who have come into contact with the children have, on the whole, been accepting and understanding of the children's limitations, but have also come to see that education is a field in which they have a role to play. Their willingness to give time to children, take the trouble to explain and discuss important issues, has strengthened the bonds of commitment between school and community. (Geddes 1984: 21–2)

Similar results were found in another 'Areas Study' project with three primary schools in the northern suburbs of Melbourne. The specific brief for this inservice project was to identify factors that 'might influence easy transfer from home and neighbourhood to school'. Comments revealing the movement toward stronger parent participation include:

> The three schools involved in the Area Study, which had as its focus transition from home to the school setting, were aware that their programs would be more effective if they involved parents, more mature students (both of primary and secondary school age), grandparents and other teachers within the schools. This involvement would encourage participation in various activities concerned with the pre-school programs . . . Perhaps it could be said that if parents are to be valued they must be of the school—as participants in the school community not just recipients of the schooling process. (O'Donnell et al. 1979: 97)

Illustrating the commitment of school communities to take decision-making responsibility seriously were the reactions recorded during inservice projects in secondary schools. A number of parent and community initiatives were put into effect between 1976 and 1981, including the following:

- Efforts were made to draw into the school the variety of ethnic groups. Greek and Italian parent committees were formed. Greek and Italian languages were introduced into the curriculum, and members from these groups were included into the school council.
- The Maltese community, the largest in the area, was served by the employment of a Maltese aide who translated school notices into Maltese and helped develop curriculum on Maltese language and culture. A school-based curriculum centre has been established for teacher–parent meetings, adult classes and other community activities.
- An Adult Listener Scheme was established to build a community link

around the issue of literacy. This parent–teacher–student interaction, aided by the Parent Communication Officers and members of the English faculty, enabled a number of adults to assist low-achieving children with their reading. Early in 1980, the scheme was promoted with a public seminar on children's reading, and Parent-Assisted Reading Programs. A large gathering of parents, teachers and volunteers from five schools in the area attended, sharing ideas, spreading interest and generally fostering the scheme.

- Other community liaison developments facilitated parent–student participation, holiday programs, human relations teaching, cross-age tutoring and school-to-work research. The Ethnic Community parent staff became important in the curriculum development of the school because they were voting members of the school council and other policy making committees. (Jones et al. 1982: 30)

Teachers and parents, having pushed programs to the allowable limits of government policy at the time, made the following evaluations concerning a western-suburb parent–school program operating between 1976 and 1982. It foreshadowed changes to ministerial policy and school decision-making practice during the 1980s:

> First, a school needs a commitment to a strategy of keeping decision making avenues open to representatives of the major school constituencies. This is a major contribution that a School Administration can make to school processes. It is preferable that administrators with commitment to such management, vision and sharing of power be appointed to Sunshine High School after due consultation with representatives of staff, students and parents. Clarification of, and commitment to student rights and parent rights especially in relation to school councils will be a key to future school improvement. Studies of the obstacles to sustained and informed parental involvement needs to be conducted, preferably at the regional level. For example, issues such as parents who are shift workers, single parents and unfamiliarity with meeting procedures are crucial problems which need investigation. (Jones et al. 1982: 59)

Shifting the 'toothless tiger'

During the 1970s many lessons were learnt from the previous decade of experience with parent 'involvement' and 'participation' in school-decision-making. In his study of the 1975 Schools Councils Act, however, Pettit (1987: 30) indicated that there was 'scant relocation of power', and in general the process was a 'toothless tiger'.

The newly elected Victorian State Labor government of 1983 stated from the outset that its philosophy and responsibility to the state education system was to extend the participative role of parents and citizens in school decision-making. The partnership concept proposed assumed a fundamental consensus between parents and teachers in deciding the goals and processes of education in local schools.

Minister of Education Robert Fordham was to move the 'devolution of control' thesis in Victorian schools towards a stronger form of participatory democracy. Fordham (1983) stated: 'there must be a genuine devolution of responsibility by government, and the active participation in our education of parents, teachers and the wider community'.

The initial memorandum to presidents of school councils was followed by a detailed set of Ministerial Papers (1–6), outlining the government's philosophies and priorities. A set of 'important principles' was outlined for 'continuing consideration':

- genuine devolution of authority and responsibility to the school community;
- collaborative decision-making processes;
- a responsive bureaucracy, the main service of which is to service and assist schools;
- effectiveness of educational outcomes; and
- the active redress of disadvantage and discrimination.

School councils were to be empowered to decide curriculum policy and content of their schools. Genuine school–community interaction was to be essential to the development of collaborative educational processes supported by the community. Council membership was to be shared by parents, teachers, community representatives and students (where appropriate). The school principal was to be an ex-officio voting member of the council (Ministerial Paper No. 4).

Parents as partners

In addition to the movement towards collaborative decision-making, there was the 'frantic activity' to promote parent activities in schools generally in Victoria in the mid-1980s. This period witnessed a powerful shift in ministerial policy, from a previous emphasis on meritocracy based on individual educational achievements, to one of improving the quality of schooling for disadvantaged groups of students. The partnership of parents–community and teachers was critical to these school-centred reform efforts. It was in one sense a shift from the compensatory education themes of the 1970s, to an effective school strategy of improving children's learning, that was to provide the focus for school programs during the 1980s (Knight 1993). This was part of a broader shift in policy direction, which saw a lessening of interest in class and an emphasis on gender and ethnicity. During this period there was an interesting degree of international convergence in substantive policies and policy-making between the United Kingdom and Australia. This would not be the last time that comparing the interplay between substantive policies and ideology in those political contexts would be made.

For example, the Oxford Review of Education (1987) summarised changes in UK policy towards parent participation (reflecting similar changes in local policy-making):

> However, a series of reviews of the implementation of the Plowden Committees' policy proposals, twenty years on, found that the only successful schemes were those involving parents more clearly in educational provision rather than those which attempted to iron out differences in home circumstances through new forms of pedagogy, schooling or curricula.

The partnership concept led to a range of reform projects based on specific curricula schemes—reading, language and mathematics—to a broad range of parent–home activities such as reading, tutoring and a general perspective that more 'education' takes place in the home (especially with mothers) than in the school (Pettit 1980; Victorian Ministry of Education 1987a, 1987b, 1987c; Berger 1987; Toomey 1987; Rowe 1990, Rowe 1991; Kirner 1989).

The partnership concept has its critics. Soliman (1991) for example, made the point that:

> ... the partnership concept assumes a fundamental consensus between teachers and parents on the goals and processes of education. Research in this area suggests that consensus is more likely to be achieved between parents and teachers of similar socio-economic background, e.g. middle class, and thus partnership works to favour the interests of middle-class students. (Soliman 1991: 53)

The Participation and Equity program (PEP) initiated in Victorian schools during this period aimed to extend the democratisation process of school-based decision-making in public school systems. The new argument accompanying the PEP policy provided an educational rationale for parent participation. The PEP authors stated that growing evidence from research showed that student learning is improved and achievement increased when parents are active partners with students and teachers in the learning process (Brown et al. 1985).

The PEP program witnessed an intense effort to develop parent participation in the educational community. Rizvi et al. (1987), in an extensive review of the Participation and Equity Program in Victorian schools, made the following summary of parent participation:

> PEP can justifiably accept credit both for improving levels of parent participation in schools and for experimentation and sponsoring considerable debate about parent participation in the educational community.

Initially this experiment and debate centred mostly on the questions of technique of how to get more people involved, but in 1986, schools became much more reflective about what parent participation might mean, who had the capacity to participate in what and why certain forms of participation were educationally worthwhile and others were not. (Rizvi et al. 1987)

Defining participatory democracy in schools

If the 'involvement' view of parent decision-making was to avoid conferring political responsibility to parents, then the movement to 'participatory' decision-making legislated by the 1983 Ministerial Papers argued for parents to exert some control over their lives (and their children) by participating in school decision-making. This definition is found in the classical theories of democracy, in that it defines power as residing with the citizen rather than being controlled by it. The notion of self-government within small communities is enacted through active representation and participation. Whether this is an adequate definition for a democratic theory of education, whether it is sufficient to address the question of who should have authority over educational issues, and whether it leads to participatory virtues in the relationships between parents, teachers and students are questions to be addressed.

Parent participation in the decision-making of school policy depends on how participatory democracy is defined. There are two broad assumptions involved. One is that parents are sufficiently qualified—on the whole—to participate in forming collective decisions binding on them, the school and the community. The other is that parents are not qualified *per se*, and that such decisions should be delegated to people who have been entrusted with making decisions—at federal, state or regional level. How you define the moral value of democracy depends largely on how inclusive or exclusive your decision is about the above assumptions. Gutmann makes the point concerning the education adequate for participating in democratic politics:

> A democratic society must not be constrained to legislate what the wisest parents want for their child, yet it must be constrained *not* to legislate policies that render democracy repressive or discriminatory. A democratic theory of education recognizes the importance of empowering citizens to make educational policy and also of constraining their choices among policies in accordance with those principles—of non-repression and non-discrimination—that preserve the intellectual and social foundations of democratic deliberations. A society that empowers citizens to make educational policy, moderated by these two principled constraints, realises the democratic ideal of education. (Gutmann 1984: 14)

An assumption behind effective community decision-making in a democratic state is that parents (and/or guardians) of students ought to have adequate opportunity to formulate agenda questions and to express preferences about the outcomes of school policy. Given that within any given community there is considerable difference in how the common good is defined, then agreement about the ends of education becomes a priority in school decision-making.

If this is the case in school practice, then the definition of democratic theory will have moved from parent involvement ('institutional democracy') to parent participation ('representative democracy') and towards a pluralist model of democracy. This is a more complex view of political power than the usual account of representative democracy. The emphasis is on individual participation through group action. Gaze and Jones define the pluralist model of democracy as one that:

> ... assumes that power resides with individuals who form themselves into pressure groups in order to assert their interest in any given issue. Government functions as a neutral adjudicator, balancing the claims and resolving problems by developing what it takes to be the most appropriate social policy. Democracy is not seen as a form of self-government, but as a political process in which individuals are able, if they so desire, to play a significant role in influencing the governments determination of social policy. Further, individuals are able to participate more directly than the other models allow, for their participation goes beyond electoral politics or the politics of protest. On this model, individuals organise themselves into groups to create policy by lobbying about anything they consider to be sufficiently important to them to justify them devoting their time and energy. (Gaze and Jones 1990: 21)

Various studies also support this contention—that people tend to participate in the political process if they believe their participation will significantly affect outcomes (Verba et al. 1971, Verba and Wie 1972).

With this in mind, our next step is to examine the role of parents within a secondary school council, working within the 1983 ministerial legislation, to ascertain whether their duties can be viewed as a movement towards a more democratic system in the sharing of decisions over educational issues.

Parent rights and duties in their local school

In the example discussed on the next few pages the school is Duke Park College, a coeducational secondary school in inner-urban Melbourne, of mixed social class with 700 students speaking some 27 languages. The brief for the school council was to establish school policy for educational goals and a school code of behaviour according to Ministry of Education guidelines (T. Knight 1993: Ch. 7).

The Victorian Minister of Education (1985, 1986) set out guidelines for the establishment of school councils that enabled each government school to hire the school principal and decide the curriculum policy for the school. The school council's general range of duties included:

- Selection of school principal
- Educational policy
- Building and grounds
- Cleaning services
- Financial management and general accountability to the school community.

Guidelines for membership of the school council included:

- Parents—no less than one-third of the school council
- Staff—no more than one-third of the school council
- Students—adequate representation in relation to school size and structure
- Principal—'ex-officio', a voting member of council
- Co-opted members—members of school community as required (up to one-fifth of membership).

Nominations and elections were held for all candidates except co-opted members. To fill the position of president, only existing members of the school council (members who are in paid employment at the school are not eligible) may be nominated; a general election (including voters from the wider school community) is then held. The council at the time of this study had a balance of gender representation. The central brief for the school council (starting 1990) was to develop a curriculum policy and educational aims for the school and local community. At the same time, the school community was facing the demands of government 'guidelines' bringing changes to the Years 11 and 12 curriculum, as well as ministerial pressure (under District Provision guidelines) to consider the possibility of a district-wide merger with four local secondary colleges. Both of these issues involved a very demanding brief for the schools.

Thus the development of school educational goals, which were to be 'long-term, sustainable and achievable', was undertaken during a period of considerable tension and contested demands. The question as to who should have authority over educational issues came into sharp focus, given the competing demands on the Duke Park school council. It was to be a set of decisions that addressed the balance between the demands of central curriculum 'guidelines' and the maintenance of local needs.

Establishing the condition for policy formation

To initiate the process of decision-making, each school constituency, (faculty, parent, student and community representatives) was asked by the school council to develop a framework for decisions concerning the main objectives for the school. A policy subcommittee of the school council was to collate submissions and forward them to school council for comment and further action. This process went back and forth from constituents, to subcommittee to council, for a period of six months. Each constituency demonstrated a different approach to this task.

Teachers, when faced with curriculum decisions of the kind requested, were more likely to be drawn towards central authorities or professional subject groupings within schools for sources of authority. Indeed, Sturman (1990: 1) has commented that there is scant evidence that teachers view the community as a source of authority for curriculum knowledge. The issues of staff autonomy and collaboration quickly surfaced during this phase. What was obvious in observing subcommittee governance procedures was how the general school culture operated within a typology of fragmented individualism—that is, a large percentage of the staff were more concerned with their individual classroom practice and operated as minimalists in terms of school-based activities. Lortie (1975) has defined this as a traditional form of teacher isolation in schools. One difficulty with this typology is that this kind of teacher isolation leaves the politics of school activities in the hands of administrators, usually of the strong centralised kind. There is a general loss of the teachers' voice in this relationship in its stronger form. Another school culture typology—often co-existing with the previous model—is one that consists of teacher subgroups and/or subject groupings operating as separate or disconnected subentities (S. Ball 1987). Duke Park at the time of this study operated within a mix of these typologies. In general, staff collegiality was not achieved in this study. It was and still remains a conflict model in operation, not a consensus model.

None of this is particularly new information. Fullan (1990) cites, for instance, good examples of staff differences in autonomy and collaboration and consequent differences in school decision-making. Duke Park is probably more in line with observations that school change depends on about 10 per cent of the staff (Joyce et al. 1989: 13). Cohen and Harrison (1979), in a large Australian study of 98 secondary schools, cited only 24 per cent of the staff surveyed considered that staff participated in writing the school objectives. Decision-making participation is a complicated procedure in schools, especially when generalising across schools. Hargreaves (1989: 26) warns of the survey tradition and its difficulty in teasing out accurate indicators of teacher opinion, differences, and conflicts of interest within the teaching community. The observational technique used in this model also has its limitation and leaves some doubt as to the ability to make generalisations across to other models.

However, it was a practical and effective means to identify key decision-making procedures in a school. 'Critical events' were followed to obtain portraits of how parents engaged the decision-making process. For example: Who initiated questions? Who was responsible for handling issues? How exactly were parents involved? The final decision-making processes were analysed in terms of effect, consequence and rationale for decisions.

Parent shift to a more political role

While the general staff struggled to gain a sense of collegiality, this was not the case for the parent representatives on council. During the initial phase of the policy planning and the later work within the combined council, the parent representatives maintained a cohesive presence, brought a pluralist perspective to issues (both ethnic and gender) and provided links to diverse community opinion.

What emerged from this collaborative effort is that the parent group gave strong support to the 'willing 10 per cent' of staff, thus enlarging the group working on policy formation and change in the school. Reasons for this support included the following explanations. Parents are one step removed from the everyday politics of school life and can bring to the deliberations a perspective unencumbered by faculty allegiances or internecine arguments. However, the strongest asset that parents bring to this school decision-making process is a keen interest in their children's schooling and high expectation for their success. This translates into a strong commitment to the school, and time given generously to committee and decision-making responsibilities. Evidence from this study indicates that when parents are given the opportunity to contribute to *important* school decisions—and not just as token participants in social activities—they are motivated by a sense of usefulness, competence and belonging to the task. This confirms the Verba and Nie (1972) data that people tend to participate politically if they believe that their participation will strongly effect the process and outcome.

Social reproduction and the democratic ethos

A vital stage in school deliberation was the general agreement on a principled theory of education to inform the school curriculum policy. In some respects this was the most difficult stage in the formation of policy guidelines. Parent representatives on the committee argued for the necessity for educational goals to be defined through a democratic public philosophy that included personal rights and responsibilities, and an education for democratic and public participation. The conflict model was in full flowering during the resolution of these proposals. Whilst difficulty is rarely encountered in achieving agreement for a democratic school, defining what this means opens up considerable diversity of opinion and conflict. It centrally addresses two questions: Whose knowledge is important? and Knowledge for what purpose? In this case, a set of general principles was finally agreed upon after strenuous debate and negotiation. The commitment to democratic values led to curriculum policy that aimed to develop within the school a sense of community and shared values through social understanding. Central to the debate was an agreed premise that a 'distinctive virtue' of a democratic society is that it requires its citizens to actively influence how their society reproduces itself. Students were to be taught that they are responsible for solving both their own and wider social problems, in consultation and debate with others, and the school's obligation was to provide the opportunity to develop knowledge, skills and understanding to solve important issues (Dahl 1989; Davie 1986; Gilligan et al. 1990; Gutmann 1987; Knight 1992; Pearl 1988; Slee 1988). The general principles informing the school curriculum, as decided by the school council were as follows:

- The purpose of the school goals was to set out long term, sustainable and achievable objectives for the educational community at Duke Park College.
- These educational goals had been defined through a democratic public philosophy that payed attention to public responsibility, personal rights and democratic tolerance.
- This democratic ethos was one in which there was a conscious striving to organise all school activities towards compliance with mutually-agreed-upon goals.
- The school goals aimed to provide every student with knowledge and experience to have equal choice in work, politics, culture, leisure and personal development.
- The school community agreed upon a comprehensive and common curriculum and its basics included personal and social development, aesthetic understanding, cultural competence, environmental awareness, political literacy and physical education.
- The academic curriculum included a full range of subjects from Year 7 culminating in a comprehensive choice at the Years 11–12 Victorian Certificate of Education.
- The school aims were to help teachers to guide and evaluate their own activities and teaching.

Initial optimism and cautionary tales

The structure for school decision-making as described in this study was developed through the ministerial fiat of 1983, advocating forms of 'participatory democracy' with parent, teaching staff and student representatives on school councils empowered with the duties of constructing school educational policy. Given that in this model the critical mass actively involved in policy decisions was about 10 per cent of staff, the parent–community representatives provided a strong core to assist the 'willing 10 per cent'.

There was a balance achieved between the demands of government policy 'guidelines' and local needs in constructing a broad and balanced curriculum. However, the 1983 ministerial policy advocating school-based autonomy came under considerable tension, for by the end of the 1980s, government policy 'guidelines' and curriculum 'frameworks' were to control much of the original school-based impetus. Schools that seriously applied the 1983 policy aims were subjected to increasing demands from a centralised subject-based curriculum. In essence, the conflict was between the mandate of the early devolution theory, in that it assumed trust in school communities to formulate policy, and the more recent centralised doctrine implying that teachers and parents are not able to perform these duties. Instead a professionally based hierarchy, situated between the Ministry and the school system, was to make important curriculum judgments.

This is especially true for a mandated curriculum at Years 11–12, with a trickle-down assumption to influence curriculum goals at Years 7–10. Important knowledge in Victorian schools has been increasingly defined in terms of subject-based curriculum, influenced by a professional and centralised bureaucracy, motivated by a 'recognition that the nation's productivity and international competitiveness depends, in large part, on the skills of its people' (Bates 1987; Devison 1992: 1; Pusey 1991; Thurow 1992; Yeatman 1990).

Goodson (1992: 25) makes a compelling argument that local school needs and 'national political cultures' have been displaced by this movement. The tension between the 1983 government policy emphasising participatory democracy and the later forms of representative democracy has not been resolved. The increasing challenge for schools and their communities is how to strike a balance between centralised and school-based decision-making. It is, of course, part of a larger struggle inside the education community to reconcile the unresolved tension in the interrelationship between society, education and an economy dominated by deregulation, free trade and technological change.

The cautionary tale to this study is that we have developed a kind of steering from a distance model of school decision-making. Yes, parents and community representatives can and are able to perform the duties associated with policy formation, and with competence. However, there is an emerging gap between policy formation and policy implementation. Unlike La Trobe University's School Task Force models (previously described), in which policy formation and policy implementation were part of the working coalitions between teachers, parents and 'outsiders', this existing 'participatory' model does not have an implementation phase built into its processes.

The same can be said of the Schools of the Future program (1993) prepared by the Liberal government in Victoria. Both the Labor policy of 1983 and the Liberal policy of 1993 have inbuilt gaps between policy formation and policy implementation—that is, between intended policy and policy in use. Little thought has been given to the implementation phase, and little has been learnt about this process from the UK experience as cited by Bowe et al. (1992). The Schools of the Future policy has another dimension of concern: there will be an imbalance between parent and teacher representatives on school councils. School councils will have six to twelve members, no more than one-third of whom are teachers. On some school councils there may even be *no* classroom teachers, as the one-third applies to all Department of School Education employees. The coalition between parents and teachers nurtured during the previous decade will be broken. The gap between policy formation and implementation will be widened considerably. What must be built into the school day is time allowance and administrative support to develop a more collaborative school culture. This needs to be done in order to counter the trend to entrepreneurial school decision-making and mechanisms leading to centralised control over school policy.

In summary, the Duke Park model proved to be a step toward a more democratic school governance process. It confirmed the ability of parents to perform at a high level of competence and commitment in the formation of school policy. It moved the parent role from client-helper to political partner.

Parents as consumers

During the period when the previously discussed study was being undertaken, the Ministry established the Structures Project Team. The framework recommended by the Project Team was that Victorian state schools were to be 'self-governing schools' by the 1990s—expressing aims such as 'efficiency', 'flexibility', 'adaptability' and 'participation'. However, parent and teacher organisations mounted considerable opposition to the concept of 'self-governing schools', and the government was forced to back down on its reforms. Nevertheless, similar policy was to emerge under the newly elected Liberal government of 1992, in the shape of 'Schools of the Future'.

The Schools of the Future program (for implementation in Victorian schools during 1993) raises serious questions concerning parent participation. The preliminary paper states that 'parents will be able to directly participate in decisions that affect their child's education'. This sounds similar to statements in the 1973 and 1987 Schools Commission reports and the 1983 Ministerial Paper (No.1), although school councils will be restricted to six to twelve members and the school principal moves from being an ex officio voting member of council, to being the executive officer of the council, with direct responsibility for all school curriculum and management decisions. There is a strong sense of hierarchical governance structure being developed, while parents and the community appear to be cast to one side and relegated to passive supporters of the system even with enlarged representation. The Schools of the Future model is an attempt to connect the institutional practice of schooling with the marketplace. The self-management concept has been translated into a single word, 'choice', by such writers as Chubb and Moe (1990). They argue for a consumer-led recovery of the schooling system, meaning privatisation of government schooling. Ball (1993: 4) makes a strong conclusion from his comparative study of UK and USA school practice: 'the implementation of market reforms in education is essentially a class strategy which has one of its major effects the reproduction of relative class (and ethnic) advantages and disadvantages'.

Parents will be defined as consumers within this entrepreneurial model, which promises diversity, choice and cost-effective schools—a 'culture of service' as described by Caldwell and Spinks (1992: 175). The role of parents and the community is less than clear in terms of their role as political partners in policy formation. It is a passive choice, in which the market influences important educational policy decisions. The price of management transformation will come at the expense of community cooperation where parents have been able to exercise choice with accountability as a means of building common understanding.

Bowe et al. (1992: 81) raise questions concerning 'self-determining schools' from research conducted in the United Kingdom. (Again, the influence and convergence in substantive policy-making between the UK and Australia should be noted.) The new educational world of self-determining schools, disciplined by the market, is intended to produce a social order in which 'natural' talents and inclinations of individuals and organisations can come to the fore. However, our research suggests that far from releasing people from the burdens of bureaucracy, local management of schools may well increase the internal administrative load. In addition, 'being enterprising' requires risk capital and time. In the case study reported here, the former has been raised partly out of the 'system' but also via a loan at the unknown cost of linking the school's finance to the presently depressed leisure and financial markets. Responding to the consumers brings difficulties in tying together the competing concerns of parents, employers and students.

In a democratic school the parent and the student are treated as producers of education and knowledge, not as consumers. When these people are perceived as producers, choice takes on an interpretation different from choice as consumers. Learning and the construction of knowledge is not achieved in isolation; it is always in consideration of others and with others. In the deliberate construction of knowledge there is an emphasis on collaboration, coordination and cooperation. If choice is limited to the consumer, none of these important issues are considered.

The importance of how human interactions affect the development of competencies is demonstrated in the work of Bornstein and Bruner (1989) and Tudge and Rogoff (1989). The idea of cooperation in sharing thought processes is central to their theory of learning and development.

Retrospect and prospect

This has been a discussion not of parents in a biological or parenting role, but of the role a parent brings to the school, as linked to the political form of the society in which the school resides. The rights and responsibilities of parents are determined by the nature of the democratic process. If a mandate for democracy is the right to determine and participate in decisions that influence one's future, then responsibility for decisions concerning children's education is included in this mandate.

An important distinction in a democratic school—as distinct from one that sees itself as an economic pathway—is its willingness to accept some responsibility for the condition of the community. In a democratic classroom the student learns to become a democratic citizen. This involves confronting increasingly complicated and difficult problems. Thus schooling provides, developmentally from preschool to Year 12, experiences for everyone to gain a critical perspective.

At present, in schools the rhetoric of accountability is used to emphasise the latitude given (by legislation) to local schools and community to manage their own policy. But increasingly this latitude is being eroded, and centrally defined criteria are becoming the gauges of accountability. In a democratic school, accountability is negotiated, and the general direction is downward (that is, being able to defend to students and parents, with reason and evidence, that what is being taught is worthwhile). Furthermore, *there has been power in school councils for local constituencies to intervene and change the school program and evaluation.* This relationship between schools, parents and community is worth preserving and extending. The study at Duke Park College (discussed earlier in this chapter) revealed such an intervention by the school, parents and community into existing government 'guidelines'—poised as they were between two competing political paradigms—to gain a voice over what counts as important knowledge in their school. Parents in this study were seen to ask the hard questions in situations that required direct and forthright opinion.

Up to 1993, what we witnessed of governance practice in education in the state of Victoria was a trend towards more democratic control of school decision-making. The self-managed entrepreneurial school currently being promoted by the Liberal government will reverse this trend. Authority will be hierarchically structured within a management model that will ensure centralised control over decentralised schools. The risk for government schooling will be to have a number of poorly resourced schools, and a concomitant deflection from education because of a strong overlay of administrative duties. As curriculum recedes towards the centre, schools will be judged to be 'successful' on their ability to market themselves and establish a consumer base, not on their ability to involve school communities and parents as responsible citizens in a strong democracy.

16 School Leadership: Securing Quality Teaching and Learning

Clive Dimmock

In the new conceptions of schools and schooling arising from restructuring, attention is placed on the quality of teaching and learning experienced by all students. This interest in teaching and learning signals a departure from past tradition in at least three ways. First, previous waves of reform have generally failed to penetrate beyond school administration into the classroom (Banathy 1988). Improvement in teaching and learning implies reform in classroom practice. Second, there is recognition that all students, irrespective of gender, ethnicity, age and ability, have the right to experience quality teaching and learning. Large numbers of students have left school in the past without realising this entitlement. Third, and perhaps most significant, is the recognition that successful reform of teaching and learning is predicated on a holistic view of the school, incorporating its organisational structures, leadership and management (Holly 1990). This chapter presents such a view by mapping the connections between learning, teaching and organisational structures, while emphasising the role of management and leadership in securing quality teaching and learning.

Schools are essentially places for all students to learn. The quality of a school is therefore appropriately judged by the quality of teaching and learning (the core technology) offered and experienced by its members. It is at the points of service delivery, the interface between teacher and learner, and the outcomes of learning, that the most pertinent and poignant indicators of school quality are provided. Placed in this context, the importance of school leadership, management and administration is judged by the extent to which they nurture and support quality teaching and learning for all. Securing uniformly high-quality service across the whole school has been a relatively neglected concern of school leaders in the past. School effectiveness studies, too, have labelled schools *effective* while commonly ignoring substantial within-school differences in quality between departments, teachers and student outcomes (Reynolds 1992).

In securing quality curriculum experiences for all learners, the degree of within-school variance justifies close attention by school leaders.

A policy emphasis at system level on student learning outcomes is focusing schools on ways to improve their present 'low levels of learning productivity' (Ashenden 1990b; Dimmock 1993a). Recent restructuring efforts highlight the growing dissatisfaction with existing school arrangements for core technology. Research findings now provide reasonably clear insights into the characteristics of schools providing quality learning and teaching for all students (Murphy 1991).

In advocating a holistic approach to improving core technology and learning productivity, the contribution made by school leadership and management is crucial. Yet the relationships between leadership, management and core technology variables are somewhat equivocal and more problematic than often assumed, and the ambiguity has not been addressed by principals' professional development. Although the past decade has witnessed an explosion in the provision of leadership training for principals, much of this professional development rests on the belief that improving the quality of school management will automatically benefit the quality of teaching and learning. This mistaken belief is evidenced in the considerable body of research revealing the discontinuity between school administration and core technology (Wildy and Dimmock 1993). Experience suggests that too much emphasis has been placed on training principals in management *per se* and too little on educational or instructional leadership.

Even the impressive body of literature on instructional leadership, mostly emanating from the United States during the 1980s, generally fails to specify expected outcomes and the nature of linkages between key variables of core technology and leadership. With notable exceptions (for example, Smith and Andrews 1989) this work is largely prescriptive, advocating checklists of instructional tasks for principals to implement in a top-down process. The assumption is that when principals execute particular instructional tasks, teaching and learning improve. There are two weaknesses to this argument. First, the exercise of leadership and management as a top-down process places undue reliance on those below—in this case, teachers and students—to react in predictable and prescribed ways to secure intended outcomes. In workplace environments typically characterised by loose coupling and autonomy, such as schools and classrooms, this strategy requires considerable faith on the part of its advocates. Adopting strategies that start with intended outcomes and work in reverse—that is, bottom-up—may be more rewarding. A second problem with top-down instructional leadership is the sheer impossibility of principals meeting the expectations to fulfil so many exacting and diverse tasks, even if some of them are delegated (Deal 1987; Smith and Piele 1989). It is worth clarifying the *status quo* in core technology, and school leadership and management, before exploring a bottom-up approach in detail.

Schools and schooling: present characteristics and context

A starting point is the identification of typical characteristics of core technology, school structure and leadership at present. In one such analysis, Elmore claims that classroom activity for the average student is 'dull, perfunctory and disconnected from what goes on in other classrooms or in the larger community' (Elmore et al. 1990: 8). He argues that teachers are faced with impossible tasks of engaging large numbers of heterogeneous students in learning. They react by lowering their expectations of students to learn and/or by focusing on small groups of more able students who give them job satisfaction. Students in turn accommodate to feelings of alienation, lack of success and boredom by withdrawing from the process. According to Elmore, powerful structural and cultural forces in schools have combined to reinforce a very narrow model of teaching and learning in most schools. For the most part, students are taught in groups of 25 to 30 for lesson periods of between 30 and 60 minutes. Most of the time all students in the class receive the same material, which is typically delivered or transmitted through teacher-directed expository methods, the more so with older students. When not listening passively to teacher talk, students normally work on material alone, in a classroom culture that has more elements of competition than cooperation. Knowledge is conceived as discrete sets of facts, which students are expected to memorise and periodically recall. Teaching is equated with telling, knowledge with facts, and learning with recall (Cohen 1988). A culture in which teachers work individually and privately is the norm. Teacher collegiality or collaboration is the exception.

The organisation and management of the school is typically hierarchical and bureaucratic. In larger schools extensive vertical structures place the principal at the apex of the institution, with many levels of senior and middle managers between the principal and the class teacher and student. Authority and decision-making tend to be exercised top-down, based on position and rank rather than expertise. Characteristically, the senior management is 'decoupled' from the instructional core. Particularly in larger schools, the principal may be several layers removed from the classroom and teaching and learning and the attendant issues surrounding the technical core. Research findings indicate that only a minority of principals find instructional leadership a reality (Wildy and Dimmock 1993; Rallis and Highsmith 1986).

Devolution and decentralisation place additional competing claims on principals, threatening to divert their attention further from concerns of curriculum, teaching and learning. Many principals become preoccupied with administration and low-level clerical duties. Others assume higher-level managerial roles, concerned with maintaining present levels of performance. Fewer still exercise leadership—the inspiration and motivation of staff and students to higher levels of performance. In previously centralised systems a legacy of strong top-down line management has created a cadre of principals who now find the exercise of leadership either alien or difficult.

In secondary schools in particular, organisational fragmentation and division results from a strongly factionalised departmental structure (Fullan and Hargreaves 1991). This shapes and dictates teachers' affiliations and loyalties, teachers' views of knowledge and its structure, the design and delivery of the curriculum, as well as the bases on which decisions on budgetary and resource allocation are taken. All of these render the creation of a whole school culture, an integrated view of knowledge, a cooperative workplace environment, difficult and unlikely.

For more than two decades studies have captured schools as organisations with ambivalent, conflicting and multiple goals and an unclear technology, making the link between process and outcome uncertain and problematic. As well, the type of clientele, young children and students requiring an orderly and structured environment, has added to the problematic nature of schools. With a new intake of students every year, schools are continually under pressure, some more than others, to exercise control and stability in their workplace environment. Faced with the vulnerabilities at the heart of their operation, the complexities of linking teaching with learning and with student outcomes, schools have reacted by establishing strong structures and rules to bolster the infrastructure supporting the core technology. The result is a strong edifice supporting a weak but critically important centre of core activity. Thus timetables, administrative expedience, staff availability, customs, ceremonies and rituals, regulations and rules drive the school and provide a strong unequivocal set of ground rules by which the school can function. The technical core (teaching and learning) survives as the soft underbelly of school operation.

School management and organisation conflicts with, and even obstructs, the implementation of a restructured curriculum and core technology. Sizer (1984), for example, believes 'the structure is getting in the way of children's learning' (p. 205). And Chubb (1988) concludes, 'Efforts to improve the performance of schools without changing the way they are organized . . . will therefore probably meet with no more than modest success' (p. 29).

Evidence suggests that if schools are to achieve improvements in student learning outcomes then new approaches to teaching and learning are required. These new approaches are unlikely to be effective if simply grafted onto present organisational structures and administrative, managerial and leadership practices.

Securing quality teaching and learning: a leadership model

Forming a vision of schools focused on effective teaching and learning for all students is helpful in eliciting a leadership model for such schools. A degree of imagination is thus called for in reconstructing quality schools for the future, although an image of these quality schools can be created with knowledge derived from research on learning styles, effective teaching and learning and school effectiveness and school improvement. The literature on policy implementation, particularly, is also instructive.

From this extensive body of research findings it is possible to derive five main principles undergirding the school for quality learning and teaching:

1. Student outcomes provide goal direction for learning.
2. Learning and the individual learner are made the centrepiece of school life.
3. Teaching focuses on learning and teaching for understanding; a balance and variety of teaching strategies is achieved, a combination of methods, from didactic and expository to constructivist.
4. Learning and teaching shape and dictate school structures and organisation, which are flexibly designed to support and facilitate the principles and practices of effective learning and teaching.
5. Learning and teaching principles and practices mould leadership, management, resource allocation and culture/climate, all of which are dedicated in turn to supporting a service delivery designed for quality learning and teaching.

It is the *interrelationship* or connectedness of these five principles, rather than discreteness, that holds the key to unlocking excellence in learning and teaching in schools. Moreover, the direction and nature of this interrelationship is important. Typically, schools and school systems have been managed by top-down policy-making and strategy. In this top-down model, bureaucrats and managers view policy-making as a linear or algorithmic process, which permeates down through the school system until finally having an impact on the class teacher and student. History is replete with examples of policies that failed to deliver their intended outcome in the classroom. Many explanations account for these failures, including underresourcing and lack of professional development to provide support. But perhaps the most poignant is the failure of policy-makers to consult with and understand the feelings, wishes and concerns of those at the implementation end of the policy process. No matter how important a policy, it comes to little if it fails at the point of implementation. The weakness of top-down procedure is that it places too great a strain on school leaders to ensure ownership and commitment or, more usually, compliance by teachers in classrooms. This is especially the case given the 'loose coupling' of schools, the so-called 'teacher autonomy' and the unappealing nature of many new policies to teachers.

A more promising school leadership model for quality learning and teaching is grounded in 'bottom-up' generated policies, issues and concerns. Policy formulation in this paradigm begins with the expression of intended outcomes—in this case, student learning outcomes. The beginning goal and the final outcome are then one and the same. Research findings suggest that learning is most effective when it is goal-directed (Locke and Latham 1990; Spady and Marshall 1991). Key questions here are: How do students best learn? What are the individual differences between students in how they best learn?

Responses to these questions about learning and individual learning styles are prerequisites for the school's next stage of decisions, focusing on teaching and teaching strategies. Key issues at this stage are: How do teachers best teach? What are the individual differences between teachers in how they best teach? Most importantly, at the interface between learning and teaching: How does a school's perspective on student learning shape its teaching? Teaching is therefore driven by learning, and it responds and reacts to the demands, needs and interests of learners.

The concerns and questions outlined above, focusing on student outcomes, learning and teaching, constitute the core technology of the school. They explicitly take account of the feelings and requirements of those responsible for the most crucial stage of policy-making—namely, implementation into practice. Two further stages are important in enabling and supporting the core technology. First, structures provide the framework for delivery of this core technology. The design of these structures enables the school to operationalise its planned core technology. Pertinent questions include: What structures most enable the successful implementation of planned teaching–learning activities? Are existing structures inhibitive of, or obstructive to, the delivery of effective teaching and learning? In this approach, core technology drives the design of organisational structures rather than the structures constraining the core technology.

A further stage involves connections between core technology and leadership and management, resource allocation and culture/climate building. The nature of the school's core technology provides a framework for school leadership and management. It provokes key questions:

How do leadership and management best support effective teaching and learning in the school? Do effective teaching and learning provide the generic purpose of, and priority for, leaders and managers? Leadership and management incorporate resource allocation and culture/climate building. Placing core technology at the forefront of schools raises considerations as to whether patterns of resource allocation and utilisation enable and support effective teaching and learning. Similarly, to what extent does the school culture and climate reflect an emphasis on securing effective teaching and learning for all students?

The importance of this strategy of working backwards (or bottom-up) from the intended outcomes of a system through each layer of school organisation (and beyond the school into district and central office if necessary) was realised by Elmore (1979–80), who referred to the process as backward-mapping. The present analysis recognises five layers, all interactive, as critical in designing schools for quality learning and teaching. Applying Elmore's concept of backward-mapping to the five interactive levels or layers suggested provides a strategy by which schools can achieve quality in learning and teaching. The core technology of teaching and learning determines the school's organisational structures along with its leadership, resource management and culture/climate, all of which find their rationale and raison d'être in enabling and supporting delivery of a quality core technology. A model of the process is shown in Figure 16.1.

Figure 16.1 Model of school leadership for quality teaching and learning: backward-mapping

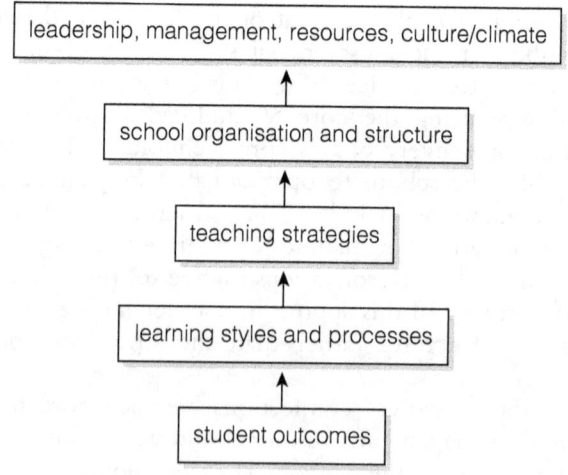

This model provides an overarching framework and strategy by which all schools and their communities can address the challenge of providing school leadership and management for quality teaching and learning in the 1990s and into the twenty-first century. The specific responses made by individual schools may vary within this general framework, depending on school context, school goals and the school's perceived strengths and weaknesses at present. Importantly, responses will be shaped by appeal to what works. A growing body of research literature on effective learning and teaching provides schools with a rich variety of practice from which to choose. The diversity of responses made by individual schools should be celebrated, for there is value in each school devising and owning its own path for providing a quality service delivery for all students in learning and teaching.

The process of backward-mapping, using the model set out in Figure 16.1, provides the framework for understanding the linkages between core technology and leadership and management. The model advocates that the roles, relationships and functions incorporated in school leadership and management, together with organisational structures, be decided according to principles and practices of effective learning and teaching.

Student outcomes, effective learning and implications for school leadership

According to the principle of backward-mapping, student outcomes provide a base for targets and goals towards the achievement of which schools construct learning experiences. Extending the principle further, what implications do student outcomes and effective learning have for school leadership and management?

Effective schools are centres of effective learning. Mortimore (1993) has defined the concept of *effective learning* as the acquisition of knowledge, understanding or skill with economy of time and effort, in ways that foster assimilation and accommodation with other learning, and with endurance for as long as it is found relevant by the learner. These effective schools place learners and learning at the heart of their operation while remaining focused on their fundamental task, how to facilitate and promote the learning of all students towards achievable goals. Schools like these display a number of important characteristics:

- Student outcomes are converted into meaningful learning goals for individual students.
- Every student is valued as a learner.
- Relevant information is collected on each student's learning characteristics and achievements.

- Research findings on effective learning principles are sought as guides to practice.
- Wherever possible, school-wide policies and shared practices on learning are adopted for consistency and reinforcement.
- The whole school is viewed as a learning community.

These six features of schools for effective learning provide us with insights into effective leadership and management. When student outcome statements are personalised and individualised they become learning goals towards which students can strive to attain. Setting, negotiating, monitoring and renegotiating appropriate learning goals for each student at regular intervals requires careful management and considerable investment of time by teachers. Through individual goal-directed learning, each student is made to feel valued as a learner. This may also be achieved through recognition of what individual students bring to the learning environment. More informed decision-making with respect to students' learning, and more information about individual students and how they best learn, is crucial (Dunn, Beaudry and Klavas 1989). This information comes from multiple sources. Schools may start learning profiles for each student before enrolment and continue to profile their learning characteristics and achievements throughout their school history. Profiles include information about interests, abilities, achievements and learning-style characteristics and preferences. Learning-style inventories are useful for identifying specific learning characteristics (McCarthy 1990). Many students arrive at school ill-equipped to learn; they possess minimal learning techniques and skills. Effective schools realise the need to develop the processes of learning as early as possible in the students' schooling.

Most importantly, schools concerned with quality learning seek reliable research findings on the conditions necessary for effective learning. After considering the implications, they base their learning policies and practices on research evidence as to what works. These schools realise the powerful effect of whole-school policies and shared practices towards learning (Dimmock 1993b). Important learning competencies and principles are repeated for consistency and reinforcement as students move between teachers and subjects (Gagné 1974). The notion of the whole school as a learning community emphasises the importance of learning for all—principal, teachers, parents and other stakeholders in the school.

The quality school for learning, therefore, places the student at the centre of its operation in two ways. First, it identifies, collects and applies information about individual students' learning styles and uses this information to decide how its students best learn. The quality school accepts responsibility for developing effective learning styles for each student, especially students with learning difficulties. Second, it adopts, across the whole school, through collaborative staff agreement, shared practices based on research findings to secure reinforcement and consistency. Both of these policies and practices have major implications for teaching. It is therefore necessary to backward-map their effects on teaching.

Effective teaching and implications for school leadership

When a school decides on the configuration of its effective learning, the principle of backward mapping suggests that it then possesses a base from which it can provide effective teaching. Extending the principle further, what are the implications of effective teaching for school leadership and management?

Effective schools for learning display the following teaching characteristics:

- Teaching focuses on student learning and understanding.
- Teachers share responsibility with students for their learning.
- A wide repertoire and range of teaching methods is practised.
- Research findings on effective teaching principles, techniques and behaviours are sought as guides to practice.
- School-wide instructional policies and shared practices are adopted.
- Teachers evaluate their own and their colleagues' teaching.

In schools for quality learning and teaching, the 'focus of schooling must shift from teaching to learning' (Carnegie Forum 1986: 3). The quality school moves from a teacher-centred to a learner-centred pedagogy. The purpose of the delivery system is to meet the learning needs of students. Teachers become 'managers of learning experiences' (Hawley 1989, p.32), and students take more responsibility for their own learning. The teacher's task is to empower and enable students to accept and take control of their learning, a condition that Elmore calls 'teaching for understanding' (1988: 11). An emphasis on understanding requires teachers to construct learning experiences that enable students to draw connections between concepts and ideas and new and previously acquired knowledge, while encouraging them to achieve rigour, reflection and application (Marton and Ramsden 1988).

A concerned, caring approach on the part of the teacher highlights the importance of the quality of the teacher–student relationship. Although there is current emphasis on students accepting responsibility for their own learning, it is important for teachers to assume a share in that responsibility. Students feel supported when teachers demonstrate their commitment to, and concern for, the achievement of learning goals and outcomes. Research confirms the importance of the environment created by teachers, principals and others in influencing learners' perceptions of learning (Marton and Ramsden 1988).

Creating and maintaining a learning-directed model of instruction (rather than a teacher-directed model) requires a broad range of teaching strategies and a more personalised and individualised approach to learning (Brophy and Evertson 1976; Brophy and Good 1986; Harvey and Crandall 1988; Murphy 1991). This range of teaching–learning strategies is required for student engagement, taking into account the individual learning styles of students. The implications for teachers and school leaders centre on the extent to which teachers possess a wide rather than narrow repertoire of teaching–learning methods and strategies as well as their ability to switch between them with flexibility. To what degree are teachers operating within a comfort zone, placing undue reliance on just one or two teaching methods? A clearer picture of the range and balance of teaching–learning strategies required is provided by research findings on effective teaching.

The quality learning school bases its practices on research findings on effective teaching. A formidable body of research literature now exists on effective teaching for learning. Some of this work takes the form of meta-analyses, incorporating the results of many individual studies (Fraser et al. 1987; Porter and Brophy 1988). This concern for, and interest in, research as the guide to practice yields many benefits. It provides a sounder footing for innovation and practice than trial-and-error, intuition, subjective opinion or simply following practices in other schools. It is likely to reduce the element of risk that is present in any innovatory situation, because effects may have already been documented in sampled schools. This allows focus to be placed on the problems of implementation rather than on the innovation itself. Embedding teacher practices in the research findings of effective teaching and learning presents many challenges to school leaders and managers.

Where teachers adopt school-wide effective instructional techniques and shared practices, their efficacy is raised through reinforcement, consistency and synergy. A number of researchers have stressed the importance of shared practices in building collaboration and a learning culture in schools through tight coupling and linkage (Dimmock 1993b; Murphy et al. 1985). There is also convincing evidence that the quality of teaching improves when teachers self- and peer-evaluate (Little 1982). Securing tight coupling through shared school-wide effective teaching practices and an evaluative teacher culture are important responsibilities for school leaders and managers. Policies and practices of effective learning and teaching have major implications for school organisation. It is therefore necessary to backward-map their effects on organisational structures.

Effective school organisational structures and school leadership

The principle of backward mapping suggests that a school that has decided on the configuration of its core technology then possesses a base from which to design organisational structures conducive to quality teaching and learning. Extending the principle further, what organisational structures facilitate quality teaching and learning, and what are their implications for school leadership and management?

The following principles underlie the structural characteristics of schools that attempt to achieve effective teaching and learning for all students (this analysis supports Murphy's 1991 suggestions):

- Structures grounded in mastery (or outcome-based) learning
- Structures facilitating developmentally based learning
- Structures conducive to individualisation and personalisation of learning

These powerful concepts provide the rationale for more flexible structures concerning:

- School clustering
- Student grouping
- Teacher grouping
- Student and teacher role changes
- Volunteers and aides
- Use of space
- Use of technology
- The calendar
- Timetables
- Curriculum
- Classroom and out-of-classroom learning
- Student assessment

A context in which these flexible structures and their underlying principles find favour and expression is central to the responsibility of school leaders and managers. Hence, quality schools are characterised by leadership and management that realises that flexible structures need to be created, accepted, implemented and regularly reviewed in terms of their efficacy in achieving quality teaching and student learning.

Murphy argues that 'for schools concerned with restructuring educational processes, learning theory and student needs take precedence over the custodial interests of parents, administrative convenience, and market forces . . . in the creation and reshaping of structures to house teaching and learning . . . ' (1991: 63). Emphasis on learning theory and student learning outcomes is endorsed by Spady (1988), who advocates outcome-based learning and demonstrated student mastery. These concepts replace the calendar as the learning unit, so that the key issue is reaching the outcomes successfully, not when or how long it takes. According to Murphy (1991), the second principle for redesigning delivery structures is developmentally paced learning. This allows students to progress from one skill level to the next when they are ready, regardless of age or grade. A third principle for changing structures concerns the individualisation and personalisation of learning. This has two objectives: firstly, to humanise the organisational climate by creating a caring learning community between adults and children so that each student feels supported and valued by teachers and school leaders; and secondly, to differentiate delivery in such a way that each student experiences an appropriate curriculum.

Bringing these concepts into operation requires flexible structures quite different from the rigid bureaucratic structures currently shaping most schools (Murphy 1993). Each school should consider its own preferred structures in response to the learning needs of its students. Inter-school cooperation in the form of clustering may offer opportunities to share knowledge and resources. In future, clusters of schools may share students and specialist teaching staff, offering wider curriculum choices and making teachers' expertise more widely available. A Schools Council report (1992) in Australia on the need for flexible strategies in the primary sector provides a useful range of options available for schools.

At least twelve different but interwoven strands constitute flexible organisational arrangements. Research findings suggest that students differ in their learning-style preferences, some preferring to learn on their own but others preferring to learn in pairs, in small groups, in whole classes and large groups. The dominant pattern of the whole-class group is beginning to break. As well, schooling that prepares children for adult life should provide them with the opportunity to work in groups of different size, assuming individual responsibility as well as contributing to very large teams. More opportunity is provided for students to study individually. *Individualised learning* figures prominently in research findings on effective teaching.

Small-group work is already widespread. The Schools Council report (1992) acknowledges that small cooperative group learning is sometimes constrained by lack of space and the physical configurations of schools and classrooms. The report also endorses the educational benefits from *multi-age and non-graded grouping*, on the basis of family members or mixed ability. Students should also be encouraged to learn from each other. This can be secured by *fluid grouping*, allowing students of different grades, year levels and abilities to interact. Cross-age tutoring and peer tutoring have consistently positive results on learning. New conceptions of teaching and learning demand changes in traditional roles for both students and teachers. Students become workers, active learners and, occasionally, teachers. Teachers, for their part, assume a learner orientation.

On a larger scale there is interest in the *extended grouping* structure along with the idea of *sub-schools*. Students in extended groups remain with a small group of teachers for a number of years, thereby securing continuity and close understanding between teachers and students. Sub-schools or mini-schools may also improve the closeness of relations between teachers and students and provide greater sense of identity for both students and staff, particularly in large schools.

Team teaching has a chequered history. Past attempts to introduce change at classroom level involved grafting new teaching methods on to existing structures and practices, which otherwise remained intact. But in a new environment of backward-mapping, where change is supported at each level, team teaching holds potential for teachers collaboratively to plan, implement and evaluate educational programs (Little 1990; Rosenholtz 1989).

One variation combines team teaching with extended grouping so that teams of four teachers take responsibility for the delivery of the whole curriculum to between 80 and 100 students. In this arrangement, teachers teach other subjects as well as their own; and consequently, teachers are closer to learners and more aware of teaching for learning. Each team is usually able to 'buy in' specialist help, such as music teaching. Specialist teachers in one Canberra school have formed themselves into a team to 'service' groups of mainstream teachers. These arrangements help to break the rigidity of subject departments as the predominant form for organising curricula and grouping staff in secondary schools.

Other developments include the creation of specialist teachers. While one version of team teaching invites teachers to become more generalist, other trends favour more specialisation, especially in areas such as languages, music and physical education. There is considerable scope to involve more parents and other adults in assisting teachers and students. More adults present in classrooms do not reduce class sizes, but, more importantly, they do reduce the student–adult ratio. As well, schools providing quality teaching and learning in future will employ more part-time and casual teachers and teachers' aides, thereby releasing teachers to use time more flexibly.

More flexible use of time and timetabling is an essential requirement for improving teaching and learning. Present patterns of school year and school day are under increasing attack for their inflexibility (Knight 1989). Typically, schools open for only 190 days, little more than one half the year. They function between limited hours of 8.30 am and 4.00 pm, and access to school facilities such as libraries is normally impossible after these hours. Yet it is after school that students are expected to complete homework and when parents are more likely to be available to provide support. Extending the school day and introducing shift patterns would enable students and teachers to make better use of facilities and to capitalise on preferred learning styles.

Introducing flexitime for teachers (for example, nine day fortnights), dividing the school day into two parts, so that one-teacher-per-class activities take place in one half and whole-school or sub-school activities take place in the other, offer more flexibility for groups of different size. The large student group taught by one or two teachers can release other staff to undertake joint lesson planning and preparation. The occasional 'special program day', with a particular theme to guide learning across the whole school, involving the abandonment of the normal timetable, facilitates cross-age tutoring and other more flexible forms of student grouping.

Many of these flexible structures threaten to break the pattern of the traditional one-teacher class with lessons of 40 minutes. The introduction of new conceptions of learning and teaching, involving higher order thinking skills, render the standard lesson time obsolete and too rigid. Problem-solving activities, for example, may take considerably longer than 40 minutes. Standard lesson times seem more for administrative expedience than for enhancing the learning of all students. Flexibility of time is necessary for self-paced learning.

More flexible arrangements for student and teacher grouping and timetabling enmesh with curricular changes. Change in any one of these structures facilitates change in the others. Team teaching, for example, promotes the feasibility and workability of an integrated curriculum. Conversely, the introduction of an integrated curriculum is likely to work best with team teaching. The introduction of problem-solving greatly enhances the efficacy of individualised and small-group collaborative learning and is favoured by an integrated curriculum.

A wider range of teaching–learning venues offers more flexibility. Individualised and small-group learning and problem-solving may involve more learning taking place outside classrooms in libraries and resource centres, in the workplace and in the field. Some schools have established student and staff research and publications centres. The wider uses of technology, especially CD ROM and other multimedia developments, foster changes in teaching and learning. Much of this technology facilitates individualised and small-group work, self-paced learning, and problem-solving. Technology affects teachers as much as students by offering more ways of transmitting lessons (one teacher in a school might teach a lesson to schools throughout an entire system), of presenting information to be learned and of recording student progress.

Flexibility extends to student assessment. In these flexible structures, instead of all students sitting examinations at the same time once a year, irrespective of their pace of learning, they are assessed when they are ready. Flexibility of assessment is matched by profiling each student's achievements in detail against agreed and negotiated learning goals. A major managerial and leadership challenge is presented by changing organisational structures in these diverse ways and ensuring their effective operation in meeting goals of quality teaching and learning. It is to this stage that the analysis now backward-maps.

Leading, managing, resourcing and culture-building for effective teaching and learning

School-site leaders play a vital role in creating, maintaining and developing schools of quality in teaching and learning. Just as these schools implement new conceptions of learning, teaching and structure, so they are dependent for their success on specific forms of leadership, management, resourcing and culture-building. The nature of these forms is best determined by backward-mapping from learning, teaching and more flexible structures. What implications follow for school leadership and management from schools displaying the learning, teaching and organisational structures described?

In schools attempting to achieve effective teaching and learning for all students, the present analysis suggests the following characteristics and competencies are required by school leaders and managers:

- Goal orientation, especially towards student learning outcomes.
- Technical knowledge and management of effective teaching and learning.
- Technical knowledge and management of curriculum design, development and evaluation.
- Understanding and advocacy of research findings on effective teaching and learning, school effectiveness and school improvement as basis of practice.
- Knowledge and management of organisational structures for service delivery of teaching and learning.
- Awareness of desired and desirable organisational behaviours.
- Strategist for organisational change and innovation.
- Ability to create an organisational culture that values learning for all and a positive climate of human relations.
- Resource management to support the goal of enhancing learning for all.
- Monitoring and reviewing performance at school and sub-school levels for quality assurance in order to provide feedback, positive reinforcement and accountability.

A major shift in the mind-set of school leaders is prompted by the centrality of students and learning in these quality schools. Principals and teachers are goal-oriented in respect of improving student learning outcomes, interpreting their work and judging their performance in terms of the contribution they make to enhancing learning (Levine and Lezotte 1990). They conceptualise school problems in these terms, using students and their learning as goals and benchmarks against which to assess effectiveness. They adopt collegial and professional, rather than hierarchical, stances in problem-solving (Moore Johnson 1990). They encourage teachers to conceptualise issues bottom-up, from the students' viewpoint, rather than top-down, from their own perspective. Above all, they hold students' welfare uppermost in their values, believing they are in school primarily to serve the interests of all students. These school leaders are goal-oriented in respect of learning at two levels: they possess a school-wide perspective, viewing the school and parents as a learning community; and they are acutely concerned, through a heightened sense of justice and equity, for the interests of each student and their learning needs (Leithwood and Montgomery 1982; Reilly 1984).

Leadership in the school for quality learning and teaching focuses on learning, pedagogy and curriculum (Hord, Stiegelbauer and Hall 1984; Leithwood and Steinbach 1993). Principals and senior staff exercise instructional leadership based on a strong technical knowledge of, firstly, effective teaching and learning and, secondly, curriculum design, development and evaluation. This technical knowledge is a prerequisite for leading and managing teachers as professionals and subject experts, and for managing a set of activities as esoteric as teaching and learning. Technical knowledge of curriculum design, development and evaluation becomes increasingly important as these curriculum processes become more and more school-based. Without such knowledge, school leaders are likely to find professional dialogue and interpersonal communication on key school issues, as well as relationships between themselves and other school members, to be seriously deficient. Principals and senior staff who are well versed in the theory and practice of curriculum design, implementation and evaluation and who have knowledge of effective teaching–learning principles are empowered leaders of their learning communities (Duke 1987). They possess the technical knowledge to relate to teachers and students on classroom level issues as well as provide whole-school perspectives. Collaborative and collegial decision-making is more likely when the principal and senior staff are not buffered from the core technology.

Principals who are instructional leaders are able to set priorities for nurturing the quality of teaching and learning in the school. They accept the broadening of managerial responsibilities that comes with devolution and decentralisation, but they contain these additional tasks by framing their importance within the context of teaching and learning. Financial management, for example, is conceived more in terms of how it can influence resource allocation to enhance the core technology rather than regarded as intrinsically important in itself (Duke 1987). The focus on instructional or educational leadership by principals and senior staff sets the school culture and prevailing values. The school is valued as a learning community, with the principal as chief learner alongside staff and students (Barth 1990). Traditional role divisions between administrators, teachers and learners become blurred and frequently inverted. Students adopt teaching as well as learning roles, while teachers adopt learning as well as teaching roles. School leaders encourage these more fluid roles and relationships, recognising their importance in enhancing the school as a community of empowered learners.

As learners, principals and senior staff demonstrate that they value the importance of research findings as guides to practice and future innovation (Rossow 1990). They encourage teachers to be familiar with research on effective teaching and learning by obtaining and disseminating research and by resourcing and arranging staff development to keep staff informed (Duke 1987). These school leaders familiarise themselves with research on school effectiveness and school improvement and seek appropriate opportunities to apply important findings. In regard to research, they demonstrate competencies of reading, understanding, conceptualising and transforming into practice. Successful implementation of new concepts of teaching and learning depends on major reconfiguration of many school organisational structures. These include new forms of student and teacher groupings as well as reformed timetable arrangements and curricula. In restructuring schools it is therefore imperative for school leaders to have an understanding of schools as organisations and their attendant structures (Ubben and Hughes 1992). The leadership of principals is empowered when they become students of organisational theory and analysis and apply this knowledge in reconstructing schools. The ability to reflect critically on the extent to which existing structures facilitate and hinder quality teaching and learning is a neglected concern of school leaders. In the initial stages of reconstructing schools it may be necessary for school leaders to play a prominent role in demolishing unproductive structures. Equally important is the capability to plan, design and implement new structures on the basis of backward-mapping, enabling visions of teaching and learning to be realised. In particular, these effective principals recognise the efficacy of tight coupling and linkage to organisational effectiveness (Dimmock 1993b; Murphy et al. 1985). Tight coupling and synergy is achieved when all parts of a school share common values, goals and practices. Forging cultural and (to a lesser extent) bureaucratic linkages between the parts of a school helps to dismantle the barriers and internal divisions that have sustained loose coupling in the past and creates a unifying energy to achieve school goals in the future. These are achievable when the school is tightly coupled, not through heavy-handed bureaucratic and hierarchical administration, but through common cultural linkages and shared professional practices supported by a minimum of bureaucracy (Wilson and Firestone 1987). Effective school leaders realise the importance of managing structures in the promotion and achievement of desirable practices, professional relationships and school-wide goals.

These school leaders deliberately and consciously demonstrate in their own professional work the core values and behaviours they promulgate in their schools. They model the very behaviours and approaches they advocate for their schools (Dimmock 1993b). In this leader-as-model role, desirable values and practices are deliberately replicated at different levels. In advocating a school focus on student learning, effective principals and teachers approach their own professional work with a learning orientation (Barth 1990). The problematic nature of most issues and the value of inquiry in determining their resolution is publicly demonstrated in the behaviour of the principal and teachers. Likewise, student collaborative learning in the classroom is enhanced when paralleled by staff collaborative decision-making at classroom, department and whole-school levels. Encouraging students to problem-solve in their learning can be achieved through teachers modelling the same processes in their teaching and in the wider school setting of administration and policy-making. These processes are more evident where students join with staff in decision-making.

At different levels in the school the same modelling and reinforcement applies to leadership, goal-directed behaviour and preparedness for risk-taking. The concept of leadership density entails its exercise throughout the school—leadership by students in the classroom, by teachers and by senior staff. Encouraging students to set goals for their learning is paralleled by teachers' goal-setting and school goal-setting. Powerful reinforcement occurs where these sets of goals align. Similarly, developing in students a confidence to take risks and learn from mistakes is supported where students observe these values and behaviours operating across other levels of the school, including school leadership and management.

New configurations of teaching and learning are dependent on school leaders taking responsibility for building a culture that supports learning for all and a positive climate that values productive human relations (Ubben and Hughes 1992). Effective school leaders recognise the multiple and mutually reinforcing strategies available to them in building supportive learning cultures. These range from more explicit forms of verbal communication with all groups in the school community, to include modelling and demonstrating through their own behaviours, as well as more subtle uses of symbols, ceremonies and rituals (Parkay and Hall

1992). High but realistic learning expectations are conveyed, rewards, recognition and resources for learning are provided and learning time protected (Smith and Piele 1989).

High levels of learning productivity in schools are underpinned by a climate of positive human relations, responsibility for the creation of which is assumed by school leaders. Earlier discussion in this chapter highlights three aspects of human relations critical to effective teaching and learning: care, collaboration and democratisation. In schools where each student is valued as an individual learner, where a strong sense of equity and social justice permeates policy and practice, where teachers assume joint responsibility with students for learning outcomes, care, concern and commitment permeate all relationships. Students care for each other, teachers care for students as well as for each other, and principals care for teachers and students.

These schools realise that new concepts of teaching and learning are predicated on collaborative relationships throughout the school (Rosenholtz 1989). Teachers, for example, are able to create successful collaborative classroom experiences for students as well as collaborate effectively themselves in planning, teaching, evaluating and school decision-making (Moore Johnson 1990). Effective school leaders realise the need to nurture collaboration by establishing a framework of trust, respect, congeniality and collegiality. Ways in which they, as leaders, relate to teachers, students and parents help to establish the norms of behaviour desired for others.

Ability and willingness to involve all participants in the school community, especially teachers, students and parents, reflects the school leaders' awareness of the importance of democracy in building a healthy school climate for enhancing teaching and learning. These leaders realise the importance of democratic values, such as tolerance and respect for the rights and values of others, participation, concern for equity, and ability and opportunity to make judgements and choices in one's own and others' interests. These and other democratic values become embedded in the curriculum, school structures and core processes of learning, teaching and decision-making (Dimmock 1993c). A healthy democratic school climate where students are encouraged to participate in, and are consulted about, the running of their school is as much a valuable part of their learning as the acquisition of subject knowledge. Effective school leaders realise that the one form of learning is likely to promote the other.

Resource allocation is crucial in supporting the quality school for learning and teaching. Patterns of allocation reveal whether the school is fostering the learning of all students and whether it has thought carefully about the resource levels necessary for the learning of different cohorts of students (B. Knight 1993). Program budgeting ties resources to objectives and curriculum programs and is a marked advance on simple line-item budgeting, which still pervades schools. A further stage beyond program budgeting involves tying resources to student outcomes; instead of decisions taken on the basis of the costs of mounting each course or program, resources are allocated on the expected costs of individuals or groups of students achieving certain levels of learning outcomes. Students and schools perform well when leaders recognise the need for agreement on goals, when resources are allocated to support goal achievement and when all parts of the school work consistently and collaboratively towards the same ends. Resources are allocated to professional development, which, in turn, supports improvements in teaching and learning. Professional development of staff is school-focused, addressing specific school policies and involving functioning teams.

Effective schools monitor and review their performance at whole-school and sub-school levels (Cuttance 1993a). Their school communities express interest in the quality of teaching and learning, the appropriateness of structures, culture and climate, as well as the quality of leadership and management, by adopting and institutionalising evaluation procedures. School leaders contribute directly, through their personal involvement in monitoring and reviewing, and indirectly, by establishing a culture and climate supportive of the engagement of others in review. These effective leaders realise the importance of monitoring and reviewing as prerequisites for providing feedback and positive reinforcement, both of which are consistently shown by research to be among the behaviours contributing most to learning (Fraser et al. 1987).

Schools perform well when leaders recognise the need for agreement on goals, when resources are allocated to support goal achievement and when all parts of the school work consistently and collaboratively towards the same ends. Resources are allocated to professional development which, in turn, supports improvements in teaching and learning. Professional development of staff is school-focused, addressing specific school policies and involving functioning teams. As effective leaders they give abundant feedback and positive reinforcement to teachers and students and at the same time build the culture for these behaviours to permeate all levels and members of the school community. Furthermore, these leaders appreciate that review and evaluation are prerequisites for accountability to their constituents.

The quality school is constantly looking for school improvement. It allows the nature of its students to shape the appropriateness of its learning and teaching. With new students entering the school each year, change is endemic. These schools are constantly searching for better ways of service delivery. Principals are transformational leaders (Leithwood and Jantzi 1990); they promote, support and evaluate change according to its likely influence on teaching and learning. They are comfortable in managing change and transmitting enthusiasm for change across their communities. Where principals combine a focus on instructional leadership with the abilities of transformational leaders, they are most likely to benefit the quality of teaching and learning. Their technical knowledge of teaching, learning and curriculum enables them to select the desirable from the undesirable changes (Fullan 1991). Their expertise as leaders and managers of the change process involved in implementing new forms of teaching and learning enables them to handle successfully any opposition or conflict that may come from students, teachers and parents. Leading and managing a community of learners entails responsibility for ensuring that all participants are well informed about, aware of, and involved in, the arguments for change. Effective school leaders recognise the importance of timing in managing change and that ultimately it is students and teachers who hold the key to improving learning and teaching.

Conclusion

Schools for quality learning and teaching are those that have clear understanding of, and commitment to, student learning and learning outcomes, not just for the student population of the school as a whole, but also for individual students. These quality schools place all students and learners at the centre of what they do; they are driven by the philosophy and practice of helping all students learn as best they can. In these effective schools, it is not only teaching and learning that assume new forms. Flexible organisational structures are designed to facilitate new teaching and learning practices. Leadership and management are reconceptualised in ways that respond to the delivery of quality teaching and learning. Traditional top-down linear conceptions of leadership and management and their influence on teaching and learning become inappropriate. In their place is a new configuration of leadership and management, one which makes them derivative from, and responsive to, principles and practices of quality teaching and learning for all students. It is in this way that school leadership and student learning outcomes are crucially related. In this backward-mapping conception of leadership, new and different roles, relationships and competencies are demanded of effective school leaders. This is the challenging conception of school leadership, towards which our school leaders and those who prepare them will have to rise, if our schools are to meet the expectations for learning placed on them.

17 Quality Assurance and Quality Management in Education Systems

Peter Cuttance

The literature on quality over the past forty years can be viewed as having developed three key areas relating to different aspects of assuring and managing quality. The first area describes approaches to quality control. Quality control refers to a system for comparing output with defined standards. The second area describes approaches to quality assurance. Quality assurance can be viewed as addressing the same objectives as quality control but doing so in a preventative rather than after-the-fact way. It goes beyond the comparison of output with defined standards, seeking to prevent defects from arising in the first place. Thus, it extends the focus from outcomes or outputs to the processes that produced them. The third area directly addresses strategies for ensuring that not only are preventative practices established but also that the whole of general management practice is orientated towards the management of quality. This is manifest in the literature by reference to such approaches as 'total quality management'.

Quality control

Quality control refers to a system for comparing output with defined standards:

> ... the activities and techniques employed to achieve and maintain the quality of a product or service. It involves a monitoring activity, but also concerns finding and eliminating causes of quality problems so that the requirements of the client are continually met. (Oakland 1989: 10)

In education systems, large-scale student testing can be viewed as one manifestation of quality control. The purpose of such testing is to certify some students as meeting a predefined quality standard, often defined by norms, and to 'reject' other students as having not met those standards. This non-certification of some students leaving the education system is evidence that not all outcomes of the system meet the predefined quality standard. Another example is students being held back to repeat a grade.

There can be a considerable cost in the inspection processes required to ascertain whether or not individual students or services meet the predefined standards. By their nature the resources required to carry out 'inspection' do not themselves contribute to the quality of the individual product or service; they merely control the quality of the supply of products and services by withholding those that do not meet the standard. In one sense, then, the inspection process itself can be seen as wasteful, in that it focuses on looking for precisely the examples of a product or service that we wish not to produce. The literature on quality assurance takes up this issue by shifting some of its focus to the processes responsible for producing a product or service, in addition to the actual output produced.

Quality assurance

Quality assurance seeks to prevent defects arising in the first place; it is a system of activities for ensuring the production of a defined service to agreed standards within resources (Morgan and Everett 1990: 25). This means:

> the prevention of quality problems through planned and systematic activities. These will include: the establishment of a good quality management system and the assessment of its adequacy, the audit of the operation of the system, and the review of the system itself. (Oakland 1989: 10).

This preventative feature of quality assurance systems, themselves being subject to quality assurance standards, is an aspect of the process of 'building-in quality'. This contrasts with the focus on weeding out the non-quality outcomes from the overall output in quality control systems.

The explicit standards required for quality assurance are, however, a departure from the usual intra-professional perspectives of quality. Explicit standards themselves demystify. Further, they can be used as the basis of a more intelligible system of public accountability. This also emphasises the role of service user in judging the appropriateness and effectiveness of services; that is, it focuses jointly on both the user and the provider as the assessor of the quality of the service.

In reference to education, Kogan (1986) has argued that many writers have assumed a close correspondence between professional autonomy and responsiveness to clients, but in practice the connection is anything but automatic. According to Pollitt, this approach also contrasts with 'the often vague or idiosyncratic judgements which in the past have sometimes constituted the reputational currency of the . . . teaching professions' (Pollitt 1990: 437).

The accountability of government to parliament requires a demonstration that services are efficient and effective and that they are capable of providing value for money. The audit and review of public sector service organisations must therefore be designed to provide the information required to indicate whether the process and structures through which outcomes and services are produced are operating effectively and to provide recommendations on ways in which this process can be improved. Thus, although quality assurance systems in the public sector address the fundamental issue of accountability, they must also operate in a way that maximises their contribution to the development and effectiveness of the organisation if they are to fulfil their function. That is, quality assurance brings together the common focus of accountability and development for a service. Accountability systems focus primarily on proving quality, while development systems focus on improving quality.

Quality management

Modern approaches to quality management complement the scope of quality assurance by directly addressing an active development component. In particular, they build an ethos of continuous review of the users' service requirements and the organisation's ability to meet them.

The management of quality must be treated like any other managerial function, with clear lines of responsibility through an accountable individual in a senior position in the organisation. Public sector managers have a duty to:

> ensure that quality assurance systems are in place, and, beyond that, to check that these systems have certain characteristics which render them useful and intelligible not only to the professional service deliverers but also to the public and its representatives. (Pollitt 1990: 441)

Most attempts to set up quality assurance systems in the public sector, however, have been based on existing systems for collecting data. This is generally unsatisfactory because such data tend to describe efficiency and economy only; and it does not focus on quality, effectiveness, risk management and user satisfaction, the significant concerns of quality management.

Managers must be prepared to establish new systems of data collection rather than repackage current but inappropriate statistics from present collections.

Core features of systems for the management of quality

Morgan and Everett (1990: 25) argue that a quality management system has five core features:

- A clear definition of the purpose of the service.
- A clear definition of the method of delivery of the service (objectives and standards).
- A system for monitoring performance (including the response to this monitoring process itself).
- A system for the maintenance of performance.
- A process for developing the service.

A fully integrated quality management system is driven by a knowledge and skill-based culture, not a rule-based culture. It must address:

- Planning throughout the organisation (to be effective, planning must be integrated across organisational levels).
- Systems for implementing plans (action plans).
- A system for monitoring the progress of plans (it is important that monitoring is undertaken frequently, even if less accurately, rather than infrequently and accurately).
- A system of audit and review (including audit and review of the quality assurance and quality management process itself).
- A system for benchmarking the performance of various processes (benchmarking is the process of comparing the performance of similar operations in different parts of the organisation, or across organisations of a similar type).
- Systems for measuring performance improvement (however, it is important that the appraisal of individuals be independent of the general review of quality, otherwise the integrity of the quality review process will be diminished).
- Training and development throughout the organisation (this should focus on both formal training and development, and informal coaching and peer tutoring; and it is important that the effectiveness of the training be evaluated).

The role of inspectorates

Most education systems derived from British systems of state-provided education have at some stage had inspectorates of schools. In fact, the early history of these systems is marked by a significant role for school inspectors. The first appointments of members of Her Majesty's Inspectorate (HMI) in England were made in December 1839. The establishment of HMI was based on the precedent set by the inspection of factories under the Factory Act, from 1802 onwards. As in the case of inspectors appointed for the latter purpose, inspectors of schools did not necessarily have a background in education; they were more likely to be clergymen than any other profession (Sutherland 1973: 58).

The appointment of inspectors of schools in Australia followed this lead. For example, Dr William Wyatt, secretary to the Medical Board of South Australia, was appointed as the first inspector in that state. His duties were not clearly specified by the governor:

> His Excellency desires me to say that he does not consider it necessary to give any detailed instructions as to your duties, since the office being a new one His Excellency, placing every confidence in your zeal and abilities, thinks it better to leave you to the exercise of your own judgement upon them. (Smeaton 1927: 60)

In both the United Kingdom and Australia, however, the role of the inspectorate has varied considerably since its inception. During the latter years of the nineteenth century in both countries the inspectorate was involved in the examination of pupils. At other times it has been involved in the examination and licensing of teachers, the recruitment of teachers, and the training and development of teachers.

The practice of the inspectorate in carrying out school inspections has also varied over the years. A principal described an inspection visit by Dr Wyatt as follows:

> . . . about 11.15 on Wednesday the doctor came along. He looked at the roll-book, had a little chat with the teacher, heard the upper class read, asked a few questions, told us we were very good boys, and gave us a half-holiday. By 12.15 we were all out at play. The system was beautiful in its simplicity. It followed the line of least resistance. It created no friction. It economised the time. (Kanem 1915: 14)

In the early days Wyatt and a subsequent appointee were not able to visit schools that were most remote from Adelaide. Such schools were 'inspected' by magistrates, justices of the peace, ministers of religion, district councillors and others (Jones 1985).

Over the years, school inspection has generally been interpreted to contain three principal elements:

- A check on the use of public funds (the accountability function).
- The provision of information to central government concerning the success or otherwise of the education system, based on its independent professional judgement (the eyes and ears of the Secretary of State function).
- The provision of advice to those responsible for the running of educational establishments (the advisory function). (Lawton and Gordon 1987)

Quality control in education systems

The narrow 'quality control' aspect of the inspection of schools in

Australia during the early years of the inspectorate, through its dominant role in the examination of pupils and the policing of regulations, is encapsulated in the following quotation from an inspector:

> the rigid nature of inspections and examinations was a wholesome terror for dilatory individuals, and inspectors had made it not possible for drunkards to continue as teachers, or persons who had failed at everything else to turn to school-keeping. (Quoted in Jones 1985: 93)

The most restrictive quality control role of the inspectorate, however, emanated from the 1858 Royal Commission in England, which recommended that better efficiency should be achieved by examining:

> every child in every school to which grants are to be paid with a view to ascertaining whether these indispensable elements of knowledge are thoroughly acquired, and to make the prospects and position of the teacher dependent to a considerable extent on the results of this examination. (Quoted in Lawton and Gordon 1987: 11)

It was this recommendation that was translated into the system of 'payment by results' in the revised code of 1862. As a result of the revised code the role of the inspector became very much one of the enforcer of the code. Some HMI inspectors (in particular, Matthew Arnold) were publicly critical of the damage being done to education by payment by results. Inspectors became feared and hated in the elementary schools rather than welcome as advisers, as they often had been previously:

> [the inspector's] manner could be terrifying. He could choose passages for dictation which contained words quite outside the children's vocabulary, or he could deliberately exploit the difficulties of the English language. (Quoted in Sturt 1967: 351)

A similar system of payment by results was introduced in Australian state systems, with the inspectorate undertaking the examination of pupils:

> Hartley relentlessly kept the inspectors' role firmly centred on examining and inspecting in his firm belief that this was the way to get an efficient system, improved standards, justice to teachers and children and value for money for the colony. (Jones 1985: 143)

Few challenged the accountability role of the inspectors, the value-for-money purpose of inspections. The inspectorate concentrated on the detailed assessment of teachers rather than advice for them, which teachers claimed was their great need (Jones 1985: 194).

Quality assurance review

The quality assurance focus, which goes beyond the narrow quality control approach described above, has also been evident at different times among school inspectorates. For example, the citizens' charter in describing the proposed new role for HMI in the United Kingdom said, 'the inspectorates are concerned with value for money and standards of output and performance' (UK Parliament 1991: 40).

The appointment of Dr Wyatt as the first inspector in South Australia was prompted in part by grave doubts held by members of the Legislative Council that the colony was not giving value for money on its spending on education (Saunders 1967: 212). Wyatt assessed the worthiness of schools in general terms in order to establish that the teachers were not collecting government money fraudulently (Jones 1985: 35).

The quality assurance role requires an explicit statement of standards and criteria, but inspectorates have never been known for their preparedness to provide a public statement of these. One of the more explicit statements was made by the Central Board of Education in South Australia in 1874 when it prepared instructions for the guidance of inspectors, who were instructed on arrival at a school to check immediately if the lesson corresponded to the timetable, examine the records and then conduct examinations in all subjects with special attention to the Three Rs. They were to point out privately faults and deficiencies and note them in the observation book for future reference. The report on each school had to cover its organisation, methods of teaching, instruction and progress, the attendance, and the notes made in the observation book (Jones 1985: 49).

In recent times HMI staff in England have worked with *aides-mémoire* to guide the inspection process in individual schools, although these have generally not been public declarations of criteria used in inspections.

The UK Education (Schools) Act 1992 provides for a substantial revision to the role and function of HMI. The Chief Inspector now has to keep the Secretary of State informed about:

- The quality of the education provided by schools.
- The educational standards achieved in those schools.
- The spiritual, moral, social and cultural development of children in schools.
- Whether the financial resources made available to those schools are managed efficiently.

The Chief Inspector also gives advice to the Secretary of State on request.

Under the Act every school in England and Wales is to be inspected on a four-year cycle. Although the Act does not set out the conditions for the inspection of schools in terms of the criteria and practices to be followed, it is expected that the regulations under the Act will require HMI to provide detailed and specific criteria for this purpose.

The Act requires inspections of schools to be undertaken by registered inspectors leading inspection teams comprising both professional members with a background in education and lay members 'without interest' in the particular school. Inspection teams may also include individuals from non-education backgrounds where that provides specific skills and knowledge relevant to the evaluation of the work of a school. In order to assure the quality of school inspections, HMI produces explicit criteria for the standards and quality of practices required in schools.

Quality Management

Individual schools have sought to manage the quality of their processes and outcomes through planning and other management processes. Other systemic structures for the management of quality have been those supporting curriculum development and implementation, and the professional development of staff.

It has been suggested that the advisory duties of HMI are almost equivalent in force to the position of executive control of schools. However, the Rayner Review made it clear that HMI had no direct responsibility or powers, except the right of access to institutions and the duty to inspect on behalf of the Secretary of State. The HMI are not responsible for decisions about the organisation or the curriculum in schools: nor for standards; nor the standard of facilities, equipment, staffing or other resources; nor for the deployment or promotion or appointment of teachers (Rayner Report 1983, para 1.12 (iv)). Similarly, inspectors and advisory staff in Australian school systems have not in the past assumed line-management responsibilities for schools.

Advice to schools

School inspectorates have traditionally offered advice to schools on the improvement of their performance. This advice has been tendered from the point of view of autonomous professionals giving expert advice. For much of the time there has been pressure from schools for inspectorates to develop their advisory function:

> [The inspector] should take a class and show the teacher how to adopt his methods, and the teacher, by that means would have a better idea of what he required, and the result examination would be very much easier on account of the suggestions which he would have made.

Although there were several times during the nineteenth century when the inspectorate attempted to develop the advisory role, it was usually short lived and not systematically implemented. After the Second World War, however, the advisory function of school inspectors slowly gained ascendancy over the quality control function. In 1969 the Director-General of Education in South Australia explicitly described the role of inspectors in the system as one of providing:

> a main role to guide, to lead and to inspire teachers and to help them with their problems, both personal and professional, . . . the inspectors' wider role . . . makes them agents for cross-fertilisation of ideas and practices between schools, and also makes them moderators of the Head's assessment of teachers' ability. (J.S. Walker 1969: 90)

Over the years there has been considerable discussion about the appropriate framework for this advisory role. The discussion has centred on the structures required for the provision of independent advice and the need to provide advice for policy-makers and developers.

Accountability and independence

In the United Kingdom the independence of Her Majesty's Inspectorate has been exhibited by the extent to which it has published evidence that might appear to support criticisms of government policy. However, Eric Bolton made it clear when he was Senior Chief Inspector that HMI can never criticise government policy as such; it can only make statements of fact that have clear implications for such policy (Lawton and Gordon 1987).

In the early years, some independence for HMI was gained when the committee to which it reported made a commitment not to change HMI reports. However, on many occasions the committee did return the report to the inspector for further revision. Final control over the independence of HMI was exercised through the 'judgement of their Lordships' in stipulating that if a report:

> does not conform to this standard, it is to be returned to the Inspector for revision, and if, on its being again received from him it appears to be open to the same objection, it is to be put aside as a document not proper to be printed at public expense. (Quoted in Lawton and Gordon 1987: 11)

The Department of Education and Science in England indicated that:

> while the decision to publish what HMI write rests with the Secretaries of State, any of their work which the Secretaries of State decide should be published is published as the Inspectorate wrote it. (Department of Education and Science 1979)

The inspection and review function, however, can have only a limited form of independence. One aspect of independence sought is from the potential interference of providers. This is fundamental to the claim to report without fear or favour. Until the recent reform, the Inspectorate in England was structurally a division of the Department of Education and Science. Under the recent Act the Inspectorate has been established as a separate department of state, providing it with a greater degree of independence from the department responsible for the provision of education.

The organisational structures of school review programs recently established in Australian state school systems and in New Zealand have approached the problem of independence in different ways. The New Zealand solution is similar to that for HMI. The New Zealand Education Review Office (ERO) is established as a separate government department within the portfolio managed by the Minister of Education. The program of work for the ERO is agreed with the Minister annually and funds provided from the Treasury for this program of work.

The South Australian and New South Wales governments have established their education review function within the department responsible for the provision of schooling. In both cases the director responsible for the review function is a member of the department's senior decision-making group.

Both solutions encapsulate a tension between accountability and advisory functions. The external (separate department) solution inhibits the communication of everyday information about the effectiveness of practice in schools to inform the operational decisions of the Education Department. It leads to both more formal and less informal input from the reviews of schools to policy and program development. Research on the use of findings from evaluations indicates that the effectiveness of evaluations is determined in part by the reporting process, and is maximised when there is a mix of formal and informal reporting processes and practices. Establishing a separate government department for the review function provides it with greater formal independence from the operational functions of the system. This may improve its credibility in the eyes of the public, but it does not necessarily lead to a more effective discharge of accountability within the system.

Accountability is defined as 'a condition in which individual role holders [or organisations] are liable to review and the application of sanctions if their actions fail to satisfy those with whom they are in an accountability relationship' (Kogan 1986: 25). Betcher et al. (1979) distinguish three elements to accountability in school systems:

- Moral accountability (answerability to one's clients).
- Professional accountability (responsibility to oneself and one's colleagues).
- Contractual accountability (accountability to one's employers or political masters).

The locus and balance of these three elements varies with the organisational structure of school systems. For example, an independent school that does not have formal organisational links to other schools is accountable in the first two senses above. Most non-government schools are, however, also contractually accountable to a governing body or belong to a church system that exercises power over the governance of the school. Schools established as 'commercial trading enterprises' are contractually accountable to their board of directors. Schools within government education systems are also clearly accountable in all three senses described above. Ultimately, accountability in the contractual sense in public education systems is an extension of the political accountability of ministers to parliament.

In most government systems reforms in the past few years have shifted the balance of authority and power from the centre, through the devolution of authority and responsibility over a wider range of operational issues to school communities. Where this has taken the form of 'organisational devolution' the contractual accountability of schools has not been weakened and moral accountability to school communities has been strengthened through their increased involvement and knowledge of the operations of individual schools. Thus, responsibility, the moral sense of duty to perform appropriately, is increased at the local level. Any change in the locus of contractual accountability is dependent on the extent to which there is also devolution of authority to the local level. In public school systems, devolution of authority (as organisational devolution) retains the line of authority within the state management structure for the school system—hence it continues to provide a formal line of accountability through the minister to parliament.

In some public systems (in the United Kingdom and New Zealand, for example) devolution has taken a political form rather than the organisational form found in Australian and many North American systems. A system that delegates power and authority to electorally mandated bodies at the local level devolves a significant degree of contractual accountability also to the local level. Further, at that level it shifts the balance of accountability from the moral to the contractual domain, as local communities are delegated formal powers of sanction over schools. This shift in the locus of power over sanctions in New Zealand and the United Kingdom has been accompanied by an emphasis on schools as operating in a 'market' situation. The powers of sanction are a direct result of the parents' power to call the governing body of the school to account by exercising their electoral authority. In such systems the Minister of Education ultimately becomes responsible for the provision and marketing of education, in much the same way that the Minister of Consumer Affairs is responsible for the structures and processes for ensuring the regulation of consumer markets (goods and services). That is, the focus of the Minister of Education moves away from direct accountability for the quality of education provided, to the choice and regulation of the provision to consumer groups (parents and students).

A review function with a dual accountability and advisory role is appropriate for both the organisational and political models of devolution (outlined above). In a politically devolved system the review function can contribute significantly to the Education Minister's ability to account for the provision of schooling and provides the account of school performance required by school governing bodies. It is for these reasons that HMI in the UK and the ERO in New Zealand report directly to the Education Minister and the governing bodies of schools, with only an indirect or secondary role to report to the Department of Education. These reporting relationships reflect the review function's primary focus on accountability for outcomes, rather than on advisory or development outcomes for schools and the department's development of policy and delivery of programs.

The paradigm of quality assurance and quality management now predominant in other industries provides a framework for the review function to make a more significant contribution to the development of schools and advice on the delivery of programs in systems that have opted for organisational devolution. Quality assurance reviews conducted at arm's length from the system's operational functions and the development of practices for the management of quality throughout the organisation can serve this purpose while also meeting the accountability requirements of the system. In this model the feedback from quality assurance reviews are fundamental to the management of quality. The aim of quality assurance reviews is to provide advice of a developmental nature for managing quality in the delivery of schooling; a source of policy advice to ministers, independent and additional to that from the operational management function; and a contribution to the ability to account publicly.

The need for professional independence for the quality review function is recognised in the quality assurance literature. An essential issue for government is whether the accountability function is viewed as dischargeable simply through the inspection of the end products or outcomes of the education system (for example, the statewide assessment of student attainment) or whether the effective operation of a quality review and audit process is itself viewed as necessary to discharge the accountability function.

Systemic policy advice

The role of inspectorates in providing policy advice has received considerable attention. In the United Kingdom this interface between the inspectorate and the executive arm of government has passed through a series of phases since 1944:

- In the immediate post-1944 phase, partnership was the dominant metaphor, and HMI occupied a relaxed and almost unnecessary place in the political background.
- From the late 1960s to the mid-1970s the education service became increasingly controversial, and, after some uncertainty, HMI returned to the political arena with a very definite professional role to play.
- Finally, in the late 1970s and throughout the 1980s education became increasingly politicised, and the professional role of HMI became very much more important. (Lawton and Gordon 1987: 104)

Recent policy developments in England make HMI's first task that of ensuring that schools and parents receive regular and frequent inspection reports and the advice and judgements that arise from them. The provision of policy advice for government is less central to the new role for HMI.

In New South Wales and South Australia the review programs have a joint focus on the evaluation of systemic programs and services and on the development context of the individual school. All school reviews contain one or more elements of systemic review, which gathers information on performance indicators for practice and functioning across schools or a review of an area of policy or other systemic program under review at the time.

Evaluation methodology for school reviews

Most school inspectorates have established criteria to support their inspection activities. These are usually in the form of *aides-mémoire*—headings elaborated by prompts, questions, etc. Wilcox (1991), however, notes that such methods fail to meet the idealised notion of objectivity in educational research—the externalisation of agreed procedures capable of replication. The Audit Commission in the United Kingdom said: 'in the management of observation of teaching and of pupils' and students' learning one major challenge is to ensure that the inspectors follow planned approaches to observation. While they are in classrooms, laboratories and workshops it is vital that they should make judgements on pre-determined aspects of teaching and learning, applying pre-determined criteria' (Audit Commission 1989: 19).

The inclusion of lay personnel in the review and evaluation process raises questions about the evaluative skills and knowledge required. Some have argued that these skills and knowledge can be gained only by experience and training, which lay members could not be expected to have. Both the new English system of school inspections and the Australian school review systems involve members of the public in the process (Office for Standards in Education 1993). It is argued that this helps to ensure that the judgement of what represents good practice is not left just to the professionals. New insights might also be brought to the process from the experience of those whose professional lives has taken them into fields other than education (Wilcox 1991).

The methodology of school inspections in the Australian and British traditions generally ignored the substantial literature on educational evaluation (Wilcox 1989). The recently developed review programs in Australia and New Zealand and the school evaluation schemes of most North American systems have, however, paid greater attention to this literature. Inspections and reviews deal with natural settings: normally functioning schools. They build on tacit knowledge and use qualitative methods (observation, interviews, analysis of documentation, etc.). The design of the evaluation needs to be flexible rather than fixed and predetermined (Wilcox 1991).

Evaluations of systemwide programs and policies may, however, make use of both qualitative and quantitative methods. The more a program aims at individualised outcomes, the greater the appropriateness of qualitative methods. The more it emphasises common outcomes for all students, the more appropriate are quantitative methods based on standardised measures of the outcomes achieved (Patton 1986).

Decisions about sampling occur throughout the process of reviewing the performance and development of a school. Strategies for sampling the experience of a school are a form of 'purposive' sampling. The criteria for including elements in the sample is one of gathering information rather than of providing statistical evidence about the distribution of a behaviour in a notional population. That is, sampling is not 'representative' but 'contingent' and 'serial'; ideally each element in the sample is chosen after the information yielded by earlier elements has been considered. Sampling therefore takes account the continuous ebb and flow of information and the on-going attempts to make sense of it. Ideally, sampling continues until informational redundancy sets in (Wilcox 1991). Sampling strategies must also be designed to meet the needs of stakeholders when they move to respond to the findings of the review (Patton 1986).

The report of a school review may be regarded as a type of case study reconstruction of the situation observed. It involves substantial data synthesis and analysis. For the report to have integrity it is essential that this reconstruction is recognisable as an acceptable representation of the multiple realities as perceived by the various stakeholders in the school.

In developing the report it is important that the representation is checked with the reality as perceived by the various stakeholders.

An important characteristic that distinguishes the process from most naturalistic approaches to evaluation is the short period of time spent in the school—typically between three and ten days. A critical question in this type of condensed field work, is how to verify accounts and judgements of the situation, through reference to supporting information. The methodological device of triangulation is widely used in this situation. This is the process of corroborating the observation of information by drawing on evidence from a series of sources and obtained by different methods.

There is always a trade-off between the accuracy of information and the resources required to conduct a review. Time is the primary resource in school reviews. Naturally, schools want accurate information, but they prefer less accurate information (to guide their decision-making) to no information at all. They also prefer some information to none. Thus, research quality and vigour are 'less important to utilisation than the literature might suggest' (Alkin et al. 1979: 24).

One of the significant differences in methodologies used in HMI inspections and more recently developed school review processes is the emphasis on qualitative research methods to 'uncover' the underlying issues from the accounts of stakeholders in the latter. Typically, 50 to 80 per cent of the time input in an HMI inspection will be directed towards direct observation of classroom practice by members of the HMI team, all of whom operate as 'experts'. An assessment is made of various aspects of classroom practice and school functioning and of the standards of student learning outcomes. In contrast, the school review teams in New South Wales and South Australia direct most of their resources to interviews and discussions of issues with various groups of stakeholders (school staff, students, and parents). Members of these review teams operate as trained practitioners rather than as experts; most are seconded from their normal school-based jobs for one or four terms. The overall objective of the review is an assessment of quality and standards—as perceived mainly through the 'eyes' and 'interpretations' of the stakeholders—in contrast to 'expert' assessments in HMI inspections. Expert professional knowledge, however, is still important, as it conditions how the information provided by stakeholders is interpreted.

The development role of school reviews and the advisory component of HMI inspections require that the methodology must be capable of providing useful information for assisting the development of the school. Patton (1986) has provided a very relevant discussion of the key features of 'utilisation-focused' evaluation methodologies. Schools with clear development plans provide the reviewer with a hierarchy of means and ends, and the decision about where to enter this hierarchy is made on the basis of what information would be most useful to the stakeholders charged with responding to the review process (Patton 1986: 154). However, this does not license a simplistic outcomes-based approach to review. 'If intervening activities and objectives will not or cannot be implemented, then evaluation of ultimate outcomes is not very useful' (Patton 1986: 157).

In a utilisation-focused approach, initial theoretical formulations originate with identified stakeholders and intended information users, and the research interests are adapted to the evaluation needs of relevant decision-makers, not vice versa. Utilisation-focused evaluation replaces the traditional researcher's quest for truth with a search for useful and balanced information. Further, it replaces the mandate to be objective with a mandate to be fair and conscientious in taking account of multiple perspectives, multiple interests, and multiple realities (Patton 1986).

The recently established school review programs in South Australia and New Zealand follow the lessons learnt from the quinquennial review program conducted by the Inner London Education Authority during the 1980s. The essential conclusion from research on the effectiveness of inspections as contributors to the development of schools was that they should be carried out regularly and more frequently than every five years. The review programs have been designed to review each school every three or four years.

Other aspects of the management of quality in education systems

Performance indicators

One of the main areas of development in reporting in education during the past decade has been the establishment of performance indicators. In general, this work has not lived up to the expectations that policy-makers and operational managers had of it. There are two main reasons for this. First, the indicators have been highly global (for example, pupil–teacher ratios and expenditure per pupil). Second, the time lag in providing these indicators to operational managers has generally meant that they have not been incorporated into routine decision-making about the delivery of schooling. Global indicators have been of some use in policy-making, but the more valuable information about the effects and impact of policies has not often been captured by the sets of indicators developed, partly because they have tended to be based on extant data collected for administrative reasons, rather than data required for management and policy decision-making.

The development of performance indicators as part of the quality review function in South Australia focused on aspects of practice and functioning in schools (Cuttance et al. 1991) and on their use by schools in action plans—the implementation plans associated with collaborative school development plans (Education Department of South Australia 1990a, 1991a). The purpose of the former set of indicators is to highlight the aspects of strong practice in the education system and aspects requiring improvement. The indicators provide information for resource allocation decisions, particularly in relation to the provision of training and development for school staff, and policies and programs for more intensive review.

Strategic planning

All Australian state education systems have introduced strategic planning over the past five years or so (Davis et al. 1989). This coincides with the broader use of strategic approaches to management in both the public and private sector. Strategic planning has been implemented at the state level as a means of moving towards an agreed vision and the medium-term objectives of new policies.

The other area in which strategic planning has become widely used is at the school level. School development plans have been established by all schools in South Australia to implement departmental objectives and to address local school priorities (Education Department of South Australia 1990a), and most other states have introduced planning at the school level to address strategic change and development. Although not as widespread at this time, school development planning has also been introduced in the United Kingdom (Department of Education and Science 1989, 1991).

Action plans for the implementation of strategic school objectives, regular monitoring of pupil outcomes and an annual review of priorities are essential elements of this approach to strategic management.

Internal school review

Hopkins (1989) provides an overview of the main characteristics of effective schemes for internal school-based review:

- They are based on a systematic review and evaluation process, and are not simply an exercise in reflection.
- Their immediate goal is to obtain information about a school's condition, purposes, and outcomes.
- They are meant to lead to action on an aspect of the school's organisation or curriculum.

- They are a group activity that involves participants in a collegial process.
- Optimally the process is 'owned' by the school.
- Their purpose is school improvement/development, and their aspiration is to progress towards the ideal goal of a 'problem-solving' or 'relatively autonomous' school.

This list of characteristics has benefited from hindsight gained through the evaluation of school-based review schemes. In reality, few schemes have conformed to this idealised set of characteristics, partly because there has been considerable variation in purpose among the schemes that have been in use.

Part of the current perception of the shortcomings of school-based internal self-evaluation and review schemes stems from changes in the prevailing view of the management of education. When school-based review schemes were introduced during the 1970s and 1980s their orientation towards accountability was referenced primarily by the standards and traditions of professional institutions. Thus, school-based reviews invested primary responsibility for the development of schools in the professionals who were involved in schooling. However, even a decade ago there was concern that schooling was, after all, an activity that is directly funded by the Treasury, and that this public responsibility required some form of formal accountability. Since then the prevailing view of the administration of public organisations has strengthened in terms of the requirement for them to provide evidence that they are accountable for their activities. This need not result in a weakening of the accountability of schools to professional standards and traditions. Indeed, paradoxically as it may seem, the more 'community needs oriented' the school system becomes, the weaker the argument for direct control through accountability mechanisms emanating from the Treasury. The increased demand for accountability is not so much to the public as electors, and therefore providers of funds, but to the consumer of the services offered by schools.

The problems encountered in school self-evaluation as the primary approach to school improvement arise from its failure to meet the criteria set out above. The major problem has been the failure of schemes to construct analytically critical reviews and evaluations of the process of schooling (Clift 1987; Hopkins 1989; Hargreaves 1988). Evaluations have tended to be defensive and have often not tackled issues central to the process of learning and teaching critically (Hargreaves 1988). In addition, the development that should follow an evaluation has not been managed successfully and has often not resulted in the intended improvements (Hargreaves 1988).

There are various reasons for these failures. Successful change in social organisations through a process of review, development and evaluation requires a high level of complex skills and management. It requires motivation (Clift 1987) and access to training in skills of evaluation and the management of change (Clift 1987; Hopkins 1989). The significant investment of time required for successful school development means that all participants must have a strong commitment to the changes required and be prepared to divert time and energy from other activities into the various phases of the program (Hopkins 1989). The lack of experience in planned change, and in managing the commitment and time required to redeploy resources, has also been cited by Clift (1987) as one of the main reasons for the failure of systems based entirely on school self-evaluation to lead to successful school development.

Self-evaluation processes that attempt to comprehensively review *all* aspects of a school's operations are rarely effective. To be effective, self-evaluation processes must be directly linked to the development plan for the school. Further, uncoupling the internal review process from accountability requirements makes it easier to assess progress in the restricted range of activities that are the focus of development in a particular period. The alternative—a requirement that school self-evaluation or internal review serve strong accountability purposes—considerably reduces its potential usefulness for development purposes.

Satisfying the dual requirements of accountability and development requires the combined use of both internal and external approaches to evaluation. External evaluations can contribute to accountability because they have a degree of independence by being conducted at arms' length from the operations of the school, although they are less effective than internal evaluations in the everyday monitoring of progress towards intended development outcomes. Both approaches can make a significant contribution to establishing priorities among competing claims for areas of potential development in schools.

Personnel appraisal and development

No Australian state system currently has a unified systemic approach to personnel appraisal across schools and non-school parts of the system. However, appraisal processes have been introduced by individual schools and for particular groups of staff. For example, all principals in most state systems now negotiate an annual performance management plan with their line managers in regional structures. Alignment between school development plans, the review process and principal's performance management plans is a necessary feature of successful development in schools. A lack of alignment between any pair of these processes implies that they are operating at cross-purposes—hence the source of dysfunction in the development process.

Discussion

Since their emergence in the nineteenth century, public education systems have established structures for monitoring and improving the quality of the education services they provide. These structures have traditionally taken the form of inspection, although inspection in education has always embodied a broader concept of the inspection process than that in other services and particularly in industry. Inspection in education has generally embodied aspects of advice about how to improve the service and provision of schooling, although there have been periods when this has been a minor aspect of the inspection process.

The broad concept of inspection, which included direct advice and support to schools, has an affinity with the concepts of quality assurance and quality management that gained wide acceptance in the general literature on management. The practice of the school inspectorates in all Australian public school systems until the 1970s, however, departed significantly from the practices of quality assurance and quality management. In particular, the inspections did not focus on strategic development issues and the structures and processes required for assuring continuous improvement in student outcomes. Further, the inspection processes did not explicitly seek to involve stakeholders in the process, and the reports from inspections were not written for those responsible for the day-to-day work of the school. Although the principal of the school usually received a copy of the report, it was written primarily for the director responsible for schools in the region.

Quality assurance brings the focus of development and accountability together. Both accountability and quality assurance require a process of educational review. Although many accountability systems in the past have operated without explicit criteria, quality assurance requires the establishment of systemic criteria for the standard of practice and level of outcomes to be expected in schools. Quality assurance is provided by using these systemic standards to inspect and review the work and achievements of schools.

To be effective in contributing to continuous improvement in schools, the system of education review itself must be conducted in such a way that it leads to effective follow-through from its findings and recommendations. This can be achieved by ensuring that the school community retains ownership of the review process and the reporting process specifically focusing on this aspect of the process.

The integrity of the quality review function is established and maintained by:

- autonomy and independence from the operational functions of the system;

- the independence of the review and audit process from practices for the appraisal of individual staff;
- the objective for reviews to be conducted in a way that ensures effective follow-up. This is ensured by:
  — involving all key stakeholders from the school community in the review and audit process;
  — publishing the criteria and practices for conducting quality reviews;
  — negotiating the statement of the findings from a quality review with the principal of the school, with the proviso that it accurately represents the findings of the review;
- the competence and credibility of the staff of quality review and audit teams;
- the public nature of the process for reporting findings from quality reviews and audits;
- the provision of advice and feedback to support and service functions on the effectiveness of their operations in terms of their impact in schools;
- the provision of public reports on the performance of the system as a whole;
- the public declaration and adherence to a code of ethics by all members of review teams.

For establishing a culture that focuses on the quality of practices and outcomes it is of fundamental importance that the quality reviews emphasise the relevance of the full range of processes and structures for the effective management of quality.

Bibliography

Abrahamson, E. and Fombrun, C. J. 1992, 'Forging the iron cage: Interorganizational networks and the production of macro-culture', *Journal of Management Studies*, vol. 29, no. 2, pp. 175–185

Adelman, C., Jenkins, D. and Kemmis, S. 1982, 'Rethinking Case Study: Notes from the second Cambridge Conference in Case Study', *Methods*, vol. 1. Deakin University, Geelong, pp. 2–3

Alkin, M.C., Daillak, R. and White, P. 1979, *Using Evaluations: Does Evaluation Make a Difference?* Sage, Beverly Hills, Calif.

Allen, R.F. 1985, 'Four phases for bringing about cultural change', in *Gaining Control of the Corporate Culture*, eds R.H. Killman, M.J. Saxton, and R. Serpa, Jossey-Bass, San Francisco, pp. 332–50

Anderson, G. 1989, 'Critical ethnography in education: Origins, current status and new directions', *Review of Educational Research*, vol. 59, no. 3, pp. 249–70

——1990, 'Towards a critical constructivist approach to school administration: Invisibility, legitimation and the study of non-events', *Educational Administration Quarterly*, vol. 26, no. 1, pp. 38–59

Angus, L. 1982, 'Definitions of unacceptable pupils: The case of the 'Sweathogs'', *Unicorn*, vol. 8, no. 2, pp. 267–72

——1984, 'Student attitudes to teachers and teaching', *Unicorn*, vol. 10, no. 2, pp. 240–50

——1986a, 'Pupils, power and the organisation of the school', *Journal of Educational Administration*, vol. 24, no. 1, pp. 5–17

——1986b, *Schooling, the School Effectiveness Movement and Educational Reform*, Deakin University Press, Geelong

——1988, *Continuity and Change in Catholic Schooling: An Ethnography of a Christian Brothers College in Australian Society*, Falmer Press, London

——1990, 'Democratic participation and administrative control in education', *International Journal of Educational Management*, vol. 3, no. 2, pp. 20–6

——1992, ' "Quality" schooling, conservative educational policy and educational change in Australia', *Journal of Educational Policy*, vol. 7, no. 4, pp. 379–97

——1993a, 'Women in a male domain: Gender and organizational culture in a Christian Brothers College', in *Education, Inequality and Social Identity*, ed. L. Angus, Falmer Press, London, pp. 57–90

——1993b, 'Sociological analysis and education management: The social context of the self-managing school', *British Journal of Sociology of Education* (in press)

——1994, 'Cultural perspectives in educational administration in this volume

Angus, L. and Rizvi, F. 1989, 'Power and the politics of participation', *Journal of Educational Administration and Foundations*, vol. 4, no. 1, pp. 6–23

Antal, A.B., Dierkes, M. and Weiler, H.N. 1987, 'Cross-national policy research: Traditions, achievements and challenges', in *Comparative Policy Research: Learning from Experience*, eds M. Dierkes, H.N. Weiler and A.B. Antal, Gower Publishing, Aldershot, England, pp. 13–25

Apple, M.W. 1987, *Is the New Technology Part of the Solution or Part of the Problem?* CDC/Prentice Hall, Canberra

——1988, 'Standing on the shoulders of Bowles and Gintis', *History of Education Quarterly*, vol. 28, pp. 231–41

——1991, 'The social context of democratic authority: A sympathetic response to Quantz, Cambron-McCabe and Dartley', *The Urban Review*, vol. 23, no. 1, pp. 21–9

——1992, 'Education, culture and class power: Basil Bernstein and the neo-marxist sociology of education', *Educational Theory*, vol. 42, no. 2, pp. 127–45

Ashenden, D. 1989, *State Aid and the Division of Schooling in Australia*, Deakin University Press, Geelong

——1990a, form letter, 25 June 1990

——1990b, 'Award restructuring and productivity in the future of schooling', 1990 Frank Tate Memorial Lecture, *Victorian Institute of Educational Research Bulletin*, 64. (Text also available from Ashenden & Associates, 118 Subiaco Road, Subiaco, WA 6008)

——1990c, *Restructuring Careers and Training for Education Workers*, Ashenden and Associates, Subiaco, WA

——1990d, 'The future of the teaching profession: Time for a radical turn', *Working Papers on Public Education*, vol. 2. Victorian State Board of Education, Melbourne

Audit Commission 1989, *Assuring Quality in Education*, HMSO, London

Austin, A.G. 1961, *Australian Education, 1788–1900: Church, State and Public Education in Colonial Australia*, Isaac Pitman, Melbourne

Australian Copyright Council, bulletin no. 52, *Libraries and Copyright*

——bulletin no. 62, *Historians and Copyright*

——bulletin no. 67, *A Teacher's Guide to Copyright*
——bulletin no. 78, *Computers and Copyright*
Australian Council of Trade Unions/Trade Development Council (ACTU/TDC) 1987, *Australia Reconstructed: ACTU/TDC Mission to Western Europe.*, Australian Government Publishing Service, Canberra
Australian Education Council 1990, *Teacher Education in Australia* (draft), AEC, Melbourne
——1991, *National Report on Schooling in Australia*, The Curriculum Corporation, Carlton, Vic.
——1992, *National Report on Schooling in Australia 1991* with accompanying *Statistical Annex*, AEC, Carlton, Vic.
Australian Government Publishing Service 1983, *National Economic Summit Conference, 11–14 April: Documents and Proceedings*, submission by the Youth Affairs Council of Australia, vol. 3, pp. 745–61
Australian National Opinion Poll (ANOP) 1984, Youth Attitudes: Report on a Survey of Australian Young People, ANOP, Canberra
Bailey, F.G. 1988, *Humbuggery and Manipulation: The Art of Leadership*, Cornell University Press, Ithaca, NY
Ball, D. 1980, *A Suitable Piece of Real Estate*, Hale & Iremonger, Sydney
——1987, *A Base for Debate*, Allen & Unwin, Sydney
Ball, S. J. 1987, *The Micro-politics of the School: Towards a Theory of School Organization*, Methuen, London
Ball, S. J. 1990, *Politics and Policymaking in Education: Explorations in Policy Sociology*, Routledge, London
Ball, S. 1992, *Reforming Education and Changing Schools: Case Studies in Policy Sociology*, Routledge, London
——1993, 'Education markets, choice and social class: The market as a class strategy in the UK and USA', *British Journal of Sociology*, vol. 14, no. 1, pp. 3–19
Banathy, B. 1988, 'Improvement or transformation?', *Noteworthy*, McRel, Denver, Col.
Barcan, A. 1965, *A Short History of Education in New South Wales*, Martindale Press, Sydney
Barnard, C. 1938, *The Functions of the Executive*, Harvard University Press, Cambridge, Mass.
Barth, R.S. 1990, *Improving Schools From Within: Teachers, Parents and Principals Can Make the Difference*, Jossey-Bass, San Francisco
Bassett, G.W. 1965, 'Training educational administrators in Australia', in ed. E.L. French, *Melbourne Studies in Education, 1964*, Melbourne University Press, Melbourne, pp. 31–49
Bates, R.J. 1980, 'Educational administration, the sociology of science, and the management of knowledge, *Educational Administration Quarterly*, vol. 16, no. 2, pp. 1–20

——1982, 'Education and the corporate economy: A response to Hedley Beare', *Unicorn*, vol. 8, no. 4, pp. 351–62
——1983, *Educational Administration and the Management of Knowledge*. Deakin University Press, Geelong
——1984, 'Toward a critical practice of educational administration', in *Leadership and Organizational Culture*, eds T.J. Sergiovanni and J.E. Corbally, University of Illinois Press, Urbana, Ill.
——1986, *Management of Culture and Knowledge*, Deakin University Press, Geelong
——1987, 'Corporate culture, schooling, and educational administration', *Educational Administration Quarterly*, vol. 23, no. 4, pp. 79–115
——1988, 'Is there a new paradigm in educational administration?', paper presented to the Organisational Theory Special Interest Group, annual conference of the American Educational Research Association, 5–10 April
——1990, 'Leadership and the rationalisation of society', paper presented to the Organisational Theory Special Interest Group, annual conference of the American Educational Research Association, 16–20 April
——1992a, 'The emerging culture of educational administration and what we can do about it', national conference of the Australian Council for Educational Administration, Darwin
——1992b, 'Leadership and school culture', *Il Congreso Interuniverstario de Organizacion Escolar*, Universidad de Sevilla, Seville
——1993a, 'On knowing: cultural and critical approaches to educational administration', *Educational Management and Administration*, vol. 21, no. 3, pp. 171–76
——1993b, 'Educational reform: Its role in the economic destruction of society', *Australian Administrator*
Beare, H. 1982, 'Educations' corporate image', *Unicorn*, vol. 8, no. 1, pp. 12–28
——1987, 'Changing structures in education', in *Principal and Change: The Australian Experience*, eds W.S. Simpkins, A.R. Thomas and E.B. Thomas, University of New England teaching monographs, Armidale, NSW
——1990, *Educational Administration in the 1990s*, ACEA monograph series, no. 6, Australian Council for Educational Administration, Melbourne
——1991, 'The restructuring of schools and school systems: A comparative perspective', in *Restructuring School Management: Administrative Reorganization of Public School Governance in Australia*, eds G. Harman, H. Beare, and G. Berkely, Australian College of Education, Canberra
Beare, H. and Boyd, W.L. (eds) 1993, *Restructuring Schools: An International Perspective on the Movement to Transform the Control and Performance of Schools*, Falmer Press, London and Washington, DC

Beare, H., Caldwell, B. and Millikan, R. 1989, *Creating an Excellent School: Some New Management Techniques*, Routledge, London
Bechtel, W. and Abrahamsen, A. 1991, *Connectionism and the Mind*, Blackwell, Oxford
Beilharz, P. 1987, 'Reading politics: social theory and social policy', *Australia and New Zealand Journal of Sociology*, vol. 23, no. 3, pp. 388–406
Ben Habib, S. 1987, 'The generalised and the concrete other: The Kohlberg-Gilligan controversy and feminist theory', in *Feminism as Critique*, eds S. Ben Habib and D. Cornell, University of Minnesota Press, Minneapolis
Benkel, R. et al. 1988, *Rights and Responsibilities in the School Community*, Leon Cussen Institute, Melbourne
Bennis, W. and Nanus, B. 1985, *Leaders: The Strategies for Taking Charge*, Harper & Row, New York
Benson, J. 1977, 'Organizations: A dialectical view', *Administrative Science Quarterly*, vol. 22, pp. 1–21
Berger, E.H. 1987, *Parents as Partners in Education* 2nd edn, Merrill Publishing Co, Columbus, Ohio
Berger, P. L. and Luckman, T. 1972, *The Social Construction of Reality: A Treatise in the Sociology of Knowledge*, Penguin, Harmondsworth
Berkeley, G.F. and Kenway, N. 1987, *A Management Review of the ACT Schools Authority: Report to the Minister for Territories*, ACT Schools Authority, Canberra
Bernstein, B. 1977, *Class, Codes and Control*, vol. 3, Routledge, London
Bernstein, R.J. 1976, *The Restructuring of Social and Political Theory*, Blackwell, Oxford
Betcher, T., Eraut, M., Booth, J., Canning, T. and Knight, J. 1979, 'Accountability in the Middle Years of Schooling', working papers, Final report to the Social Science Research Council (UK)
Biddle, B.J. and Anderson, D.S. 1991, 'Social research and educational change', in *Knowledge for Policy: Improving Education Through Research*, eds D.S. Anderson and B.J. Biddle, Falmer Press, New York
Bidwell, C.E. 1965, 'The school as a formal organisation', *Handbook of Organizations*, ed. J.G. March, Rand McNally, Chicago
——1979, 'The school as a formal organisation: Some new thoughts', in *Problem-Finding in Educational Administration*, eds G.L. Immegart and W.L. Boyd, Heath, Lexington, DC
Blackmore, J. 1987, 'Educational leadership: A feminist critique and reconstruction', in *Critical perspectives on educational leadership*, ed. J. Smyth, Falmer Press, London, pp. 93–129
——1991, 'Man the administrator?', *Images of Educational Administration*, section 3. Deakin University Press, Geelong
——1992, 'Policy as dialogue: Feminist administrators working for edu-

cational change', American Educational Research Association annual conference, San Francisco

Boland, J. and Gilhome, C. 1988, *Legal Liability Update*, Leo Cussen Institute, Melbourne

Bolman, L.G. and Deal, T.E. 1991, *Reframing Organizations: Artistry, Choice, and Leadership*, Jossey-Bass, San Francisco

BonJour, L. 1985, *The Structure of Empirical Knowledge*, Harvard University Press, Cambridge

Bornstein, M.H. and Bruner, J. (eds) 1989, *Interaction in Human Development*, Lawrence Erlbaum Associates, Hillsdale, NJ

Borthwick, Ann 1992, 'A short tour of the findings of the Mayer Committee', *Curriculum Perspectives*, vol. 12, no. 4

Bottery, M. 1988, 'Educational management: An ethical critique', *Oxford Review of Education*, vol. 14, no. 3, pp. 341–51

Bourdieu, P. 1977, 'Cultural reproduction and social reproduction', in *Power and Ideology in Education*, eds J. Karabel and A. Halsey, Oxford University Press, New York, pp. 487–511

Bowe, R. and Ball, S. with Gold A., 1992, *Reforming Education and Changing Schools*, Routledge, London

Bowles, S. 1991, 'What markets can—and cannot—do', *Challenge*, July/August, pp. 11–16

Bowles, S. and Gintis, H. 1976, *Schooling in Capitalist America*, Basic Books, New York

Boyd, W.L. 1992, 'The power of paradigms: Reconceptualizing educational policy and management', *Educational Administration Quarterly*, vol. 27, no. 3

Braverman, H. 1974, *Labor and Monopoly Capital*, Monthly Review Press, New York

Bray, M. 1991, *Making Small Practical: The Organization and Management of Ministries of Education in Small States*, Commonwealth Secretariat, London

Brizman, D. 1986, 'Cultural myths in the making of a teacher: Biography and social structure in teacher education', *Harvard Educational Review*, vol. 56, no. 4, pp. 442–56

Brophy, J. and Evertson, C. 1976, *Learning From Teaching: A Developmental Perspective*, Allyn & Bacon, Boston

Brophy, J. and Good, T. 1986, 'Teacher behaviour and student achievement', in *Handbook of Research on Teaching* 3rd edn, ed. M.C. Wittrock, Macmillan, New York, pp. 328–75

Brown, D.J. 1990, *Decentralization and School-based Management*, Falmer Press, London and New York

Brown, J., Cahir, P. and Reeve, P. 1985, *An Educational Rationale for Parent Participation*, Australian Council of State School Organisations, Melbourne

Brumby, J. 1989, *An Apple for the Teacher? Choice and Technology in Learning*, report of the House of Representatives Standing Committee on Employment, Education and Training, AGPS, Canberra

Bubner, R. 1982, 'Habermas's concept of critical theory', in *Habermas: Critical Debates*, eds J. Thompson and D. Held, Macmillan, London

Buchanan, J.J. 1987, 'The constitution of economic policy', *Science*, vol. 236, pp. 1433–6

Bullough, R., Gitlin, A. and Goldstein, S. 1984, 'Ideology, teacher role and resistance', *Teachers College Record*, vol. 87, pp. 339–58

Burns, J. 1978, *Leadership*, Harper & Row, New York

Burrell, G. and Morgan, G. 1982, *Sociological Paradigms and Organisational Analysis*, Heinemann, London (reprinted)

Butts, R.F. 1961, *Assumptions Underlying Australian Education*, Australian Council for Educational Research, Melbourne

Byrt, W. 1989, 'Management education in Australia' in *Management Education : An International Survey*, ed. W. Byrt, Routledge, London, pp. 78–103

Caldwell, B.J. 1991, 'Restructuring education in Tasmania: A turbulent end to a decade of tranquillity' in *Restructuring School Management: Administrative Reorganisation of Public School Governance in Australia* eds G. Harman, H. Beare and G.F. Berkeley, Australian College of Education, Canberra, pp. 207–28

——1993a, *Decentralising the Management of Australia's Schools*, National Industry Education Forum, Melbourne

——1993b, *Review of Resource Allocation Within the Tasmanian Education System*, chair B.J. Caldwell, report of the Review Committee to the Minister for Education and the Arts, April

Caldwell, B.J. and Spinks, J.M. 1988, *The Self-Managing School*, Falmer Press, London and Washington DC

——1992, *Leading the Self-Managing School*, Falmer Press, Lewes

Campbell, J., McMeniman, M. and Baikaliff, N. 1992, *Visions of a Future Australian Society: Towards an Educational Curriculum for 2000 AD and Beyond*, a report for the Ministerial Consultative Council on Curriculum, Brisbane

Campbell, R. 1987, *A History of Thought and Practice in Educational Administration*, Teachers College Press, New York

Campbell Report 1973, *Secondary Education for Canberra,* report of the Working Committee on College, proposals for the Australian Capital Territory, chairman Dr Richard Campbell, AGPS, Canberra

Carnegie Forum on Education and the Economy 1986, *A Nation Prepared: Teachers for the 21st Century*, Carnegie Forum, Washington, DC

Carrick Report 1989, *Report of the Committee of Review of New South Wales Schools*, Chair Sir John Carrick, NSW Government Printer, Sydney

Casey, P. M. 1990, The Australian Catholic School Sector: Organizational Structures and Their Rationales at State and Territory Level, unpublished MEd thesis, University of Melbourne

Cazden, C.B. 1992, *Whole Language Plus: Essays on Literacy in the United States and New Zealand*, Teachers College Press, New York

Chapman, J. (ed.) 1990, *School-Based Decision-Making and Management*, Falmer Press, New York

Chapman, J., Angus, L. and Burke, G. with Wilkinson, V. (eds) 1991, *Improving the Quality of Australian Schools*, Australian Council for Educational Research, Melbourne

Chapman, J.D. and Dunstan, J.F. (eds) 1990, *Democracy and Bureaucracy: Tensions in Public Schooling*, Falmer Press, London

Chisholm, R. (ed.) 1987, *Teachers, Schools and the Law*, New South Wales University Press, Sydney

Chubb, J.E. 1988, 'Why the current wave of school reform will fail', *The Public Interest*, vol. 90, pp. 28–49

Chubb, J.E. and Moe, T.E. 1990, *Politics Markets and America's Schools*. Brookings Institute, Washington, DC

Churchland, P. M. 1986, *A Neurocomputational Perspective: The Nature of Mind and the Structure of Science*, MIT Press, Cambridge

Churchland, P. S. 1986, *Neurophilosophy: Toward a Unified Science of the Mind/Brain*, MIT Press, Cambridge

Clark, C.M.H. (ed.) 1962), *Select Documents in Australian History, 1851–1900*. Angus & Robertson, Sydney

Claydon, L.F. 1973, *Renewing Urban Teaching*, Cambridge University Press, London

——(ed.) 1975, *The Urban School*, Pitman Pacific Books, Carlton, Vic

Clegg, S. 1981, 'Organization and control', *Administrative Science Quarterly*, vol. 26, pp. 545–62

——1988, 'The good, the bad and the ugly', *Organization Studies*, vol. 9, no. 1, pp. 7–13

Clegg, S. and Dunkerley, D. 1980, *Organization, Class and Control*, Routledge & Kegan Paul, London

Clegg, S. and Higgins, W. 1987, 'Against the current: Organizational sociology and socialism', *Organizational Studies*, vol. 8, no. 3, pp. 201–22

Clift, P. 1987, 'School-based review: A response from the UK perspective', in *Improving The Quality of Schooling: Lessons from the OECD International School Improvement Project* ed D. Hopkins, Falmer Press, Lewes

Cohen, D.K. 1988, *Teaching Practice: Plus Ça Change . . .* National Centre for Research on Teacher Education, issue paper 88–3, Michigan State University, East Lansing

Cohen, D. and Harrison, M. 1979, 'Curriculum decision-making in Australian education: What decisions are made within schools?', *Journal of Curriculum Studies*, vol. 11, no. 3

Cohen, M.D. and March, J.G. 1974, *Leadership and Ambiguity: The American College President*, McGraw-Hill, New York

Collins, J. 1973, 'Parent power 1972–1973', *The Educational Magazine*, vol. 30, no. 6, p. 10

Connell, R.W. 1985, *Teachers' Work*, Allen & Unwin, Sydney

——1987, *Gender and Power*, Allen & Unwin, Sydney

Connell, W.F. 1980, *The Australian Council for Educational Research, 1930–1980*, ACER, Melbourne

Connolly, W. 1988, *Politics and Ambiguity*, University of Wisconsin Press, Madison

Coombs, R., Knights, D. and Willmot, H.C. 1992, 'Culture, control and competition: Towards a conceptual framework for the study of information technology in organizations', *Organization Studies*, vol. 13, no. 1, pp. 51–72

Cronbach, L.J. and Associates 1980, *Toward Reform of Program Evaluation*, Jossey-Bass, San Francisco

Culbertson, J.A. 1981, 'Antecedents of the Theory Movement', *Educational Administration Quarterly*, vol. 17, no. 1, pp. 25–47

——1983, 'Theory in educational administration: Echoes from critical thinkers', *Educational Researcher*, December

Culbertson, J. et al. 1973, *Social Science Content for Preparing Educational Leaders*, Charles E. Merrill, Columbus, Ohio

Cunningham, K.S. and Radford, W.C. 1963, *Training the Administrator: A Study with Special Reference to Education*, ACER, Melbourne

Cuttance, P. 1993a, 'School development and review in an Australian state education system', *School-Based Management and School Effectiveness*, ed. C. Dimmock, Routledge, London, pp. 142–64

——1993b, 'The development of quality assurance reviews in the NSW public school system: What works?', Quality Assurance Directorate, NSW Department of School Education, Sydney

——1993c, 'Quality assurance and quality management: Complementary but different functions', Quality Assurance Directorate, NSW Department of School Education, Sydney

Cuttance, P., Willmshurst, J., Arnold, N. and Turner, G. 1991, 'Performance indicators for effective practice review in South Australian schools', in *Performance Indicators in Education: What Can They Tell Us?* ed. J. Hewton, Australian Conference of Directors-General of Education, BrisbaneDahl, R. 1989, *Democracy and Its Critics*, Yale University Press, New Haven, Conn.

Dahlöff, U. 1986, 'Towards a contextual rationale in distance higher education: The small-scale cases of Australia and Sweden', *Distance*

Higher Education and the Adult Learner, eds G. van Enckevort, K. Harry, P. Morin and H. Schutze, Open University, Heerlen, The Netherlands

Dale, R. 1989, *The State and Education Policy*, Open University, Milton Keynes

Dalmau, T. and Dick, B. 1989, *From the Profane to the Sacred*, an Interchange Resource Document, Chapel Hill,

Davie, George 1986, *The Crisis of the Democratic Intellect*, Polygon, Edinburgh

Davies, L. 1992, 'School power cultures under economic constraint', *Education Review*, vol. 44, no. 2, pp. 127–36

Davis, G., Weller, P. and Lewis, C. 1989, *Corporate Management in Australian Government*, Macmillan, Melbourne

Dawkins, J.S. 1987, Higher Education: A Policy Discussion Paper (the Green Paper), AGPS, Canberra

——Higher education: A policy statement (the White Paper). AGPS, Canberra

Dawkins, J.S. 1988, and Costello, R. 1983, 'Education, Progress and Equality', in *Labour Essays*, eds J. Reeves and K. Thompson, Drummond, Blackburn, Vic.

Deal, T.E. 1987, 'Effective school principals: Counselors, engineers, pawnbrokers, poets ... or instructional leaders?', in *Instructional Leadership: Concepts, Issues and Controversies*, ed. W. Greenfield, Massachusetts: Allyn & Bacon, Massachesetts, pp. 230–48

Deal, T.E. and Kennedy, A.A. 1982, *Corporate Cultures: The Rites and Rituals of Corporate Life*, Addison-Wesley, Reading, Mass.

Demaine, J. 1988, 'Teachers' work, curriculum and the New Right', *British Journal of Sociology of Education*, vol. 9, no. 3, pp. 247–64

Dent, J.F. 1991, 'Accounting and organizational culture: A field study of the emergence of a new organizational reality', *Accounting, Organizations and Society*, vol. 16, no. 8, pp. 705–32

Department of Education and Science 1979, *Management Review of the DES 1977–78*, DES, London

——1989, *Planning for School Development: Advice to Governors, Headteachers and Teachers*, DES, London

——1991, *Development Planning—A Practical Guide: Advice to Governors, Headteachers and Teachers*, DES, London

Department of Employment, Education and Training, 1989, *Better and Fairer: Achievements in Employment and Training*, Australian Government Publishing Service, Canberra

Devison, I. 1992, Taskforce on Pathways in Education and Training, Department of School Education–Ministry of Employment, Post-Secondary Education and Training, Vic.

Dewey, J. 1929, *Experience and Nature*, Dover, New York

———1957, *Human Nature and Conduct*, University of Chicago Press, Chicago

———1973, *The Philosophy of John Dewey*, University of Chicago Press, Chicago

Dick, B. and Dalmau, T. 1991, *Values in Action: Applying the Ideas of Argyris and Schon*, an Interchange Resource Document, Chapel Hill

Dierkes, M., Weiler, H. and Antal, A. (eds) 1987, *Comparative Policy Research: Learning from Experience*, Gower Publishing, Aldershot, UK

Dimmock. C. 1993a, 'Deregulating the workplace: The impact on school culture.' *Principal Matters*, vol. 5, no. 1, pp. 8–9

———1993b, 'School-based management and linkage with the curriculum', in *School-Based Management and School Effectiveness*, ed. C. Dimmock, Routledge, London, pp. 1–21

———1993c, 'Building democracy in the school setting: The principal's role', paper presented at the joint Australian—Russian Conference on Democratic Values in Education, Perth, WA, June

Dix, W.L. 1985, 'Australian industry-challenges for the future', *Practising Manager 6*, 1, 4–8, quoted in ACTU/TDC 1987, *Australia Reconstructed*, AGPS, Canberra, p. 155

Drucker, P. F. 1990, *The New Realities*, Mandarin, London

———1993, *Post-Capitalist Society*, Harper Business, New York

Duignan, P. A. and Macpherson, R.J.S. (eds) 1992, *Educative Leadership*, Falmer Press, London

Duignan, P. A. and Teather, D.C.D. 1985, 'Teaching educational administration externally at the University of New England', *Distance Education*, vol. 6, no. 1, pp. 34–55

Duke, D.L. 1987, *School Leadership and Instructional Improvement*, Random House, New York

Dunn, R., Beaudry, J.S. and Klavas, A. 1989, 'Survey of research on learning styles', *Educational Leadership*, vol. 46, no. 6, pp. 50–8

Dunphy, D. 1990, *Under New Management: Australian Organizations in Transition*, McGraw Hill, Sydney

Durand-Drouhin, M. 1991, 'New directions in vocational and technical education and training', paper presented at the OECD seminar on Linkages in Vocational and Technical Education and Training, 19–22 March, 1991, at Phoenix, Arizona (restricted OECD document)

Ecker, G. 1985, 'Theories of educational organization: Modern', in *International Encyclopedia of Education*, eds T. Husen and T.N. Postlethwaite, Pergamon, Oxford

Edmonton Public Schools 1993, *Budgeting Manuals: Schools and Central Services 1993/94*, Edmonton Public School District, Edmonton, Alberta

Education Department of South Australia 1990a, *Guidelines for School*

Development Planning, Education Department of South Australia, Adelaide

——1990b, *A Framework for Reviewing the Effectiveness of Schooling*, Education Department of South Australia, Adelaide

——1991a, *Guidelines for Internal Review of School Development*, Education Department of South Australia, Adelaide

——1991b, *School Reviews: Information for School Communities*, Education Department of South Australia, Adelaide

Eliason, L., Fagerlind, I., Merritt, R. and Weiler, H. 1987, 'Education, social science and public policy: A critique of comparative research', in *Comparative Policy Research: Learning from Experience*, eds M. Dierkes, H. Weiler and A. Antal, Gower Publishing, Aldershot, UK, pp. 244–61

Elmore, R.F. 1979–80, 'Backward mapping: Implementation research and policy decisions', *Political Science Quarterly*, vol. 94, no. 4, pp. 601–16

——1988, *Early Experiences in Restructuring Schools: Voices From the Field*, National Governors' Association, Washington, DC

Elmore, R.F. et al. 1990, *Restructuring Schools: The Next Generation of Educational Reform*, Jossey Bass, San Francisco

English, J. 1975, 'Brunswick Girls High School: A personal view', in *The Urban School* ed. L. Claydon, Pitman Pacific Books, Carlton

Erickson, F. 1987, 'Conceptions of school culture: An overview', *Educational Administration Quarterly*, vol. 23, no. 4, pp. 11–24

Everard, K.B. and Morris, G. 1985, *Effective School Management*, Harper & Row, London

Everhardt, R. 1983, *Reading, Writing and Resistance*, Routledge & Kegan Paul, New York

Evers, C.W. 1987, 'Naturalism and philosophy of education', *Educational Philosophy and Theory*, vol. 19, no. 2, pp. 11–21

——1990a, 'Educating the brain', *Educational Philosophy and Theory*, vol. 22, no. 2, pp. 65–80

——1990b, 'Schooling, organisational learning and efficiency in the growth of knowledge', in *School-based Decision-making and Management*, ed. J.D. Chapman, Falmer Press, London

——1993, 'Administrative decision-making as pattern processing', in *Australian Council of Educational Administration Yearbook*, ACEA, Melbourne

——1994, 'Administrative decision-making as pattern processing' in *ACEA Yearbook, 1994*, eds P. Crowther et al., ACEA, Hawthorn

Evers, C.W. and Lakomski, G. 1991, *Knowing Educational Administration: Methodological Controversies in Educational Administration Research*, Pergamon Press, Oxford

——1993, 'Justifying educational administration', *Educational Management and Administration*, vol. 21, no. 3, pp. 140–52

Feigl, H. 1951, 'Principles and problems of theory construction in psychology', in *Current Trends in Psychological Theory*, ed. W. Dennis, University of Pittsburgh Press, Pittsburgh, pp. 179–213

—— 1974, *Inquiries and Provocations: Selected Writings*, Reidel, Boston

Finegold, D., Richardson, W. and McFarland, L. (eds) 1993, *Something Borrowed, Something Blue: The Thatcher Government's Appropriation of American Education and Training Policy*. Oxford series on comparative education, Triangle Press, New York

Fiske, E.B. 1992, *Smart Kids, Smart Schools: Why Do Some Schools Work?*, Touchstone, New York

Fogarty, R. 1959, *Catholic Education in Australia, 1806–1950*, 2 vols, Melbourne University Press, Melbourne

Fordham, R. 1983, memo to Presidents of School Councils, Minister of Education, Melbourne

Foster, W.P. 1980a, 'Administration and the crisis of legitimacy: A review of Habermasian thought, *Harvard Education Review*, vol. 50, no. 4, pp. 496–505

—— 1980b, 'The changing administrator: Developing managerial practice', *Educational Theory*, vol. 30, no. 1, pp. 11–23

—— 1984, 'Toward a critical theory of educational administration', in *Leadership and Organizational Culture*, eds T.J. Sergiovanni and J.E. Corbally, University of Illinois Press, Urbana, Ill.

—— 1986, *Paradigms and Promises*, Prometheus, Buffalo, NY

Fraser, B.J., Walberg, H.J., Welch, W.W. and Hattie, J.A. 1987, 'Syntheses of educational productivity research', *International Journal of Educational Research*, vol. 11, no. 2, pp. 147–247

Freeman, G. 1973, 'Parent Involvement?', *The Open Book*, no. 4, and the *Educational Magazine*, p. 11

Fullan, M.G. 1990, 'Staff development, innovation and institutional development', ASCD yearbook *Changing School Culture through Staff Development*, ed. B. Joyce, pp. 3–25

—— 1991, *The New Meaning of Educational Change*, Cassell, London

Fullan, M.G. and Hargreaves, A. 1991, *What's Worth Fighting For? Working Together for your School*, Australian Council for Educational Administration, Melbourne

Gadamer, H.-G. 1976, 'The historicity of understanding', in *Critical Sociology*, ed. P. Connerton, Penguin, Harmondsworth, Middx

—— 1979, 'The problem of historical consciousness', in *Interpretive Social Science: A Reader*, eds P. Rabinow and W.M. Sullivan, University of California Press, Berkeley

Gagné, R.M. 1974, *Essentials of Learning for Instruction*, Holt, Rinehart & Winston, New York

Garms, W.I., Guthrie, J.W. and Pierce, L.C. 1978, *School Finance*, Prentice Hall, Englewood Cliffs, N.J.

Gaze, B. and Jones, M. 1990, *Law, Liberty and Australian Democracy*, Law Book Company, Melbourne

Geddes. J. 1984, 'Action research teams: students as researchers', *In Service Education with Primary Schools*, pp. 21–2

Geertz, C. 1973, *The Interpretation of Cultures*, Basic Books, New York

Gemmill, G. and Oakley, J. 1992, 'Leadership: An alienating social myth', *Human Relations*, vol. 45, no. 2, pp. 113–29

Getzels, J.W. and Guba, E.G. 1957, 'Social behaviour and administrative process', *The School Review*, vol. 65, no. 4, pp. 423–41

Getzels, J.W., Lipham, J.M. and Campbell, R.F. 1968, *Educational Administration as a Social Process*, Evanston and London, Harper & Row, London and New York

Giddens, A. 1976, *New Rules for Sociological Method*, Hutchinson, London

——1984, *The Constitution of Society: Outline of the Theory of Structuration*, University of California Press, Berkeley

Giddings, G. and Fraser, B. 1992, 'A survey of teaching views of a modular curriculum innovation', *Curriculum Perspectives*, no. 1, April, pp. 27–36

Gill, P. 1975, 'Involving parents: practical steps towards articulating schooling and the culture of the students' in *The Urban School*, ed. L. Claydon, Pitman Pacific Books, Carlton

Gilligan, C. 1982, *In a Different Voice*, Harvard University Press, Cambridge

Gilligan, C., Lyon, N.P. and Hanmer, T.J. 1990, *Making Connections*, Harvard University Press, Cambridge

Giroux, H. 1981, *Ideology, Culture and the Process of Schooling*, Falmer Press, London

——1983, *Critical Theory and Educational Practice*, Deakin University Press, Geelong

——1984, 'Rethinking the language of schooling', *Language Arts*, vol. 61, no. 3, pp. 33–40

Gittins, R. 1988, 'A few tips from Paris as Dawkins takes the class', *Sydney Morning Herald*, 6 April

Golden, K. 1992, 'The individual and organizational culture: Strategies for action in highly ordered contexts', *Journal of Management Studies*, vol. 29, no. 1, pp. 1–21

Goll, I. and Zeitz, G. 1991, 'Conceptualizing and measuring corporate ideology', *Organization Studies*, vol. 12, no. 2, pp. 191–207

Goodson, I. 1992, 'Studying School Subjects', *Curriculum Perspectives*, vol. 12, no. 1, April, pp. 23–6

Gouldner, A. 1976, *The Idea of Ideology and Technology*, Macmillan, London

Greenfield, T.B. 1973, 'Organizations as social inventions: Rethinking assumptions about change', *Journal of Applied Behavioural Science*, vol. 9, no. 5, pp. 551–74

——1979, 'Ideas versus data: How can the data speak for themselves?', in *Problem-Finding in Educational Administration*, eds G.L. Immegart and W.L. Boyd, Lexington Books, Lexington, pp. 167–90

——1980, 'The man who comes back through the door in the wall', *Educational Administration Quarterly*, vol. 16, no. 3, pp. 26–59

——1983, 'Environment as subjective reality', revised version of a paper presented to symposium on School Organizations and their Environments at the annual conference of the American Educational Research Association, Montreal, pp. 1–50

——1984, 'Leaders and schools: Willfulness and nonnatural order in organizations', *Leadership and Organizational Culture: New Perspectives on Administrative Theory and Practice*, eds T.J. Sergiovanni and J.E. Corbally, University of Illinois Press, Urbana, Ill.

——1985a, 'Putting meaning back into theory: The search for lost values and the disappeared individual', paper presented to the annual conference of the Canadian Society for the Study of Education, Montreal, pp. 1–30

——1985b, 'Theories of educational organization: A critical perspective', in *International Encyclopedia of Education: Research and Studies*, vol. 9, eds T. Husen and T.N. Postlethwaite, Oxford, Pergamon, pp. 5240–51

——1986, 'The decline and fall of science in educational administration', *Interchange*, vol. 17, no. 2, pp. 57–80

——1991a, 'Foreword' to *Educational Leadership: The Moral Art*, by C. Hodgkinson, State University of New York Press, Albany, NY, pp. 3–9

——1991b, 'Re-forming and re-valuing educational administration: Whence and when cometh the phoenix?', *Educational Management and Administration*, vol. 19, no. 4, pp. 200–17

——1991c, 'Science and service: The making of the profession of educational administration', paper presented to the 35th anniversary conference of the Department of Educational Administration, University of Alberta, Edmonton, September 1991, pp. 198–224

——1993, 'Theory about organization: A new perspective and its implications for schools', in *Greenfield on Educational Administration*, eds T.B. Greenfield and P. Ribbins, Routledge, London and New York (reprint of 1974 IIP presentation)

Greenfield, T.B. and Ribbins, P. (eds) 1993, *Greenfield on Educational Administration*, Routledge, London and New York

Gregory, K.L. 1983, 'Native view paradigms: Multiple cultures and culture conflicts in organizations', *Administrative Science Quarterly*, vol. 28, pp. 359–77

Griffin, Gary A. 1988, 'Leadership for curriculum improvement: The school administrator's role', *Critical Issues in Curriculum Evaluation*, 87th yearbook of the National Society for the Study of Education, Chicago

Griffiths, D.E. (ed.) 1957, *Documents on the Establishment of Education in New South Wales, 1789–1880*, Australian Council for Educational Research, Melbourne

——1959, *Administrative Theory*, Appleton-Century-Crofts, New York

——1979, 'Intellectual turmoil in educational administration', *Educational Administration Quarterly*, vol. 15, pp. 43–65

——1985, *Administrative Theory in Transition*, Deakin University Press, Geelong

Grimshaw, J. 1991, 'The idea of female ethic', in *A Companion to Ethics*, ed. P. Singer, Blackwell, Oxford

Gronn, P. C. 1982, 'Neo-Taylorism in educational administration', *Educational Administration Quarterly*, vol. 18, pp. 17–35

——(ed.) 1983, *Rethinking Educational Administration: T.B. Greenfield and his Critics*, Deakin University Press, Geelong

Gronn, P. C. and Ribbins, P. 1993, 'The salvation of education: better science or alternatives to science?', *Educational Management and Administration*, vol. 21, no. 3, pp. 161–69

Guthrie, J.W. and Koppich, J.E. 1993, 'Building a model of education reform and "high politics" ', in *Restructuring Schools: An International Perspective on the Movement to Transform the Control and Performance of Schools*, eds. H. Beare and W.L. Boyd, Falmer Press, London and Washington, DC, pp. 12–29

Gutmann, Amy 1987, *Democratic Education*, Princeton University Press, Princeton, NJ

Habermas, J. 1972a, 'Technology and science as "Ideology" ', in *Toward a Rational Society*, ed. J. Habermas, Heinemann, London (translated by J.J. Shapiro)

——1972b, *Knowledge and Human Interests*, Heinemann, London (translated by J.J. Shapiro)

——1976, *Zur Rekonstruktion des historischen Materialismus*, 2nd edn, M. Suhrkamp, Frankfurt

——1979, *Communication and the Evolution of Society*, Beacon Press, Boston (translated by T.A. McCarthy)

——1986, *The Theory of Communicative Action*, vol. 1, Beacon Press, Boston

——1987, *The Theory of Communicative Action*, vol 2, *The Critique of Functionalist Reason*, Polity Press, Cambridge

Hallenstein, H. and Miles, D. 1988, *Legal Liability: Outdoor Education — Accidents Outdoors*, Leo Cussen Institute, Melbourne

Halpin, A.W. 1957, 'A paradigm for research on administrator behavior',

in *Administrative Behavior in Education*, eds R.F. Campbell and R.T. Gregg, Harper and Bros, New York
——(ed.) 1958, *Administrative Theory in Education*, Midwest Administration Centre, Chicago
——1966, *Theory and Research in Administration*, Macmillan, New York
Handy, C.B. 1985, *Understanding Organizations*, 3rd edn, Penguin, Harmondsworth, Middx
——1989, *The Age of Unreason*, Century Hutchinson, London
Handy, C.B. and Aitken, R. 1986, *Understanding Schools as Organizations*, Penguin, Harmondsworth, Middx, England
Hannan, Bill and Wilson, Bruce 1992, 'The development of a national curriculum framework', *Curriculum Perspectives*, vol. 12, no. 2
Hargreaves, A. 1989, *Curriculum and Assessment Reform*, Open University Press, Milton Keynes, pp. 26–33
Hargreaves, D. 1980, 'The occupational culture of teachers', in *Teacher Strategies: Explorations in the Sociology of the School*, ed. P. Woods, Croom Helm, London, pp. 125–48
——1982, *The Challenge of the Comprehensive School*, Routledge & Kegan Paul, London
——1988, 'Assessment and performance indicators: The English experience' in *Indicators in Education*, eds A. Ruby and T. Wyatt, Australian Conference of Directors-General of Education, Sydney
Harman, G., Beare, H. and Berkeley, G.F. (eds) 1991, *Restructuring School Management: Administrative Reorganisation of Public School Governance in Australia*, Australian College of Education, Canberra
Harman, G. and Meek, V.L. (eds) 1988, *Australian Higher Education Reconstructed? Analysis of the Dawkins Green Paper*, Department of Administrative and Higher Education Studies, University of New England, Armidale
Harman, G.S., Wirt, F.M. and Beare, H. 1990, 'Changing roles of Australian education chief executives at the state level', in *Education Policy in Australia and America*, eds W.L. Boyd and D. Smart, Falmer Press, London
Harmon, M.M. and Mayer, R.T. 1986, *Organization Theory for Public Administration*, Little, Brown, Boston and Toronto
Harper, I. 1993, 'Economic rationalism: The economist's view of the world', in *Educating for Profit?*, ed. A. Hukins, Australian Christian Teachers Fellowship, Sydney, pp. 39–50
Hartshorne, K. 1973, 'Start by sacking yourself', *Age*, Melbourne, 18 November
Harvey, G. and Crandall, D.P. 1988, 'A beginning look at the what and how of restructuring', in *The Re-design of Education: A Collection of Papers concerned with Comprehensive Educational Reform*, ed. C. Jenks, Far West Laboratory, San Francisco

Hawley, W.D. 1989, 'Looking backward at educational reform', *Education Week*, vol. 9, no. 9, pp. 32–5

Hayes, R. and R. Watts 1986, *Corporate Revolution: New Strategies for Executive Leadership*, Heinemann, London

Hayward, D. 1993, *Schools of the Future: Preliminary Statement*, Directorate of School Education, Melbourne

Heidegger, M. 1927, *On Being and Time*, 1962 edn, Harper & Row, New York

Held, D. 1980, *Introduction to Critical Theory*, Hutchinson, London

Hill, D. 1990, 'Something old, something new, something borrowed, something blue: Schooling, teacher education and the radical right in Britain and the USA', *Hillcole Papers*, no. 3, Tufuell Press, London

Hodgkinson, C. 1978, *Towards a Philosophy of Administration*, Basil Blackwell, Oxford

—— 1983, *The Philosophy of Leadership*, Basil Blackwell, Oxford

—— 1986, 'Beyond pragmatism and positivism', *Educational Administration Quarterly*, vol. 22, no. 2, pp. 5–21

—— 1991, *Educational Leadership: The Moral Art*, State University of New York, Albany, NY Press

—— 1993, 'The epistemological axiology of Evers and Lakomski: Some un-Quineian quibblings', *Educational Management and Administration*, vol. 21, no. 3, pp. 177–84

Holly, D. 1986, 'A critical chorus: Government policy towards teachers in Britain', *European Journal of Education*, vol. 21, no. 2, pp. 117–28

Holly, P. 1990, ' "Catching the wave of the future": Moving beyond school effectiveness by redesigning schools', *School Organisation*, vol. 10. nos. 2 and 3, pp. 195–212

Hopkins, D. 1989, *A Teachers' Guide to Evaluation in Schools*, Open University Press, Milton Keynes

Hord, S.M., Stiegelbauer, S.M. and Hall, G.E. 1984, 'How principals work with other change facilitators', *Education and Urban Society*, vol. 17, November, pp. 89–109

Hoy, W.K, and Miskel, C.G. 1987, *Educational Administration: Theory, Research and Practice*, 3rd edn, Random House, New York

—— 1991, *Educational Administration: Theory, Research and Practice*, 4th edn, Random House, New York

Huberman, Michael 1983, 'Recipes for busy kitchens: A situational analysis of routine knowledge use in schools', *Knowledge: Creation, Diffusion, Utilization*, vol. 4, no. 4, pp. 478–510

—— 1989, 'Predicting conceptual effects in research utilization: Looking with both eyes', *Knowledge in Society*, vol. 2, no. 3, pp. 6–24

Hughes, B. 1980, *Exit Full Employment*, Angus & Robertson, London

Hughes, P. (chairman) 1973, *A Design for the Governance and Organization*

of Education in the Australian Capital Territory, Commonwealth Department of Education, Canberra
——1982, *Review of the Efficiency and Effectiveness of the Education Department*, Centre for Education, University of Tasmania, Hobart
Hunt, A. and Lacy, N. 1980, *White Paper on Strategies and Structures for Education in Victorian Government Schools*, Government Printer, Melbourne
Hunt, J.W. 1979, *Managing People at Work*, McGraw Hill, London
——1983, 'Parents and teachers in curriculum', *Project Report*, 1980–82, p. 60
Hutchins, C.L. 1988, 'Design as the missing piece in education', in *The Redesign of Education: A Collection of Papers Concerned with Comprehensive Educational Reform*, vol. 1, Far West Laboratory, San Francisco, pp. 47–9
Jackson, P. 1968, *Life in Classrooms*, Holt, Rinehart & Winston, New York
Johnston, Bill J. 1991, 'Institutional and interorganizational contexts of educational administrator preparation', *The Urban Review*, vol. 23, no. 1, pp. 31–8
Johnston, N. 1991 'Foreword', in *Improving the Quality of Australian Schools*, eds J. Chapman, L. Angus and G. Burke, with V. Wilkinson, Australian Council for Educational Research, Melbourne
Jones, A.W. 1985, The Development of the Role of Inspectors of Schools in the Education Department of South Australia: 1875 to 1970. unpublished thesis, University of New England, Armidale
Jones, D., Metcalf, M., Williams, T. and Williamson, J. 1982, 'Sunshine High School: A school curriculum and self-evaluation project', in *Task Force Team Report*, ed. T. Knight, no. 7. School of Education, La Trobe University, Bundoora, Vic.
Joyce, B., Murphy, B., Showers, B. and Murphy J. 1989, 'Reconstructing the workplace: School renewal as cultural change', paper presented at the annual meeting of the American Educational Research Association, San Francisco
Kanem, G.R. 1915, 'Reminiscences', *The S.A. Teachers' Journal*
Kant, I. 1781, *Critique of Pure Reason*, 1955 edn, Heinemann, London
Karmel, P. (chair) 1973, *Schools in Australia*. Report of the Interim Committee of the Australian Schools Commission. AGPS, Canberra
Katz, D. and Kahn, R.L. 1966, *The Social Psychology of Organizations*, 2nd edn 1978, Wiley, New York
——1983, 'Organizations and the systems concept', in *Perspectives on Behavior in Organizations*, eds J.R. Hackman, E.E. Lawler III and L.W. Porter, McGraw-Hill, New York
Kempner, K. 1992, 'Getting into the castle of educational administration', *Peabody Journal of Education*, vol. 66, no. 3, pp. 104–22

Killman, R.H., Saxton, M.J. and Serpa, R. (eds). 1985 *Gaining Control of the Corporate Culture*, Jossey-Bass, San Francisco

Kingdon, John W. 1984, *Agendas, Alternatives, and Public Policies*, Little, Brown, Boston

Kinlaw, Dennis C. 1989, *Coaching for Commitment*, University Associates Inc., USA

Kirby, P. C., Paradise, L.V. and King, M.I. 1992, 'Extraordinary leaders in education: Understanding transformational leadership', *Journal of Education Research*, vol. 85, no. 5, pp. 303–31

Kirby, P. E. (chairman) 1985, *Report of the Committee of Inquiry into Labour Market Programs*, AGPS, Canberra

Kirner, J. 1973, 'Parents in education', *The Educational Magazine*, vol. 30, no. 6, p. 4

——1989, *Reading Together: A Major Initiative for Literacy Prep-Year 3*, open letter from the Minister For Education in Victoria, Government Printer, Melbourne

Knight, B. 1989, *Managing School Time*, Longman Harlow

——1993, 'Delegated financial management and school effectiveness', in *School-Based Management and School Effectiveness*, ed. C. Dimmock, Routledge, London, pp. 114–41

Knight, T. (ed.) 1984, 'In service education with primary schools', *A Series In Primary School Innovation*, Team no. 8, School of Education, La Trobe University, Bundoora, Vic.

——1992, 'Curriculum integration: balancing local and central policy', paper presented at Australian Association for Research in Education (and) New Zealand Association for Research in Education, Joint Conference, Deakin University, Geelong, 22-26 November

——1993, 'Setting the democratic base for effective schooling', *School Centered Leadership*, ed. S. Crump, Thomas Nelson, Sydney

Kogan, M. 1986, *Educational Accountability*, Hutchinson, London

Kovach, B.E. 1989, *The Organizational Gameboard*, Prentice Hall, Englewood Cliffs, NJ

Kroeber, A.L. and Kluckhohn, C. 1952, *Culture: A Critical Review of Concepts and Definitions*, Papers of the Peabody Museum, Harvard University, Cambridge

Kuhn, T. 1970, *The Structure of Scientific Revolutions*, 2nd Edition, University of Chicago Press, Chicago

Lakomski, G. 1986, 'A meta-structuralist analysis of Palermo's structuralist analysis of "Dewey's impossible dream" ', in *Philosophy of Education 1985*, ed. D. Nyberg, proceedings of the 41st annual meeting of the Philosophy of Education Society, Normal., Ill., pp. 219–21

——1988, 'Critical theory', in *Educational Research, Methodology, and Measurement: An International Handbook*, ed. J.P. Keeves, Pergamon, Oxford

Lauder, H. 1987, 'The New Right and educational policy in New Zealand', *New Zealand Journal of Educational Studies*, vol. 22, no. 1, pp. 3–23

Lawrence, P.R. and Lorsch, J.W. 1967, *Organization and Environment*, Richard D. Irwin, Homewood, Ill.

Lawton, D. and Gordon, P. 1987, *HMI*, Routledge & Kegan Paul, London

Leithwood, K. and Jantzi, D. 1990, 'Transformational leadership: How principals can help reform school cultures', *School Effectiveness and School Improvement*, vol. 1, no. 4, pp. 249–80

Leithwood, K. and Montgomery, D.J. 1982, 'The role of the elementary school principal in program improvement', *Review of Educational Research*, vol. 52, Fall, pp. 309–39

Leithwood, K. and Steinbach, R. 1993, 'The consequences for school improvement of differences in principals' problem-solving processes', in *School-Based Management and School Effectiveness*. ed. C. Dimmock, Routledge, London, pp. 41–64

Levine, D.U. and Lezotte, L.W. 1990, *Unusually Effective Schools: A Review and Analysis of Research and Practice*, National Centre for Effective Schools Research and Development, Madison, Wis.

Lindblom, C. and Cohen, D. 1979, *Usable Knowledge: Social Science Problem Solving*, Yale University Press, New Haven, Conn.

Lindblom, C.E. 1980, *The Policy-making Process*, Prentice-Hall, Englewood Cliffs, NJ

Lingard, B. 1991, 'Policy-making for Australian schooling: A new corporate federalism', *Journal of Education Policy*, No. 1. 6, No. 1, pp. 85–90

Litterer, J.A. 1969, *Organizations: Systems, Control and Adaption*, vol. 2, John Wiley, New York

Little, J.W. 1982, 'School success and staff development', *American Educational Research Journal*, vol. 19, no. 3, pp. 25–40

——1990, 'The persistence of privacy: Autonomy and initiative in teachers' professional relations', *Teachers' College Record*, vol. 91, no. 4, pp. 509–36

Locke, E.A. and Latham, G.P. 1990, *A Theory of Goal-Setting and Task Performance*, Prentice Hall, Englewood Cliffs, NJ

Lorsch, J.W. 1985, 'Strategic myopia: Culture as an invisible barrier to change', in *Gaining Control of the Corporate Culture*, eds R.H. Killman, M.J. Saxton and R. Serpa, Jossey-Bass, San Francisco, pp. 84–102

Lortie, D. 1975, *School Teacher*, University of Chicago Press, Chicago

Luhmann, N. 1985, *A Sociological Theory of Law*, Routledge & Kegan Paul, London

McBrien, R.P. 1980, *Catholicism*, Dove, Melbourne

McCarthy, B. 1990, 'Using the 4MAT system to bring learning styles to schools', *Educational Leadership*, vol. 48, no. 2, pp. 31–7

Mackay, L.D. and Spicer, B.J. 1975, *Educational Turbulence among Australian Servicemen's Children*, AGPS: Canberra

McRae, D. 1990, 'Gains under siege from new set of strains', *Age*, 13 November, p. 20

Maddock, T.H. 1994, 'Three dogmas of materialist pragmatism: a critique of a recent attempt to provide a science of educational administration', *Journal of Educational Administration*, in press

Marginson, S. 1990, *Productivity in Education: Measurement and Improvement*, Public Sector Research Centre, University of New South Wales, Sydney

——1993, *Education and Public Policy in Australia*, Cambridge University Press, Cambridge

Martin, H.J. 1985, 'Managing specialized corporate cultures', in *Gaining Control of the Corporate Culture*, eds R.H. Killman, M.J. Saxton and R. Serpa, Jossey-Bass, San Francisco, pp. 148–62

Marton, F. and Ramsden, P. 1988, 'What does it take to improve learning?', in *Improving Learning: New Perspectives*, ed. P. Ramsden, Kegan Paul, London

Mayer, E. 1992, *Employment-related Key Competencies: A Proposal for Consultation*, Melbourne

Mayo, E. 1933, *The Human Problems of an Industrial Civilisation*, Macmillan, New York

Meek, V.L. 1988, 'Organizational culture: Origins and Weaknesses', *Organization Studies*, vol. 9, no. 4, pp. 453–73

Meyer, M. and Rowan 1977, 'Institutionalized organisations: Formal structure as myth and ceremony', *American Journal of Sociology*, vol. 83, no. 2, pp. 340–63

Meyer, M.W. 1978, 'Introduction: Recent Developments in Organisational Research and Theory', in *Environments and Organisations*, ed. M.W. Meyer, Jossey-Bass, San Francisco, Washington and London

——(ed.) 1978, *Environments and Organisations*, Jossey-Bass, San Franciso, Washington, London

Miller, D. 1991, 'Theoretical dispositions—on Bourdieu and Marxism: The moulding of an intellectual habitus', *Habitus*, vol. 1, pp. 8–22

Millikan, R. 1984, 'School culture and imagery: What does it mean and what can it do for my school?', *The Secondary Administrator*, vol. 2, no. 1, pp. 3–11

Mills, A. 1988, 'Organization, gender and culture', *Organization Studies*, vol. 9, no. 3, pp. 352–69

Mintzberg, H. 1979, *The Structuring of Organizations*, Prentice-Hall, Englewood Cliffs, NJ

Mitchell, J.T. and Willower, D.J. 1992, 'Organizational culture in a good high school', *Journal of Educational Administration*, vol. 30, no. 6, pp. 6–16

Moloney, G. 1990, 'Counterpoint: A response to Dean Ashenden', *Queensland Teachers Union Professional Magazine*, vol. 8, no. 1, pp. 13–14

Moore Johnson, S. 1990, *Teachers at Work: Achieving Success in Our Schools*, Basic Books, New York

Morgan, J. and Everett, T. 1990, 'Introducing quality management in the NHS', *International Journal of Health Care Quality Assurance* (UK), vol. 3, no. 5, pp. 23–35

Mortimore, P. 1993, 'School effectiveness and the management of effective learning and teaching', paper delivered at the International Congress for School Effectiveness and Improvement, Norrkoping, Sweden

Murphy, C. 1993, The HRE Policy: A Critical Analysis of its Value Assumptions, unpublished MEd thesis, University of Queensland

Murphy, J. (ed.) 1990, *The Education Reform Movement of the 1980s: Perspectives and Cases*, McCutchan, Berkeley, Calif.

——1991, *Restructuring Schools: Capturing and Assessing the Phenomenon*, Teachers College Press, New York

——1993, 'Restructuring schooling: The equity infrastructure', *School Effectiveness and School Improvement*, vol. 4, no. 2, pp. 111–30

Murphy, J., Weil, M., Hallinger, P. and Mitman, A. 1985, 'School effectiveness: A conceptual framework', *Educational Forum*, vol. 49, no. 3, pp. 361–74

Naisbitt, J. and Aburdene, P. 1986, *Re-Inventing the Corporation*, Macdonald, London

National Commission on Excellence in Education 1983, *A Nation at Risk: The Imperative for Educational Reform*, US Department of Education, Washington DC

Ninomiya, A. and Okato, T. 1990, 'A critical analysis of job satisfied teachers', *Comparative Education*, vol. 26, Nos. 2/3, pp. 249–58

Noddings, N. 1984, *Caring: A Feminine Approach to Ethics and Moral Education*, University of California Press, Berkeley

NSW, Department of School Education 1992, *Your School's Right to Choose*, The Department

O'Brien, P. 1992, 'Four academics in search of an outrage', *Ideas in Education*

O'Donnell, P., Robertson, I. and Warren, L. 1979, 'A new way in: A report on school transition programs', in *A Series In Primary School Innovation*, Study Team no. 3. ed. T. Knight, School of Education, La Trobe University, Bundoora, Vic.

Oakland, J.S. 1989, *Total Quality Management*, Heinemann, London

Office for Standards in Education 1993, *Aspects of School Review in South*

Australia: A Report from the Office of Her Majesty's Chief Inspector of Schools, HMSO, London

Office of the Minister for Education and Youth Affairs 1984, speech for the Minister of Education, Senator Susan Ryan, on Youth Policy, November

Office of Youth Affairs and the Social Welfare Policy Secretariat 1984, *Income Support for Young People*, AGPS, Canberra

Ogawa, R. 1985, 'Theories of educational organization: Classical', in *International Encyclopedia of Education*, eds T. Husen and T.N. Postlethwaite, Pergamon, Oxford

Ohmae, K. 1990, *The Borderless World: Power and Strategy in the Interlinked Economy*, Collins, London

Organization for Economic Cooperation and Development 1980, *Youth Unemployment: The Causes and Consequences*, OECD, Paris

——1985, *New Policies for the Young*, OECD, Paris

——1986, *Youth and Work in Australia*, OECD, Paris

——1987a, *Draft Programmes of Work for 1988*, Education Division and Centre for Educational Research and Development 1987, OECD, Paris

——1987b, *Universities under Scrutiny*, OECD, Paris

——1988, *INES News*, Centre for Educational Research and Development, OECD, Paris

——1989a, *Education and the Economy in a Changing Society*, OECD, Paris

——1989b, *The Conditions of Teaching*, OECD, Paris

——1989c, *Schools and Quality: An International Report*, OECD, Paris

——1989d, *The Teacher Today: Tasks, Conditions, Policies*, OECD, Paris

——1992a, *Education at a Glance: OECD Indicators*, OECD, Paris

——1992b, *The OECD International Education Indicators: A Framework for Analysis*, OECD, Paris

Ouchi, W. 1981, *Theory Z*, Addison-Wesley, Reading, Mass.

Oxford Review of Education 1987, 'Plowden Twenty Years On', vol. 13, no. 1, pp. 1–138

Palmer, R.E. 1969, *Hermeneutics*, 8th printing, Northwestern University Press, Evanston, Ill.

Parents and Teachers in Curriculum (PATIC) 1983, Project Report 1980–82, in Research and Development/Curriculum Services Unit, ed. M. Hyde, Education Department of Victoria, Melbourne

Parkay, F.W. and Hall, G.E. 1992, *Becoming a Principal: The Challenges of Beginning Leadership*, Allyn & Bacon, Massachusetts

Parker, M. 1992, 'Post-modern organization or postmodern organization theory?', *Organization Studies*, vol. 13, no. 1, pp. 1–17

Parliament of the Commonwealth of Australia 1987, Skills formation in Australia: 1987–88 budget related paper no. 9 (Parliamentary Paper no. 204/1987), Canberra

Parsons, S. 1990, 'Feminism and the logic of morality: A consideration of alternatives' in *Socialism, Feminism and Philosophy: A Radical Philosophy Reader*, eds D. Sayers and P. Osborne, Routledge, London

Patton, M.Q. 1986, *Utilization-Focused Evaluation*, Sage Publications, California

Payer, C. 1982, *The World Bank: A Critical Analysis*, Monthly Review Press, New York

——1991, *Lent and Lost: Foreign Credit and Third World Development*, Zed Books, London

Pearl, A. 1988, 'The requirements of a democratic education' in *Discipline and Schools: A Curriculum Perspective*, ed. R. Slee, Macmillan, Melbourne

Perrow, C. 1979, *Complex Organizations: A Critical Essay*, 2nd edn, Scott-Foresman, Glenview, Ill.

——1983, 'The short and glorious history of organisational theory', in *Perspectives on Behavior in Organizations*, eds J.R. Hackman, E.E. Lawler III and L.W. Porter, McGraw-Hill, New York

Peters, R. 1966, *Ethics and Education*, George Allen & Unwin, London

Peters, T. 1992, *Liberation Management: Necessary Disorganization for the Nanosecond Nineties*, Macmillan, London

Peters, T. and Waterman, R. 1982, *In Search of Excellence: Lessons From America's Best-run Companies*, Harper & Row, New York

Pettit, D. 1980, *Opening Up Schools: School and Community In Australia*, Penguin, Ringwood, Vic.

——1987, 'Schooling at a crossroad' in *Parent Participation In Victorian Schools*, Schools Division, Ministry of Education, Melbourne, pp. 28–30

Phillips, D. 1985, *Making More Adequate Provision*, Tasmanian Government Printer, Hobart

Phillips, D.C. 1983, 'After the wake: Postpositivistic educational thought', *Educational Researcher*, vol. 12, no. 5, pp. 4–12

Pickering, D. (chair) 1993, *Report of the Cullen-Brown Advisory Committee*, Report to the Minister for Education in Victoria, Melbourne

Picot Report 1988, Taskforce to Review Education Administration (chair Brian Picot), *Administering for Excellence: Effective Administration in Education*, New Zealand Government Printer, Wellington

Pollitt, C. 1990, 'Doing business in the temple? Managers and quality assurance in the public services', *Public Administration*, 68, pp. 435–52

Popham, W.J., and Baker, E.I. 1970, *Systematic Instruction*, Prentice-Hall, Englewood Cliffs, NJ

Poppleton, P. and Riseborough, G. 1990, 'A profession in transition: Education policy and secondary school teaching in England in the 1980s', *Comparative Education*, vol. 26, nos. 2/3, pp. 211–26

Porter, A.C. and Brophy, J. 1988, 'Synthesis of research on good teaching: Insights from the work of the institute for research on teaching', *Educational Leadership*, vol. 45, no. 8, pp. 74–85

Porter, P. , Rizvi, F., Knight, J. and Lingard, R. 1992, 'Competencies for a clever country: Building a house of cards?' *Unicorn*, vol. 18, no. 3, September, pp. 50–8

Preston, B. 1984, 'Residualisation, what's that?', *Australian Teacher*, No. 8, pp. 5–6

Pring, R. 1989, *The New Curriculum*, Open Books, London

Purkey, S. and Smith, M. 1982, 'Effective schools: A review', *Elementary School Journal*, vol. 82, pp. 64–9

——1985, 'School reform: The district policy implications of the effective schools literature', *Elementary School Journal*, vol. 85, pp. 353–89

Pusey, M. 1981, 'The control of education in the 1980s', *Politics*, vol. 17, no. 2, pp. 223–34

——1987, *Jurgen Habermas*, Tavistock, London

——1991, *Economic Rationalism in Canberra: A Nation Building State Changes its Mind*, Cambridge University Press, Cambridge

Quantz, R.A., Cambron-McCabe, N. and Dartley, M. 1991, 'Preparing school administrators for democratic authority: A critical approach to graduate education', *Urban Review*, vol. 23, no. 1, pp. 3–19

Quine, W.V. 1960, *Word and Object*, MIT Press, Cambridge

Quine, W.V. and Ullian, J.S. 1978, *The Web of Belief*, Random Press, New York

Rabinow, P. and Sullivan, W.M. (eds.) 1977, *Interpretive Social Science: A Reader*, University of California Press, Berkeley

Raizen, S. 1991, Learning and work: The research base, paper presented at the OECD seminar on Linkages in Vocational and Technical Education and Training, 19–22 March, 1991, in Phoenix, Arizona (restricted OECD document)

Rallis, S.E. and Highsmith, M.C. 1986, 'The myth of the "great principal": Questions of school management and instructional leadership', *Phi Delta Kappan*, vol. 68, no. 4, pp. 300–4

Rayner Report 1983, *Study of HM Inspectorate in England and Wales*, DES, London

Reilly, D.H. 1984, 'The principalship: The need for a new approach', *Education*, vol. 104, spring, pp. 242–7

Resnick, L. and Wirt, J. (eds) (In press). Linking school and work: Roles for standards and assessment, Jossey Bass, Palo Alto, Calif.

Reynolds, D. 1992, 'School effectiveness and school improvement: An updated review of the British literature', in *School Effectiveness: Research, Policy and Practice*, eds D. Reynolds and P. Cuttance, Cassell, London, pp. 1–24

Rizvi, F. 1986, *Administrative Leadership and the Democratic Community as a Social Ideal*, Deakin University Press, Geelong

Rizvi, F., Kemmis, S., Walker, R., Fisher, J. and Parker, Y. 1987, 'Dilemmas of Reform: An Overview of Issues and Achievements of the Participation and Equity Program in Victorian Schools 1984–1986', Deakin Institute for Studies in Education, Deakin University, Geelong

Roethlisberger, F.J. and Dickson, W.J. 1939, *Management and the Worker*, Harvard University Press, Cambridge

Rosenholtz, S. 1989, *Teachers' Workplace: The Social Organisation of Schools*, Longman, New York

Rossow, L.F. 1990, *The Principalship: Dimensions in Instructional Leadership*, Prentice-Hall, Englewood Cliffs, NJ

Rowe, K.J. 1991, *Students, Parents, Teachers and Schools Make a Difference*, State Board of Education and Schools Programs Division, Ministry of Education and Training, Melbourne

Rowe, R. 1990, 'The importance of reading at home', *Working Papers in Public Education*, vol. 2, pp. 19–26, State Board of Education, Melbourne

Rule, J.B. 1979, *Insight and Social Betterment: A Preface to Applied Social Science*, Oxford University Press, New York

Rumelhart, D.E. and McClelland, J.L. (eds) 1986, *Parallel Distributed Processing*, vols. 1 and 2, MIT Press, Cambridge

Sachs, J. and Smith, R. 1988, 'Constructing teacher culture', *British Journal of Sociology of Education*, vol. 9, no. 4, pp. 423–36

Sako, M. 1991, The role of employers and unions in facilitating the transition to employment and further learning, paper presented at the OECD seminar on Linkages in Vocational and Technical Education and Training, 19–22 March 1991, in Phoenix, Arizona (restricted OECD document)

Saunders, G.E. 1967, 'The state and education in South Australia 1836–1875', in *Melbourne Studies in Education 1966*, ed. E.K. French, Melbourne University Press, Melbourne, pp. 204–38

Schattschneider, E.E. 1960, *The Semisovereign People: A Realist's View of Democracy in America*, Holt, Rinehart & Winston, New York

Schein, E.H. 1985, 'How culture forms, develops and changes', in *Gaining Control of the Corporate Culture*, eds R.H. Killman, M.J. Saxton and R. Serpa, Jossey-Bass, San Francisco, pp. 17–43

—— 1986, *Organizational Culture and Leadership*, Jossey-Bass, San Francisco

Schools Commission 1981, *Report for the Triennium*, 1982–1984, AGPS, Canberra

Schools Council 1989, *Teacher Quality: An Issues Paper*, AGPS: Canberra

Schools Council, National Board of Employment, Education and Training 1990, *Australia's Teachers: An Agenda for the Next Decade*, AGPS, Canberra

——1992, *The Compulsory Years: Developing Flexible Strategies in the Early Years of Schooling: Purposes and Possibilities*, Project Paper 5, AGPS, Canberra

——1993, *In the Middle: Schooling for Young Adolescents*, AGPS, Canberra

Schools of the Future 1993, *Education News Supplement*. February, Directorate of School Education, Melbourne, p. 5

Schools of the Future 1993, *Preliminary Paper*, January, Directorate of School Education, Melbourne

Schultz, M. 1991, 'Transitions between symbolic domains in organizations', *Organization Studies*, vol. 12, no. 4, pp. 489–506

Schumacher, E.F. 1973, *Small is Beautiful: Economics as if People Mattered.*, Harper & Row, New York

Scott Report 1989, *Schools Renewal: A Strategy to Revitalize Schools Within the New South Wales Education System*, Management Review: New South Wales Education Portfolio (chair Dr Brian Scott), NSW Ministry of Education, Sydney

Scott, B. 1990, *School-centred Education: Building a More Responsive School System*, report of the Management Review: New South Wales Education Portfolio, NSW Ministry of Education, Sydney

Scott, W.G. 1983, 'Organization theory: An overview and an appraisal', in *Perspectives on Behavior in Organizations*, eds J.R. Hackman, E.E. Lawler III and L.W. Porter, McGraw-Hill, New York

Scott, W.R. 1978, 'Theoretical perspectives', in *Environments and Organisations*, ed. M.W. Myer, Jossey-Bass, San Franciso, Washington and London, pp. 21–8

——1981, *Organizations*, Prentice-Hall, Englewood Cliffs, NJ

Seddon, T. 1991, 'Contradictions in the Australian teacher debate: Implications for policy and practice', *Journal of Education Policy*, vol. 6, no. 4, pp. 359–69

——1994a, 'Teachers' work and political action', in *International Encyclopedia of Educational Research*, eds T. Husen and N. Postlethwaite, Pergamon, Oxford

——1994b, *Context and Beyond: Studies in the Theory and Politics of Education*, Falmer, London

Sejnowski, T.J. and Rosenberg, C.R. 1987, Parallel networks that learn to pronounce English text', *Complex Systems*, vol. 1, pp. 145–68

Senge, P. M. 1992, *The Fifth Discipline: The Art and Practice of the Learning Organization*, Century Communications, New York

——1984c, 'Leadership and excellence in schooling', *Educational Leadership*, vol. 41, no. 5, pp. 4–13

Sergiovanni, T. and Corbally, J. (eds) 1984, *Leadership and Organizational*

Culture: New Perspectives on Administrative Theory and Practice, University of Illinois Press, Urbana, Ill.

Sergiovanni, T.J. 1984a, 'Cultural and competing perspectives in administrative theory and practice', in *Leadership and Organizational Culture*, eds T.J. Sergiovanni and J.E. Corbally, University of Illinois Press, Urbana, Ill.

——1984b, 'Developing a relevant theory of administration', in *Leadership and Organizational Culture*

——1984c 'Leadership and excellence in schooling' *Educational Leadership*, vol. 41, no. 5, pp. 4-13

——1991, 'Constructing and changing theories of practice: The key to preparing school administrators', *Urban Review*, vol. 23, no. 1, pp. 39-49

——1992, 'Reflections on administrative theory and practice in schools', *Educational Administration Quarterly*, vol. 28, no. 3, pp. 302-14

Sergiovanni, T.J. and Starratt, R.J. 1988, *Supervision: Human Perspectives*, 4th edn, McGraw-Hill, New York

Sexton, M. 1981, *War for the Asking: Australia's Vietnam Secrets*, Penguin, Ringwood, Vic.

Shakeshaft, C. 1986, *Women in Educational Administration*, Sage, Newbury Park, Calif.

Shaw, J. 1992, 'School cultures: Organizational value orientation and commitment', *Journal of Educational Research*, vol. 85, no. 5, pp. 295-302

Simon, H.A. 1976, *Administrative Behavior*, 3rd revised edn 1976, Macmillan, London

——1983, *Reason in Human Affairs*, Stanford University Press, Stanford

Sizer, T.R. 1984, *Horace's Compromise: The Dilemma of the American High School*, Houghton Mifflin, Boston

Skilbeck, M. 1988, 'Administrative decision and cultural values', *Reflective Readings in Educational Administration*, Deakin University Press, Geelong, pp. 303-12

Slee, R. (ed.) 1988, *Discipline and Schools: A Curriculum Perspective*, Macmillan, Melbourne

Sleezer, C.M. and Swanson, R.A. 1992, 'Culture surveys', *Management Decision*, vol. 30, no. 2, pp. 22-9

Sloan, M. 1989, 'The changing face of postgraduate study', *Compass 89*, pp. 30-1

Smart, D. 1989, 'The Dawkins' "reconstruction" of higher education in Australia', paper presented to the American Educational Research Association annual meeting, March, San Francisco

Smeaton, T.H. 1927, *Education in South Australia from 1836 to 1927*, Rigby, Adelaide

Smircich, L. 1983a, 'Concepts of culture and organizational analysis', *Administrative Science Quarterly*, vol. 28, pp. 339–59
——1983b, 'Studying organizations as cultures', in *Beyond Method*, ed. G. Morgan, Sage, London, pp. 160–72
Smith, P.B. and Peterson, M.F. 1988, *Leadership, Organizations and Culture*, Sage, Newbury Park, Calif.
Smith, S.C. and Piele, P. K. (eds) 1989, *School Leadership: Handbook for Excellence*, 2nd edn, ERIC Clearinghouse on Educational Management, Eugene, Oreg.
Smith, W.F. and Andrews, R.L. 1989, *Instructional Leadership: How Principals Make a Difference*, Association for Supervision and Curriculum Development, Alexandria, Va.
Smyth, J. 1993, *A Socially Critical View of the Self-Managing School*, Falmer Press, London
Soliman, I.K. 1991, 'State control and parent participation: Analysis of recent reports', *Australian Educational Researcher*, vol. 18, no. 1, pp. 53–73
Spady, W.G. 1988, 'Organising for results: The basis of authentic restructuring and reform', *Educational Leadership*, vol. 46, no. 2, pp. 4–8
Spady, W.G. and Marshall, K. 1991, 'Beyond traditional outcome-based education', *Educational Leadership*, vol. 49, no. 2, pp. 67–71
Spaull, A. 1987, 'The state school teachers decision (High Court 1929) revisited', *Australian Journal of Education*, vol. 31, no. 3, pp. 236–51
Starratt, R.J. 1991, 'Building an ethical school: A theory for practice in educational leadership', *Educational Administration Quarterly*, vol. 27, no. 2, pp. 185–202
——1993, *The Drama of Leadership*, Falmer Press, London and Washington, DC
Stenhouse, L. 1975, *An Introduction to Curriculum Research and Development*, Heinemann, London
Stokes, G. and Edmonds, A. 1990, 'Dawkins and the Labor tradition: Instrumentalism and centrism in Federal ALP higher education policy 1942–1982', *Politics*, vol. 25, no. 1, pp. 6–20
Stretton, H. 1988, 'What on earth does this government think it's doing?', *Australian Society*, vol. 7, no. 12, pp. 66–8
Sturman, A. 1990, 'Devolved decision-making and its impact on the curriculum', in *Working Papers in Public Education*, vol. 2, Ch. 5, State Board of Education, Melbourne
Sturt, M. 1967, *The Education of the People*, Routledge & Kegan Paul, London
Sungaila, H. 1989, *Litigation in Education*, Gavemer Publishing, Sydney
Sutherland, G. 1973, *Policy-Making in Elementary Education 1870–1895*, Oxford University Press, Oxford

Swanson, A.D. and King, R.A. 1991, *School Finance: Its Economics and Politics*, Longman, New York and London

Swedish Trade Union Confederation 1986, 'Joint responsibility for employment', document discussed at the 1986 Congress, quoted in ACTU/TDC 1987, *Australia Reconstructed*, AGPS, Canberra, p. 115

Taba, H. 1962, *Curriculum Development: Theory and Practice*, Harcourt Brace Jovanovich, New York

Taylor, C. 1979, 'Interpretation and the sciences of man', in *Interpretive Social Science: A Reader*, eds P. Rabinow and W.M. Sullivan, University of California Press, Berkeley

Taylor, F.W. 1947, *Scientific Management*, Harper & Bros, New York

Taylor, S. 1991, 'Feminist classroom practice and cultural politics: Some further thoughts about "girl number twenty" and ideology', *Discourse*, vol. 11, no. 2, pp. 22–47

Thelen, H.A. and Getzels, J.W. 1957, 'The social sciences: Conceptual framework for education', *School Review*, vol. 65, no. 3, pp. 339–55

Thurow, L. 1992, *Head to Head: The Coming Economic Battle Among Japan, Europe and America*, William Morrow & Company, New York

Toffler, A. 1985, *The Adaptive Corporation*, Pan Books, London

—— 1990, *Powershift: Knowledge, Wealth, and Violence at the Edge of the 21st Century*, Bantam Books, New York

Toomey, D. 1987, *Parent Competence in the Schools.* Participation and Equity Program, Ministry of Education, Melbourne, pp. 33–5

Tronc, K.E. and Sleigh, D. 1989, *Australian Teachers and the Law*, Butterworths, Sydney

Tudge, J. and Rogoff, B. 1989, 'Peer influences on cognitive development: Piagetian and Vygotskian perspectives', in *Interaction In Human Development*, Ch. 2

Tyler, Ralph W. 1949, *Basic Principles of Curriculum and Instruction*, University of Chicago Press, Chicago

Ubben, G.C. and Hughes, L.W. 1992, *The Principal: Creative Leadership for Effective Schools*, 2nd edn, Allen & Bacon, Massachusetts

UK Parliament 1991, *The Citizen's Charter: Raising the Standard*, HMSO, London

Vaill, P. 1984, 'The purposing of high performing systems', in *Leadership and Organizational Culture*, eds T. Sergiovanni and J. Corbally, University of Illinois Press, Urbana, Ill.

Verba, S. and Nie, N.N. 1972, *Participation in America*, Harper & Row, New York

Verba, S., Nie, N. and Kim, J.O. 1971, *The Modes of Democratic Participation: A Cross National Comparison*, Beverley Hills, Calif.

Vickers, M. 1989, *Universities and the national interest: The Dawkins Plan for higher education in Australia*, Public Policy Program, Australian National University, Canberra

Victorian Commission of Audit 1993, *Report,* Government Printer, Melbourne
——1986b, *Taking Schools into the 1990s,* Ministry Structures Project Team, Ministry of Education, Melbourne
Victorian Ministerial Papers 1–6 1985, issued by Minister of Education, Victoria
Victorian Ministry of Education 1986a, *School Council: General Information Interim Manual,* Council Services Unit, Ministry of Education, Melbourne
——1987a, *Parent Participation in Victorian Schools,* Schools Division, Ministry of Education, Melbourne
——1987b, *Case Studies of Parent Participation,* Participation and Equity Program, Special Programs Branch, Ministry of Education, Melbourne
——1987c, *Parents: One of our most valuable resources,* Participation and Equity Program. Melbourne, Victoria: Special Programs Branch, Ministry of Education, Melbourne
von Bertalanffy, L. 1956, 'General systems theory', *General Systems,* vol. 1, pp. 1–10
——1973, *General Systems Theory,* revised edn, George Braziller, New York
Walker, J.C. 1981, 'Two competing theories of personal autonomy: a critique of the liberal rationalist attack on progressivism', *Educational Theory,* vol. 31, nos. 3/4, pp. 285–306
Walker, J.C. and Evers, C.W. 1984, 'Towards a materialist pragmatist philosophy of education', *Education Research and Perspectives,* vol. 2, no. 1, pp. 23–33
——1988, 'The epistemological unity of education research', in *Educational Research, Methodology, and Measurement: An International Handbook,* ed. J.P. Keeves, Pergamon Press, Oxford
Walker, J.S. 1969, 'The challenge of freedom', *Education Gazette,* vol. 85, no. 983, pp. 90–1
——1988, *Louts and legends: Male Youth Culture in an Inner-city School,* Allen & Unwin, Sydney
——1993, 'Cultural perspectives on work and schoolwork in an Australian inner-city boys' high school', in *Education, Inequality and Social Identity,* ed. L. Angus, Falmer Press, London, pp. 128–59
Walker, W.G. 1964, 'Teaching and research in educational administration', *Journal of Educational Administration,* vol. 2, no. 1, pp. 9–22
——1965, 'Theory and practice in educational administration', *Journal of Educational Administration,* vol. 3, no. 1, pp. 18–39
——1970, *Theory and Practice in Educational Administration,* University of Queensland Press, St Lucia, Qld
Waller, W. 1932, *The Sociology of Teaching,* Wiley, New York

Watkins, P. 1986, *A Critical Review of Leadership Concepts and Research: The Implications for Educational Administration*, Deakin University Press, Geelong

Weber, M. 1949, *On the Methodology of the Social Sciences*, Free Press, New York, (translated and edited by E.A. Shils and H.A. Finch)

Weick, K.E. 1969, *The Social Psychology of Organizing*, Addison-Wesley, Reading, Mass.

——1976, 'Educational organizations as loosely coupled systems', *Administrative Science Quarterly*, vol. 21, no. 1, pp. 1–19

——1982, 'Administering education in loosely coupled schools', *Phi Delta Kappan*, pp. 673–6

Weiss, C.H. 1979, 'The many meanings of research utilization', *Public Administration Review*, vol. 39, no. 5, pp. 426–31

——1986, 'The circuitry of enlightenment: Diffusion of social science research to policymakers', *Knowledge: Creation, Diffusion, Utilization*, vol. 8, no. 2, pp. 274–81

——(ed.) 1977, *Using Social Research in Public Policy Making*, Lexington-Heath, Lexington, Mass.

——1989, 'Congressional committees as users of analysis', *Journal of Policy Analysis and Management*, vol. 8, no. 3, pp. 411–31

——1990, 'The uneasy partnership endures: Social science and government', in *Social Scientists, Policy, and the State*, eds S. Brooks and A.G. Gagnon, Praeger, New York pp. 97–111

Weiss, C.H. and Vickers, M. 1992, 'The impact of research on educational policy', in *The Encyclopedia of Educational Research*, ed. M.C. Alkin, 6th edn, pp. 1093–99, MacMillan, New York

Weiss, C.H. with Bucavalas, M.J. 1980, *Social Science Research and Decision-making*, Columbia University Press, New York

Werlin, H.H. 1988, 'The theory of political elasticity: Clarifying concepts in micro/macro administration', *Administration and Society*, vol. 20, no. 1, pp. 46–70

Westoby, A. (ed.) 1988, *Culture and Power in Educational Organizations*, Open University Press, Milton Keynes and Philadelphia

Wexler, P. 1987, *Social Analysis of Education*, Routledge, New York

Whitty, G. 1985, *Sociology and School Knowledge*, Methuen, London

Wilcox, B. 1989, 'Inspection and its contribution to practical evaluation', *Educational Research*, vol. 31, no. 3, pp. 163–75

——1991, 'Judging schools: The role of the Inspectorate', paper presented at BERA annual conference, Nottingham Polytechnic, 28–31 August 1991

Wildy, H. and Dimmock, C. 1993, 'Instructional leadership in Primary and Secondary Schools in Western Australia', *Journal of Educational Administration*, vol. 31, no. 2, pp. 43–61

Wilenski, P. S. 1982, Policies for youth: Some approaches', paper

prepared for the Organization for Economic Cooperation and Development, Paris (restricted document)
Willis, P. 1977, *Learning to Labour*, Saxon House, Westmead
Willower, D.J. 1993, 'Explaining and improving educational administration', *Educational Management and Administration*, vol. 21, no. 3, pp. 153–60
Wilson, B.L. and Firestone, W.A. 1987, 'The principal and instruction: Combining bureaucratic and cultural linkages', *Educational Leadership*, vol. 45, no. 1, pp. 18–23
Wittgenstein, L. 1953, *Philosophical Investigations*, 1973 edn, Blackwell, Oxford
Wolcott, H. 1973, *The Man in the Principal's Office: An Ethnography*, Holt, Reinhart & Wilson, New York
Wood, G.H. 1992, *Schools That Work: America's Most Innovative Public Education Programs*, Dutton, New York
Wood, S. 1985, 'Work organization', in *Work, Culture and Society*, eds R. Deem and G. Salaman, Open University Press, Milton Keynes
Woods, P. 1980a, *Sociology and the School: An Interactionist Viewpoint*, Routledge & Kegan Paul, London
——(ed.) 1980b, *Pupil Strategies: Explorations in the Sociology of the School*, Croom Helm, London
——1984, 'Negotiating the demands of schoolwork', in *Life in Schools: The Sociology of Pupil Culture*, eds M. Hammersley and P. Woods, Open University Press, Milton Keynes, pp. 225–37
Yeatman, A. 1990, 'Administrative reform and management improvement', *Bureaucrats, Technocrats, Femocrats: Essays on the Contemporary Australian State*, Allen & Unwin, Sydney, pp. 1–12
Young, M.F.D. (ed.) 1971, *Knowledge and Control*, Collier-Macmillan, London
Young, Robert E. 1990, *A Critical Theory of Education: Habermas and Our Children's Future*, Teachers College Press, New York and London

Index

Accord, 244
accountability, 217, 304–7, 314
action, administrative, 3, 4; communicative, 15, 55, 90; human, 10, 13; meaning of, 11
administration, educational *see* educational administration
administrative work, 83–5
administrators, 45; ethical issues and, 92; function of, 40–1; implications for, 233–4; power of, 47–8; responsibilities of, 89; values and, 42, 43
Adult listener scheme, 250–60
alignment, 180
alternative schools, 160
alternatives, 10
anarchist theory of administration, 8
anti-discrimination, 197–8
anti-leadership, 43, 44, 45
Ashenden, Dean, 248, 249
assessment, 288–9
audits, 165–8
Australia Reconstructed, 244
Australian Council for Educational Research, 112
Australian Council of Trade Unions (ACTU), 135, 244
Australian Education Council (AEC), 149–50, 224, 225
Australian Industrial Relations Commission (AIRC), 246
Australian Schools Commission, 113, 123, 149

Australian Teachers Union (ATU), 246
AUSTUDY, 126
autonomy, 230–1
award restructuring, 244–50

Barnard, Chester, 18, 40–1, 42, 43
Bassett, William, 2, 36
Bates, Richard, 14, 63–4
behaviour, management of, 6; organisational, 6; in schools, 30
belief, 42
Bertalanffy, Ludwig von, 20–3
Bidwell, C.E., 26
Board of Advice, 254
bottom-up process, 275, 279, 280, 285, 290
broad-banded equity programs, 177
budgeting, program, 226; school-based, 182
bureaucracies, 14, 139–40
business, 40
Butts, Freeman, 175

Campbell, Richard, 137
capitalism, 14, 56
caring, 91–3, 293
Carmichael Report, The, 135
categorical approaches, 238
Catholic schools, 147–8, 154, 156–61; funding of, 160
centralisation, 214
change, 168, 212, 258–9;

educational, 133–9; management of, 227–31
children, 200–1
churches, 153–6
coercion, 42, 43
cognitive interests, 54
coherence theory of justification, 17
coherentism, 16–17
collaboration, 293
Collaborative School Management Cycle, 184
commercialisation, 139
commitment, 249
Commonwealth, Australian, 119–23
communication, 55, 89, 90
community, 142
complementarity, 147, 148
concept development, 222
congruence, 31
Conscious, 56
consent, 43–4
context, 236–7
control, 230–1, 232
cooperation, 42
copyright, 196–7
core technology, 275, 276–8, 279–80
corporatisation, 139
cottage classroom, 249, 250, 253
Courses of Study, 221
critical theory, 13–16, 89
cross-national exchange, 110, 114, 116, 119; case studies in, 123–30
Culbertson, Jack, 3
culture, 73; anthropology of, 10; -building, 289–95; concepts in, 61–3; corporate, 60; functionalist concept of, 69–70; macro-, 76, 77, 78; organisational, 60, 67–70, 71–4, 75, 79, 80; reproduction of, 66, 67; school, 69, 78; sociology of education and, 63–7; teacher and pupil, 64–6; and power, 74–8
curriculum, hidden, 67, 74, 102; management of, 214–34; policy, 261; setting of, 268–70

Dawkins, John, 111, 126–30
decentralisation, 179, 180, 277
decision-making, 89, 115, 116, 177; parent, 257, 263; participatory, 263–4; school, 254, 259, 260–1, 268–70
democratisation, 267–8, 293
Department of Employment, Education and Training (DEET), 113, 122–3
deprofessionalism, 92
deregulation, 143
deskilling, 252
devolution, 214, 229, 230, 277, 306; second-wave, 232
Dewey, John, 2, 93–5, 99
dialogue, 90–1
differentiation, 26
disenchantment, 54
dualisms, 93–5, 103
Duke Park College, 264–70

Ebbeck Report, 240–4
economics, industrial, 141; rationalism of, 133–9, 172–3, 186–7; security of, 232
Edmonton Public School District, 181–3
education, 51; activities in, 196–8; change and, 213; cost of, 177; curriculum management in, 214–15; distance, 112; -economy relations, 113; higher, 117, 194–5; the law and, 189–203; legislation for, 191–4; marketing of, 59; markets for, 135–6; politics and, 134; post secondary, 194–5; privatisation of, 59, 136, 139; professional negligence in, 199–202; provision of, 191–2; reconstruction of, 126–30; reform of, 179–80; responsibility for, 171; role of governments in, 149–50, 175–6, 190–1; sociology of, 63–7; statutory framework of, 190–5; vocational, 194
Education Acts, 157, 191, 193
Education Reform Act, 192, 193, 194

INDEX

Education Review Officer (ERO), 305
Education Support Centres, 142, 146
education systems, 144–7
educational administration,
  alternative, 8–9; anarchist theory of, 8; appearance of, 57–9; Australian research of, 1; birth of, 1; coherentism in, 16–17; conventional notions of, 59; critical theory in, 9, 13–16; cultural perspective of, 8, 9–13; ethics and, 87–91, 107–9; philosophy and, 1, 98–101; political framework of, 9; postgraduate programs for, 2, 35–6; scientific theory of, 3–4, 8, 9, 40, 97–8; subjectivist perspective on, 7, 8; systems perspective in, 25–31; theories of, 52–3; in North America, 1
Educational Administration: Theory, Research and Practice, 19, 28
Educational Administration Quarterly, 1
educational authorities, statutory responsibilities of, 195–8; as employers, 196
educational change, 133–9
educational malpractice, 201–2
educational organisations, 5
educational rationalism, 231–3
educators, the *Family Law Act* and, 198–9; profession of, 150–1
efficiency, 247
emancipation, 58; ethics of, 87–91; interest in, 54
empiricism, 17, 21; evidence of, 8; logical, 16; research in, 26
empowerment, 230
ends, 94–5
enlightenment, 117, 126
entropy, 24, 25
epistemology, 8, 98, 99, 100
equality, 178, 182
equifinality, 25, 27
ethics, 81, 84–5, 87–91; Hodgkinson and, 85–7; in educational administration, 107–9; of caring, 91–3; of emancipation, 87–91; *see also* values
ethnic groups, 259, 260
evaluation methodology, 308–11
examination system, 219
excellence, 145
expectations, 163, 166
extended grouping, 287

Family Law Act, 198–9
Federated Teachers Union, 134
feedback loop, 27
Feigl, Herbert, 4, 28
feminist scholars, 91
Feyerabend, Paul, 7, 8
financial management, 291
fluid grouping, 286
Fordham, Robert, 261
Foster, W.P., 87–91
Frameworks, 222
Frankfurt School, 14
freedom, 229
Freedom of Information, 196
functionalist definitions, 69–70
fundamental accountability, 232

geography, 140
Geography Teachers Association of Victoria, 221
Gipps, George, 154–5
global indicators, 311
goal-setting, 292, 294
Goulburn school strike, 159
Goyen, Peter, 175
grants, 176
Greenfield, Thomas Barr, 6–9, 34–48
Griffiths, Daniel, 3
grouping, 286–7, 288, 291

Habermas, Jürgen, 14, 15, 53–4, 88–9
Halpin, Andrew, 3
Her Majesty's Inspectorates (HMI), 299, 301, 302–4, 310
hermeneutics, 10, 11

hierarchy, 24, 228–9
higher education, 117, 194–5; institutes (HEI), 240, 242–3
Higher Education Contributions Scheme (HECS), 129
Hodgkinson, Christopher, 46, 85–7, 107
holism, 23–4
Hoy, W.K., 19, 28–31
Hughes, Phillip, 136–7
human relations movement, 18
humans, 88
hypothetico-deductive theories, 10, 99

ideographic elements, 30
independence, 304–7
independent schools, 160
indicators, global, 311; performance, 311–12
individualisation, 5, 6, 236–7, 253, 286
industry, 129
initiative, 180
inputs, 24
inspectorates, 299–304
institutions, 5
internal school reviews, 312–14
International Baccalaureate, 142
interpretation, 6, 11–12, 31–2
interpretive social science, 11
interrelatedness, 23–4
intersubjectivity, 15–16
isomorphism, 32

Journal of Educational Administration, 1, 2

Karmel Report, 159–60, 176, 178, 254–5, 257
key competencies, 222–4
knowledge, 106, 107–8; creep, 117; schools as factories of, 140–4; utilisation of, 115–19; as a resource, 188
Knowledge and Human Interests, 54
Kuhn, Thomas, 7, 8, 99

labour process, 247–50
language, 15, 55–7, 58, 112
law, 189–203
leadership, 43, 70, 71–4, 109; effective, 285–8, 289–95; implications for, 283–4; instructional, 275; model of, 278–81; school, 275, 276–8, 281–3; transformational, 294–5
learning, 54–7, 102, 103; effective, 281–3, 289–95; mutual, 56, 59; outcome-based, 286; productivity of, 293; quality of, 274–5, 278–81; through language, 58
logical empiricism, 3, 40, 98–9, 100, 101
logical positivism, 3, 40

Macquarie, Lachlan, 154
malpractice, 201–2
management, 253, 275, 280, 289–95; educational, 132; financial, 291; good, 144; head-office, 144; quality, 298–9, 303, 311–14; resource, 229; school-based, 181, 230, 232; self-, 179, 184–6; of the curriculum, 214–234
managerial intervention, 238–44
market analogies, 77–8
meaning, 64; -constructing, 10 management of, 71–4
means, 94–5
Meek, V.L., 60
message systems, 74
Metherell, Terry, 137–8
mindscapes, 12
Miskel, C.G., 19, 28–31
mobilisation, 180
motivation, 53, 61, 104
multi-age grouping, 286
multiple perspectives, 12
multiskilling, 248

National Board of Employment, Education and Training (NBEET), 238
negligence, 199–202

INDEX

networks, 217–19
neural acts, 104
neutrality, 83–5
New Movement *see* Theory Movement
New South Wales Department of School Education, 137–9
Noddings, N., 91–3
nomothetic elements, 5, 6, 30
non-government schools, 153–69, 306; registration of, 193–4
non-graded grouping, 286
normative (nomothetic) dimension, 5, 6

objectivity, 7
observation, 54; theory-ladenness of, 7, 8, 9
OECD, 235
organisational identity, 161–8
organisational life, 9–19
organisational structures, 285–9
organisations, 6–7, 52–3, 62–3; anatomy of, 18; cooperation within, 42; creation of, 36–8; educational, 101; effective, 285–9; influence of, 63; humans in, 18; modern, 20–3; morality of, 34; network, 145; objective, 7; physicalness of, 39; rational model of, 25–6; scientific approach to, 26, 28; subjective, 7; in environments, 5, 38–9
Organization for Economic Cooperation and Development (OECD), 111–14, 119–23; John Dawkins and, 126–30; youth policy and, 123–6
oughts *see* values
outcome-based learning, 286
outputs, 24
Oxford Review of Education, 262

paradigm relative, 99
parent-school/community program, 255
parents, duties of, 192–3, 264–70; involvement of, 254, 257–60; participation of, 254–60; politics and, 267; rights of, 264–70; as consumers, 270–2; as partners, 261–3
Parents and Teachers in Curriculum (PATIC) Project, 257–8
Parkes, Henry, 156
Participation and Equity Program (PEP), 262
participatory democracy, 263–4
partnership, 242, 251
pedagogy, 58, 59
performance indicators, 311–12
personal (idiographic) dimension, 5, 6
personnel, 314
perspectivism, 22, 32
phenomenology, 10–11
philosophy, 3, 91, 98–101
physics, 21
planning, 312
pluriformity, 147–8
policy, borrowing, 110; coordination, 144; formulation, 114, 115–23, 130–1, 265–7; systemic advice for, 307–8
politicians, 116
politics, 172–3
positivism, 7, 54, 81, 82–3; logical, 21
posits, 108
post-positive conceptions, 5
post-secondary education, 194–5
power, 43, 44, 55–7, 227, 229, 230; culture and, 74–8
practicality, 251
practice, 103–7
predictable production, 231
principals, 233–4
priorities, 145
private enterprise, 134
private schools, 157
privatisation, 136, 139, 142–3
problem-solving, 292
production, 245
productivity, 247–8, 249
professionalism, 251

public schools, 139–40

quality assurance, 297–8, 301–3, 307
quality control, 296–7, 300–1
quality management, 298–9, 303, 307, 311–14

rational progress, 49
rationalisation, 51–2, 56, 75, 78, 106, 231–3
reason, 53–5
reflection, 54
reform, 244–5
regionalisation, 177
regulation, 24
relativism, 44–5, 46, 89
religion, 156
representation, 104
residualisation, 241
resource allocation, 170–88, 293–4
resourcing, 289–95
responsibility, 144, 146
restructuring, 143, 177; award, 244–50
rewards, 164–5
rituals, 164
roles, 6

sampling, 309
sanctions, 164–5
satisficing, 27
School Council, 255
School Education Committee, 255
schooling, 276–8
schools, advice to, 303–4; alternative, 160; behaviour in, 30; Catholic, 147–8, 154, 156–61; characteristics of, 276–8; context of, 276–8; control of by churches, 153–6; costs of operating, 158; democratic values and, 267–8, 271–2; effectiveness of, 72; government jurisdiction of, 153–6; independent, 160; moral orders, 39–40; non-government, 153–69, 306; personnel in, 166; private, 146, 157; public, 139–40, 146–7;

rationalising of, 156; reforms in, 134; resourcing of, 171; review of, 308–11, 312–14; role of, 153; secondary, 141, 218, 241–2; sub-, 287; as factories of knowledge, 140–4
Schools Authority, 136–7
Schools Council, 238
Schools of the Future, 26, 77, 181, 270–1
science, 7; behavioural, 8; empiricist, 13; natural, 101; post-positivist, 100; purposive-rational, 14; traditional, 97–8, 100
scientific theory, of ea, 8,9
secondary schools, 218, 241–2
self-evaluation, 312–14
sense data, 11
sense-making, 10
Simon, Herbert, 3, 106
skills formation, 245–6
small group work, 286
social reproduction, 267–8
societal predisposition, 231
Sociology of Teaching, The, 64
speech situation, 15, 88–9, 90
stakeholders, 165
state education departments, 176
steering capacity, 51
storytelling, 163–4, 168
strategic core, 145–6
strategic planning, 312
structures, 217–19
Structures Project Team, 270
student outcomes, 281–3
sub-schools, 287
subjectivism, 8, 13, 35, 53
subsidiarity, 147
supercities, 140–1
syllabuses, 218
symbols, 106
systemic policy advice, 307–8
systems, closed, 5, 20, 25–7; definition of, 32; education, 51, 144–7; equilibrium in, 24; general, 23–5; message, 74; natural view, 37; open, 5, 20,

23–5, 27–8; perspective in, 25–31: philosophy, 21; reform of, 306; social, 5, 19–20, 29; theory, 5–6, 20–3, 32–3; utility of, 31–3; for the management of quality, 298–9

teachers, assistant, 241, 243; award restructuring and, 244–50; conceptions of, 236–8; curriculum and, 220–1, 229; education of, 242; educator profession and, 150–1; employment of, 179; independence of, 225–6; preparation of, 241; qualified, 243; quality of, 250–1; reform and, 235–6; specialist, 287; student, 242
teacher's work perspective, 237–8, 251
teaching, effective, 283–4; improvement of, 238; quality of, 274–5, 278–81; team, 287, 288
Technical and Further Education (TAFE) colleges, 194
technocratic consciousness, 56–7, 58
technology, 258–9, 288; core, 275
'Technology and Science as "Ideology"', 14
test situations, 8
theoreticians, 7–8
theory, administrative, 3, 101–3; coherence, 17; critical, 9, 13–16, 53–5; definition of, 4; educational, 101–3; information, 16; neo-classical, 18–19; organisation, 18–19; orthodox administrative, 15; positivist administrative, 13; practice and, 103–7; purpose and function of, 2–3; reproduction, 66; systems,

5–6, 20–3; traditional administrative, 8
Theory Movement, 1, 19, 29, 82–3, 89, 99; operational definitions concept in, 4; in Australia, 2–5
theory-ladenness, 13
thermodynamics, 24–5
top-down process, 275, 279, 290
transformation, 24
truth-telling, 7, 16

Unconscious, 56
underdetermination, 7, 8
understanding, 11
unemployment, 245
unions, 178–9, 246, 248
universities, 128–9
Universities Under Scrutiny, 128, 129

value added teacher (VAT), 238–9
value-neutrality theory, 81
values, 3, 8, 36, 40–2, 44–6, 52–3; commitment to, 42–4; cultivation of, 84; ethical, 81, 84–7; new alignment of, 175–9; positivism and, 82–3; rank-ordering of, 46; traditional, 56; in the allocation of resources, 173–4; *see also* ethics

wage fixation, 246
Walker, William, 1, 2
Waller, W., 64
Weber, Max, 49–52
Whitlam, Gough, 149
whole language, 112
Wilenski, Peter, 124–5
women, 91–2, 93
work group, 31
work perspective, 253
worlds, 37, 38

youth policy, 111–12, 123–6

For Product Safety Concerns and Information please contact our EU representative GPSR@taylorandfrancis.com
Taylor & Francis Verlag GmbH, Kaufingerstraße 24, 80331 München, Germany

www.ingramcontent.com/pod-product-compliance
Lightning Source LLC
Chambersburg PA
CBHW052140300426
44115CB00011B/1458